Book of
CHANCE MEETINGS

Random Encounters in 5E

Book of
CHANCE MEETINGS

Random Encounters in 5E

by Douglas Sun

www.ramensandwich.com

FIRST EDITION

Library of Congress Cataloging-in-Publication Data: Sun, Douglas
    Book of Chance Meetings: Random Encounters in 5E / by Douglas Sun
    – 1st ed. ISBN 978-1-949976-17-5
    1. Gaming – Dungeons and Dragons.
    2. Gaming – roleplaying 3. Sci-Fi and Fantasy – Teens
    I. Sun, Douglas II. Book of Chance Meetings: Random Encounters in 5E

This book is dedicated to every gamer exiled
to Discord, Skype, TTS or any other online
environment by the pandemic of 2020-2021.
I wrote this book in anticipation of the time
when we will be rolling our polyhedral dice
in each other's company once again.

— Douglas Sun

CONTENTS

INTRODUCTION

Random encounters have been part of *Dungeons & Dragons* for a long, long time. I have on my desk before me my copy of the *AD&D Dungeon Masters Guide*, much worn at the corners after 40 years and David Sutherland's iconic cover art marred by scuff marks. Towards the back, there's a big appendix that addresses the subject of unplanned creature encounters and how to introduce them into a campaign. I remember being much intrigued by the notion — the serendipity of the DM making things happen without having planned them in advance. Just as in life, an event could come at you seemingly out of nowhere, and it would be as much a surprise to the DM as the players. And there were the encounter tables. So many tables, so rife with possibilities....

But for all those tables — crunchy, concrete things that should tell you everything you need to know — I felt there was something lacking that kept them from being truly useful.

Okay, so I roll my percentile dice and check the result for the environment through which the party is traveling. It turns up, "Orc."

Right. Presumably, there's more than one orc. So it really should be, "Orcs." But how many orcs are there? What are they doing here — which, in turn helps answer the related and all-important question, how do they react to meeting the party? It would help to have some cues to jump-start the encounter.

But there is no further guidance. Instead, I imagine Gary Gygax glaring at me, visibly annoyed: "Whaddyou mean? It's orcs. Deal with it."

I suppose the expectation was that I would just go to the *Monster Manual* and figure it out from there. But even with the information in the *Monster Manual*, the process felt less helpful than it should have been. For another thing, there wasn't any discussion of how to decide the appropriate terrain type. Again: "Whaddyou mean? A forest is a forest. Sheesh." Which seems sufficient on the surface, but then you pick apart the question this only leads you to more questions, like, what makes a forest a

forest instead of a few trees in the middle of a plain? Or, what exactly is rough terrain?

Since then, the various incarnations of *Dungeons & Dragons* have included guidance on how to cope with random encounters. The 5th Edition rules touch on them and offer reasonable advice, given the short space given

to the subject. But I have always felt that more could and should be said on the matter, and that there is room for a deeper exploration of how and why random encounters happen.

"Whaddyou mean? A forest is a forest. Sheesh."

Hence this book. My purpose in *Book of Chance Meetings* is to give you more precise and thorough guidance on how to create random encounters in your campaign than what you find in the 5th Edition core rules. Since we're publishing it under the OGL, I have to restrict it to the creatures covered by the SRD. But even so, this includes a pretty wide range of living (and undead) things that can pop out of nowhere and bare fangs at your party.

Each of the ten chapters defines and encompasses a different type of environment and includes a series of tables that cover a broad range of credible encounters for that environment. Yes, random encounters can and do happen in towns and cities, but I'd like to treat them as a different subject for a different book; *Book of Chance Meetings* limits itself to wilderness encounters. For each creature, you'll find a discussion of how it's likely to react to your party, how many of them your party encounters — an array of possibilities from how to acquire a pet rat to what's running through the mind of that ancient red dragon wheeling overhead.

But first, let's take a step back and discuss what random encounters represent and why they should exist at all.

What a Brave New World

I once gave a talk at GenCon on anime and games that was really a talk about adapting licensed properties into marketable games. In preparing it, I came to realize why it is more difficult to adapt some movies, shows and novels into an RPG that it is with others. An RPG setting requires that the players can carve out a space inside it that belongs to their characters first and foremost. They can (and probably should) have the chance to intersect with canonical characters and events, but the game needs to belong to your group and their characters alone. Some imaginary worlds make it fairly easy to do this, while others don't. For instance, it's easier to turn the Star Trek universe into a viable RPG than *The Lord of the Rings* and Middle Earth. I won't go off the rails and discuss exactly why this is so, but in my experience it is so.

Likewise, your *Dungeons & Dragons* campaign reveals to your players part of a larger world — that is to say, they experience only part of your entire campaign setting. It feels like a complete experience, but that is because they make that part wholly their own. You may have a vast and wonderful world between Heaven above and the Earth below laid out like a glorious buffet for the players, but chances are they're only going to experience a part of it. What they actually experience is limited to their individual angles of vision — that is, what they can see, hear and touch. Even if they can scry — and scry like the scrying-est wizard that ever cast *scrying* — they're only going to come into direct contact with a fraction of what is in your world. There's simply too much going on the background, beyond the player characters' ability to perceive it. Like sprites in a video game, except that you can't zoom in wherever you want to get a closer look at them.

Random encounters represent a collision between what is seen and what was, until just now, unseen in your world. Something that was unknown to your players — even to you as DM — now emerges into their awareness. What happens when those bubbles bounded by the range of perception collide becomes the core of the encounter.

In that sense, random encounters represent what military terminology calls a meeting engagement. Both sides stumble upon each other, not knowing for sure that the other was there. It's a spontaneous occurrence, one not fully anticipated by either side when they set out from their base. One side may have more time to prepare because it becomes aware of the other side's presence first, but it's all relative in a situation like this.

You don't know about the gnoll raiding party until it crests the top of the hill that you're climbing, and likewise, they didn't know about you.

Open System, Not Closed

Random encounters give the appearance of coming out of thin air because they represent the inevitable loose ends in the vast fabric of your campaign world, the places where you haven't filled in the details, but there could be something happening there. Those gnolls cresting the hill came from somewhere; they have a lair that serves as their home base. You just didn't figure out that they were there before you rolled up the encounter. Or perhaps you knew that there were gnolls in the area, but you didn't know that they had sent out these scouts, or this raiding party with which your player characters now find themselves nose-to-nose.

In this sense, your campaign world is an open system, or at least, a system with Swiss cheese-like openings in it. Unless you have determined and continually oversee every square mile of it, there are bound to be places — quite a lot of them, actually — where it's not certain what is going on there. You can think of random encounters as events that emerge from those undetermined spaces.

That's why I never fully bought into using random encounters in dungeons. That random encounters appendix in the AD&D *Monster Manual* spends rather a lot of time on them, apparently on the assumption that you can encounter almost anything at any time in a dungeon (as long as the encounters get more difficult the lower down you go).

This isn't to disparage good, old-fashioned dungeon crawls. There's nothing wrong with descending into the depths and just hacking away at whatever happens to be there. But I think of dungeons as closed systems. Compared to the vast wilderness, they're small and self-contained. As the DM, you have no doubt put some work into pre-determining who and what is in them, and this puts tight limits on what your party could plausibly encounter outside of your script. Whatever gets added to the experience through a random encounter really ought to be subtracted from a known location in the dungeon, because otherwise the how and why behind its presence is just too improbable.

That's the main reason that I do not cover dungeons in this book (natural cavern systems are another matter, and Chapter 1 addresses them). Wilderness is an open system, or at least mostly open. A dungeon is a closed system.

Unplanned, Not Planned

Another way to look at random encounters is to understand that they are not to be confused with the encounters that you have mapped out and planned for your party as part of the narrative framework of your campaign. They're things that happen along the way as your party goes from Point A to Point B. In a world in which traveling from one place to another can take quite a long time, it leaves open the possibility that something exciting can happen in between.

However, they are a different matter from the encounters that you have planned as signposts for your party. Of course, you will have places that your party must go and obstacles that they must overcome in order to complete the quest and fulfill their destinies as heroes. That's the frame on which you hang your campaign. They're the things that have to happen if everything is going to make sense in the end. You're going to lay those out in advance, you can't leave them to a random encounter table. This book is not meant to supplant them.

The Monsters We Met Along the Way

In *The Odyssey*, Odysseus' overarching goal is to return to Ithaka and reclaim his kingdom and the boss monster battle is his fight with Penelope's suitors. Taken one-by-one, they don't look much boss monsters, but you can think of them as a single, massed opponent — not quite like the component parts of Voltron coming together, but still a good fixed encounter. Put in that context, many of the episodes in Odysseus' journey up to his meeting with Nestor can be viewed as random encounters. When you put the entire picture together, they show us Odysseus' persistence and fortitude, but in the moment episodes like the Cyclops and the Sirens seem like things that just popped out at him and his crew from out of nowhere.

But if random encounters are not part of the structural framework of a campaign, they're not essential to the narrative; so why have they always been part of *Dungeons & Dragons*? I suspect that the answer lies in the origins of the game in the mythology of quests and adventure. Those great, timeless stories have boss monsters and overarching goals, as well as incidents along the way that are crucial to the narrative line. But the journey through dangerous and unfamiliar territory — and the persistent feeling of unseen menace that comes with it — is also a key ingredient of those myths. In *The Hero With a Thousand Faces* Joseph Campbell calls it the Journey into the Unknown.

For instance, you find this feeling in Arthurian romance, particularly the tales of the quest for the Holy Grail. The landscape through which the Knights of the Round Table make their way feels vast and mysterious even to the modern reader, who can step back a realize that we're talking about an area no larger than part of the British Isles. There's no escaping the sense that this is a spawning ground for hazards as yet unknown. Translated into roleplaying games, random encounters represent this mood of journeying into the unknown made material. You won't find a Questing Beast because it isn't the in SRD, but even so *Book of Chance Meetings* offers you a wide range of unpredicted encounters, both wondrous and somewhat mundane. A random meeting with a chimera ought to do in its stead.

Not the End of the World, Perhaps the Beginning of... Something

That being said, I do want to make it clear that I don't intend anything in *Book of Chance Meetings* to upend your plans for your campaign. I don't see the role of random encounters as anything so drastic. They should add spice to your campaign — an ongoing feeling of dreadful anticipation about what lies over the next hill, or what could be concealed by those trees along the way to where your party really needs to go — but they should not cancel what you have in mind. Unless, of course, you want them to provide you with guidance, in which case, I say, have at it and use them to improvise as much meaningful detail as you like.

To that end, you will find that the guidance for scaling encounters to fit your party's level tries to err on the side of not testing them too severely. The total CR of an encounter should not exceed your party's average level (see the next part of the Introduction, "How to Use This Book"). In cases where the CR is bound to exceed your party's average level, you always have the option of re-rolling for a more reasonable encounter, as far as I'm concerned. For a 1st Level party to tramp through a marshy river delta only find itself face-to-face with a kraken that has come inland to hunt — well, that's just not going to end in a satisfying manner for anyone but the kraken.

On the other hand, you can look at random encounters as serendipitous opportunities to gain resources. Treasure from a defeated monster, a wild horse or giant lizard that someone in your party wrangles and tames into a beast of burden, or a meeting with locals who are willing to share what they know about the area — all of these things can come from random encounters as well.

Friendly encounters can offer your party a sidequest that provides them with a quick break from the main thrust of your campaign. Every long story needs a change of pace, and maybe accompanying an understaffed caravan through dangerous country, or tagging along with some bugbear mercenaries as they turn on their hobgoblin commanders, is just the thing for your party right now.

Also, if your party happens to be down a player character or two and you're looking for an opportunity to introduce their replacements, random encounters can provide you with one. Did your party rescue someone held captive by bandits? Did they somehow persuade a cleric-turned-hermit to leave his or her life of devotional solitude for adventure and glory? There you go, then. Instead of adding a friendly NPC, let a player run the character as a PC.

Random encounters are still one of the most intriguing aspects of *Dungeons & Dragons*. However, I think that it also continues to receive a less thorough treatment than it deserves, at least in the canonical sources. I hope that *Book of Chance Meetings* is, at least, a step toward redressing that lack. I hope that it makes life easier for you DMs when your roll for a random encounter and the die tells you, "Well, *something* happens," and that it helps you come up with something for your players that it not only engaging, but logically consistent with your campaign world.

HOW TO USE THIS BOOK

Having discussed some of the deep background and meta-level thinking behind *Book of Chance Meetings*, let's get closer to ground level. So: How exactly do you use this book?

First of all, you need the 5th Edition core rulebooks. *Book of Chance Meetings* doesn't include creature stats and it refers to but doesn't reproduce NPC templates; you'll have to go to the source for that information. It refers to various rules mechanics (especially skill and attribute checks, but also certain rules regarding conditions and hazards) that are explained in the core rulebooks, but not here. Last but by no means least, *Book of Chance Meetings* refers you to the tables in the core rules for determining the composition of treasure.

With that stated for the record and out of the way, here's the executive summary of how to use this book: First, decide what type of terrain you should use and go the corresponding chapter. Then, roll on the first table in that chapter (Table X.1) to determine the encounter category. Then, roll on the appropriate category table (Table X.2-6) to determine the creature encountered. Finally, consult the entry for that creature and, if necessary, roll on the indicated sub-table (Table X.X.X) for more specific information. At that point, you should be ready to set up the encounter for your party and, as appropriate, go for the total party kill. Good luck.

Each chapter is set up to reflect this flow (although the part about the TPK is strictly up to you), but here's a more detailed breakdown:

Step 1: Decide Where You Are

The frequency with which random encounters occur is really a matter of taste. The 5th Edition core rules offer reasonable guidance in this regard, but in the end it's up to you as DM to decide how often to check and what probability to use.

Once you have decided that a random encounter is in order, you need to figure out the terrain in which it takes place. *Book of Chance Meetings* divides your campaign world into ten different basic terrain types, with each chapter covering a different type. A brief definition of that terrain opens each chapter, and I hope this helps in instances where the questions of which one to use seems muddled. For instance, let's say your party is investigating a stand of trees in the middle of a vast

plain. Are they in a forest, or grasslands? The beginning of each chapter should help you work that out.

You should also decide the climate zone in which the encounter takes place, because this can influence the likelihood of encountering certain creatures. Beneath some tables, you will find a die-roll modifier based on the regional climate, as influenced by its latitude. For this purpose, *Book of Chance Meetings* divides your world into three climate zones: sub-arctic, temperate and tropical.

The climate will affect the creatures you meet.

Sub-arctic covers tundra as well as more temperate regions that are still influenced by polar climate (north and south). It's cold or kind of cold most of the year, and it snows rather than rains. Alaska, Scandinavia, Southern Argentina and Chile are all examples of sub-arctic areas.

This book uses "temperate" as more or less interchangeable with subtropical. These regions are marked by distinct, but not necessarily extreme, seasonal temperature variations. When the seasons change, you notice it. The Mediterranean Basin, Southern Africa, most of the United States and most of China fall in the temperate band.

Tropical describes regions along the equator and just off to either side of it. It receives more sunlight than any other part of the world, and so it's hotter and wetter than anywhere else — unless you're talking about mountains and deserts, but even then they're going to be hotter than similar places in the other climate zones.

Hence, in this sense, tropical climate covers the Sahara Desert just as it does the rainforests of Brazil and Southeast Asia and the islands of Polynesia.

Step 2: What Manner of Beast Is It?

Once you've settled the question of environment, go to the appropriate chapter, consult the first table — the top-level table — and get your d20 working to determine the category of creature. *Book of Chance Meetings* organizes encounters into six categories:

Most humanoids and giants carry something of value.

Aggressive Creatures. This covers natural predators like lions and tigers as well as out-and-out monsters, like purple worms and otyughs. While varying in appearance, all of them share the instinct to attack first. With relatively intelligent monsters such as trolls or ogres, they may try to intimidate your party before they try to kill them, but in any case violence and predation always lie just beneath the surface of the encounter. This category also includes insects, snakes and spiders — which may seem like unlikely company for the likes of medusas and hell hounds, but they're here under the assumption that if you're close enough to notice them they instinctively lash out at you. An encounter from this category means that your party is almost certainly in for a fight.

Defeating creatures from this table does not yield treasure unless so noted.

Neutral Creatures. On the other hand, not every interesting encounter automatically leads to a fight. Prey animals (like elk and boar) and wild animals like bears and elephants attack your party only if provoked. In these cases, you as DM have the option of requiring a skill check from your party if they wish to avoid an animal attack. If they demonstrate sufficient survival skill or book-knowledge of how to deal with animals, they get off clean; if not, someone makes a false move that persuades the animal to charge. This category also includes creatures that can be tamed or befriended, such as horses, giant lizards, hippogriffs and the occasional unicorn. The entry for that creature may include mechanics for turning it into a useful companion.

In addition, *Book of Chance Meetings* treats certain intelligent monsters — in particular, dragons and giants, as neutral rather than aggressive because it is quite possible that intimidation and violence just won't be part of the encounter. For one thing, their alignment may dictate that they are indifferent or even friendly unless convinces them otherwise. More important, they are intelligent beings capable of making complex plans and dealing with your party would be a pointless distraction from them. Perhaps they just have more important things to do than to kill your player characters.

Defeating creatures from this table does not yield treasure unless so noted.

Humanoids. Simply put, this category covers anything classified as humanoid in 5th Edition's taxonomy. As such, it includes popular PC races such as elves and dwarves, but also classic bad guys like orcs and goblins. It's just as simple as that, with the nature of the encounter depending on the type of humanoid you rolled up.

Unless so noted, you may assume that humanoids carry treasure even when away from their lairs; use the Individual Treasure table from the core rules according to the CR of the encounter if away from their lair, or the appropriate Treasure Hoard table from the core rules if in their lair.

Humans. Think of this category as one that covers professions rather than creatures. Some encounters with sentient beings are bound to focus on what they're doing when your party comes upon them, and the matter of who they are is less important than that. They may be merchants traveling between settlements, hunters out looking for game, or bandits on the lookout for a different kind of prey. That activity and how it defines them determines how they're equipped and how they react to your party. They may or not be human — the composition of the group is a matter of your discretion. I call this category "Humans" only to reflect the fact that in

Dungeons & Dragons, as in fantasy in general, humans are the measure of all things; everyone else is defined by how they differ from them, and humans have a versatility and scope of self-definition that is allowed to no one else.

Unless so noted, you may assume that humans carry treasure even when away from their home base; use the Individual Treasure table from the core rules according to the CR of the encounter. Individual entries provide guidance if you are likely to encounter them in their base of operations (their lair, as it were).

Watch Out! This category covers incidental hazards presented by objects rather than creatures, or even by the terrain itself (such as quicksand). There's nothing here that will make headlines, just a little harassment to add some flavor to your campaign and remind your party that the adventuring life is not all glory.

Step 3: Determine What's There

After you settle on a terrain type and roll up the encounter category, go the appropriate category table and get your polyhedral dice going to determine the encounter more precisely. Consult the entry for that creature. In some cases, you will have to roll on a sub-table to determine the creature encountered.

Step 4: Consider Why and Reckon How Many

The rest of the entry provides you with guidance for shaping the encounter. Each entry contains three types of information: a discussion of why this creature is here and what it is doing — which, in turn, influences how it reacts when it discovers your party; how many of them are present; and of course, what treasure is to be had by defeating them (if any).

First off, I try to address the lack of guidance that I mentioned earlier as my biggest problem with how random encounters are generally presented. Here, you'll find suggestions regarding why that creature is in that place at that moment, what it has in mind and how it might react to meeting your party. In any event, the precise details of the encounter depend on where it happens in *your* campaign world and what *your* party is doing. I can't provide you with that level of finish, but I can at least give you some raw material from which you can shape the final product.

Each entry begins with the assumption that you are running a 1st Level party through its paces. If this is not the case, *Scaling the Encounter* gives you advice for ratcheting up the challenge based on the average level of your party. Determine the average level of your party by

adding together each party member's level and dividing the sum by 4, fractions rounded down. For instance, the average level of a party consisting of six 5th Level characters would be 7 for this purpose: 5 x 6 = 30; 30 ÷ 4 = 7.5, rounded down to 7.

Sometimes I Repeat Myself, and At Other Times I Repeat Myself

No doubt, you will notice some repetition from chapter to chapter, that the entry for a particular creature bears a striking resemblance to the entry for that creature in a different chapter. This is not a coincidence — nor do I consider it laziness on my part. For one thing, standardizing expression is an important part of writing rules; it lets you know at a glance that this thing here is basically the same as that thing over there, and you can move on. Like shorthand, it allows you to digest information more efficiently.

For another, a creature's essential nature doesn't change much depending on the terrain. So it's likely motivations and actions will not vary significantly from one environment to the other and there's no point in pretending otherwise. Orcs are not vicious marauders when you encounter them in hill country, but gentlemen farmers in the plains.

In many cases, the formula for scaling up the encounter involves calculating the number of antagonists according to a ratio with your party's average level that is based on the CR of the creature. Here, you should round up fractions. For instance, I suggest that you scale up an encounter with merrow so that the encounter group consists of one for each multiple of 3 in your party's average level. For a party with an average level of 7, this generates 2.33 merrow, which you should round up to three.

As a general rule, I like to keep the CR of a random encounter below your party's average level, but higher than one-half of it (just to make it an interesting fight). They should tax your party's resources just enough to be engaging, but not so much as to cause genuine despair. Unless you can somehow integrate them into the main thrust of your campaign, the random encounters in this book are meant to be entertaining accents to your campaign; they need not interfere at all with your overall plan. Notwithstanding what I said earlier about total party kills, if you have a strong plan for your campaign, it would pretty well screw things up if your party was wrecked by a random bunch of drow just as they turned a blind corner in a cavern complex, no matter how sophisticated a backstory you work up for why they are even there in first place.

Finally, you may find important information under the *Treasure* sub-heading. No doubt, someone in your party, like Igor in *Dork Tower*, spent an action to ready his treasure sack. Not every entry has notes regarding treasure, because some creatures just won't have anything to loot; for instance, wild animals don't bring money with them when they leave their lairs. But monsters that strike from within their lairs (like will-o-wisps, for instance) or swallow their victims whole should have something worth taking once you've dealt with them — slit open a purple worm and it's Christmas morning, but with guts and ichor instead of bows and wrapping paper. Most humanoids and giants carry something of value and they almost certainly keep treasure in their home base.

As for tallying up the treasure, the guidelines in the core rules provide guidance as good as any. The advice given here generally boils down to: Total up the CR of the encounter and consult the appropriate table in the core rules. With some exceptions, my rule of thumb is that if a monster is in its lair, use the Treasure Hoard tables; if it's away from its lair, use the Individual Treasure tables.

A Note on Morale, or: "Run Away!"

And that, in sum, is how to use the material in Chapters 1-10.

However, I'd like to address one more topic before setting you loose on them: that of group morale. Your players, of course, decide how much of a fight their characters put up, and as GM you control the actions of NPCs. But what about monsters? Do they have the option to fight or flee? And if so, when and how does it kick in? This is another question that has long dogged me about how to handle encounters. Does it make sense that creatures inevitably fight to the last dire wolf, or does it make more sense that if you kill enough of them, the rest cut and run?

I'd say this question is especially pertinent to random encounters. If they're defending their lair, yes, it makes sense that creatures would fight to the death. But as I remarked earlier, I see random encounters as meeting engagements in which the two sides come together by accident. In most cases, there's nothing territorial at stake, no hearth and home to protect. Without so much riding on the outcome of the fight, why would creatures — even mindlessly aggressive ones — fight your party to end?

If this question has occurred to you, too, I suggest the following:

At the beginning of the round after the first enemy creature becomes dead or incapacitated, compare the total CR of the remaining enemy creatures to the average level of the characters in your party that are not dead or incapacitated. If the enemy CR is no more than half of your party's average level, make a check on the enemies' behalf using the highest player character Charisma as DC. If the check succeeds, the creatures remain committed to the fight, but you should make the check again at the beginning of every subsequent round as long as the remaining enemy CR is no more than half of your party's average level, until the check fails or until all of the enemy are dead or incapacitated. If the check fails, they withdraw, moving directly away from your party and leaving their casualties behind.

If the enemy is a single creature and not a group, the Charisma check is triggered when the creature is reduced to half of its hp or lower.

You may use this mechanic or not, at your discretion. I offer it because I think that giving your enemy the option to break off an encounter when it's clearly going against them adds to its credibility, and using the highest Charisma in your party as a proxy for their ability to put mortal fear into an enemy gives them a subtle, but credible way to express their heroism.

CAVERNS

CHAPTER ONE

Caverns and the Underground

What are Caverns?

First of all, it's important to establish what "caverns" means in the context of this book. You can find a hole in the ground or a small cave, one that can house a couple of bears or a penny packet of goblin marauders, almost anywhere. Caverns, on the other hand, are networks of chambers and connecting passages closed off from direct sunlight. They're large enough to form an ecosystem of their own and they host a wide variety of creatures great and small. The network of caves in *The Keep on the Borderlands* that serves as an apartment building for various evil humanoid tribes, is a classic example of caverns under this definition. The vast underground network that is the drow's canonical homeland is an epic example.

Caverns run deep into the earth, but they may also be carved out of hillsides and mountainsides. In all cases they are by definition spaces closed off from direct sunlight, open sky and, to a substantial extent, fresh air. Therefore, this chapter uses terms like "subterranean" and "underground" somewhat loosely, in that a cavern that burrows into the side of a mountain at 10,000 feet above sea level is just as subterranean as one that delves into the bowels of the earth.

Caverns represent the most harrowing environment you can find on the Material Plane. Not only are they physically and psychologically grueling, but they are home turf to a menagerie of monsters, some of which you won't find anywhere else. Sounds like a relaxing vacation, doesn't it? Have fun!

What Do You Find in Caverns?

When you determine that a random encounter is in order, roll on Table 1.1 to determine the category:

TABLE 1.1
Encounter type - Caverns

d20	CATEGORY
1-7	Aggressive Creatures (Table 1.2)
8-11	Neutral Creatures (Table 1.3)
12-16	Humanoids (Table 1.4)
17	Humans (Table 1.5)
18-20	Watch Out! (Table 1.6)

Then, roll on the appropriate table to determine the creature, person or thing encountered.

> **Dungeons = Caverns?**
> For purposes of this discussion: No. Caverns are natural formations created by geological forces, such as weathering and volcanism. To the extent that dungeons are constructions — that is, they were designed and constructed by intelligent beings — they are not the same thing as caverns, although caverns can make a perfectly good setting for good old-fashioned dungeon crawl. On the other hand, abandoned mines may qualify as caverns in that, given enough time, they revert to wilderness.

Encounters in caverns almost inevitably take place at close quarters. Even a large cavern is an enclosed space. And besides, the complete absence of sunlight ensures that it is impossible to see very far.

"Subterranean" and "underground" are used somewhat loosely.

TABLE 12

Aggressive Creatures - Caverns

d100	ENCOUNTER
1-4	Basilisk
5-6	Behir
7-8	Cloaker
9-11	Darkmantle
12-14	Death Dog
15-17	Drider
18-21	Earth Elemental
22-28	Fungi
29-31	Gibbering Mouther
32-35	Grick
36-38	Hell Hound
39-42	Mephits
43-45	Mimic
46-49	Minotaur
50-58	Oozes
59-64	Otyugh
65-66	Purple Worm
67-69	Roper
70-73	Rust Monsters
74-75	Salamanders
76-79	Scorpions
80-85	Spiders
86-88	Stirges
89-90	Troll
91-97	Undead
98-100	Xorn

Basilisk. Your party follows a passageway that broadens out into a chamber, and they notice some unmoving shapes in the darkness. You may require a successful DC 15 Wisdom (Perception) check to realize that they're realistic stone figures of various creatures, some of them in pieces, as if partially eaten. Somewhere in the gloom, a basilisk lurks, waiting for prey.

Scaling the Encounter: A basilisk may be a bit too much for a beginning-level party. Feel free to re-roll for another encounter. Conversely, if you want to run a more challenging encounter for a higher-level party, your party encounters two basilisks sharing a lair.

Treasure: The lair contains scattered valuables belonging to the basilisk's previous victims. Roll on the appropriate Treasure Hoard table, according to the total CR of the encounter. If there is more than one basilisk in the encounter, consider that basilisk eggs may also be present for the taking.

Behir. As your party enters a chamber, you may allow them a DC 15 Wisdom (Perception) check to realize that one behir has detected their presence, and it waits in the darkness to spring an ambush on them. As an intelligent being, it may choose to taunt your party before it attacks them, but in any event it treats them as its prey.

Scaling the Encounter: If your party's average level is lower than 8, a behir may be a bit too much to throw at them. Feel free to re-roll for another encounter.

Treasure: Most likely, your party has stumbled into the behir's lair, so the belongings of its previous victims lie strewn about. Roll on the Treasure Hoard: Challenge 11-16 table to determine the total haul.

Cloaker. A cloaker is more likely to lurk in the chambers of a cavern system than in the narrow passageways; that way it has enough elbow room to feed on what it kills without having to take it elsewhere. However, if a group of potential targets passes by without noticing it, it may follow them around, looking for a moment when one party member is particularly vulnerable. At that point, the cloaker strikes.

Scaling the Encounter: If your party's average level is lower than 7, a cloaker may be more than you want to throw at them. Feel free to re-roll for a different encounter. However, if your party's average level is 15 or higher, consider using two cloakers for the encounter to make use of the dreadful effect of their subsonic communication with each other.

Darkmantle. Your party is about to pass directly under a darkmantle. The darkmantle knows that they're there; what about vice-versa? You may allow your party a DC 15 Wisdom (Perception) check to notice a particular stalactite hanging from the ceiling — that is, assuming they're using some kind of illumination, or they have darkvision. Success means that you may then allow each individual who succeeded to make a DC 15 Intelligence (Nature) check to recognize that it's really a darkmantle.

Scaling the Encounter: If you wish to make the encounter more challenging, the encounter group consists of 1d4 darkmantles for each multiple of 2 in your party's average level.

Treasure: Most likely, your party has stumbled upon the darkmantles' lair, so the belongings of their previous victims like strewn about. Roll on the Treasure Hoard table appropriate to the total CR of the encounter.

Death Dog. Your party is stalked by one death dog prowling the caverns, looking to sate its unthinking bloodlust even if it means attacking a target that outnumbers it. It may not attack immediately upon being spotted by your party, but it will attack sooner or later. It may be waiting for an opening — will one of the party members stumble and fall behind in the treacherous darkness?

Scaling the Encounter: If you wish to make the encounter more challenging, the encounter group consists of a pack of death dogs with bad intentions, two for each multiple of 3 in your party's average level.

Drider. Your party crosses paths with one of these former cast-offs from the drow. Perhaps this drider has gone mad from its fate, and it automatically attacks anyone who disturbs its lonely exile in a fit of unthinking rage. Perhaps it is more calculating — though perhaps no less mad — and it somehow thinks that killing an elf or another enemy of the drow and presenting its head to a representative of the Spider Queen will somehow restore it to favor. Or you may consider that hunger and insanity have given it a taste for human or humanoid flesh. Whatever motivation you give it, that should drive how it reacts to your party.

Scaling the Encounter: A drider may be a bit much for a lower-level party to handle, so if your party's average level is less than 6, feel free to re-roll for a different encounter.

Treasure: If your party encounters the drider in a chamber rather than a corridor, they have probably found it sulking in its lair. To determine its treasure, roll on the Treasure Hoard: Challenge 6-10 table.

Earth Elemental. An earth elemental found on the Material Plane was most likely summoned here, and it found itself unable to return to the Elemental Plane of Earth after its summoner was done with it. It is also possible that it has crossed over via a natural portal with the Plane of Earth. A cavern complex carved from the guts of the earth would be the most logical place for such a planar intersection.

Your party may feel the tremors before it sees one earth elemental approach them. You may allow them to interact with it if someone knows Terran or has the capability to control elementals. Otherwise, it's likely that the elemental will treat your party as an enemy; it either hears echoes of its original summoner, who brought it to this plane to attack enemies, or it bears an uncontrollable grudge against the Material Plane, whose residents are always trying to dominate elementals.

Scaling the Encounter: If your party's average level is lower than 5 an earth elemental may be more than you want to throw at them. Feel free to re-roll for a different encounter. Conversely, if you want to run a more challenging encounter for a higher-level party, the

encounter group consists of one earth elemental for each multiple of 6 in your party's average level.

The size of the fungi is bound to limit the size of the encounter group.

Fungi. Not all fungi are passive, odd-looking things that you can pick and eat. Roll on Table 1.2.1 to determine which of these oversized and possibly predatory fungi greets your party:

TABLE 1.2.1
Fungi - Caverns

d6	ENCOUNTER
1-4	Shrieker
5-6	Violet Fungus

Shrieker. Your party stumbles into a colony of 2d6 shriekers. At your discretion as DM, they may serve as unwitting tripwires for a nearby community of subterranean dwellers. If you wish, roll for an encounter to determine who or what takes alarm at the shriekers' shrieks.

Violet Fungus. Seeing human-sized mushrooms may or may not startle your party; it probably depends on how experienced they are as adventurers. Assuming your party has some way to see in the darkness, you may allow them a DC 15 Wisdom (Perception) check when they get within 10 feet of the giant mushrooms to notice that what look like tendrils extending from their bases are moving towards them. In other words, two violet fungi have detected them and they attack.

Scaling the Encounter: With shriekers and violet fungi, their size is bound to limit the size of the encounter group — you can only cram so many of them into a
➤

cavern or tunnel. However, if you want to increase the challenge of silencing a bunch of piercers before they blow your party's cover, you may increase the size of the colony to 4d4. With violet fungi, you may use an encounter group equal to 1d4 for each multiple of 2 in your party's average level.

Gibbering Mouther. With the environment limiting visibility, your party is likely to hear a gibbering mouther well before they can see it. In this case, you may allow your party a DC 15 Intelligence (Nature) check to identify what is making that maddening cacophony in the darkness beyond the torchlight. Perhaps the gibbering mouther makes its lair in a nearby subterranean pool, but it is just as comfortable in a dry, rocky cavern or tunnel. Needless to say, it attacks your party without hesitation — it is simply in its nature to do so.

Scaling the Encounter: If you wish to make the encounter more challenging, the encounter group consists of one gibbering mouther for each multiple of 4 in your party's average level.

Treasure: Belongings from the gibbering mouther's previous victims might well remain trapped in its body, remaining intact while the flesh that once claimed them as its own has long since dissolved. Roll once on the Treasure Hoard: Challenge 0-4 table for each gibbering mouther present.

Grick. A grick tries to hide as potential prey approaches. If it fails, your party notices that one oversized worm-like thing with a maw surrounded by four tentacles instead of a face is trying to cloak itself in shadow or squeeze down behind some rubble. When it gets within striking distance, it strikes.

Scaling the Encounter: If you wish to make the encounter more challenging, the encounter group consists of one grick for each multiple of 3 in your party's average level. If your party's average level is 15 or higher, consider adding one grick alpha to the encounter as the group's leader. Alternately, you may use an encounter group that consists of one grick alpha for each multiple of 10 in your party's average level.

Treasure: Since gricks are opportunity predators rather than hunters, your party may find treasure that has piled up from the belongings of former victims. Roll once on the Treasure Hoard: Challenge 0-4 table for each grick in the encounter group, and once on the Treasure Hoard: Challenge 5-10 table for each grick alpha.

Hell Hound. Your party crosses paths with one hell hound in a mean and paranoid mood. Most likely, it

came to the Material Plane as a companion of a devil and somehow got separated from its master. Or perhaps it was part of a pack kept by a fire giant up in the hills or mountains and became hopelessly separated from them. In any event, it is none too pleased about wandering this plane alone and it takes out its separation anxiety on your party.

Scaling the Encounter: A hell hound may be a bit too much for a beginning-level party. Feel free to re-roll for another encounter. Conversely, If you wish to make the encounter more challenging, the encounter group consists of one hell hound for each multiple of 5 in your party's average level.

Mephits. These annoying little elementals have a habit of crossing over into the Material Plane, like ink bleeding through paper, and making nuisances of themselves. They are not predatory, but they are very annoying and they interpret any attempt to brush them aside as an attack. Subterranean environments attract various types of mephit. Roll on Table 1.2.2 to determine the kind of mephit your party encounters:

TABLE 1.2.2
Mephits - Caverns

d6	ENCOUNTER
1-3	Dust Mephit
4	Magma Mephit
5-6	Mud Mephits

Dust Mephit. Your party finds one dust mephit blocking their path. It fixes them with a piercing gaze, but it won't make the first move (unless there is a group of them and they outnumber your party; see Scaling the Encounter). When dust mephits attack, they concentrate on one target to the extent possible. They want to make sure of at least one kill, and if the rest run off they're okay with that; their goal is to satisfy their morbid curiosity about death.

Magma Mephit. Magma mephits can emerge into the Material Plane wherever there is the slightest indication of volcanism, and something as modest as magma bubbling at the bottom of a subterranean crevasse qualifies. One magma mephit blocks your party's path. It ignores all attempts to brush it aside and it interprets any attempt to step over it or around it as an attack.

Mud Mephit. 1d4+1 mud mephits lounging by an underground pool or stream spot your party. They ▶

have slowly been driving each other mad with incessant and pointless complaints about everything and nothing, and they see your party as a diversion.

They're too lazy to move, so they yell out to your party and start complaining to them that it's too hot, or too cold, too dry or too wet inside the cave — or how they're too poor, or bored, or exhausted. They start to beg your party for handouts. All of this is in Aquan or Terran, of course. If your party ignores them, the mephits chase after them and eventually become exasperated enough to attack. If your party confronts them, they become agitated and attack.

Scaling the Encounter: If you want to run a more challenging encounter for a higher-level party, the encounter group consists of 1d4 dust mephits or magma mephits for each multiple of 2 in your party's average level, or 1d4 mud mephits plus one mud mephit for each level in your party's average level.

Mimic. Your party sees a chest sitting off to the side of a passageway. Is it filled with treasure that was abandoned for some reason? Unfortunately, no — it's a mimic. Caverns may seem like a dangerous environment for a mimic, but experience teaches them that there are enough dumb and greedy humanoids and humans down here to provide prey. If your party inspects it up close, it attacks. You may allow your party a DC 15 Wisdom (Perception) to notice a twitch or some other movement that gives it away.

Scaling the Encounter: If you wish to make the encounter more challenging, your party finds a veritable hoard of fake treasure chests — one mimic for each multiple of 3 in your party's average level

Minotaur. Your party finds itself heading down a twisty tunnel that winds around and about, as if designed to disorient anyone who follows it. At the end of the confusing passage is cavern housing a minotaur that sizes them up as its latest victims. However, if this is not an appropriate location for a legitimate minotaur's lair, you may consider that the minotaur is hungry enough to go abroad to hunt for food, or that it has been forced for some reason to relocate and it has set up in an impromptu lair without a proper labyrinth.

Scaling the Encounter: A minotaur may be a bit too much for a beginning-level party. Feel free to re-roll for another encounter. Conversely, if you want to run a more challenging encounter for a higher-level party, consider that two minotaurs inhabit this lair. They work

as a team, seeking to attack your party from different angles.

Treasure: At the heart of the minotaur's lair is its treasure hoard — as well as the remains of its previous victims. Roll once on the Treasure Hoard: Challenge 0-4 table if one minotaur is present, or on the Treasure Hoard: Challenge 5-10 table if two are present.

Oozes. Oozes are an icky occupational hazard of adventuring in caverns and dungeons. They're like black scum and hair clogs to a plumber, except that they can reach out, swallow you whole and dissolve all your tools. Roll on table 1.2.3 to determine the type of ooze encountered:

TABLE 1.2.3
Oozes - Caverns

d6	ENCOUNTER
1	Black Pudding
2-3	Gelatinous Cube
4-5	Gray Ooze
6	Ochre Jelly

Black Pudding. You may allow your party a DC 15 Wisdom (Perception) check to notice that what looks at first like a patch of shadow is moving like spreading sludge. Failure means that there is no way that they can react in time to avoid it; combat begins with the black pudding no more than 20 feet away from a party member.

Gelatinous Cube. A gelatinous cube may be hard to make out in dim light. It is also large enough to block a typical tunnel or passage, so there's no good way to get around it even once you know it is there.

If you wish, consider that the gelatinous cube has fed just moments before your party discovers it. In particular, consider this as an option if your party contains members with enough hit points left so that they can sustain some acid damage in order to rescue someone from the belly of the cube. In this case, there is a human or humanoid of your choice inside the cube and it has not yet taken any damage from being digested. It may be the last surviving member of an adventuring party, an explorer, or even a foolish spelunker looking for a thrill. Feel free to roll on Table 1.5 if you want some guidance.

Gray Ooze. You may allow your party a DC 15 Wisdom (Perception) check to notice that some nearby rocks or rubble seem to have a wet sheen. If there is

➤

stonework present, the mortar between the stones seems to be oozing. That's because it's a gray ooze, and it strikes at the nearest party member with a metal shield or weapon.

Ochre Jelly. Your party notices that something seems about to drip down from the ceiling. You may require a DC 15 Wisdom (Perception) or Wisdom (Survival) check to realize that it's a dull yellow color — not quite right for it to be water. Of course, it's an ochre jelly and it's about to reach down and strike at them.

Scaling the Encounter: Because of their size, oozes generally work alone. There just isn't room enough for more than one of them at a time. Furthermore, a black pudding may be a bit much for a beginning-level party, so you may re-roll on Table 1.2.3 for a different ooze. However, if you wish to make a gray ooze encounter more challenging, consider that the group consists of 1d4+1 gray oozes.

Treasure: Most oozes feed on the move, so that they have no lair where they accumulate treasure. And in any event, black puddings and gray oozes are notorious for dissolving metal and any other substance of which a valuable item might be made. However, gelatinous cubes and ochre jellies are equally noted for destroying flesh but leaving harder substances undamaged. Therefore, you should roll once on the Treasure Hoard: Challenge 0-4 table for each gelatinous cube and ochre jelly killed.

Otyugh. Your party comes upon a pile of offal and other rotting discards. Given the limited visibility, you may allow them a DC 15 Wisdom (Perception) check to smell it before they can see it. Unfortunately for them, it's also the lair of an otyugh, which reaches out from the unspeakable muck and attacks them. This otyugh may be an independent predator, or it may have a symbiotic relationship with a nearby humanoid colony that uses it as a combined garbage disposal and guard aberration. If the latter, you may roll on Table 1.4 to determine who or what takes alarm when they hear disquieting noises coming from their garbage dump.

Scaling the Encounter: If your party's average level is lower than 5, an otyugh may be more than you want to throw at them. Feel free to re-roll for a different encounter. Conversely, if you want to run a more challenging encounter for a higher-level party, consider that your party has come across a large and genuinely appalling pile of rot, and that it conceals one otyugh for each multiple of 7 in your party's average level.

Treasure: The belongings of the otyugh's previous victims lie scattered about its lair; it's just a question of whether your party has the stomach to go through it all after defeating the monster. Roll once on the Treasure Hoard: Challenge 5-10 table for each otyugh present to determine its contents.

Purple Worm. It's never a good sign when the ground beneath your feet rumbles, quivers and buckles. It's all the more disquieting when the ground is solid rock. One of the most disturbing possibilities when this happens is that a purple worm, using its tremorsense, has spotted your party as its next meal. The worm's approach should give them enough time to sense that something is amiss and do something about it; you may allow them a DC 15 Intelligence (Nature) check to realize that it's a purple worm causing the disturbance underfoot. Combat begins when it breaches the surface within striking distance of your party.

Scaling the Encounter: If your party's average level is lower than 15, a purple worm may be more than you want to throw at them. Feel free to re-roll for a different encounter.

Treasure: Cutting open and gutting a purple worm is quite a chore, but it should reveal valuables that belonged to its previous prey — and purple worms eat a lot. Roll on the Treasure Hoard: Challenge 11-16 table to determine total hoard.

Roper. As your party passes through a chamber, they realize that what looks like a stalactite or a stalagmite is no such thing; it's a roper. From its point of view, your party looks like its next meal, and it acts accordingly.

Scaling the Encounter: If your party's average level is lower than 5, a roper may be more than you want to throw at them. Feel free to re-roll for a different encounter. Conversely, if you want to run a more challenging encounter for a higher-level party, use an encounter group of one roper for each multiple of 7 in your party's average level.

Treasure: Ropers wait for their prey to come to them, so wherever your party encounters them, that's going to be their lair. Valuables from their previous victims are either scattered about or inside their bodies. Determine the total CR of the encounter and roll on the appropriate Treasure Hoard table.

Rust Monster. Assuming that at least one member of your party wears armor or carries a weapon with ferrous metal in it, 1d4 rust monsters scuttle at them, drawn by their unique idea of what constitutes a hearty meal.

Scaling the Encounter: Rust monsters do not occur in large groups. But if you want to provide a more challenging encounter, use a swarm (relatively speaking) of 2d4 rust monsters.

Salamanders. The subterranean world seems like it would bore a salamander, since there is so little to set aflame in a place encased in rock. However, they are drawn to any trace of volcanic activity, and even lava at the bottom of a crevasse creates a comfortable spot for them. Your party comes across one fire snake at its ease in such a place. It decides to set fire to their clothes and other flammable possessions just for amusement.

Scaling the Encounter: If you wish to make the encounter more challenging, the encounter group consists of two fire snakes for each multiple of 3 in your party's average level. You may substitute one salamander for five fire snakes.

Scorpions. For whatever reason, your party's approach disturbs 1d8 scorpions sheltering among some rubble, and they attack your party. They have stingers, and they don't hesitate to use them.

Scaling the Encounter: If your party's average level is 5 or higher, they have attracted the attention of one or more giant scorpions. In this case, the encounter group consists of one giant scorpion for each multiple of 7 in your party's average level.

Spiders. Spiders in caverns have the right setup to weave large webs that are hard for larger creatures to avoid. A web that provides a meaningful encounter for your party is going to be too large to skirt — perhaps it spans a tunnel from side to side, blocking it entirely. It may be an empty web, as in Table 1.6: Hampering Web, or it may be crawling with spiders — or it may be that just one very big and dangerous spider calls it home and hunting ground.

Roll on Table 1.2.4 to determine what kind of spider your party encounters:

TABLE 1.2.4
Spiders - Caverns

d6	ENCOUNTER
1-3	Spiders
4-5	Giant Spider
6	Phase Spider

Spiders. Your party is confronted by a large web
➤

that is home to 2d8 spiders that swarm anything caught in it. Unless your party has adequate illumination or darkvision, you may require your party to make a DC 15 Wisdom (Perception) check to avoid walking right into it.

Giant Spider. Instead of a bunch of small spiders, the large web houses one giant spider. It may not wait for someone from your party to get entangled in its web; instead it uses its web ranged weapon attack to immobilize anyone who gets within range.

Phase Spider. Your party encounters one phase spider that literally appears out of nowhere. Phase spiders are quite fearless, and they use their ability to jump back and forth between planes to conduct hit-and-run attacks, wearing the party down until they are all incapacitated or dead.

Scaling the Encounter: Giant spiders live alone, as too much weight would drag down their web. If you want to create a more challenging encounter with ordinary spiders, you may add another 2d8 to the encounter group — having too many, however, not only creates an unwieldy encounter, but it assumes an awfully large population of spiders for a single web.

A phase spider may be a bit too much for a beginning-level party. Feel free to re-roll for another encounter. Conversely, if you want to run a more challenging encounter for a higher-level party, use an encounter group consisting of one phase spider for each multiple of 4 in your party's average level.

Treasure. Giant spiders may have trapped humanoid-sized victims in the past and left some of their valuables caught in their web. You may roll on the Individual Treasure: Challenge 0-4 table if you wish.

Stirges. Your party spots what appears to be a swarm of 2d6 oversized bats hanging from the ceiling. You may allow them a DC 15 Intelligence (Nature) check to realize that they're actually stirges right before they swoop down and attack. Anyone who passes below looks like a good blood meal to them.

Scaling the Encounter: If you wish to make the encounter more challenging (and the encounter takes place in a space large enough to accommodate so many stirges), the encounter group consists of 1d8 stirges plus 1d4 stirges for each level in your party's average level.

Troll. A cavern complex can be a tough place for a troll to make a living. There are too few soft marks and too many creatures who would rather fight back than let a troll shake them down. And that's to say nothing of the plentiful predators, who not only have no money to fork over, but they'd sooner gut you than parlay with you. But trolls live here nonetheless. Your party comes across one troll either gnawing on bones in the cavern in which it makes its lair, or blocking a tunnel so it can extort anyone who wants to get past.

Scaling the Encounter: If your party's average level is lower than 5, a troll may be more than you want to throw at them. Feel free to re-roll for a different encounter. Conversely, if your party's average level is 10 or higher, feel free to add one troll to the encounter — a tag-team of trolls.

Treasure: The troll's racket has worked well enough in the past: Its victims pay one way or another. If your party defeats the troll in its lair, roll on the Treasure Hoard: Challenge 5-10 table for each troll present to determine the hoard.

Undead. Considering how many different ways there are to meet a bad end in caverns, encountering the restless dead in this environment should come as no surprise. Roll on Table 1.2.5 to determine the undead abomination encountered:

TABLE 1.2.5
Undead - Caverns

D2	ENCOUNTER
1	Ghost
2-6	Ghouls/Ghasts
7	Shadows
8-11	Skeletons
12-14	Specter
15-16	Wight
17	Wraith
18-20	Zombies

Ghost. A ghost is hard to miss in the pitch dark of a cavern, and it leaves a vivid impression on anyone who sees it. Almost certainly, it is the remnant of someone who died unhappily in this horrible place. Perhaps it fell to its death in the darkness, or it was slain by any of the monsters or humanoids that dwell here. You may make this into a hostile encounter by having the ghost try to possess a member of your party so that it may resolve unfinished business from its former life. This may lead to a small side quest for your party if this unfinished business involves retribution against the denizens of these caverns.

➤

Ghouls/Ghasts. Ghouls and ghasts are things of the night. But in the subterranean darkness, the differences between night and day are purely theoretical and these undead walk at anytime. Furthermore, there never seems to be any shortage of rotting corpses from which to create them. Two ghouls (or one ghast) approach your party, driven by mindless hunger for their flesh.

Shadows. The lurid glow of your party's torches casts a shadow of someone who isn't there! That's because the shadow is a creature in its own right, and even in complete darkness it could spot your party as its prey. Without thinking or feeling, it attacks the nearest party member, eager to drain the life from another victim and create one more of its own kind.

Skeletons. Your party comes across 1d4 skeletons that were once human or humanoid. They're still equipped in the arms and armor they had at their demise. Perhaps they were explorers or adventurers. Perhaps they were bandits, for whom these caverns provided less safety than they'd anticipated. In any event, they attack, driven by necromantic echoes of their battle lust or rage at their fate.

Specter. Specters find the perpetual gloom of subterranean spaces much to their liking, as there is never any sunlight to hamper them. Your party comes upon one specter that was once someone who perished in this forsaken place, but all connections to who and what it was in life no longer exist. Only blind hatred of the living drives it to attack your party on sight.

Wight. It's hard to notice details in the dark, so you may require your party to make a successful DC 15 Wisdom (Perception) check to spot the skeletal pallor, death's-head grin and demonic red eyes on the otherwise humanoid figure before them before it can size them up. They have come face-to-face with a wight. The wight can have any one of a number of different backstories and motivations taken from its life. One possibility is that it was the leader of a bandit gang whose followers betrayed and killed him, and that it's looking to create zombie followers who will help it exact revenge. Or perhaps it was an adventurer stabbed in the back by his companions to create larger shares of the loot. Ultimately, it's up to you to decide what's going on with this wight and how it fits into your campaign world.

Wraith. Given the darkness of their surroundings, you may require that your party make a successful DC 15 Wisdom (Perception) check to see the gray, wispy

➤

form approaching them before it comes close enough to attack. This wraith was once someone who perished in this forsaken place. Perhaps your party passes a cairn improvised from rubble, or the wraith rises from bones stripped bare by a predator. Whatever the case, it takes out the resentment that it bore at the end of its life on your party.

Zombies. Your party come across 1d4 zombies that have been programmed to kill every living thing they encounter. The source of the necromancy that created these zombies is up to you. Perhaps they slipped the leash of their creator and they now wander mindlessly, looking for victims.

Scaling the Encounter: Ghosts and wraiths always work alone, and so does a wight in many circumstances. The base encounter group for specters also consists of only one of its kind.

A wight or a wraith may be a bit too much for a beginning-level party. Feel free to re-roll for another encounter. However, if you want to make a wight encounter more challenging, add one zombie minion for each level in your party's average level above 3. With specters, you may create a more challenging encounter by using two specters for each multiple of 3 in your party's average level, with all of them being part of a group that perished *en masse*.

Shadows: The encounter group consists of two shadows for each multiple of 3 in your party's average level.

Skeletons: If you wish to make the encounter more challenging, the encounter group consists of 1d4 skeletons plus one skeleton for each level in your party's average level. You may substitute one warhorse skeleton for two skeletons.

Zombies: If you wish to make the encounter more challenging, the encounter group consists of 1d4 zombies plus plus one zombie for each level in your party's average level. If the average party level is 3 or higher, you may use an encounter group consisting of one ogre zombie for each multiple of 3 in the party's average level.

Treasure: It's quite possible that ghosts and wraiths are encountered in or near the place where they died or were buried — in which case, the valuables they had on them are lying about somewhere. You may require a successful DC 15 Wisdom (Perception) check to find its exact location, and roll on the appropriate Individual Treasure table. ➤

With skeletons and zombies, they may have with them some remains of what they had on their person at the time of their death. Roll on the Individual Treasure: Challenge 5-10 table for a wraith. Roll on the Individual Treasure: Challenge 0-4 table once for each multiple of four skeletons or zombies, rounded up.

Xorn. The good news for your party is that they have stumbled upon a cache of precious metals and/or uncut gemstones, or at least a vein of rock containing precious metal ore or gemstones. The bad news is, so has a xorn. And the xorn is willing to fight to the death for possession of it. As far as it is concerned, your party is trying to steal its kill.

Scaling the Encounter: If your party's average level is lower than 5, a xorn may be more than you want to throw at them. Feel free to re-roll for a different encounter.

TABLE 1.3
Neutral Creatures - Caverns

d20	ENCOUNTER
1	Azer
2-4	Bats
5-9	Centipede
10	Dragon
11-13	Fire Beetle
14-16	Lizards
17-19	Rats
20	Stone Giant

Azer. Most likely, azers encountered on the Material Plane are working on a specific task for someone who has summoned them, or they have been cut loose from their obligations after something untoward happened to their summoner. So when your party crosses paths with one azer, it is probably on an urgent errand for its master and refuses to be detained. Or perhaps, it is at loose ends (either because it has completed the task for which it was summoned, or because its summoner is no more) and, for some reason, it cannot return to its native plane.

In any case, it may be persuaded to help your party in exchange for credible leads on a good source of precious metals or gems, or for help in returning to the azer kingdom. In these cases, your party must make a successful DC 15 Charisma (Persuasion) check and have someone who can communicate with the azer.

Scaling the Encounter: Azers are not automatically hostile to your party (unless it has an efreeti with it), so scaling the encounter may not be a big deal. However, if you want to use an encounter group that will challenge a higher-level party, it consists of one azer for each multiple of 3 in your party's average level. Consider that they are a work party come to the Material Plane is to exploit a known source of precious metals or gems.

Treasure: Roll on the Individual Treasure: Challenge 0-4 table to determine what valuables the azer carries on its person.

Bats. Of course you encounter bats; you're exploring caverns. Your party approaches a colony consisting of 1d4+1 swarms of bats, all of them hanging from the ceiling and walls. However, even though they're uncomfortably close to the bats' lair, it's possible to avoid setting them off. You may have your party make a DC 15 Wisdom (Survival) or Intelligence (Nature) check. Failure means that someone makes a false move that triggers the bats' fight-or-flight response, and having nowhere to flee, they fight.

Scaling the Encounter: If you want to make the encounter more challenging for a higher-level party, use an encounter group consisting of 1d4 giant bats and/or swarm of bats in any combination, plus one swarm of bats or giant bat for each level in your party's average level.

A Monster-Eat-Monster World
You may notice that there aren't many neutral encounters in this chapter. That's just how things worked out. The fact is, if you go through all of the creatures in the SRD and pick out the ones that seem characteristic of a subterranean environment, most of them are aggressive and predatory. More likely than not, whatever you find down here, it would be out of character if it backed down from a fight.

Centipede. Have your party make a DC 15 Wisdom (Perception) group check. Failure means that no one notices the giant centipede wending its way across their path and someone in the front of the march order comes dangerously close to stepping on it. The giant centipede responds by attacking that character. Success means that they notice the giant centipede in time to avoid provoking it, thus making a hostile encounter purely optional.

Dragon. Dragons encountered at random in a subterranean space are coming from or returning to their lair. It's not at all unusual for them to keep their lair in caves and such, and they have to have some way of getting in and out so they can terrorize the puny beings

who live in the open, right? To determine what kind of dragon your party encounters, roll on Table 1.3.1:

TABLE 1.3.1
Dragon - Caverns

d12	ENCOUNTER
1	Black
2	Blue
3	Green
4-5	Red
6-7	White
8	Brass
9	Bronze
10	Copper
11	Gold
12	Silver

To determine its age, see Scaling the Encounter.

To be clear, this need not be a hostile encounter. A chance meeting with a dragon so close to its lair is bound to raise its suspicions. But they're shrewd and highly intelligent creatures, so a dragon stumbling upon adventurers close to its hearth and home may want to figure out their angle — their reason for being here — before doing something it can't take back. This encounter should test how well your party can talk its way out of a dicey situation (if they don't want a close-quarters fight with a dangerous and iconic creature, that is).

Scaling the Encounter: Because dragons get tougher with age, the age of the dragon encountered should depend on your party's average level — especially if you decide that this is going to be a hostile encounter. If your party's average level is 10 or lower, they encounter a wyrmling. If theirs average level is 11-18, they encounter a young dragon. If their average level is 19-25, they encounter an adult dragon. If their average level is higher than 25, they encounter an ancient dragon.

Fire Beetles. Your party comes across 1d6 giant fire beetles scuttling along the cave floor. Fire beetles are not aggressive, but they defend themselves if threatened — if they're hunted for their luminous glands, for instance.

Lizards. Your party crosses paths with 1d6 giant lizards foraging for insects and small animals. They are not aggressive and they can be wrangled and trained to serve as pack animals or mounts. To wrangle a giant lizard, it must be successfully grappled and kept in grappled condition for 10 consecutive rounds. At that point, it becomes docile and submits to whomever grappled it. Because of its size, two medium-size creatures may grapple with the same giant lizard simultaneously, and as long as one of them maintains its grappled condition, this counts toward the requirement for wrangling it.

Alternately, you may consider that the giant lizards are already tame. They wear harnesses that allow them to be led, with straps and ties for securing cargo to their backs. Merchants and miners who traverse the underground use them as pack animals — they have low overhead clearance and good balance, and they don't freak out in subterranean spaces as easily as horses and mules — so it's a reasonable bet that giant lizards encountered here have become separated their owners. Returning them might produce a reward — although if the true owners turn out to be drow, that reward would take the form of eternal servitude to the Spider Queen. In any event, this could create a worthwhile sidequest for your party.

Rats. You will find rats everywhere they can find food. Roll on Table 1.3.2 to determine the nature of the rat encounter:

TABLE 1.3.2
Rats - Caverns

d6	ENCOUNTER
1	Lone Rat
2-4	Swarm of Rats
5-6	Giant Rats

Lone Rat. A single rat, foraging by itself or lost from its nest, approaches your party while they take a rest. It's not much of a threat, but if someone in your party is looking for a familiar or even just a pet, this is an opportunity. Interacting with the rat — especially earning its trust with food — and making a successful DC 10 Intelligence (Nature) check earns its loyalty.

Swarm of Rats. One swarm of rats sniffs out your party's food rations as they cross paths with each other. They don't attack party members who don't interfere with their basic mission of acquiring food. But unless they are stopped, they eventually account for all of your party's rations, making off with what they don't eat on the spot.

Giant Rats. In this case, the rats drawn by the food your party carries are giant rats. There are 2d6 of them.

Stone Giants. As unlikely as it seems that an environment with relatively low overhead clearance would accommodate giants, subterranean spaces are home turf to stone giants. Your party crosses paths with one stone giant outside of its lair, either traveling or patrolling the area.

Stone giants insist on having their space. They don't like sharing cavern networks with other creatures, and they'll throw elbows to make sure they are left alone. They treat your party with suspicion, but they are not necessarily aggressive. If your party persuades it that they are not hostile, the stone giant may (depending on the situation in which its tribe finds itself) ask them to help in dealing with unruly neighbors.

Scaling the Encounter: If your party's average level is lower than 7, a stone giant may be more than you want to throw at them. Feel free to re-roll for a different encounter. On the other hand, if your party's average level is 15 or higher, you may want to add one stone giant to the encounter. At your discretion, each stone giant may be accompanied by a pet black bear on a leash.

Treasure: Roll on the Individual Treasure: Challenge 5-10 table for each stone giant present to determine the valuables on their person.

A large, cavernous space serves well as a permanent dwelling if you have the right temperament. With all of the encounters described below, there is a chance that they take place in or very near the creatures' lair. In that case, roll on the appropriate Treasure Hoard table according to the total CR of the encounter.

TABLE 1.4
Humanoids - Caverns

d20	ENCOUNTER
1-2	Bugbears
3-5	Drow
6	Duergar
7-8	Dwarves
9	Gnomes
10-12	Goblins
13	Grimlocks
14	Hobgoblins
15-17	Kobolds
18-19	Orcs
20	Svirfneblin

Bugbears. Your party crosses paths with one or more bugbears (see Scaling the Encounter). Caverns are a natural place for bugbears to make their lair, so depending on circumstance, it is possible that your party finds them on their home turf. The situation of the bugbears encountered depends on the size of the encounter group.

One or two bugbears are likely sentries guarding their lair, or they're patrolling the surrounding area, or scouting a target ahead of a raid. They might also be headed to the world outside the caverns — perhaps their tribe has been hired as mercenaries for a forthcoming war, and they are carrying messages back and forth to their new boss. In any case, they are likely to demand that your party state their business before starting a fight.

If the encounter group is larger than that and your party is entering a large cavern, they may have stumbled upon a bugbear tribe's lair. If you decide this is not their lair, then perhaps the group is a raiding party on its way to the outside world, or to a target in a nearby cavern. Perhaps they are mustering for war and heading off to join the main army. In the first case, they fight to the death to defend their home base. In the other cases, they may ignore your party, brushing them aside as they have more important things in mind.

Scaling the Encounter: A beginning-level party should only have to cope with one bugbear. If you wish to make the encounter more challenging, the encounter group consists of two bugbears for each multiple of 3 in your party's average level. If your party's average level is 10 or higher, add one bugbear chief as the group's leader.

Drow. Drow are in their element in this kind of environment. However, if your campaign world includes large concentrations of drow, such as the underground cities for which they are known, those are fixed locations rather than random encounters. A random encounter with drow may be an extension of those fixed locations.

A small group of drow encountered away from a settlement may be a military outpost in a nook carved into the wall of a passage. It may be a patrol based in one of those outposts. If there is a large drow presence in the general area, they may be messengers shuttling between the drow and other denizens of the caverns. Or perhaps they are going abroad for no particular reason at all — just subterranean sightseeing. If they are a military patrol or outpost, they fan out upon spotting your party, take cover among rocks and rubble and ready their hand crossbows. In any event, they treat your party with deep suspicion — anyone who is not drow is a potential enemy.

A large group of drow likely has a more serious purpose in mind. They may be a raiding party on the way to their target for the day. Or they may be a raiding party on

their way back, with loot and 2d6 human and/or humanoid captives. Another possibility is that your party crosses paths with a drow merchant caravan, in which case the encounter group also consists of 2d6 giant lizards and human and/or humanoid slaves acting as lizard drovers and bearers, equal to the number of giant lizards present + 1d8. Consider that there is a 5% chance that any given captive/slave is someone of consequence, who could provide your party with a significant reward for their safe return home. In all such cases, the encounter group has more important things to do than deal with your party.

Scaling the Encounter: Use an encounter group of 1d4 drow for each level in your party's average level. If your party's average level is 10-14 add one drow elite warrior to the group as its leader. If you don't want to run a mass encounter, feel free to substitute one drow elite warrior for 20 drow as much as you like.

No Angels? No Demons or Devils?
Demons and devils make great antagonists, but as natives of other planes they have no easy hook for placing them in an environment on the Material Plane. With elementals (including mephits), at least, they have an innate connection with an aspect of the Material Plane that can tie them to a particular type of terrain. Mud mephits in a swamp, a water elemental in a tide pool? Makes at least a modicum of sense. All it takes is a little imagination to conjure an excuse for why they would linger outside of their native plane. But an erinyes or a glabrezu? What would they be doing in the Material Plane? There has to be a very particular purpose behind their presence, in which case that purpose should be tied to your deliberate design of your campaign world or narrative line rather than emerging out of the probabilities reflected in a random encounter table.

Same thing with angels. They're a striking addition to a campaign, but it's hard to tie them to a particular likelihood of appearing in a particular environment in the Material Plane because they have to have a very specific reason for being here. That reason, whatever it is, is bound to involve so many details that need to flow organically from your particular campaign world.

Treasure: If the encounter group is a returning raiding party, determine the total challenge level and roll on the appropriate Treasure Hoard table. If it includes a merchant caravan, determine the value of their cargo by rolling on the appropriate Treasure Hoard table, where the challenge level equals the number of giant lizards present; this is in addition to any individual treasure found on caravan members.

Duergar. Your party crosses paths with a lone figure that looks like a dwarf, but with gray skin that seems to blend into the gloom of the cavern. It's a duergar, and most likely it's there for either of two reasons: It's on its way to or from a work gang engaged in mining or stone working; or it is a sentry for a nearby duergar colony. A small group of duergar are probably a work gang in transit. A large group of duergar may be a large work gang or even a war party on its way to attack a rival. If your party happens to be in a large cavern, they could have stumbled into the duergar lair.

Duergar do not automatically attack strangers, but they do regard your party with deep suspicion. However, it is possible that the presence of a dwarf in your party triggers them, and they challenge that character (or characters) to a fight at the slightest provocation. On the other hand, it is also possible that your party meets a duergar colony that could use some help dealing with a local rival in this subterranean world. In this case, they try to hire your party as mercenaries, offering them each an uncut gem (the value of which should depend on the term of service) as payment.

Scaling the Encounter: The encounter group consists of two duergar for each multiple of 3 in your party's average level.

No Vampires?
As described in 5th Edition, vampires are boss monsters — powerful villains who should serve as fixed points in your campaign. They are also closely linked to a particular location. Without that prominent location nearby, there should be no vampire.

Same with liches. You're not going to randomly meet a lich coming the other way as you walk down a country road. It's just not going to happen.

However, vampires (like doppelgängers) just might show up when I get around to writing about random encounters in cities and towns.

Dwarves. Your party crosses paths with a small group of dwarves in their natural environment. However, if your campaign world includes large subterranean concentrations of dwarves, such as full-fledged mining settlements, they should qualify as fixed locations rather than random encounters. A random encounter with dwarves may be an extension of those fixed locations,

most likely a work or exploration party or a military patrol on the lookout for enemies — a subterranean wilderness is bound to include many familiar enemies, like orcs, goblinoids and duergar.

Unless your party includes any such enemies, dwarves are unlikely to treat them with hostility. It's much more likely that they freely share their local knowledge and even material help — you may require the party to make a successful DC 10 Charisma (Persuasion) check in the latter case. You may also use an encounter with dwarves to provide your party with a sidequest, with the dwarves trying to enlist them in defending their colony against external threats.

Scaling the Encounter: Consider an encounter group consisting of 1d8 guards (armed with battle-axes instead of spears) plus two guards for each level in your party's average level for a military group. A work group consists of 2d6 commoners armed with pickaxes (treat as spears that cannot be thrown) plus two guards for each level in your party's average level. If the encounter takes place in the dwarves' lair, consider an encounter group consisting of 1d4 guards and 1d4 commoners for each level in your party's average level, with one priest or one knight as the colony's leader, or both. If you don't want to run a mass encounter, feel free to substitute one priest for 16 guards or one veteran for 24 guards as freely as you like.

Gnomes. Your party crosses paths with a small party of gnomes, consisting of 2d6 commoners and one priest. They may be freelance mechanics who travel between mines, looking to sell their services. Or they may be a daring (perhaps foolhardy?) bunch of gem cutters looking to cut out the middleman and find raw stones themselves. In either case, they have brought along a priest of one of their patron deities as their sole protection.

The gnomes are not aggressive. It won't take much prompting to get them to trade with your party and share local knowledge. Their priest may be willing to help your party with spells in return for the standard price for such services.

Goblins. Goblins like to make their lairs in caverns, so it is quite possible that your party could stumble upon a cavern containing a goblin tribe's base of operations. If the guidelines for scaling the encounter suggest a small group of goblins, they're probably associated with a nearby lair. They may be patrolling the tunnels near the lair or sentries posted at a fixed location. They may be a hunting party. Or they may be messengers traveling between their tribe and an allied tribe. But goblins are common enough and sufficiently comfortable in this environment that they may be out and about for no particular reason at all.

A large group of goblins is likely to be a raiding party on their way out. Or they may be a raiding party on their way back, with loot and 1d6 human and/or humanoid captives. Consider that there is a 5% chance that any given captive is someone of consequence, who could provide your party with a significant reward for their safe return home. In either case, the encounter group has more important things to do than deal with your party. However, if your party finds a goblin lair, they fight to the death to defend it. In addition to the normal treasure found in the lair, there are 1d8 human and/or humanoid captives bound and eager for rescue.

Scaling the Encounter: Use an encounter group of 1d4 goblins for each level in your party's average level. If you don't want to run a mass encounter but you still want to provide a higher-level party with a meaningful challenge, feel free to substitute one goblin boss for four goblins as much as you like.

Treasure: If the encounter group is a returning raiding party, determine the total CR and roll on the appropriate Treasure Hoard table.

Grimlocks. Your party crosses paths with 1d4 grimlocks. A small group of these degenerate humanoids may be sentries posted somewhat apart from their lair, or they may be a hunting party looking for food. Either way, your party probably looks to them like a good target of opportunity to victimize.

A larger group is likely a serious raiding party with a particular target in mind, or coming back from a successful raid. In the latter case, consider that they have 1d6 human and/or humanoid captives with them. Consider that there is a 5% chance that any given captive is someone of consequence, who could provide your party with a significant reward for their safe return home. Likewise, if your party finds the grimlocks in their lair, 1d12 captives may be present.

Scaling the Encounter: Use an encounter group of 1d4 grimlocks plus one grimlock for each level in your party's average level.

Hobgoblins. Hobgoblins prefer defensible strongholds with clear sight lines of the surrounding country, so caverns are not their preferred location to establish a lair. However, it's not inconceivable that a legion fallen on hard times might take refuge here, or that a successful legion might set up a sort of subterranean recruiting station to pull in additional troops from the local evil humanoids.

If your party comes across a small group of hobgoblins, they may be sentries or a patrol securing the area near their lair. But it is also possible that they're messengers shuttling back and forth between other humanoid settlements, trying to recruit allies or just communicating with other hobgoblins. A larger group of hobgoblins indicates that the winds of war are brewing. Unless your party has stumbled upon the hobgoblin lair, a large hobgoblin encounter group would be a war party on their way to or from the war zone. That war zone might be located in the outside world, or they may be party to a war in the caverns themselves. In any event, they have more important business than attacking your party; in fact, they might even size them up and try to recruit them to fill out the ranks.

Scaling the Encounter: The baseline encounter group should consist of 1d4 hobgoblins for each multiple of 2 in your party's average level. If your party's average level is 10-19, add a hobgoblin Captain as the group leader, accompanied by two goblin servants or one bugbear. If your party's average level is 20 or higher, add instead one hobgoblin warlord with two bugbear aides.

Kobolds. Your party comes across a small group of these nasty little reptilian humanoids. Unless your party stumbles upon their lair, they are most likely out hunting. To them, your party looks like a good source of plunder. If your party does not surprise them, they fan out to take cover among rocks and rubble, hoping to ambush them as they pass. If there are ledges in the tunnel, they climb onto them and drop rocks onto your party. If there are any gnomes in your party, kobolds focus on attacking them as much as possible.

With a large encounter group, it's possible that your party has stumbled upon the kobolds' lair. In this case, all entrances to the cavern should have a trap of your choice associated with it.

Scaling the Encounter: Use an encounter group of 2d4 kobolds plus 1d4 kobolds for each level in your party's average level. If you'd rather not run a mass encounter, you may cut down on the kobold's numbers by substituting one winged kobold for two kobolds as much as you like.

Lycanthrope. To determine what manner of werebeast your party encounters, roll on Table 1.4.1:

TABLE 1.4.1

Lycanthropes - Caverns

d6	ENCOUNTER
1-4	Wererat
5-6	Werewolf
➤	

All lycanthropes assume their animal form if the encounter comes down to combat, although they may choose their hybrid form instead if they have access to a weapon.

Wererat. One wererat from a colony looking to enlarge its population tries to ambush your party. You may require your party to make a DC 20 Wisdom (Perception) check to see it at a distance and notice that it changes from its hybrid form into its humanoid form before disappearing into the shadows, where it will wait for them to come within striking distance. If your party has darkvision, the DC is only 15.

Werewolf. Caverns can provide werewolves a refuge if they're being hunted in the outside world. However, this environment is not without its hazards. Your party crosses paths with one werewolf in its hybrid form. It feels little need to conceal its identity because making a show of its true strength can scare off enemies. Instinctively, it regards your party as enemies, so it attacks first and asks questions later.

Scaling the Encounter: A werewolf may be more than you want to throw at a low-level party. If your party's average level is 3 or less, feel free to re-roll the encounter. Alternately, if you want to make a lycanthrope encounter more challenging for a higher-level party, use a pack of them consisting of one werewolf for each multiple of 5 in your party's average level or one wererat for each multiple of 3 in your party's average level.

Orcs. It's a dangerous way to make a living in the subterranean depths, but that does not deter orcs who exist by taking what they can from their neighbors. In particular, they like to pick on dwarf mining colonies, if they can find them — not only are dwarves good at finding precious metals, but wreaking havoc on them is fun. A small group could be a scout party out to get the lay of the land, while a larger group would be an actual raiding party on its way to — or on its way back from — its target.

Your party crosses paths with these orcs. But if they're on an actual raid there's no guarantee that they'll pay your party much attention. Their leader may look your party over and decide that they're not worth the bother. But they may also decide to interrogate your party for information about the surrounding area, and they'll easily resort to violence if your party is slow to cooperate. They are less likely to give your party a break if there are dwarves in it. They'll also make elf characters a special focus of their hostility, although it would surprise them to find an elf in this environment.

Scaling the Encounter: The baseline encounter group should consist of 1d4 orcs for each multiple of 2 in your party's average level. If your party's average level is 5-9, consider adding an orog as the group's leader. If your party's average level is 10 or higher, use an orc war chief as its leader.

Treasure: If the orcs are coming back from a successful raid, you may roll on the Treasure Hoard: Challenge 0-4 table to determine the fruits of their labor. This is in addition to the individual treasure they carry.

Svirfneblin. Your party crosses paths with a small group of svirfneblin from a nearby settlement. They're looking for new sources of gems, or on their way to work a known vein. Deep gnomes are instinctively suspicious of outsiders. Unless they have an elemental companion to protect them (see Scaling the Encounter), they use their stone camouflage ability to try to conceal themselves at your party's approach.

That being said, svirfneblin are not aggressive, and they can provide local knowledge and material assistance if your party wins their trust. You may require a DC 15 Charisma (Persuasion) check to make this so, although you may reduce the DC to 10 if your party has a gnome do the talking. The biggest risk in an encounter with a larger group of svirfneblin is that their elemental companion may slip its leash and go after your party.

Scaling the Encounter: The encounter group should consist of a number of svirfneblin equal to your party's average level. If your party's average level is higher than 10, the group has a pet xorn or earth elemental with it.

TABLE 1.5
Humans - Caverns

d10	ENCOUNTER
1-2	Adventurers
3-5	Bandits
6	Exiles
7	Explorers
8	Fugitives
9-10	Miners

Adventurers. Unless your party are the only adventurers in your campaign world, it shouldn't come as a complete surprise to meet another party. Caverns are a classic destination for anyone looking to defeat monsters and gain wealth and glory. How they react to your party depends on a variety of factors. Are they rivals pursuing the same goal? If not, perhaps this party is willing to share useful information. In fact, if your party is stuck and having a hard time advancing the storyline of your campaign, a friendly encounter like this can help steer them in the right direction. Differences in alignment may also shape how the two parties react to each other. Composition of this adventuring party is up to you and can vary widely according to circumstance. A party plunging into the underground might be foolhardy newcomers, or canny veterans. It may have at least one dwarf, brought along to use darkvision and stonecunning. It may also have at least one rogue to deal with traps and hazards.

Scaling the Encounter: Unless there is some possibility that this encounter turns hostile, the relative level of the party is mainly a matter of affect. A higher-level party might project self-confidence and calm (even arrogance), while a beginning-level party might stumble about, unsure of themselves. If you're leaning towards a hostile encounter, however, consider that the average level of the party should be roughly two-thirds of your party's average level.

Bandits. Caverns offer bandits a suitable place to make a lair, since officers of the law would have to be brave indeed to try to find them here. However, making their way to the outside world is a chore and a hazard, as is living in a place surrounded by creatures that would just as soon kill you for loot (or for food) as look at you.

Your party runs into a small group of bandits who have been sent to make sure the coast is clear. They may not treat your party as a target, as adventurers are usually too well-armed. However, if they belong to a gang that sees the residents of nearby caves as potential enemies, they may try to hire your party as mercenaries to supplement their numbers — and, ideally, take some blows for them.

Scaling the Encounter: As a rough guideline, the encounter group should contain 1d8 bandits for each level in your party's average level. If your party's average level is 4 or higher, add a bandit captain as their leader. If you don't want to run a mass encounter but you still want these criminals to provide a higher-level party with a meaningful challenge, feel free to substitute one thug for four bandits as much as you like.

Treasure: If your party finds the bandits' hideout, roll on the Treasure Hoard table appropriate to the total CR of the encounter. Do so also if you decide that the bandits encountered are on their way back from a successful raid. Consider that there is also a 20% chance that the bandits have with them a high-value captive whom they intend to ransom. The identity of this captive is left to

you as DM, as it should depend on local circumstances and fit into your campaign world.

Exiles. Your party encounters 1d4 humans or humanoids who could serve as a source of adventure hooks. From their appearance, they have obviously seen better days. They have fled their home for any of a variety of reasons: perhaps they are royalty or nobility who have been usurped; perhaps the opposite is the case and they are failed usurpers on the run. Or perhaps they have gotten caught up in a blood feud in their homeland and that's why they fear for their lives. Whatever the circumstance, they have come to this horrifying place as a last resort, looking for a refuge from their enemies. You may consider that some of their group have already fallen to the hazards of the subterranean world by the time your party finds them.

No matter their reason for being here, they should offer your party an adventure hook of some sort. It may involve protecting the exiles from their real (or imagined) pursuers. It may involve returning to their former home and securing an important item that was left behind (a family heirloom, a badge of office), perhaps even helping them return home and force their way back into their former position of prominence. At the very least, exiles can provide your party with information about their former home territory, which in turn could be a key location in your campaign.

Use any NPC template you like for the exiles, depending on the backstory you assign them.

Explorers. Explorers differ from adventurers, much to their detriment. Pure desire to discover drives them, so they go forth lightly armed. This leaves them ill-prepared to face the menaces that live in caverns. Your party crosses paths with a small group consisting of 1d4 scholars (treat them as commoners) and 1d4 scouts (at least one of them should be a dwarf) who act as bodyguards. Perhaps they are here thanks to the sponsorship of an academy or a ruler eager to know more about the world. Or perhaps the explorer is a wealthy eccentric who undertook this expedition on his or her own.

Such an encounter is not likely to be hostile. You may treat this as an opportunity for your party to receive some help from a knowledgeable stranger — the explorers are likely to have excellent maps of nearby areas (and knowledge of those areas) and they're willing to share them. Conversely, they may have reached the point at which they realize that they're in over their heads and the caverns offer more dangers than they can handle. They may ask for food or supplies — or your party's protection — as they continue to explore.

Fugitives. Your party crosses paths with 1d6 bedraggled humans or humanoids stumbling along the broken cavern floor. They are unarmed, and they are barely clothed. At your discretion, they may have a manacle around one wrist, with the other manacle dangling on its chain. They're on the run from something. The manacles indicate that they are escaped prisoners. From whom they are fleeing and why they were imprisoned in the first place is up to you, and ought to depend on where in your campaign world this encounter takes place.

How the encounter plays out depends on how your party reacts, but one thing on which you may rely is that these fugitives did not go to the trouble of a jailbreak just to allow a bunch of strangers to take their freedom back from them. Each of them has learned to whip their freed manacle by the chain and wield it as a club. Treat the fugitives as bandits, but without weapons (except for the manacle) or armor.

Treasure: Fugitives have no treasure.

No Country for Much of Anyone
Compared to the other environments described in this book, you won't find many humans here. With the possible exception of mining, there is no routine business that would bring them to such a horrible place. Except for the foolhardy and the desperate, this is no place for humans.

Miners. Mines that are actively worked do not qualify as caverns in the context of this book; they're settled areas, not wilderness. However, miners who are foolhardy or just ignorant of the dangers may explore the cavernous wilderness, hoping to find treasures of the earth. Your party crosses paths with a small group of 1d10 miners convinced that they'll strike whatever it is they're looking for if they just keep stumbling through the darkness. If there is a mining colony nearby, they might well be an offshoot from it.

This is not likely a hostile encounter. Instead, the miners could have local knowledge that your party finds useful, as well as torches, lamp oil, rope and other supplies for exploring underground. They might also want your party to serve as armed escort, having realized a little too late that dangerous creatures lurk here. In fact, if you want to stage a situation in which your party has the chance to rescue them from their foolhardiness, roll for an additional encounter.

Treat the miners as commoners armed with pickaxes (treat as spears that cannot be thrown).

TABLE 16
Watch Out! - Caverns

d20	ENCOUNTER
1	Abandoned Lair
2-3	Bioluminescence
4	Did You Hear That?
5-8	Falling Rocks
9	Hampering Web
10-11	Loose Footing
12-13	Rock Slide
14-15	Sudden Drop
16-17	Sudden Gust
18	Trap
19-20	Tripping Hazard

Abandoned Lair. A cavern network is a creature-eat-creature world. Your party finds an uninhabited chamber that demonstrates this grim fact. Roll again to determine the type of creature that once dwelt here. The cavern is littered with their abandoned possessions. Humanoids may have left behind something of their culture: cave paintings, art objects, religious objects, and the like. Your party may find their remains are here, as well — in other words, they were slaughtered where they lived.

There is a 50% chance that one entrance to the cavern is guarded by an active trap (see Trap, below).

Treasure: Determine the CR of whatever occupied this abandoned lair. If you decide that they were attacked and slaughtered here, there is a 20% chance that the invaders left some treasure behind. Roll on the appropriate Individual Treasure table. Otherwise, whoever attacked them took everything, and there is no treasure.

If there are no remains of the previous occupants, then the lair was abandoned. Perhaps they went to attack an enemy and never came back? In this case, roll on the appropriate Treasure Hoard table. In other words, your party stumbles upon a freebie.

Bioluminescence. Your party has the good fortune to find a colony of bioluminescent fungi or moss. The illumination turns darkness into dim light, or dim light into bright light, in a 30-foot radius from the center of the colony.

Did You Hear That? The acoustics in this part of the caverns can be deceptive. Choose a party member to make a DC 15 Wisdom (Survival) check. Failure means that that character believes that he or she has heard a monster of your choice vocalize nearby, or some other auditory phenomenon that indicates trouble nearby. A successful check means that the party member in question realizes that this is an illusion, and the noise is either much farther away than it seems, or it is something else entirely.

If you wish, roll on Table 1.6.1 for guidance on what your party thinks it hears:

TABLE 1.6.1
Did You Hear That? - Caverns

d10	What They Think They Hear...
1	Clash of weapons
2	Crash of falling rocks
3	Dragon roaring
4	Gibbering mouther babbling
5	Human or humanoid screaming
6	Monstrous howling
7	Shriekers shrieking
8	Voices speaking in Dwarvish
9	Voices speaking in Undercommon or Elvish with a Drow accent
10	Zombies or ghouls groaning

Falling Rocks. Your party is exploring an environment entirely encased in rock. Who would have thought that loose stones and rubble would fall on them? Make a melee attack roll (no bonuses) against each party member. A successful attack causes 1d6 damage, but a successful DC 15 Dexterity (Acrobatics) check halves the damage, rounded down.

Hampering Web. There is a finely-woven spider's web right in your party's path, spanning the entire width of the passage, but there is no spider present. Your party may make a DC 15 Wisdom (Perception) check to spot the web before someone at the front of the march order walks right into it. Anyone who fails to avoid the web is stuck, and becomes restrained.

The restrained character may attempt to escape by making a DC 20 Strength (Athletics) or DC 20 Dexterity (Acrobatics) check. Other party members may try to free their restrained colleague by making a total of three successful attack rolls with a slashing weapon against the web, which has AC 15. But for each attempt, there is a 10% chance, cumulative with each new attempt, that one giant spider appears from out of the darkness and enters the web from the top edge to see what it caught this time. Each attack roll counts as an attempt.

Loose Ground. In the gloom, your party fails to notice that they're following a passage that slopes downward. It's just steep enough to make you lose your balance if you don't spot it. One character in the front of the march order takes a tumble, suffering 1d6 falling damage. A successful DC 15 Strength (Athletics) or Dexterity (Acrobatics) check halves the damage, rounded down.

Rock Slide. It's not a catastrophe, but enough to cause problems. One side of the passageway was starting to crumble and your party's footfalls set if off. Choose a party member on the flank of the march order. Loose rock cascades onto him or her, causing 2d6 damage. That character is also restrained until freed. A successful DC 15 Dexterity (Acrobatics) check halves the damage, rounded down.

Pulling the restrained character free requires a successful DC 20 Strength (Athletics) check, or your party must spend 10 minutes removing the rocks one by one.

Compared with the other areas described in this book, you won't find many humans here.

Sudden Drop. Your party may or may not notice that a crevasse cuts across the passage in front of them. Have your party make a DC 15 Wisdom (Perception) check to notice it in time to warn the characters at the front of the march order. If the check fails, one character in front falls 20 feet and takes commensurate falling damage, although a successful DC 15 Dexterity (Acrobatics) check halves it through proper bracing for impact.

The crevasse is narrow enough to cross with a running long jump, but this requires a successful DC 10 Strength (Athletics) or Dexterity (Acrobatics) check.

Sudden Gust. Whoosh! A sudden rush of air puts out all lit torches. You may allow anyone holding a torch a DC 20 Dexterity check to keep it lit by shielding it just in time.

Any torch that goes out requires a DC 10 Dexterity check to re-light it; failure means that it's useless.

If you wish, you may roll for another encounter, using the occasion to throw something at your party from out of the sudden darkness.

Trap. Your party stumbles upon an old, but still active, trap. Who set it and why they set it is no longer apparent. But it's there nonetheless and your party still has to deal with it. Roll on Table 1.6.2 to determine the sort of trap, as described in the core rulebooks.

TABLE 1.6.2
Trap - Caverns

d8	ENCOUNTER
1-2	Collapsing Roof
3	Falling Net
4-6	Pit
7	Poison Dart
8	Rolling Sphere

Or use a trap of your own devising. Keep in mind that traps in this environment are most likely simple, even crude, because of limits on the materials available — and the sophistication of those who built them.

Tripping Hazard. Pick a party member at the front of the march order. That character trips over an object unseen in the dim light — a rock, or the remains of a creature, for instance. He or she must make a successful DC 10 Strength (Athletics) or Dexterity (Acrobatics) check to avoid a hard fall that causes 1d4 damage — and perhaps no small embarrassment in the eyes of the other party members.

There's No Ground Like the Underground

Caverns are a unique environment. Essentially, they embody what is deepest in and darkest about the human imagination — which explains a lot about the monsters that you find here, and practically nowhere else.

DESERT

CHAPTER TWO

Desert

What is a Desert?

The desert, with its sweeping vistas, unforgiving climate and apparent hostility to living things, has always been a place of awe and danger. The *Tales of the Arabian Nights* tell us that dust devils and other such natural phenomena are powerful elemental spirits, and in so doing created a mythology that comes down to us in the present day, and not just through fantasy roleplaying games. In more practical terms, the desert is an environment characterized primarily by lack of rainfall and humidity. The rate of evaporation often exceeds rainfall, so the ground is arid, the air is dry and creatures and plants that cannot adapt to these conditions do not live here. Some humanoids and humans live in, or at least travel through the desert but they are relatively few and far between.

However, it is also the case that deserts can be found at various latitudes, so even though traveling through a desert always means traversing a dry place, the weather is not universally the same. Deserts close to the equator, like the Sahara and the Mojave, tend to be hot year-round, while deserts closer to the poles, like the Gobi, can get quite cold in the winter. Because of this, please note that some tables in this chapter require a die-roll modifier depending on the desert's placement in your campaign world.

Desert terrain tends to provide broad vistas with open sight lines. As a general rule, encounters begin with both sides spotting each other from a distance (unless otherwise specified). This requires that either or both sides deliberately closes the range before combat begins.

What do you Find in a Desert?

When you determine that a random encounter is in order, roll on Table 2.1 to determine the category:

TABLE 2.1

Encounter Type - Desert

d20	ENCOUNTER
1-8	Aggressive Creatures (Table 2.2)
9-13	Neutral Creatures (Table 2.3)
14	Humanoids (Table 2.4)
15-16	Humans (Table 2.5)
17-20	Watch Out! (Table 2.6)

Then, roll on the appropriate table to determine the creature, person or thing encountered.

TABLE 2.2

Aggressive Creatures - Desert

d100	ENCOUNTER
1-4	Gorgon
5-8	Basilisk
9-15	Bird of Prey
16-19	Bulette
20-24	Cheetahs
25-28	Chimera
29-32	Death Dog
33-35	Elemental
36-39	Grick
40-43	Griffon
44-45	Hell Hound
46-54	Insects
55-58	Lion
59-62	Manticore
63-65	Medusa
66-69	Mephits
70-73	Ogres
74-76	Oni
77-78	Purple Worm
79-80	Roc
81-86	Scorpions
87-92	Spiders
93-98	Undead
99-104	Snakes

+4 to the die roll if in a tropical desert

Gorgon. Gorgons find hot climates inhospitable because bright sunlight and hot air heat up their carapace of iron plates too much for comfort. But they can be found in sub-arctic or temperate deserts.

Your party approaches a gorgon's lair — perhaps it is a cluster of rocks, or a small cave hollowed out of a rocky outcropping. Petrified chunks lie scattered about outside the lair; you may allow your party a DC 15 Wisdom (Survival) check to realize that they're crumbs leftover from the gorgon's previous meals. The monster is, of course, quite happy to prey on your party and save them for later if it isn't hungry right now. You may also allow your party a DC 10 Wisdom (Perception) check to hear the gorgon before they see it — it's the sound of sand and grit that has gotten in between its metal plates rubbing against them.

Scaling the Encounter: If your party's average level is lower than 5, a gorgon may be more than you want to throw at them. Feel free to re-roll for a different encounter.

Treasure: The lair contains scattered valuables belonging to the gorgon's previous victims. Roll on the Treasure Hoard: Challenge 0-5 table to determine the total haul.

Deserts do not provide many places to hide.

Basilisk. Your party comes across a cluster of rocks that, unfortunately, a basilisk has chosen for its lair. Here it preys upon creatures — and hapless travelers —taking shelter from the sun or blowing sand; they don't realize what they've gotten themselves into until it is too late.

Because the basilisk doesn't have to go far from its sheltering place, this encounter is likely to start at a closer range than a typical desert encounter. However, you may allow a DC 15 Wisdom (Perception) or Wisdom (Survival) check to hear something stirring behind the rocks, or at least to intuit that something is there.

Scaling the Encounter: A basilisk may be a bit too much for a beginning-level party. Feel free to re-roll for another encounter. Conversely, if you want to run a more challenging encounter for a higher-level party, your party encounters two basilisks sharing a lair.

Treasure: The lair contains scattered valuables belonging to the basilisk's previous victims. Roll on the appropriate Treasure Hoard table, according to the total CR of the encounter. If there is more than one basilisk in the encounter, consider that basilisk eggs may also be present for the taking.

Birds of Prey. A bird of prey, or a flock of them, wheels overhead, then swoops down on your party. Keen-eyed, but bird-brained all the same, the bird has spotted something in your party as food — a familiar or small summoned creature is an obvious choice, but it could be travelers rations, like strips of cured meat left in the open. To determine which species, roll on Table 2.2.1:

TABLE 2.2.1
Birds of Prey - Desert

d10	ENCOUNTER
1-3	Eagle
4	Giant Eagle
5-7	Blood Hawks
8-10	Hawks

Eagle. One eagle swoops down on your party, aiming itself at something it has identified as food.

Giant Eagle. A giant eagle has spotted your party. Giant eagles are intelligent and may respond if your party tries to flag them down. Though it cannot speak when spoken to, a successful DC 15 Charisma (Persuasion) check by someone who speaks Common or Auran persuades it to do your party a service, if it is within its power to accomplish it. This may involve delivering a written message or token, or guiding your party to a place that it knows, or even traveling with them for a while as an airborne lookout.

Blood Hawks. A flock of 2d6 blood hawks swoops down on your party. They concentrate on a single target — most likely a pack animal, but they may settle for a small humanoid as the next best thing.

Hawks. A flock of 2d10 hawks targets your party. They're probably going after your party's rations, but they may have spotted rodents or small reptiles that are scurrying along the desert floor. To the extent that your party is in their way, the hawks attack them.

Bulette. It's not as easy here as it is in more fertile regions, but land sharks can find enough to eat in a desert — and one has just spotted your party as its next meal. To create a little drama, you may require a successful DC 15 Wisdom (Perception) check for them to sense the ground rumbling; you may then allow a DC 15 Intelligence (Nature) check to identify it as a bulette before it breaches the surface.

Scaling the Encounter: A bulette may be a bit much for a lower-level party to handle, so if your party's average level is less than 5, feel free to re-roll for a different encounter. Conversely, if your average party level is higher than 10, you may add another bulette to make it more challenging.

Treasure: Bulettes hunt on the move, so treasure that belonged to its previous victims is scattered far and wide. However, you may allow your party a DC 10 Wisdom (Survival) check to follow the trail back to its last kill. If successful, roll on the Individual Treasure: Challenge 0-4 table to determine what they find.

The Meaning of Desert

One of the Roman historian Tacitus' most quotable passages comes from a speech that he attributes to a British chieftain who declares that, "The Romans make a desert, and call it peace." However, Tacitus doesn't mean by this that the Roman conquest of Britain made it look like an establishing shot from *Lawrence of Arabia*, or southern Nevada outside of Las Vegas. In some English translations, "wasteland" substitutes for "desert."

Similarly, if you go back far enough, references to St. Jerome living as a hermit use "desert" and "wilderness" interchangeably. Depictions through the Renaissance period often show him with plenty of trees in the background, not Saharan dunes. In other words, a desert is any place devoid of the fundaments of human habitation.

This book, however, sticks to the more modern, scientifically-driven meaning of "desert." Creature, monster and plant alike, they are here because they have adapted to survive in an exceptionally arid land.

Cheetahs. A small coalition of 1d4 of these sleek, fast predators spots your party. They're hungry, and your party looks as good as anything else they are likely to find at the moment. Your party hears the cheetahs make sharp, high noises like birds chirping as they circle and prepare to attack.

Treat cheetahs as panthers, except that their speed is 60 ft.

Scaling the Encounter: If you wish to make the encounter more challenging, the encounter group consists of a large coalition of 2d6 cheetahs.

Chimera. Your party spots a winged monstrosity with three different animal heads circling above them. This can only mean one thing: A chimera has spotted them as potential prey. You may allow a DC 15 Wisdom (Perception) check for your party to notice the chimera at a range of about 200 feet, allowing them time to react before they are within range of its attacks. If not, they first become aware of the chimera at a range of only 100 feet.

Scaling the Encounter: If your party's average level is lower than 6, a chimera may be more than you want to throw at them. Feel free to re-roll for a different encounter.

Alternately, consider that your party comes upon a chimera that has been injured in a fight with a manticore or a wyvern. Your party may get to watch the dazzling air-to-air combat from a safe distance. The chimera is reduced to half of its hit points by the time it drives off its enemy and turns on your party. Deep gashes and embedded manticore spikes are visible. It's wounded, but it's still hungry — in fact, perhaps it needs to feed in order to heal and your party looks like an easier target than one of its monstrous rivals.

Death Dog. One death dog roaming the wilderness stalks your party, looking to sate its unthinking bloodlust even if it means attacking a target that outnumbers it. It may not attack immediately upon being spotted by your party, but it will attack sooner or later. It may be waiting for an opening — will a pack animal fall behind from thirst and exhaustion, or one of the party members break formation and wander just far enough from the support of the others?

Scaling the Encounter: If you wish to make the encounter more challenging, the encounter group consists of a pack of death dogs with bad intentions, two for each multiple of 3 in your party's average level.

Elemental. With its endless vistas of the earth below and the sky above, the desert offers elementals a relatively comfortable place in the Material Plane. To determine the elemental being that your party encounters, roll on Table 2.2.2:

TABLE 2.2.2
Elementals - Desert

d8	ENCOUNTER
1-4	Earth Elemental
5-7	Air Elemental
8-9	Fire Elemental

+1 to the die roll if in a tropical desert.

Air Elemental. That dust devil racing across the desert floor is really an angry air elemental. It heads right for your party.

Earth Elemental. As your party passes it, it looks like a pile of rocks. It's really an earth elemental brooding on its fate. It unleashes its mindless fury on your party just because it feels like it.

➤

Fire Elemental. In tropical deserts, the heat can become so intense that it actually creates conditions that fire elementals can tolerate; it may even open up gaps between the Material Plane and the Elemental Plane of Fire.

Your party crosses paths with a fire elemental. From a distance, it looks like a desert plant has been set aflame. Once they get close, however, it becomes apparent that this supposed brushfire has no fuel source, and it lashes out and attacks them.

Scaling the Encounter: If your party's average level is lower than 5, an elemental may be more than you want to throw at them. Feel free to re-roll for a different encounter. Conversely, if you want to run a more challenging encounter for a higher-level party, the encounter group consists of one elemental for each multiple of 6 in your party's average level.

Grick. A grick making its lair among some rocks, or burrowed into the sand, tries to hide as potential prey approaches. If it fails, your party notices one oversized worm-like thing with a maw surrounded by four tentacles trying to make itself inconspicuous. When your party gets within striking distance, it attacks.

Scaling the Encounter: If you wish to make the encounter more challenging, the encounter group consists of one grick for each multiple of 3 in your party's average level. If your party's average level is 15 or higher, consider adding one grick alpha to the encounter as the group's leader. Alternately, you may use an encounter group that consists of one grick alpha for each multiple of 10 in your party's average level.

Treasure: Since gricks are opportunity predators rather than hunters, your party may find treasure that has piled up from the belongings of former victims. Roll once on the Treasure Hoard: Challenge 0-4 table for each grick in the encounter group, and once on the Treasure Hoard: Challenge 5-10 table for each grick alpha.

Griffon. One griffon has strayed from its normal hunting grounds in more fertile lands. Pickings are slim, however, and when it sees your party its deepening hunger drives it to go for one of their mounts or pack animals — or at least, it thinks it has spotted a mount or a pack animal.

Scaling the Encounter: If you wish to make the encounter more challenging, your party encounters a flock (or pack?) of griffons hunting together. There is one for each multiple of 3 in your party's average level.

Hell Hound. Your party crosses paths with one hell hound in a mean and paranoid mood. It may have come

to the Material Plane as a companion of a devil and somehow got separated from its master. Or perhaps it was part of a pack kept by a fire giant up in the hills or mountains and became hopelessly separated from them. In any event, it is none too pleased about wandering this plane alone and it takes out its separation anxiety on your party. You may also treat its breath weapon as a fire risk.

Scaling the Encounter: A hell hound may be a bit too much for a beginning-level party. Feel free to re-roll for another encounter. Conversely, If you wish to make the encounter more challenging, the encounter group consists of one hell hound for each multiple of 5 in your party's average level.

Insects. You may not think of insects as predatory, but they feed without giving much thought to who might be put out by their actions, and they cause trouble in their own way. Some are viciously aggressive when they feel threatened. Roll on Table 2.2.3 to determine the insects encountered:

TABLE 2.2.3
Insects - Desert

d6	ENCOUNTER
1-4	Swarm of Insects
5-6	Giant Wasps

Swarm of Insects. One swarm of insects — call them gnats, midges, whatever you will — descends upon your party and makes their lives decidedly unpleasant.

Giant Wasps. Your party comes upon two giant wasps guarding a nest hanging from a large desert plant, or a rock overhang. They are in a sufficiently bad temper to attack anything that comes within 50 feet of the nest.

Scaling the Encounter: If you wish to make the encounter more challenging (or more of a nuisance, depending on how you look at it), the encounter group consists of 1d4 giant wasps for each multiple of 2 in your party's average level, or 1d4 swarms of insects plus one additional swarm for each level in your party's average level.

Lion. Your party sees a lion feeding on a fresh kill — a wild goat, or some other suitable creature. Perhaps it has hunted an unfortunate human or humanoid. You may allow a DC 15 Wisdom (Perception) check to determine if your party makes out what's happening at a sufficient distance to steer clear, if they choose. Otherwise, the lion looks up at them with suspicion, not only unhappy that they have interrupted its meal, but determined that no one steals a kill from a top predator.

Scaling the Encounter: If you wish to make the encounter more challenging, your party comes upon a pride of lions feeding on a carcass, with two lions for each multiple of 3 in your party's average levels.

Manticore. Your party spots a large winged beast in the sky. You may require a successful DC 15 Intelligence (Nature) check to recognize it as a manticore on the hunt before it gets close enough to attack. Once it gets close enough to launch its spikes, it may choose to toy with its prey just to watch them squirm. In this case, it demands some kind of bribe in exchange for sparing them — a bargain it will keep, if your party makes the right offer. A suitable offer might take the form of treasure or humiliating servitude that amuses the manticore.

Alternately, perhaps it is the case that the manticore has information that might interest your party, and if your party gets the upper hand in combat, it offers that information in exchange for its life. One possibility: the manticore once guarded the lair of a lamia, but left after a falling out with its master. It offers to guide your party to the lair — and therefore, the treasure that lies within.

Scaling the Encounter: If you wish to make the encounter more challenging, consider that there are multiple manticores working as a team. In such a case, the encounter group consists of one manticore for each multiple of 5 in your party's average level, rounded up.

Medusa. It may be inconspicuous enough so that you should require a successful DC 10 Wisdom (Perception) check to notice it, but your party passes what appears to be a realistic statue of an animal. In fact, a medusa has made its lair in among some rocks nearby, where it surrounds itself with the petrified remains of its victims. It decides that your party would supplement its existing collection nicely. If your party investigates, they'll find more and more such statues until they reach the edge of the medusa's lair.

Scaling the Encounter: If your party's average level is lower than 6, a medusa may be more than you want to throw at them. Feel free to re-roll for a different encounter.

Treasure: The medusa's gaze petrifies flesh, but not valuables. To total up the bits and pieces that once belonged to its humanoid victims, roll on the Treasure Hoard: Challenge 5-10 table.

Mephits. These annoying little elementals have a habit of crossing over into the Material Plane, like ink bleeding through paper. They are not predatory, but they are very annoying and they interpret any attempt to brush them aside as an attack. Roll on Table 2.2.4 to determine the kind of mephit your party encounters:

TABLE 2.2.4
Mephits - Desert

d6	ENCOUNTER
1	Ice Mephit
2-5	Dust Mephit
6-8	Smoke Mephits

+1 to die roll if in a temperate desert.
+2 if in a tropical desert.

Ice Mephit. In sub-arctic deserts, the weather sometimes becomes cold enough to draw ice mephits from the Elemental Planes. They congregate anywhere ground water emerges onto the surface. One ice mephit hides among desert plants as it pelts your party with small rocks and it cackles contemptuously at someone who would invade its space. This isn't enough to cause damage, but it refuses to stop, even if your party tries to walk away.

Dust Mephit. Your party finds one dust mephit planting itself firmly in their path. If they try to go around it, it shifts so that it is always in their way. It fixes them with a piercing gaze, but it won't make the first move (unless there is a group of them and they outnumber your party; see Scaling the Encounter). When dust mephits attack, they concentrate on one target to the extent possible. They want to make sure of at least one kill, and if the rest run off they're okay with that; their goal is to satisfy their morbid curiosity about death.

Smoke Mephits. 1d4+1 smoke mephits drawn by the intense desert heat jump from the rock on which they have been perching and buzz about your party. They pepper your party with questions about where they are going, what are they doing here, etc. And they respond to whatever your party says with a string of bad advice and misleading statements. Like a swarm of insects, they refuse to stop unless forced to do so.

Scaling the Encounter: If you wish to make the encounter more challenging, the encounter group consists of 1d4 dust mephits or ice mephits for each multiple of 2 in your party's average level, or 1d4 smoke mephits plus a number of additional smoke mephits equal to your party's average level.

Ogres. Deserts do not provide a favorable environment for giants; because of their size, they tend not to do well in the heat and they need more water to stay hydrated than smaller creatures. Therefore, ogres encountered in the desert — especially a sub-tropical or tropical desert — might well be outcasts from larger groupings of their kind in the nearest forest or hill country. The desolation of the desert provides them with fewer opportunities for food and plunder, so they take what they can get. They'll attack your party, no matter what.

Scaling the Encounter: The encounter group consists of one ogre for each multiple of 3 in your party's average level. If your party is only 1st Level, consider that one half-ogre confronts them.

Treasure: These ogres are away from their lair. Total up the CR of all ogres killed and roll on the appropriate Individual Treasure table.

Oni. An ogre mage wandering the desert may be desperate in that it has worn out its welcome in more fertile and densely populated lands. Or it may deliberately target merchant caravans passing through the desert, and while it's waiting for another one, it spots your party as a suitable target. It tries to befriend your party while using its *Change Shape* ability to disguise itself as someone inoffensive — a traveler suffering from thirst and exhaustion, for instance. If they allow the oni to travel with them, it bides its time until they make camp for the night. It volunteers to take the first watch, then it strikes once everyone else is asleep.
If you wish, you may allow your party a DC 20 Intelligence (Arcana) check to suspect that this apparently friendly stranger might be using magic to alter its appearance.

Scaling the Encounter: An oni may be a bit too much for a low-level party. Feel free to re-roll for another encounter. Conversely, if you want to run a more challenging encounter for a higher-level party, use an encounter group consisting of two oni if your party's average level is 10 or higher.

Purple Worm. It's never a good sign when the ground beneath your feet rumbles, quivers and buckles. In this case, a purple worm, using its tremorsense, has spotted your party as its next meal. The worm's approach should give them enough time to sense that something is amiss and do something about it; you may allow them a DC 15 Intelligence (Nature) check to realize that it's a purple worm causing the disturbance underfoot. Combat begins when it breaches the surface within striking distance of your party.

Scaling the Encounter: If your party's average level is lower than 15, a purple worm may be more than you want to throw at them. Feel free to re-roll for a different encounter.

Treasure: Cutting open and gutting a purple worm is quite a chore, but it should reveal valuables that belonged to its previous prey — and purple worms eat a lot. Roll on the Treasure Hoard: Challenge 11-16 table to determine total hoard.

Roc. A roc encountered in the desert has roamed far afield from its mountain or hilltop eyrie in search of food. If anything, this means that it is less likely to be picky in its choice of prey. It may prefer a single big, juicy target, but in a pinch a bunch of smaller ones — like your party and its pack animals — will tide it over.

Scaling the Encounter: Rocs are fearsome opponents. If your party's average level is lower than 11, a roc may be more than you want to throw at them. Feel free to re-roll for a different encounter.

Scorpions. Your party takes a rest halt by some rocks and disturbs the scorpions that live among and under them. 1d8 scorpions attack your party. They have stingers, and they don't hesitate to use them.

Scaling the Encounter: If your party's average level is 5 or higher, consider that they have taken some shade from a large rock, or a rock formation, and in so doing they have disturbed one or more giant scorpions. In this case, the encounter group consists of one giant scorpion for each multiple of 5 in the party's average level, rounded up.

Spiders. Spiders that live in the desert tend to make their lairs between and beneath rocks, in a single desert plant, or even burrowing underground rather than weave huge webs. Having a place where they can escape the midday sun is more important than exercising their web-spinning chops. Your party is most likely to encounter them by coming too close to their lairs for comfort — perhaps by resting in a rare and welcome bit of shade. You may allow your party a DC 15 Wisdom (Perception) check to avoid being surprised when the spider rushes out to launch a pre-emptive strike on them. Roll on Table 2.2.5 to determine what kind of spider your party encounters:

TABLE 2.2.5
Spiders - Desert

d6	ENCOUNTER
1-3	Giant Spider
4-5	Giant Wolf Spiders
6	Phase Spider

Giant Spider. Giant spiders native to the desert live alone. Your party encounters one giant spider that darts out from behind a rock.
➤

Giant Wolf Spider. Wolf spiders burrow into the ground and they either take whatever stumbles into their lair, or they emerge to ambush prey. As your party approaches, vibrations in the ground tell them that something juicy has come to their doorstep, and 1d4 giant wolf spiders attack. You may allow your party a DC 15 Wisdom (Perception) check to notice a hole in the ground large enough to fit a big spider, and if successful, a DC 15 Intelligence (Nature) check to realize that it's a wolf spider burrow.

Phase Spider. Your party encounters one phase spider that literally appears out of nowhere. Phase spiders are quite fearless, and they use their ability to jump back and forth between planes to conduct hit-and-run attacks, wearing your party down until they are all incapacitated or dead.

Scaling the Encounter: To create a more challenging encounter with giant wolf spiders, use an encounter group consisting of 1d4 + your party's average level.

A phase spider may be a bit too much for a beginning-level party. Feel free to re-roll for another encounter. Conversely, if you want to run a more challenging encounter for a higher-level party, use an encounter group consisting of one phase spider for each multiple of 4 in your party's average level.

Undead. You won't find ghouls and ghasts in a desert because anything that's dead desiccates instead of rots. There are still many ways to die horribly in the desert, and sufficient opportunity for necromantic evil to disturb what rest they might otherwise manage. Roll on Table 2.2.6 to determine the undead abomination that greets your party:

TABLE 2.2.6
Undead - Desert

d10	ENCOUNTER
1	Ghost
2-3	Mummy
4	Shadows
5-8	Skeletons
9	Wraith
10	Zombie

Ghost. A ghost in the desert is easily mistaken for some random object glinting in the sun during the day, or a gust of sand at night. But it s no less real for all of

that, and anyone who mistakes it for a natural phenomenon is in for a nasty surprise. Almost certainly, it is the remnant of someone who died unhappily in this wasteland, alone and in terrible distress. Thirst, exposure and hunger are all likely causes of its demise. Perhaps this unfortunate person got lost and ran out of water or food far from any hope of resupply. Perhaps bandits or hostile nomads waylaid this person. Whatever the case, you may make this into a hostile encounter by having the ghost try to possess a member of your party so that it may resolve unfinished business from its former life.

Mummy. Unlike most undead found in the wild, mummies had a proper burial when they died and even underwent elaborate preparation before they were interred. Some necromantic magic has stirred them, and the purpose behind it generally involves guarding its burial place. Mummies encountered at random have wandered from their tombs, as if they have forgotten their original purpose, but the magic that created them as undead remains. Instinct drives them to attack, even though they no longer, strictly speaking, protect the place they were created to protect.

Shadows. The bright desert sunlight casts a dark shadow — but then your party realizes that the shadow doesn't belong to anyone! That's because it is a creature in its own right, an insubstantial undead intent on draining the life from the living. It's not particularly at home here and shadows prefer darkness, where they can strike unseen. All the same, it attacks the nearest party member, eager to spawn one more of its own kind.

Skeletons. Your party crosses paths with 1d4 skeletons — undead created from remains that have been stripped of flesh by scavengers and wind-blown dust, and bleached in the desert sun. They may be casualties from skirmishes involving bandits or nomads. They may be what is left of adventurers or travelers who got stranded in the merciless desert and perished. Driven by rage at their fate, they attack.

Wraith. There are plenty of ways to come to a bad end in the desert, and your party has the misfortune to come across a wraith that was once someone who perished in this forsaken place, and which is now bound to it. Perhaps they pass an improvised cairn, or just a skeleton bleached in the sun and half-covered by drifting sand. Whatever the case, it takes out the resentment that it bore at the end of its life on your party.
➤

Zombie. Your party come across 1d4 zombies that have been programmed to kill every living thing they encounter. The source of the necromancy that created these zombies we leave to you. Perhaps they slipped the leash of their creator and they now wander the desert, freed of the need for water and shelter, mindlessly looking for victims.

Scaling the Encounter: Ghosts and wraiths always work alone.

Mummy: A mummy may be a bit too much for a beginning-level party. Feel free to re-roll for another encounter. Conversely, if your party's average level is higher than 5, consider adding another mummy to the encounter. No more than that, though — a horde of stray mummies wandering from their tombs is a bit much to imagine as a purely random encounter. If your party's average level is 20 or higher, the wandering mummy is one mummy lord.

Shadows: The encounter group consists of a number of shadows equal to your party's average level.

Skeletons: If you wish to make the encounter more challenging, the encounter group consists of 1d4 skeletons plus one additional skeleton for each level in your party's average level. You may substitute one warhorse skeleton for two skeletons.

Zombies: If you wish to make the encounter more challenging, the encounter group consists of 1d4 zombies plus one additional zombie for each level in your party's average level. If your party's average level is 3 or higher, you may use an encounter group consisting of one ogre zombie for each multiple of 3 in your party's average level.

Treasure: It's quite possible that ghosts and wraiths are encountered in or near the place where they died or were buried — in which case, the valuables they had on them are lying about somewhere. You may require a successful DC 15 Wisdom (Perception) check to find its exact location, and roll on the appropriate Individual Treasure table.

Similarly, a mummy that has slipped its leash probably has not strayed far from its tomb. Roll on the Treasure Hoard table appropriate to the total CR of the encounter for the contents of their stash. You may require a successful DC 15 Wisdom (Survival) check to work back how it got from there to here.

With skeletons and zombies, they may have with them some of what they had on their person at the time of their death. Roll on the Individual Treasure: Challenge 0-4 table once for each multiple of four skeletons or zombies, rounded up.

Any ghost encountered is usually someone who died unhappily and alone in this terrible wasteland.

Snakes. Venomous snakes make themselves at home in the desert. They like to shelter among rocks and strike from ambush, but they also need to sun themselves from time to time. In general, they go about without fear, knowing that anyone who tries to harm them must answer to their deadly bite first. Roll on Table 2.2.7 to determine the size of the snake(s) encountered:

TABLE 2.2.7
Snakes - Desert

d10	ENCOUNTER
1-4	Swarm of Poisonous Snakes
5-8	Poisonous Snake
9-10	Giant Poisonous Snake

Swarm of Poisonous Snakes. Your party stops to rest among some rocks that conceal a snake pit with one swarm of poisonous snakes present. You may allow a DC 10 Wisdom (Perception) check to notice the snakes before they get close enough to attack.

Poisonous Snake. One poisonous snake slithers out from under a rock. Either that, or your party spots it dead ahead, right in their path and close enough to attack. It holds its ground, all but daring your party to attack it. If your party wishes to avoid it rather than fight it, you may allow them a DC 15 Wisdom (Survival) or Intelligence (Nature) check to back away without provoking the snake.

Giant Poisonous Snake. One giant poisonous snake slithers out from behind a rock. You may allow a DC 10 Wisdom (Perception) check to notice the snakes before they get close enough to attack. Like its normal-sized cousin, your party may also spot it dead ahead and holding its ground.

The desert is not kind to wandering travelers.

TABLE 2.3
Neutral Creatures - Desert

d100	ENCOUNTER
1-4	Awakened Shrub
5-9	Axe Beaks
10-18	Camel
19-26	Centipede
27-29	Centaur
30-34	Cockatrice
35-36	Dragon
37-43	Elephant
44-46	Genie
47-52	Goats
53-56	Hippogriff
57-61	Horses
62-66	Hyenas
67-71	Jackals
72-76	Lizard
77-81	Mules
82-84	Pseudodragon
85-90	Rats
91-95	Rhinoceros
96-100	Vultures

Awakened Shrub. Only the hardiest plants can thrive in a place with so little water. Despite the fact that only the strongest can survive here (or perhaps because of it), some desert plants acquire sentience. Your party comes into contact with one or more such awakened shrubs. Perhaps a party member takes advantage of it to answer the call of nature. Perhaps it produces berries that look appetizing. These or similar actions cause the shrub to express alarm.

Even if your party has done mischief to it, an encounter with an awakened shrub is not necessarily hostile. If your party asks it for help, a successful DC 10 Charisma (Persuasion) check wins it over, but the DC is 15 if your party has harmed it in some way. Help from an awakened shrub includes providing knowledge of the surrounding area.

Scaling the Encounter: If you wish to make the encounter more challenging, the encounter group consists of one awakened shrub for each multiple of 3 in your party's average level, rounded up.

Axe Beaks. Axe beaks can find enough to eat in the desert, but it's not easy. Your party comes across a hunting pack of 1d4+2 of these odd-looking, bad-tempered flightless birds. They don't like having their hunt interrupted, but it's not a sure thing that they'll attack. Have your party make a DC 15 Intelligence (Nature) or Wisdom (Survival) check. Failure means that a party member has made a false move that angers the axe beaks, which then attack the party.

Camel. Your party sees 1d8 camels wandering through the desert without any apparent purpose. Though domesticated and widely kept as mounts and beasts of burden, wild camels do exist. They are bad-tempered, but they can be wrangled and trained to serve. To wrangle a camel, it must be successfully grappled and kept in grappled condition for 6 consecutive rounds. At that point, it becomes docile and submits to whomever grappled it. Because of its size, two medium-size creatures may grapple with the same camel simultaneously, and as long as one of them maintains its grappled condition, this counts toward the requirement for wrangling it.

Perhaps your party has found camels that belonged to someone else. They wandered off from their masters, who would owe a favor or two to whomever returned their animals. Or perhaps the former owners met with a bad end, leaving the camels to their own devices. Perhaps they were merchants who perished from the desert's hazards, or simple travelers who fell afoul of bandits. In that case, you may roll on the Treasure Hoard: Challenge 0-4 table for contents of their saddle bags, which could include personal items that give hints as to their identity, and that their next of kin would appreciate having back.

Centaur. Your party spots in the distance a lone figure, half-human and half-equine. It is a centaur, and like all too many of its kind, it became irrevocably separated from its tribe during a migration and now wanders the world alone. A centaur in the desert may keep company from time to time with caravans passing through, in which case it would have knowledge of settlements, roads and oases that would help your party, and it could be persuaded to share it. It is also likely to have a basic knowledge of Common, picked up from contact with desert folk who know nothing of Sylvan or Elvish. A centaur might also offer your party the chance to take on a sidequest, asking for help in finding its long-lost tribe.

Scaling the Encounter: It is up to you whether or not to scale up an encounter with centaurs. Though most often encountered alone, it is possible that as many as three or four centaurs might have split off from their tribe as a group. However, if you anticipate a hostile encounter, throwing more than one centaur at your party would provide a stiff challenge if their average level is less than 4.

Treasure: Centaurs carry their valuables with them. Roll once on the Individual Treasure: Challenge 0-4 table for each centaur present.

Centipede. As your party takes a rest stop in the shade of a large rock, one giant centipede crawls out from under it. It emerges close enough to your party to provide an unpleasant surprise for all involved. Have your party make a DC 15 Intelligence (Nature) or Wisdom (Survival) check. Failure means someone has made a false move that provokes the giant centipede to attack. Success means that they notice it in time to give it some space, thus making a hostile encounter purely optional.

Cockatrice. Cockatrices can adapt to desert life, finding enough food to survive among desert plants and small creatures. Your party comes across one cockatrice foraging on the desert floor. Its appearance is a nasty surprise — inevitable, considering the cockatrice's nasty temperament and petrifaction ability. If your party wishes to avoid a fight, require a DC 15 Intelligence (Nature) or Wisdom (Survival) check. Failure means that someone in your party has made a false move that sets off the beast, and it attacks.

Scaling the Encounter: If you wish to make the encounter more challenging, use an encounter group that consists of 1d4 cockatrices plus a number of additional cockatrices equal to your party's average level.

Dragon. Your party notices a large shape — almost large enough to blot out the sun — circling in the sky. It's a dragon on the prowl. To determine what kind of dragon roll on Table 2.3.1:

TABLE 2.3.1
Dragons - Desert

d12	ENCOUNTER
1	Black
2-3	Blue
4	Green
5	Red
6	White
7-8	Brass
9	Bronze
10	Copper
11	Gold
12	Silver

To determine its age, see Scaling the Encounter.

To be clear, this need not be a hostile encounter. The dragon is not defending its lair, so it may just be curious about your party. It may have more important things to do and decline to take notice of them at all. Or it may be hungry and on the hunt, or it's angry because your party has intruded on territory it claims as its own.

Alternately, you may present your party with a scenario that you can weave into the larger story of the campaign. Your party finds a dragon wyrmling sprawled on a dune, or propped up against a rock. It's obviously in a bad way — gashed open, bleeding profusely (or it has almost bled out), barely conscious.

Assume that it has stabilized after being reduced to 0 hp, and that it now has 1 hp. Dehydrated and exposed to the desert heat, it's a miracle that it's still alive. How it got that way is up to you, and it may depend on how dragons fit into your campaign world. Perhaps it fled from a fight in which it was badly wounded. Who would its enemies be, and why were they fighting? Were its relatives or companions killed?

How your party decides to deal with this child in distress could open up possibilities for later in your campaign. If they rescue it, will its kin reward them later, or will its enemies confront them on the principle that, "The friends of my enemy must also be my enemy?" Conversely, what are the consequences if they put it out of its misery, like scavengers roaming a medieval battlefield? Will its kin seek retribution, or will its enemies treat your party as allies?

Scaling the Encounter: Because dragons get tougher with age, the age of the dragon encountered should
➤

depend on your party's average level — especially if you decide that this is going to be a hostile encounter. If your party's average level is 10 or lower, they encounter a wyrmling. If theirs average level is 11-18, they encounter a young dragon. If their average level is 19-25, they encounter an adult dragon. If their average level is higher than 25, they encounter an ancient dragon.

Elephant. Some elephants have adapted to live well enough on the scarce resources that the desert offers. Your party comes across one elephant and it is always the case with elephants in the wild that avoiding a stampede requires some care. If they want to avoid a confrontation with the elephant, have them make a DC 15 Wisdom (Survival) or Intelligence (Nature) check. Failure means that someone has made a false move, triggering an attack.

Scaling the Encounter: If your party's average level is lower than 4, a hostile elephant encounter may be more than you want to throw at them. Feel free to re-roll for a different encounter. Conversely, if you want to run a more challenging encounter, the encounter group is a small herd of elephants, consisting of one for each multiple of 5 in your party's average level.

Genie. Travelers in the open desert beware: It could be that that gust of wind or column of swirling sand you see in the distance is one of these legendary elemental beings. Roll on Table 2.3.2 to determine the genie encountered:

TABLE 2.3.2
Genie - Desert

d6	ENCOUNTER
1-4	Djinni
5-6	Efreeti

Djinni. Your party notices a sandstorm blowing up suddenly. Maybe they spot it in the distance, maybe it flares up right on top of them. It could be a trick of nature in an unforgiving land. Or it could be a djinni out for a joyride, in which case kicking up the sandstorm in their midst is its equivalent of flying low overhead just to give them a little scare.

When a djinni meets your party while gallivanting about the open desert, quite possibly it is bored and looking for excitement. It has some interest in taking your party as slaves, but more than anything, it

➤

expects them to entertain it. This means the djinni dogs your party until it is satisfied, but your party can also use this as leverage. You may require a successful DC 15 Charisma (Persuasion) check to pull it off, but they could exchange the promise of amusement for the djinni's help, in which case it joins your party as a friendly NPC — at least until it gets bored of their company, or tired of waiting to have fun.

Efreeti. An efreeti in the Material Plane likely has slaving in mind, and not much else. If your party encounters one, the mostly likely course is that it tries to cow your party into becoming its captives, summoning a fire elemental for extra muscle if necessary. If it comes to a fight, the efreeti tries to kill only as many as absolutely necessary to get the rest of your party to submit to it — they're more valuable to it as captives than as corpses. If they try to talk their way out of this predicament — perhaps they want to convince the efreeti that they can lead it to more and better captives — you may require a successful DC 15 Charisma (Persuasion) for the ruse to work

Scaling the Encounter: An encounter with a genie need not be hostile. But it could go south. Perhaps your party is not keen on being hustled off to the Elemental Plane of Fire as an efreeti's slaves. So you should consider whether a hostile genie is more than you want to throw a party with an average level lower than 10. Feel free to re-roll for a different encounter.

Treasure: Roll on the Individual Treasure: Challenge 11-16 table to determine what valuables the genie has on its person. In addition, if your party encounters an efreeti with captives, consider that at least one of them is a high-value prisoner — someone whose standing is such that his or her rescue and safe return would fetch a handsome reward.

Goats. Your party comes across a small herd of 1d8 billies and 2d8 nannies quietly grazing. Perhaps they are wild goats — or perhaps they have gotten separated from a larger herd, and somewhere nearby there is a goatherd who would give a reward for their safe return. In any event, billies can be ornery beasts and if your party approaches them, you may require your party to make a DC 15 Intelligence (Nature) check to avoid setting off an attack in which the males charge to cover the fleeing females.

Scaling the Encounter: If you wish to make the encounter more challenging, use a herd of wild (and potentially irritated) giant goats instead. The encounter group should consist of 1d4 giant goats for each multiple of 2 in your party's average level with the same 1:2 ratios of males to females. Giant goats are quite wild; there is no chance that they are being kept by someone else.

Hippogriff. Your party sees a hippogriff circling overhead, looking for its next meal, or on the ground dealing with its prey. Hippogriffs are not as aggressive as birds of prey, and it is no sure bet that they would attack your party on the hope that it could make off with a pack animal or their stash of rations.

Hippogriffs may also be a kind of prey. If hippogriffs are used as mounts in your world, it must follow that captive adults have value as breeding stock. Chicks captured from the wild also have value because they are still young enough to be tamed. To that end, you may allow your party a DC 20 Wisdom (Survival) check to trace a path to the hippogriff's lair (likely to be sited atop a large rock or on a hilltop) after observing it for a while. If your party has someone capable of flight, reduce the DC to 15. To subdue an adult hippogriff to the point where it can be bound and held captive, it must be successfully grappled and kept in grappled condition for 10 consecutive rounds.

Scaling the Encounter: The hippogriff population in a desert is likely to be sparse. But if you want to stage a hostile encounter and you need to make it more of a challenge for a higher-level party, consider that the encounter group consists of two hippogriffs for each multiple of 3 in your party's average level.

Horses. Some horse breeds have adapted to live in the desert. Your party comes across a small herd of them. They only questions are, how many of them are there, and do they belong to someone else? Horse encounters are unlikely to be hostile, although they may put up a fight if you try to wrangle them before they've been broken. Roll on Table 2.3.3 to determine the nature of the horse encounter:

TABLE 2.3.3
Horses - Desert

d4	ENCOUNTER
1-3	Riding Horse
4	Warhorse

Riding Horse. Your party comes across a small herd of 2d4 riding horses grazing, or moving at a walk. It's up to you to decide whether they're wild, or if they belong to someone — and if the latter, is their herder nearby (see Table 2.5) or have they escaped from someone who would pay a reward for their return?
➤

If they are wild, they can be wrangled. To wrangle a riding horse, it must be successfully grappled and kept in grappled condition for 6 consecutive rounds. At that point, it becomes docile and whoever grappled it may ride it or use it as a pack animal. Because of its size, two medium-size creatures may grapple with the same riding horse simultaneously, and as long as one of them maintains its grappled condition, this counts toward the requirement for wrangling it.

Warhorse. Your party comes across 1d4 warhorses. Whether their owners were killed in battle, or they just escaped from the stable, is up to you. If the former, they wear empty saddles. Warhorses do not need to be wrangled; they have been broken and disciplined, so they're used to working with human or humanoid riders. However, they're also trained fighters and if you don't approach them just right in a situation like this, they'll take you for the enemy and attack. If your party approaches the warhorses, require a DC 15 Intelligence (Nature) check to avoid setting the horses off.

Hyenas. Hyenas find slim pickings in the desert, but this makes them all the more canny as predators. A pack of 2d6 hyenas comes across your party, but they do not attack unless they are at least twice as numerous as your party, or unless they can isolate a party member and use their pack tactics ability — perhaps one character has gone ahead to scout the lay of the land, or separated him or herself to answer the call of nature. Otherwise, they hover about on the flank of the party, looking for an opportunity to strike. If they find none, they eventually tire of the hunt and move off.

Scaling the Encounter: If you wish to make the encounter more challenging, the encounter group consists of two giant hyenas for each multiple of 3 in your party's average level.

Jackals. Your party comes across a small pack of 2d6 jackals scavenging a carcass. This is as good as it gets for them living in the desert, so they're keen to protect their find. If your party wishes to avoid a fight, have them make a DC 15 Wisdom (Survival) check; failure means that someone has made a move that the jackals take as a threat, and they attack.

Lizards. Your party crosses paths with 1d4 giant lizards foraging for large insects and smaller lizards. They are not aggressive and they can be wrangled and trained to serve as pack animals or mounts. To wrangle a giant lizard, it must be successfully grappled and kept in grappled condition for 10 consecutive rounds. At that point, it becomes docile and submits to whomever grappled it. Because of its size, two medium-size creatures may grapple with the same giant lizard simultaneously, and as long as one of them maintains its grappled condition, this counts toward the requirement for wrangling it.

Mules. Mules are domestic creatures. So when your party sees 1d6 mules mulling about for no apparent purpose, it is highly likely that they have escaped from someone who brought them into the wilderness as pack animals — a merchant caravan or miners, for instance. Their owners will pay a reward for their return. Or your party could claim them as their own without anyone (possibly) being the wiser.

Mules do not attack. But they may be skittish around strangers, especially if they have been out in the wild for a while. If your party tries to take possession of them, have them make a DC 10 Intelligence (Nature) check to avoid a hostile reaction. Remember, these creatures have a kick like a mule.

Pseudodragon. If someone in your party is looking for a familiar, here is a chance. They pass a pseudodragon hiding in a cleft in a rock, or partially camouflaged in a desert plant. It would like to remain hidden, but there just isn't enough cover to make sure. It is reluctant to fight, and if it is approached by a superior force, it uses its limited telepathic ability to communicate its fear and anxiety.

How the pseudodragon responds if your party tries to befriend it is up to you. You may require a Charisma (Persuasion) check with a DC of anywhere between 10-20, depending on how difficult you want to make it. Pseudodragons are picky in choosing the company they keep, but you may decide that DC 20 is a bit steep, especially for a lower-level party.

Rats. You find rats everywhere they can find food, and they can sniff out food even in barren desert. Roll on Table 2.3.4 to determine the nature of the rat encounter:

TABLE 2.3.4
Rats - Desert

d6	ENCOUNTER
1	Lone Rat
2-4	Swarm of Rats
5-6	Giant Rats

Lone Rat. A single rat, perhaps foraging by itself or lost from its nest, approaches your party while they take a ➤

rest. It's not much of a threat, but if someone in your party is looking for a familiar or even just a pet, this is an opportunity. Interacting with the rat — especially earning its trust with food — and making a successful DC 10 Intelligence (Nature) check earns its loyalty as a pet.

Swarm of Rats. Without being aware of it, your party has stopped to rest in the shade of a rock under which some rats have made their nest. Drawn by the party's rations, a swarm of rats makes for the nearest source of food. They don't attack party members unless they interfere with their basic mission of acquiring food. But unless the rats are stopped, they eventually account for all of your party's rations, making off with what they don't eat on the spot.

Giant Rats. In this case, the rats drawn by your party's food are giant rats. There are 2d6 of them.

Rhinoceros. Your party interrupts one rhinoceros as it grazes on such forage as the desert offers. It is not aggressive — as a herbivore, it does not hunt for food. But if it feels threatened it becomes a dangerous foe. Have your party make a DC 15 Intelligence (Nature) or Wisdom (Survival) check. Failure means that someone has made a false move that the rhinoceros interprets as a threat. It charges.

Scaling the Encounter: If you wish to make the encounter more challenging, your party faces a herd of potentially angry rhinoceros, one for each multiple of 3 in your party's average level.

Vultures. Your party comes across 1d6+2 vultures picking at a carcass. It could be an animal — or it could be a humanoid or a human. The desert offers many ways for the reckless and unfortunate to die, and the vultures here never seem to go hungry for long. How they respond depends on how they interpret your party's actions. You may have your party make a DC 10 Intelligence (Nature) or Wisdom (Survival) check. Failure means that a party member has made a false move that persuades the vultures to attack, thinking that they need to defend their food source.

Scaling the Encounter: If you wish to make the encounter more challenging, consider substituting giant vultures for the vultures. The encounter group then consists of two giant vultures for each multiple of 3 in your party's average level. Giant vultures may be hunting instead of feeding. Perhaps they — mistakenly or not — spotted your party as hapless travelers on their last legs, in which case they swoop down to try to hasten their demise.

TABLE 2.4

Humanoids - Desert

d10	ENCOUNTER
1	Bugbear
2	Dwarves
3	Gnolls
4	Gnomes
5-6	Goblins
7	Hobgoblins
8-9	Orcs
10	Werewolf

Bugbear. Your party crosses paths with one or more bugbears (see Scaling the Encounter). Bugbears encountered in such a sparsely populated are likely here for professional reasons. They're probably mercenaries on their way to meet their client, or they may be so desperate for work that they have come here on speculation.

Conversely, they could be heading home after a victorious battle — or straggling in the wake of a catastrophic defeat. Their exact circumstances and motivation should depend on what else is going on in your campaign world. If there is no such war in which they could take part, they're out for some casual plunder, or perhaps on their way to shake down a hobgoblin tribe that once employed them.

Their interest in fighting your party should vary according to the reason why they're here. For instance, mobilizing for war means they have a larger purpose in mind than victimizing your party. On the other hand, if they're at loose ends and just wandering through the desert, killing your party and taking their stuff may be the best option open to them.

Scaling the Encounter: A beginning-level party should only have to cope with one bugbear. If you wish to make the encounter more challenging, the encounter group consists of two bugbears for each multiple of 3 in your party's average level. If your party's average level is 10 or higher, add one bugbear chief as the group's leader.

Dwarves. It's not that dwarves like the aridity, heat and open spaces of the desert — they don't. If your party comes across dwarves here, it's most likely that they have been hired as mining specialists to exploit deposits of gemstones or useful metals. It's a small group of dwarves, 1d8+2 of them, and they're probably on their way to or from a job site, perhaps taking loads of ore for smelting. Treat them as commoners armed with battleaxes and pickaxes (treat as spears that cannot be thrown), and the weapon proficiency to use them, leading an equal number of mules. They could provide

your party with a sidequest, offering a suitable reward in exchange for protection from monsters or other enemies.

Gnolls. A small band of gnolls trekking through the desert are likely to be scouts looking for settlements with anything worth taking, or spying on caravan routes so their tribe can plot an ambush. However, they're not above trying to rob your party as a target of opportunity.

If the gnoll group is relatively large (see Scaling the Encounter) this may be the actual raiding party. They may be on their way back from a successful raid, spattered with blood and taking with them captives whom they will sacrifice to their evil deity. In either case, they ignore your party if your party declines to interfere with them, guided as they are by their primary purpose.

Scaling the Encounter: The baseline encounter group should consist of two gnolls for each multiple of 3 in your party's average level. If your party's average level is 7-9, add a gnoll pack lord to the mix as the group's leader Feel free to substitute one gnoll pack lord for four gnolls as much as you like if you don't want to run a mass encounter.

Treasure: If the gnolls are coming back from a successful raid, you may roll on the Treasure Hoard: Challenge 0-4 table to determine the fruits of their labor. This is in addition to the individual treasure they carry.

Gnomes. Your party crosses paths with a group of 1d4+1 gnomes accompanied by one gnome acolyte. They have been hired as artificers and they are traveling to a community where they expect to take up work, such as a mining settlement or a village along a caravan stop. Or perhaps they are traveling back to their home village.

They have no particular love of the desert, but work is work and not be passed up. Vague unease about its hazards grips them. Perhaps they know of a threat from a specific monster, or they're just worried in general about getting jumped by orcs or bandits. In this case, they'll pay your party what they can for their protection (perhaps they know where their potential enemies make their lair).

Rats are often found as familiars or pets.

Hobgoblins. If war plagues your campaign world, hobgoblins go about, selling their martial services to anyone willing to employ them. If your party crosses paths with hobgoblins crossing the desert, they have probably come across some mercenaries on their way to their mustering point. If that's the case, they have business to take care of and they'll ignore your party as long as they don't try to interfere.

On the other hand, the hobgoblins might initiate a fight with your party if things have not been going well for them. Perhaps the desert potentate who hired them changed his mind and sent them home without pay. If they're broke, as long as they properly challenge your party to a fight, killing your party for their belongings is not mere robbery but taking spoils of war. Alternately, these hobgoblins may be fleeing a lost battle and, like many mercenaries in such a situation, they can rationalize killing and looting your party in any number of ways — perhaps they won't get paid because their employer was killed; or they need to settle for what they can get now that the battle won't yield any spoils; or perhaps they're just hungry and desperate after getting separated from the main army.

Scaling the Encounter: The baseline encounter group should consist of 1d4 hobgoblins for each multiple of 2 in your party's average level. If your party's average level is 10-19, add a hobgoblin captain as the group's leader, accompanied by two goblin servants or one bugbear aide. If your party's average level is 20 or higher, add instead one hobgoblin warlord with two bugbear aides.

Orcs. There are more promising places than the desert for orcs interested in plunder and slaughter; it's too sparsely populated to offer a lot of targets. However, orcs can make do in almost any environment. Orcs encountered in the desert may be from a tribe in exile, or one that is based in nearby hills or grasslands and finds itself blocked from projecting its power into more profitable areas.

A small group of orcs in the desert are likely to be scouts, looking for settlements that their tribe can target in the future, or spying on caravan routes. They may be looking for oases that their tribe can use as a base. They may attack your party just for the fun of it, but they are just as likely pump them for useful information about the surrounding area.

If the orc group is relatively large (see Scaling the Encounter) this may be an actual raiding party. They may be on their way back from a successful raid, spattered with blood and and draped with loot. In either case, they ignore your party if your party declines to interfere with them, guided as they are by their primary purpose.

Scaling the Encounter: The baseline encounter group should consist of 1d4 orcs for each multiple of 2 in your party's average level. If your party's average level is 5-9, consider adding an orog as the group's leader. If your party's average level is 10 or higher, use an orc war chief as its leader. If you don't want to run a mass encounter but you still want to provide a higher-level party with a meaningful challenge, feel free to substitute one orog for four orcs as much as you like.

Treasure: If the orcs are coming back from a successful raid, you may roll on the Treasure Hoard: Challenge 0-4 table to determine the fruits of their labor. This is in addition to the individual treasure they carry.

Werewolf. A werewolf in the open desert is likely a wanderer, an exile from a distant land. It is restless, always desperate to escape its terrible curse, yet trapped by it. When it comes across your party, rage at its own fate drives it, almost without thinking, to spread its curse so that others will know its suffering. It is clever enough to approach in its human form, pretending to be a lost traveler, or a merchant. Once your party gets close and drops its guard, it attacks. If it has a weapon at hand, it changes into its hybrid form; otherwise it changes into its animal form.

Scaling the Encounter: A werewolf poses a stiff challenge to a beginning-level party. If your party's average level is 3 or less, feel free to re-roll the encounter. Alternately, if you want to make a werewolf encounter more challenging for a higher-level party, use a pack of them consisting of one werewolf for each multiple of 5 in your party's average level.

Treasure: Assume that your party meets the werewolf away from its lair. Roll once on the Individual Treasure: Challenge 0-4 table for each werewolf killed in the encounter.

TABLE 2.5

Humans - Desert

d20	ENCOUNTER
1	Adventurer
2-4	Bandits
5	Exiles
6	Explorers
7	Fugitives
8-10	Herders
11-12	Hermit
13-15	Merchants
16-20	Nomads

Adventurers. Unless your party contains all of the adventurers in your campaign world, it's at least theoretically possible that they'll run into another adventuring party tramping through the desert. Perhaps they're pursuing the same objective as your party. Perhaps they have a different mission; perhaps they're headed for a site that your party knows nothing about (like ancient ruins said to hold lost treasures). Perhaps they're lost and starving, or wounded, or cursed.

How they react to your party depends on a variety of factors. Are they rivals pursuing the same goal? If not, perhaps this party is willing to share useful information. In fact, if your party is stuck and having a hard time advancing the storyline of your campaign, a friendly encounter like this can help steer them in the right direction. Differences in alignment may also shape how the two parties react to each other.

Composition of this rival party is up to you and can vary according to circumstance. A party braving the desert would be well-advised to have someone accomplished in Survival, such as a ranger, with them. Conversely, a party that is struggling may be in a bad way precisely because none of them is well-versed in Survival or Nature.

Scaling the Encounter: Unless there is some possibility that this encounter turns hostile, the relative level of the party is mainly a matter of affect. A higher-level party might project self-confidence (or arrogance), while beginning-level party might stumble about, unsure of themselves. If you're leaning towards a hostile encounter, however, consider that the level of the party should be roughly two-thirds of your party's average level.

Bandits. The desert is not the most comfortable place in which to be a bandit. But it does have a way of discouraging the forces of law from coming after them, and if they can get timely information about merchant caravans passing through, the rewards make it worthwhile to get some sand in their boots. Bandits encountered here are probably either on their way to or coming back from the nearest caravan route — although a small group may be scouts or lookouts protecting the nearby cave in which they take shelter.

They may not target your party, as adventurers are usually too well-armed and too hard to bully. But they may make an exception if your party carries a conspicuous and obviously valuable treasure, or they outnumber your party by at least three to two. It's more likely that they assume that your party is a posse sent out after them — or that your party intends to rob them of what they took from others by force.

Scaling the Encounter: As a rough guideline, the encounter group should contain 1d8 bandits for each level in your party's average level. If your party's average level is 4 or higher, add a bandit captain as their leader. If you don't want to run a mass encounter but you still want these criminals to provide a higher-level party with a meaningful challenge, feel free to substitute one thug for four bandits as much as you like.

Treasure: If your party finds the bandits' hideout, roll on the Treasure Hoard table appropriate to the total CR of the encounter. Do so also if you decide that the bandits encountered are on their way back from a successful raid. Consider that there is also a 10% chance that the bandits have with them a high-value captive whom they intend to ransom. The identity of this captive is left to you as DM, as it should depend on local circumstances and fit into your campaign world.

A friendly encounter could help steer your party in the right direction

Exiles. Your party encounters 1d6 people who could serve as a source of adventure hooks. From their appearance, they have obviously seen better days. They have fled into the desert for any of a variety of reasons: perhaps they are royalty or nobility who have been usurped; perhaps the opposite is the case and they are failed usurpers on the run. Or perhaps they have gotten caught up in a blood feud in their homeland and that's why they fear for their lives. Whatever the circumstance, they have left their home for this desperate and forsaken place because they need to hide.

No matter their reason for being here, they should offer your party an adventure hook of some sort. It may involve protecting the exiles from their real (or imagined) pursuers. It may involve returning to their former home and securing an important item that was left behind (a family heirloom, a badge of office), perhaps even helping them return home and force their way back into their former position of prominence. At the very least, exiles can provide your party with information about their former home territory, which in turn could be a key location in your campaign.

Use any NPC template you like for the exiles, depending on the backstory you assign them.

Explorers. Your party bumps into a small party driven by human curiosity to explore and map the desert wastes. The group consists of 1d4 scholars (treat them as commoners) and 1d4 scouts who act as bodyguards. Perhaps they are here thanks to the sponsorship of a ruler or noble who has heard rumors that precious metals and gemstones can be found out here, or an academy looking for a lost civilization. Perhaps the explorer is a wealthy eccentric who undertook this expedition on his or her own.

This encounter is not likely to be hostile. Explorers are open and curious, despite the fact that the desert offers so many ways for them to perish. Instead, you may treat this as an opportunity for your party to receive some help from a knowledgeable stranger — the explorer is likely to have excellent maps of nearby areas (and knowledge of those areas) and is willing to share them. Conversely, an expedition that has been in the field for a while may be running short on supplies — not just cartography supplies, but fresh water — and would pay well if your party can provide help. Also, if your party is in the mood for a sidequest, an explorer may offer one: If the expedition is headed into particularly dangerous territory, it may want additional guards to keep it safe.

Fugitives. Your party crosses paths with 1d4 bedraggled people stumbling through the desert. They look to be in less-than-optimal shape, but they're moving as fast as they can manage. Most, if not all of them have a manacle around one wrist, with the other manacle dangling on its chain. They're escaped prisoners who have fled into the open desert. From whom they are fleeing and why they were imprisoned in the first place is up to you, and ought to depend on where in your campaign world this encounter takes place.

How the encounter plays out depends not only on how your party reacts, but on the state of mind you assign to the fugitives. On the one hand, it's hard to imagine that they went to the trouble of a jailbreak just to allow a bunch of strangers to take their freedom back from them. On the other hand, they might be desperate with thirst and ready to give up. Each of them has learned whip their freed manacle by the chain and wield it as a club.

Treat the fugitives as bandits, but without weapons or armor.

Treasure: Fugitives have no treasure.

Herders. Your party spots in the distance a herd of goats, or some other herbivore suitable to an arid environment. There are 2d6 herders in their midst. Your party startles them, but they are not necessarily hostile. It's just that they didn't expect to meet anyone out here; it's usually

just them and their animals. If you wish, you may require your party to make a DC 10 Charisma (Persuasion) check to calm them.

That being said, the herders can provide your party with helpful local knowledge. They know all the nearby sources of water, the places where monsters are reputed to reside, gossip from any settlements in the area. They may even have specific knowledge that can help your party get where they want to go.

Treat herders as commoners. They carry crooks or staves that they can wield two-handed as clubs, but they wear no armor.

Hermit. A desert cave is a prime location for someone who has decided to withdraw from worldly cares, but that that doesn't mean bold adventurers like your party won't stumble upon it. One hermit lives here, devoted to a pure and simple life of contemplation. The hermit may be a divine spellcaster, for whom seclusion and meditation is a form of service to a deity. It takes a successful DC 15 Charisma (Persuasion) check to get past the fact that your party has broken this seclusion, but the hermit may be willing to use divine spells to aid them.

Alternately, your party may have found a secular hermit — someone who, having been wounded by failure or grown weary of success, decided to retire completely from the world. Such a person won't have divine spells, but may have magic items, local lore, or even knowledge and personal connections from his or her former life that might help your party.

Yet another possibility is that this hermit is a retired adventurer or soldier, in the manner of knights in the Arthurian romances who became hermits to repent of lives spent fighting each other and dallying with married ladies. Hermits in this mold have discarded their fighting gear, but they may be persuaded to leave their seclusion and join your party as friendly NPCs.

Treat a religious hermit as an acolyte, priest or cult fanatic, but feel free to generate a higher-level divine spellcaster if you want to create a more spectacular effect with this encounter. Treat a secular hermit as a commoner, or use a character class and level of your choice.

Treasure: Roll on the Treasure Hoard: Challenge 0-4 to determine if the hermit has any magic items and/or valuable devotional items.

The hermit could be a retired adventurer or soldier.

Merchants. If your party is playing it safe and sticking to roads or major trails as they traverse the desert, it's a reasonable bet that they share that route at some point with a caravan consisting of 2d6 merchants and 2d8 guards accompanying a string of camels, mules or giant lizards carrying trade goods.

As a natural first reaction to armed strangers, the caravan guards interpose themselves between your party and the pack animals. You may require a DC 15 Charisma (Persuasion) check to convince them that your party means no harm. In turn, traveling merchants could help your party by selling them necessary items, exchanging hard money for treasure items or providing knowledge of just about anywhere in your campaign world (where is this caravan going, and where did it originate?). A caravan that is low on guards might offer to hire your party as additional security.

Treat the merchants as commoners. Treat the guards as guards, although you may freely substitute veterans for guards if you want the caravan to have more capable escort.

Treasure: Roll once on the Individual Treasure: Challenge 0-4 table for each merchant or guard. In addition, roll once on the Treasure Hoard: Challenge 0-4 table for each

merchant present to determine the value of goods and/or hard money in the caravan. You may substitute valuable goods — spices, fine cloth, expensive hardwood, etc. — for art objects or coin as you wish.

Nomads. Perhaps all your party sees at first is dust kicked up from the desert floor, or perhaps they're close enough to notice that it's a group of tribal warriors mounted on riding horses or camels creating the disturbance. They're nomads who are native to this desert and although they live on the move, constantly looking for places to hunt and water their mounts, they consider the entire desert their territory and treat outsiders with suspicion. You may require a DC 15 Charisma (Persuasion) check, ratcheted down to DC 10 if your party offers them gifts, to win over the nomads, who may then help your party by trading animals suitable as mounts or pack animals, or providing useful local knowledge about water sources, monster lairs, etc.

The nomads carry shortbows in addition to spears.

Scaling the Encounter: As a rough guideline, the encounter group should contain 1d8 tribal warriors multiplied by your party's average level. If your party's average level is 6 or higher, add a veteran as the group's leader. If you don't want to run a mass encounter, feel free to substitute one thug with a shortbow for four tribal warriors as much as you like.

TABLE 2.6
Watch Out! - Desert

d12	ENCOUNTER
1	Did You Hear That?
2	Falling Rock
3	Flash Flood
4	Footprints
5	Hidden Hole
6-7	Mirage
8-9	Sand Pit
10-11	Sandstorm
12	Tripping Hazard

Did You Hear That? Choose a party member to make a DC 15 Wisdom (Survival) check. Failure means that that character believes that he or she has heard a noise made by a nearby creature or a dangerous natural phenomenon. It can be as consequential as a dragon's roar, or as eerily intimate as a rattlesnake's rattle. However, this is an illusion; the sound is coming from much farther away than it seems, and it may not be real at all. A successful check means that that party member realizes that this is an illusion, and the noise is either much farther away than it seems, or it is something else entirely.

TABLE 2.6.1
Did You Hear That? – Desert

d10	They Think They Hear...
1	Dragon roaring overhead
2	Footsteps of a large group of humans or humanoids
3	Giant insects buzzing
4	Hoofbeats of horses or other herd animals
5	Lion or other big cat roaring
6	Movement behind a cluster of rocks
7	Roc shrieking overhead
8	Voices speaking in Common
9	Voices speaking in Orcish
10	Windstorm

Falling Rock. Your party takes a rest in the shadow of a rock formation, or passes close by it to take advantage of the shade. Unfortunately, it isn't as stable as it seems. A chunk of rock large enough to leave a mark tumbles onto the closest party member (or pick one at random). The rock causes 1d8 bludgeoning damage, but a successful DC 15 Dexterity (Acrobatics) check halves the damage, rounded down.

Flash Flood. It can be tempting to take a rest stop in a gully or travel along it, to make advantage of the shade it provides. A dry depression is also an obvious place to heed the call of nature. However, this leaves you vulnerable to flash floods, which can brew up in the desert before you know it. Unless your players make it a point that their characters are keeping to higher ground, sudden rain upstream creates a rush of water that may sweep up one or more party member. In this situation, swimming is not possible and drowning becomes a possibility.

Anyone caught in the gully when the waters come rushing down can make a DC 15 Wisdom (Perception) or Wisdom (Survival) check to sense it in time to get out. Failure, however, means that they are caught in the torrent and carried downstream. Every 30 seconds, they are carried 30 feet downstream, but they may make a DC 20 Strength (Athletics) or Wisdom (Survival) check to

catch hold of something and haul themselves out of the water to safety.

Footprints. Your party spots human or humanoid footprints. Require a successful DC 15 Wisdom (Survival) check to realize that they are very old, and they will not lead to anything useful. Failure may lead to an amusing (for you as DM, anyway) wild goose chase.

Hidden Hole. The ground beneath the feet of a party member at the front of the march order gives way. It's a hole in the ground — perhaps an animal burrow, one that is easily stepped in by accident, or it's so extensive that it weakens the ground above it and too much weight on it causes it to collapse underfoot. Have your party make a DC 15 Wisdom (Perception) check to spot one that is right in their path in time to avoid it. Failure means that a party member steps into it, with all of the hazards that come with an unexpected tumble. That party members suffers 1d6 damage, with a DC 15 Dexterity (Acrobatics) check to halve the damage.

Mirage. Your party sees a large body of water in the distance — or rather, that's what they think they see. You may allow them a DC 15 Intelligence (Nature) or Wisdom (Survival) check to recognize that this is a mirage, and they will have to look elsewhere to refill their canteens. If they fail and decide to chase after this illusory oasis, you may allow them another check for every two miles traveled.

If this encounter takes place at night, re-roll for another encounter.

Sand Pit. Unless your party is traveling a road or an established path, they step into a patch of sand that will not support their weight. You may allow your party a DC 20 Intelligence (Nature) or Wisdom (Survival) check to spot the danger in time to avoid it. Failure means that a character at the front of the march order has stepped right into it, and it acts like quicksand.

Sandstorm. A sudden sandstorm blows up and catches your party in it for 1d6 x 5 minutes. During this time, heavily-obscured conditions prevail in the area around them, all movement allowances are halved and no aerial movement is allowed except with a successful DC 20 Strength (Athletics) check.

In addition, sand and grit blown about with such force can cause lingering problems even for those properly girded for desert travel. Once the storm ends, have each party member make a DC 15 Constitution or Wisdom (Survival) check. Those who fail suffer lingering effects from irritation to the eyes and upper respiratory tract until the next long rest: -1 penalty to Constitution-based checks and a -2 penalty to Wisdom (Perception) checks. If your party has the misfortune to be hit by more than one such storm before they can take a long rest, these penalties are cumulative.

Thirsty?

Thirst is one of the obvious hazards of traveling through the desert. So why doesn't it figure into Table 2.6? Granted, it seems like a strange omission. But the effects of thirst are, like the effects of fatigue, a constant concern and not a thing or random happening with a fixed location in place and time. Modeling it is a matter for a guide to wilderness survival, which would be a different book than this one.

Tripping Hazard. Pick a party member at the front of the march order. That character trips over an unseen obstacle — a half-buried skeleton, for instance. He or she must make a successful DC 10 Strength (Athletics) or Dexterity (Acrobatics) check to avoid a hard fall that causes 1d4 damage — and perhaps no small embarrassment in the eyes of the other party members.

Just Deserts

Its relative hostility to life makes the desert an exotic environment, and perhaps it's just not a big part of your campaign world. Or maybe you're a Frank Herbert fan, and your campaign world is nothing but desert. Either way, it's worth considering how and why life, whether sentient or unintelligent, survives here as a point of comparison against more hospitable places.

FOREST

CHAPTER THREE

Forest

What is a Forest?

This may seem painfully self-evident, but it is useful to clarify that in this book, "forest" refers to a large land area dominated by trees and mostly, if not entirely, free of human settlement. Other intelligent beings may live here; various humanoids might go about their business in a forest. And, of course, elves and fey consider forests to be their home turf. But they share the area with a variety of wild animals and monsters that includes — but is not limited to — the encounters described here. However, cultivated areas in which trees are grown and tended do not count. Even large orchards still qualify as agriculture, not wilderness.

Welcome to Sherwood

In England in the Middle Ages, the word "forest" was not, strictly speaking, a description of the terrain. It indicated that a place was royal land, land that belonged to the Crown. Hence, the actual Sherwood Forest was not a solid mass of trees in which Robin Hood could hide from the Sheriff of Nottingham, but a patchwork of wooded areas and rolling grassland, and some of the grassland was actually cultivated. But the whole area was still a forest. In other words, the term belonged to the real estate business, not to topology or biological science.

Just thought you'd like to know that.

Any description of who and what you are likely to encounter in a forest is complicated by the fact that forests are prominent features of the land just about everywhere you go and one must make allowances for differences in climate. Therefore, some tables in this chapter require die roll adjustments based on which of the three different classifications of forest describes your party's current surroundings: boreal, temperate or tropical.

Boreal forests occur in cold weather areas — in the sub-arctic bands, or at high altitudes. In fact, it might make more sense to use the tables in this chapter instead of those in Chapter 8 if the mountains in which your party finds itself is heavily forested. The tables here make similar allowances for the cold — you'll find winter wolves in the sub-arctic, but not many boa constrictors,

for instance. Conifers predominate in boreal forests, as they do in forests at high altitudes.

Hot, humid weather with high rainfall characterizes tropical forests — jungles or rain forests, if you prefer to call them that. The climate encourages lush growth of evergreen trees and sustains certain fauna that you won't find in colder climates. Cold-blooded creatures can thrive here because of the heat. As a sort of flip side to boreal forests, boa constrictors thrive here, but winter wolves can't stand the heat as well as the humidity). As the name suggests, temperate forests enjoy a moderate climate — temperatures that are cold in winter, but not too cold; hot in summer, but not too hot; and rainfall that is enough to support abundant flora, but not excessive. Both coniferous and deciduous trees may thrive here, as well as animal life that prefers a relatively mild climate. Temperate forests also include tropical dry forests. Tropical dry forests lie in the tropical climate band, but they don't receive nearly the same rainfall as jungles/rainforests, so their flora and fauna are more comparable to that of temperate forests.

What Do You Find in a Forest?

When you determine that a random encounter is in order, roll on Table 3.1 to determine the category:

TABLE 3.1

Encounter Type - Forest

d20	CATEGORY
1-6	Aggressive Creatures (Table 3.2)
7-12	Neutral Creatures (Table 3.3)
13-16	Humanoids (Table 3.4)
17	Humans (Table 3.5)
18-20	Watch Out! (Table 3.6)

Then, roll on the appropriate table to determine the creature, person or thing encountered.

Note that line of sight does not extend very far in the middle of a forest. At most, your party has a clear view to the other side of a clearing. Otherwise, trees, heavy undergrowth, dead logs and other physical obstacles make it hard to see very far. Therefore, whomever or whatever your party comes across, the encounter is likely to start at fairly close quarters.

It's rare you have a clean line-of-sight in a forest.

TABLE 3.2
Aggressive Creatures - Forest

d100	ENCOUNTER
1-3	Winter Wolf
4-7	Saber-Toothed Tiger
8-17	Wolves
18-21	Ankheg
22-26	Birds of Prey
27-29	Bulette
30	Drider
31-32	Ettercap
33-34	Ettin
35-36	Green Hag
37-39	Griffon
40	Hell Hound
41-42	Hill Giant
43-51	Insects
52-55	Lion
56-57	Mephits
58	Medusa
59	Minotaur
60-63	Ogre
64-65	Otyugh
66-69	Salamanders
70-78	Snakes
79-87	Spiders
88-89	Troll
90-96	Undead
97-98	Will-o'-Wisp
99-100	Worgs
101-102	Wyvern
103-105	Panther
106-108	Tiger
109-110	Shambling Mound

+6 to the die roll if in a temperate forest.
+10 to the die roll if in a tropical forest.

Winter Wolf. Their white fur and gift for stealth make winter wolves a dangerous predator in boreal forests, where snow often covers the ground. You may allow your party a DC 15 Wisdom (Perception) check to notice a large pair of pale blue eyes and the outline of a winter wolf lurking in between the trees. The wolf is hungry (or confident) enough to think that it can take them, although its real target may be your party's pack animals.

Scaling the Encounter: A winter wolf may be a bit too much for a beginning-level party. Feel free to re-roll for another encounter. Conversely, if you want to run a more challenging encounter for a higher-level party, use an encounter group consisting of one winter wolf for each multiple of 4 in your party's average level.

Treasure: Furriers in your world may be willing to pay for winter wolf pelts. How much is ultimately up to you, but 5 gp is a reasonable baseline and should scale up the farther away you go from its native climate (and the rarer they become).

Saber-Toothed Tiger. These predators are found in boreal and temperate forests and they are fearless as well as skilled hunters. You may allow your party a DC 15 Wisdom (Perception) to notice that a saber-toothed tiger has been stalking them, weaving in and out of the trees.

Scaling the Encounter: Saber-toothed tigers usually hunt by themselves. If you wish to make the encounter more challenging, use a group consisting of one saber-toothed tiger for each multiple of 3 in your party's average level.

Wolves. In a boreal or temperate forest with game animals, you are bound to find wolves that prey on them. Roll on Table 3.2.1 to determine whether your party encounters wolves or dire wolves:

TABLE 3.2.1
Wolves – Forest

d4	ENCOUNTER
1	Dire Wolf
2-4	Wolves

Dire Wolves. One dire wolf sets upon your party from amongst the trees. As their name suggests, dire wolves are vicious and fearless and the attack regardless of the numerical odds.

Wolves. Your party meets a pack of 1d4+1 wolves on the prowl. They split into two groups and maneuver to attack your party from the flanks.

Scaling the Encounter: If you wish to make the encounter more challenging, the encounter group consists of two dire wolves for each multiple of 3 in your party's average level, or 1d4 wolves plus a number of additional wolves equal to your party's average level.

Treasure: Furriers in your world may be willing to pay for wolf pelts. How much is ultimately up to you, but 2 gp is a reasonable baseline price for a normal wolf
➤

pelt and 3 gp for a dire wolf pelt. Dire wolf pelts are not necessarily more desirable, but they are larger and offer more fur to work with.

Ankheg. These burrowing monstrosities are notorious hazards in farming country, but they also prey on forest creatures. As your party passes overhead, an ankheg in its tunnel mistakes your party for a herd of deer. It breaches the surface and attacks.

Scaling the Encounter: If you wish to make the encounter more challenging, the encounter group consists of one ankheg for each multiple of 3 in your party's average level. Each ankheg emerges from a point no closer than 20-40 feet to any other attacking ankheg.

Treasure: Ankhegs under the forest floor leave a lot of animal bones behind them, but in the wilderness they find few targets that leave behind treasure. You may roll once on the Individual Treasure: Challenge 0-4 table for each ankheg present, if you wish.

Birds of Prey. A bird of prey — or a flock of them — wheels overhead, then dives down past the treetops at your party. Keen-eyed, but bird-brained all the same, the bird has spotted something in your party as food — a familiar or small summoned creature is an obvious choice, but it could just be travelers rations, like strips of cured meat left in the open. To determine which species, roll on Table 3.2.2:

TABLE 3.2.2
Birds of Prey – Forest

d10	ENCOUNTER
1-2	Eagle
3	Giant Eagle
4-5	Blood Hawks
6-7	Hawks
8-9	Owl
10	Giant Owl

Eagle. One eagle swoops down on your party, aiming itself at something it has identified as food.

Giant Eagle. A giant eagle has spotted your party. Giant eagles are intelligent and may respond if your party tries to flag them down. Though it cannot speak when spoken to, a successful DC 15 Charisma (Persuasion) check by someone who speaks Common or Auran persuades it to do your party a service, if it is

➤

within its power to accomplish it. This may involve delivering a written message or token, or guiding your party to a place that it knows, or even traveling with them for a while as an airborne lookout.

Blood Hawks. A flock of 2d6 blood hawks swoop down on your party. They concentrate on a single target — most likely a pack animal, but they may settle for a small humanoid as the next best thing.

Hawks. A flock of 2d10 hawks targets your party. They're probably going after your party's rations, but they may have spotted rodents or small reptiles that are scurrying along the forest floor. To the extent that your party is in their way, the hawks attack them.

Owl. Owls hunt at night, so you should re-roll this encounter if it takes place during the day. Otherwise, one owl has spotted food among your party's belongings. Most likely, it has spotted a small animal companion or familiar, or rations left out in the open.

Giant Owl. Likewise, a giant owl encounter is most suitable for night, so you should re-roll this encounter if it takes place during the day. One giant owl spots food among your party's belongings.

Bulette. Bad luck — a land shark senses your party walking overhead and figures they're its next meal. To create a little drama, you may require a successful DC 15 Wisdom (Perception) check to sense the ground rumbling; you may then allow a DC 15 Intelligence (Nature) check to identify it as the sound of a bulette before it breaches the surface.

Scaling the Encounter: A bulette may be a bit much for a lower-level party to handle, so if your party's average level is less than 5, feel free to re-roll for a different encounter. Conversely, if your average party level is higher than 10, you may add another bulette to make it more challenging.

Treasure: Bulettes hunt on the move, so treasure that belonged to its previous victims is scattered far and wide. However, you may allow your party a DC 10 Wisdom (Survival) check to follow the trail back to its last kill. If successful, roll on the Individual Treasure: Challenge 0-4 table to determine what they find.

Drider. In an isolated corner of the forest, your party comes across one of the Spider Queen's cast-offs. Perhaps this drider has gone mad from its fate, and it automatically attacks anyone who disturbs its lonely exile in a fit of unthinking rage. Perhaps it is more calculating — though no less mad — and it somehow thinks that killing an elf or another enemy of the drow and presenting its head to a representative of the Spider Queen will somehow restore it to favor. Or you may consider that hunger and insanity have given it a taste for human or humanoid flesh. Whatever motivation you give it, that should drive how it reacts to your party.

Scaling the Encounter: A drider may be a bit much for a lower-level party to handle, so if your party's average level is less than 6, feel free to re-roll for a different encounter.

Treasure: It is most likely that your party has stumbled upon a lone drider sulking in its lair. To determine its treasure, roll on the Treasure Hoard: Challenge 5-10 table.

Ettercap. A lone ettercap tries to ambush your party, attacking from behind once they have passed its hiding spot. You may allow a DC 15 Wisdom (Perception) or Wisdom (Survival) check to sense that something is trying to hide from your party as they approach. Failure means that the ettercap gets to use its web ability to pin as many party members as possible, intending to close and finish off each one with its *Web Garrote* attack.

Treasure: You may consider that the ettercap jumps your party from its habitual spot, and that meager treasure from its previous victims lies scattered in the vicinity. Roll on the Individual Treasure: Challenge 0-4 table to determine what your party finds.

Ettin. Your party hears two loud voices coming from somewhere amongst the trees. Your party must make a successful DC 15 Intelligence (Nature) check to recognize that it's an ettin arguing with itself. If they choose not to avoid the ettin, it calls out to your party and demands that they help settle a dispute. It should be something that your party would find awkward or at least pointless to answer — for instance, whether elf flesh or dwarf flesh tastes more savory. No matter what answer the party gives, one or both heads accuses them of unfairly favoring the other and the ettin attacks.

Alternately, the ettin stops short when it spots the party. It realizes that it's hungry after arguing with itself for such a long time, and your party looks tasty.

Treasure: The ettin carries some coins in a pouch looped around its loincloth. Roll twice on the Individual Treasure: Challenge 0-4 table.

Green Hag. Your party comes upon a boggy patch in the forest when it hears what sounds like the voice of a young woman crying for help. Upon inspection, they see her half-sunk into the mire, evidently struggling to get out. Unfortunately, it's really a green hag trying to lure them into a patch of quicksand-like bog. It looks forward to the pleasure of watching them struggle, then perish. If necessary, it will help the process along.

Scaling the Encounter: Even a lone green hag may be a bit too much for a beginning-level party, especially combined with the hazards of quicksand. Feel free to re-roll for another encounter.

Treasure: This bog is the hag's lair, and it keeps trophies from its previous victims here. To determine its treasure, roll on the Treasure Hoard: Challenge 0-4 table.

Griffon. A griffon, roaming afield from its eyrie in nearby hills, spots your party and goes for one of their mounts or pack animals — or at least, it thinks it has spotted a mount or a pack animal.

Scaling the Encounter: If you wish to make the encounter more challenging, your party encounters a flock (or pack?) of griffons hunting together. There is one for each multiple of 3 in your party's average level.

Hell Hound. Your party crosses paths with one hell hound in a mean and paranoid mood. Most likely, it came to the Material Plane as a companion of a devil and somehow got separated from its master. Or perhaps it was part of a pack kept by a fire giant up in the hills not far from here and it became hopelessly separated from them. In any event, it is none too pleased about wandering this plane alone and it takes out its separation anxiety on your party. You may also treat its breath weapon as a fire risk.

Scaling the Encounter: A hell hound may be a bit too much for a beginning-level party. Feel free to re-roll for another encounter. Conversely, if you want to run a more challenging encounter for a higher-level party, the encounter group consists of one hell hound for each multiple of 5 in your party's average level, rounded up.

Hill Giant. Giants don't come down to the lowlands very often, so the hill giants who forage here operate without the constraints that their less chaotic (and more powerful) cousins might impose on them. Your party crosses paths with one hill giant that feels no compunction about taking whatever they have, and it is confident that its size and strength allows it to take all smaller comers.

Scaling the Encounter: If your party's average level is lower than 5, a hill giant may be more than you want to throw at them. Feel free to re-roll for a different encounter. Conversely, if you want to run a more challenging encounter for a higher-level party, use an encounter group of one hill giant for each multiple of 6 in your party's average level.

Insects. You may not think of insects as predatory, but they feed without giving much thought to who might be put out by their actions and they cause trouble in their own way. Some are viciously aggressive when they feel threatened. Roll on Table 3.2.3 to determine the insects encountered:

TABLE 3.2.3
Insects – Forest

d6	ENCOUNTER
1-4	Swarm of Insects
5-6	Giant Wasps

Swarm of Insects. One swarm of insects — call them gnats, midges, mosquitos, whatever you will — descends upon your party and makes their lives decidedly unpleasant.

Giant Wasps. Your party comes upon two giant wasps guarding a nest hanging from a tree branch. They are in a sufficiently bad temper to attack anything that comes close to the nest.

Scaling the Encounter: If you wish to make the encounter more challenging (or more of a nuisance, depending on how you look at it), the encounter group consists of 1d4 giant wasps for each multiple of 2 in your party's average level, or 1d4 swarms of insects plus one additional swarm for each level in your party's average level.

Lion. Your party sees a deer scamper away and then disappear amongst the trees. Then they hear a leonine roar that sounds more than a little angry. They chased off a deer being stalked by a lion, and the lion takes it out on them by attacking them.

Scaling the Encounter: If you wish to make the encounter more challenging, your party comes upon lions hunting as a pack, with two lions for each multiple of 3 in your party's average level.

Medusa. It may be inconspicuous enough so that you have your party make a successful DC 10 Wisdom (Perception) check to notice it, but they pass by what appears to be a realistic statue of a small animal. In fact, a medusa has made its lair in a small clearing nearby, where it surrounds itself with the petrified remains of its victims. It decides that your party would supplement its existing collection nicely. If your party investigates, they'll find more and more such statues until they reach the edge of the medusa's clearing.

Scaling the Encounter: If your party's average level is lower than 6, a medusa may be more than you want to throw at them. Feel free to re-roll for a different encounter.

Treasure: The medusa's gaze petrifies flesh, but not valuables. To total up the bits and pieces that once belonged to her humanoid victims, roll on the Treasure Hoard: Challenge 5-10 table.

Mephits. These annoying little elementals have a habit of crossing over into the Material Plane, like ink bleeding through paper, and making nuisances of themselves. They are not predatory, but they are very annoying and they interpret any attempt to brush them aside as an attack. Roll on Table 3.2.4 to determine the kind of mephit your party encounters:

TABLE 3.2.4
Mephits – Forest

d4	ENCOUNTER
1	Ice Mephit
2-4	Mud Mephit
5	Smoke Mephits

+1 to die roll if in a temperate or tropical forest

Ice Mephit. In boreal forests, the weather is sometimes cold enough to draw ice mephits from the Elemental Planes. They congregate around ponds, streams and bogs. One ice mephit hides among the vegetation as it pelts your party with dirt clods and rocks and it cackles contemptuously at someone who would invade its space. This isn't enough to cause damage, but it refuses to stop, even if your party tries to walk away.

Mud Mephits. 1d4+1 mud mephits lounging by a marshy clearing spot your party. They have slowly been driving each other mad with incessant and pointless complaints about everything and nothing, and they see your party as a diversion. They're too lazy to move, so they yell out to your party and start complaining to them that it's too hot, or too cold, too dry or too wet — or how they're too poor, or bored, or exhausted. They start to beg your party for handouts. All of this is in Aquan or Terran, of course. If your party ignores them, the mephits chase after them and eventually become exasperated enough to attack. If your party confronts them, they become agitated and attack.

Smoke Mephits. 1d4+1 smoke mephits came here the last time there was a fire in the forest and never left.
➤

They jump from the branch on which they have been perching and buzz about your party. They pepper your party with questions about where they are going, what are they doing here, etc. And they respond to whatever your party says with a string of bad advice and misleading statements. Like a swarm of insects, they refuse to stop unless forced to do so.

Scaling the Encounter: If you wish to make the encounter more challenging, the encounter group consists of 1d4 ice mephits for each multiple of 2 in your party's average level, or 1d4 mud mephits or smoke mephits plus a number of additional such mephits equal to your party's average level.

Minotaur. Your party spots a trail that appears to lead into a dense, gloomy part of the forest. It winds among the trees, apparently without purpose. But if your party chooses to follow it, they eventually find themselves face-to-face with a minotaur that sizes them up as its latest victims. It's rare to find a minotaur out in the open, but this one has chosen to create its labyrinth among the confusion of closely-packed trees. Was it driven out of its former, more typical lair? Did its old lair collapse and become uninhabitable?

Scaling the Encounter: A minotaur may be a bit too much for a beginning-level party. Feel free to re-roll for another encounter. Conversely, if you want to run a more challenging encounter for a higher-level party, consider that two minotaurs inhabit this lair. They work as a team, seeking to attack your party from different angles.

Treasure: At the heart of the minotaur's lair is its treasure hoard — as well as the remains of its previous victims. Roll once on the Treasure Hoard: Challenge 0-4 table if one minotaur is present, or on the Treasure Hoard: Challenge 5-10 table if two are present.

Ogres. Your party crosses paths with a foraging party of ogres. Whether you want to stage any meaningful interaction with these undersized giants is up to you, but it should surprise no one if they decide that your party is as good a target as any they are likely to find in the near future, whether they are looking for things or food (or both).

Scaling the Encounter: The encounter group consists of two ogres for each multiple of 3 in your party's average level, rounded up. If your party is only 1st Level, consider that one half-ogre confronts them.

Treasure: These ogres are away from their lair. Total up the CR of all ogres killed and roll on the appropriate Individual Treasure table.

Otyugh. Your party passes a dank, marshy swale. Here, the foliage is dense enough so that hardly any sunlight reaches it. Debris and animal remains from the forest floor collect here and stew in a state of decay. As if this wasn't bad enough, it's also the lair of an otyugh, which reaches out from under what looks like a pile of rotting leaves and attacks.

Scaling the Encounter: If your party's average level is lower than 5, an otyugh may be more than you want to throw at them. Feel free to re-roll for a different encounter. Conversely, if you want to run a more challenging encounter for a higher-level party, consider that your party has come across a large and genuinely appalling pile of rot, and that it conceals one otyugh for each multiple of 7 in your party's average level.
Treasure: The belongings of the otyugh's previous victims lie scattered about its lair. Roll once on the Treasure Hoard: Challenge 5-10 table for each otyugh present to determine its contents.

Owlbear. This encounter is most likely to take place at night, when owlbears hunt. Your party hears its terrible shriek echo through the forest; you may require a DC 15 Intelligence (Nature) check to recognize it. If it is daytime, you can either re-roll for a different encounter or consider that your party has stumbled onto a cave carved into a rocky outcropping that serves as its lair. If hunting, it attacks; if disturbed in its lair it fights.

Scaling the Encounter: An owlbear may be a bit too much for a beginning-level party. Feel free to re-roll for another encounter. Conversely, if you want to run a more challenging encounter for a higher-level party, your party has encountered a mated pair of owlbears.

Treasure: If the encounter takes place in the owlbear lair, roll on the Treasure Hoard: Challenge 0-4 table to determine what it has taken from its previous victims. If it involves a pair of owlbears, roll twice.

Salamanders. These elemental creatures are drawn to forests, where they enjoy making dangerous mischief. They revel in forests on fire. Your party chances upon one fire snake and it it practically dares them to stop it from setting the surrounding trees alight.

Alternately, you may stage this encounter with the fire snake already playing among burning trees and undergrowth. In this case, anyone who wants to make a melee attack against it must first make a successful DC 10 Dexterity (Acrobatics) check to dodge the flames, or else suffer 1d6 fire damage.

Scaling the Encounter: If you wish to make the encounter more challenging, the encounter group consists of two fire snakes for each multiple of 3 in your party's average level. You may substitute one salamander for five fire snakes.

Snakes. Venomous snakes shun the cold, but they thrive in temperate and tropical forests. They possess an unfortunate combination of traits: On the one hand, their coloration makes them hard to spot against the forest floor, but on the other hand they lash out if you get too close to them. This is what happens to your party. You may allow a DC 15 Wisdom (Perception) or Wisdom (Survival) check to realize that the front of the march order is about to step on a snake. This should give them enough time to take evasive action, although you may consider that this simply means they aren't surprised when the snake lashes out.

Roll on Table 3.2.5 to determine the size of the snake(s) encountered:

TABLE 3.2.5
Snakes – Forest

d10	ENCOUNTER
1-6	Swarm of Poisonous Snakes
7-8	Poisonous Snake
9	Giant Poisonous Snake
10-11	Constrictor Snake
12-13	Giant Constrictor Snake

+3 to die roll if in a tropical forest.

Swarm of Poisonous Snakes. Your party comes across a shallow depression which is, literally, a snake pit with one swarm of poisonous snakes present. You may decrease the DC to notice them to 5, to reflect the abundance of snakes and a terrain feature that is relatively easy to notice.

Poisonous Snake. Your party comes close to stepping on one poisonous snake.

Giant Poisonous Snake. Your party comes across one giant poisonous snake. You may decrease the DC to notice it to 10 to reflect its size.

Constrictor Snake. Constrictor snakes are found only in tropical regions, where it's hot enough for such a large cold-blooded creature to survive. But where they do occur, they are dangerous predators. A constrictor tries to sneak up on your party and make a meal of one of its members.

➤

Giant Constrictor Snake. If there is anything more daunting than running afoul of a constrictor snake, it is being targeted as food by a giant constrictor snake and they can grow huge in the jungle. One of these beasts targets one of your party members, confident that the rest won't be able to harm it.

Treasure: It's quite possible that a giant constrictor snake has fed on humans or humanoids before and that the less perishable possessions remain in its digestive tract. If your party bothers to slit the snake open and root around inside, roll on the Individual Treasure: Challenge 0-4 table.

Spiders. A forest is full of spiders, everyone knows that. Your party comes across a large web spun between two trees (unless the encounter turns out to be giant wolf spiders; see below). It may be an empty web, as in Table 3.6: Hampering Web, or it may be crawling with spiders — or it may be that just one very big and dangerous spider calls it home and hunting ground. Roll on Table 3.2.6 to determine what kind of spider inhabits this web:

TABLE 3.2.6
Spiders – Forest

d10	ENCOUNTER
1-4	Spiders
5-7	Giant Spider
8-9	Giant Wolf Spiders
9-10	Phase Spider

Spiders. These spiders are small, but their venom packs a punch. They won't leave their web, but if someone in your party gets close enough, they'll attack. 2d8 spiders live here.

Giant Spider. Giant spiders prefer the darkest corners of the forest. They live alone, so your party encounters one in its web.

Giant Wolf Spiders. Wolf spiders do not weave webs; they burrow into the ground and they either take whatever stumbles into their lair, or they emerge to ambush prey. As your party approaches, vibrations in the ground tell them that something juicy has come to their doorstep, and 1d4 giant wolf spiders attack. You may allow your party a DC 15 Wisdom (Perception) check to notice a hole in the ground large enough to fit a big spider, and if successful, a DC 15 Intelligence (Nature) check to realize that it's a wolf spider burrow.

➤

Phase Spider. Phase spiders are quite fearless, and they use their ability to jump back and forth between planes to conduct hit-and-run attacks, wearing your party down until they are all incapacitated or dead.

Scaling the Encounter: Giant spiders live alone, as too much weight would drag down their web. If you want to create a more challenging encounter with ordinary spiders, you may add another 2d8 to the encounter group — having too many, however, not only creates an unwieldy encounter, but it assumes an awfully large population of spiders for a single web. To create a more challenging encounter with giant wolf spiders, use an encounter group consisting of 1d4 plus a number of additional giant wolf spiders equal to your party's average level.

A phase spider may be a bit too much for a beginning-level party. Feel free to re-roll for another encounter. Conversely, if you want to run a more challenging encounter for a higher-level party, use an encounter group consisting of one phase spider for each multiple of 4 in your party's average level.

Treasure. With larger spiders, they may have trapped humanoid-sized victims in the past and left some of their valuables caught in their web. You may roll on the Individual Treasure: Challenge 0-4 table if you wish.

Troll. Who knows what brings a troll to this corner of the forest? What is certain is that it emerges from among the trees and demands a fee in order to let you pass through territory that it considers its own. Perhaps it demands one of the party's pack animals as its toll, or a suitable amount of coins. It fights rather than let anyone pass for free.

Scaling the Encounter: If your party's average level is lower than 5, a troll may be more than you want to throw at them. Feel free to re-roll for a different encounter. Conversely, if your party's average level is 10 or higher, feel free to add one troll to the encounter — a tag-team of trolls.

Treasure: The troll's racket has worked well enough in the past: Its victims pay one way or another, and it has accumulated a decent hoard. Searching the area turns up its stash, thrown in to a pile, on a successful DC 10 Wisdom (Perception) check. Roll on the Treasure Hoard: Challenge 5-10 table to determine the contents.

Undead. Forests are places of gloom and mystery as well as natural beauty. If your party encounters undead in the forest, they have touched that dark mystery through the remnants of souls who died terrible deaths in a hostile wilderness, and whose rest has been disturbed by an evil whose source can no longer be traced. Roll on Table 3.2.7 to determine the undead abomination that greets your party.

TABLE 3.2.7
Undead – Forest

d12	ENCOUNTER
1	Banshee
2	Ghost
3-5	Ghouls/Ghasts
6	Shadows
7-8	Skeletons
9	Specter
10	Wraith
11-12	Zombies

Banshee. Assuming that elves are a part of your campaign world, it's a good bet that they live, or at least once lived in this forest. This banshee is a relic of evil deeds and tragic events from their history. Perhaps your party hears its forlorn wail from a distance, and they only confront it if they investigate. Or perhaps they stumble upon the banshee's domain, and in its madness and despair it demands that they hand over their valuables, particularly their jewelry.

Ghost. A ghost encountered in the forest — whether glimpsed flitting between the trees, or whether it rears up suddenly out of the gloom — is most likely the remnant of someone who died a miserable death in the wilderness. Perhaps that unfortunate person got lost; or died while fleeing from pursuers; or ended his or her own life in despair. Whatever the case, you may make this into a hostile encounter by having the ghost try to possess a member of your party so that it may resolve unfinished business from its former life.

Ghouls/Ghasts. An encounter with ghouls is most likely to take place at night, although the gloom of the deep forest may work well enough for that purpose. Two ghouls (or one ghast) approach your party, driven by mindless hunger for their flesh.

Shadows. Jumping at shadows is a common reaction to traveling through the deep forest. However, sometimes a shadow is more than just a shadow — it's an undead creature! Without thinking or feeling, it attacks the nearest party member, eager to drain the life from another victim and create one more of its own kind. ➤

Skeletons. Your party comes across the undead remnants of an ancient conflict: 1d4 skeletons carrying broken weapons and draped with fragments of the armor they wore in life. Perhaps they were soldiers killed in a skirmish. Perhaps they were adventurers or explorers ambushed by brigands — or perhaps they were bandits themselves, who were hunted down in the name of justice or revenge, or who fell out among themselves. Driven by necromantic echoes of the end of their lives, they're looking for a fight.

Specter. Specters often find enough gloom to suit them where trees block out the sun. It isn't darkness, but it's close enough. Your party comes upon one specter that was once someone who perished in the wilderness, but all connections to who and what it was in life no longer exist. Only blind hatred of the living drives it to attack your party on sight.

Wraith. Your party has the misfortune to come across a wraith that was once someone who perished in the wilderness, and is now bound to the place of its doom. Perhaps they pass a hastily dug grave — you may require a DC 15 Wisdom (Perception) check to notice that the ground has been disturbed in this way — or just a skeleton that has been picked clean by scavengers. Whatever the case, it takes out the resentment that it bore at the end of its life on your party.

Zombies. Your party comes across 1d4 zombies who have been programmed to kill every living thing they encounter. The source of the necromancy that created these zombies we leave to you. Perhaps they slipped the leash of their creator and they now wander the forest mindlessly looking for victims.

Scaling the Encounter: Banshees, ghosts and wraiths always work alone. The base encounter group for specters also consists of only one of its kind.

A banshee or a wraith may be too much for a beginning-level party, so feel free to re-roll the encounter in that case. With specters, you may create a more challenging encounter by using two for each multiple of 3 in your party's average level, with all of them being part of a group that perished *en masse*.

Ghouls/Ghasts: If you wish to make the encounter more challenging, the encounter group consists of two ghouls (for or one ghast) each multiple of 3 in your party's average level, rounded up. Feel free to mix and match ghouls and ghasts as long as you maintain the right proportion of total CR to average party level.

Shadows: The encounter group consists of two shadows for each multiple of 3 in your party's average level.

Skeletons: If you wish to make the encounter more challenging, the encounter group consists of 1d4 skeletons plus one additional skeleton for each level in your party's average level. You may substitute one warhorse skeleton for two skeletons.

Zombies: If you wish to make the encounter more challenging, the encounter group consists of 1d4 zombies plus additional zombies equal to your party's average level. If the average party level is 3 or higher, you may use an encounter group consisting of one ogre zombie for each multiple of 3 in the party's average level.

Treasure: Most likely, banshees, ghosts and wraiths are encountered in or near what passes for a lair with them and you may consider that there they keep possessions that they had in life. Roll on the Treasure Hoard: Challenge 0-4 table for the contents of their stash. You may require a successful DC 15 Wisdom (Perception) check to find its exact location.

With ghouls, ghasts, skeletons and zombies, they may have with them some remains of what they had on their person at the time of their death. Roll on the Individual Treasure: Challenge 0-4 table once for each ghoul and ghast, or each multiple of four skeletons or zombies, rounded up.

Will-o'-Wisp. Your party comes upon a boggy little clearing and they see a luminous globe dancing and bobbing above the mire. It's the remnant of an unquiet soul that perished here — perhaps a wounded fugitive who stumbled into the bog and drowned, alone and in agony.

If you want to add some spice to the encounter, consider that this evil spirit tries to lure victims into a patch of quicksand to render them helpless. In this case, the will-o'-wisp restricts itself to a 50-foot diameter area at the center of the clearing. At the center of this area, the swamp turns into a 20-foot diameter pit of quicksand. If the will-o'-wisp is not already directly above the quicksand when it is engaged in melee combat, it retreats until it is above the quicksand, thus forcing its attacker to step into it in order to continue the melee.

Scaling the Encounter: If you wish to make the encounter more challenging, the encounter group consists of one will-o'-wisp for each multiple of 3 in the party's average level.

Treasure: Belongings from the will-o'-wisp's previous victims have been piling up here, with various valuables scattered in the much. To determine the treasure, roll once on the Treasure Hoard: Challenge 0-4 table for each will-o'-wisp present.

Worgs. Your party crosses paths with 1d4 of these fearsome quadrupeds out on their own. One may deduce that they became separated from their goblinoid masters — perhaps they got dealt the losing hand in a battle, or the worgs escaped their pen after being badly treated. Whatever the reason, they're in a foul mood and eager to take it out on your party.

Scaling the Encounter: If you wish to make the encounter more challenging, the encounter group consists of a pack of escaped or abandoned worgs, 1d4 for each multiple of 2 in your party's average level.

Wyvern. A wyvern on the hunt spots your party from above as they enter a clearing. The wyvern is either very hungry or very aggressive, so it swoops down to attack despite the odds.

Scaling the Encounter: If your party's average level is lower than 6, a wyvern with its blood up may be more than you want to throw at them. Feel free to re-roll for a different encounter.

Panther. Panthers prefer to hunt at night, so at your discretion this encounter takes place as your party travels after sunset, or when the panther stalks their campsite. You may require a DC 15 — DC 20, if at night — Wisdom (Perception) or Wisdom (Survival) check to notice that a panther lurks in the branches of a nearby tree just before it leaps down onto your party

Tiger. Your party draws the attention of a hunting tiger, most likely for either of two reasons. Perhaps they have startled prey it was stalking — in which case, they see the prey animal dart across its path, and they hear an angry snarl off to one side. Either that, or the tiger has targeted one of the party's pack animals as its prey.

Shambling Mound. As your party hacks its way through the jungle, they may or may not realize that a shambling mound has spotted them as a possible food source. You may require your party to make a DC 15 Wisdom (Perception) or Wisdom (Survival) check to realize that the jumble of plant growth off to the side just moved. Success means that your party may then make a DC 15 Intelligence (Nature) check to realize that it's a shambling mound.

Scaling the Encounter: If your party's average level is

lower than 5, a shambling mound may be more than you want to throw at them. Feel free to re-roll for a different encounter.

Treasure: Shambling mounds feed on the move, but their previous prey's less perishable possessions remain inside them. Roll on the Individual Treasure: Challenge 5-10 table to determine what spills out of its innards when it is slain.

TABLE 3.3
Neutral Creatures - Forest

d100	ENCOUNTER
1-4	Brown Bear
5-9	Elk
10-14	Black Bear
15-17	Awakened Tree
18-21	Axe Beaks
22-24	Badgers
25-26	Bats
27-34	Boar
35	Centaur
36-41	Centipede
42-44	Cockatrice
45-53	Deer
54	Dragon
55-63	Fey
64-67	Fire Beetles
68-70	Hyenas
71-72	Lizards
73-74	Mules
75-76	Pseudodragon
77-82	Rats
83	Raven
84-85	Unicorn
86-91	Vultures
92-96	Weasels
97-102	Elephant
103-106	Ape
107-109	Rhinoceros
110	Flying Snake

+10 to the die roll if in a tropical forest

Brown Bear. Your party spots a brown bear prowling around for food. If they are resting, the bear comes sniffing around, drawn by their rations. If your party just wants to scare it off, require a DC 15 Intelligence (Nature) or Wisdom (Survival) check. Success means that the bear takes the hint and lumbers away. Failure means that the bear charges them.

A hungry enough tiger may target the party's pack animals as prey

Elk. Your party spots a herd of 1d6 bulls and 3d6 cows grazing among the trees. If your party attacks them, only the males fight, covering the fleeing females.

Even if your party does not behave in a threatening manner, there is a chance that the bulls mistake their actions and attack anyway. Have your party make a DC 15 Intelligence (Nature) or Wisdom (Survival) check. Failure means that someone has made a false move that sets off the males and they charge.

Scaling the Encounter: If you wish to make the encounter more challenging, your party sees a lone (and rare) giant elk at a distance. As they approach it they realize that it's larger than it seemed. Confident in its power as an alpha of its kind, it attacks your party if it senses any hostile intent (remember that giant elk have the ability to understand certain languages).

Perhaps it is bad luck in your campaign world to hunt a giant elk. If your party kills it, each party member is cursed as if affected by the spell *bane*, except that the effect lasts until it is magically dispelled, or until those who did the deed atone for it.

Treasure: Elk are hunted for food wherever they share territory with humans. Perhaps a nearby butcher will pay 2 gp or thereabouts for a fresh carcass.

Black Bear. Your party spots a black bear prowling around for food. If they are resting, the bear comes around, drawn by their rations. If your party just wants to scare it off, require a DC 15 Intelligence (Nature) or Wisdom (Survival) check. Success means that the bear takes the hint and lumbers away. Failure does not necessarily mean that the bear attacks, but it does stand its ground. If they attack it, the bear defends itself. At that point, require another DC 15 Intelligence (Nature) or Wisdom (Survival) check. Failure means that someone has made a false move, provoking the bear to attack. Otherwise, it eventually takes the hint and retreats.

Awakened Tree. In old forests, there are trees that have been touched by enchantments so ancient that humans have not observed or recorded them. They are part of the forest's weird, mysterious beauty.

Your party has some sort of physical contact with a huge tree. Perhaps someone stumbles over a root and falls heavily against it. Perhaps someone just leans against it to rest. Perhaps someone breaks off a branch, or carves a sigil into the trunk, or does some other casual mischief. Perhaps a dog or some other animal companion uses the tree for its own purposes. Whatever it is, the tree expresses its alarm.

An awakened tree is not necessarily hostile. If your party asks it for help, a successful DC 10 Charisma (Persuasion) check wins it over. If your party includes someone visibly carrying an axe of some sort, the DC is 15. If the party has harmed the tree in any way, the DC is 20. Help from an awakened tree includes providing knowledge about the immediate area, or even accompanying your party as an ally as long as this doesn't require leaving the forest.

However, awakened trees instinctively react to open flame with hostility. Lighting a torch or starting campfire causes it to attack.

Scaling the Encounter: If the average level of your party is higher than 4, consider that the encounter group consists of one awakened tree for each multiple of 4 in your party's average level, rounded up. If your party's average level is 9 or higher, you may simply substitute one treant.

Axe Beaks. Your party comes across a hunting pack of 1d4+2 of these odd-looking, bad-tempered flightless birds as they hunt small animals that scurry across the forest floor. They don't like having their hunt interrupted, but it's not a sure thing that they'll attack. If your party wishes to avoid a fight, require a DC 15 Intelligence (Nature) or Wisdom (Survival) check. Failure means that a party member has made a false move that angers the axe beaks, which then attack the party.

Badgers. Your party comes across two badgers sheltering in a hollow log, or the trunk of a dead tree, or just inside their burrow. When they get close enough, they see two pairs of eyes like black marbles glinting in the gloom. Whether the badgers attack or not depends on whether they have any place to run, and whether your party behaves in a threatening manner.

You may have your party make a DC 15 Intelligence (Nature) or Wisdom (Survival) check. Failure means that a party member has made a false move that activates the badgers' fight-or-flight response. If the badgers have an escape route — deeper into their burrow, or the opposite end of a hollow log, they flee; otherwise they fight like badgers if they feel cornered.

Scaling the Encounter: If you wish to make the encounter more challenging, use an encounter group of two giant badgers.

No Dinosaurs?
I understand that the decision to exclude dinosaurs from this book is a subjective call and, as such, it is subject to controversy. I dunno. Maybe it's just me, but I have always had a hard time mixing and matching dinosaurs with *Dungeons & Dragons*. I have nothing against them, and nothing against DMs who include them in their campaign world. But for me, dinosaurs bring to mind *The Land That Time Forgot* and the pulp action genre rather than fantasy, so I have always overlooked their presence in the *Monster Manual*, whatever the edition. Dinosaurs wouldn't faze me at all in a *Savage Worlds* campaign, but they feel like an odd fit with *D&D*. It's probably just me. If you hold a different view, feel free to make some elbow room for them.

Bats. Bats that settle in the deep forest don't need a cave to make themselves at home; a large tree with foliage thick enough to block out the sun will do nicely. Your party passes under such a tree and they risk setting off a small colony of 1d4 swarms of bats. You may have your party make a DC 15 Wisdom (Survival) or Intelligence (Nature) check. Failure means that someone makes a false move that triggers the bats to attack.

Scaling the Encounter: If you want to make the encounter more challenging for a higher-level party, use an encounter group consisting of 1d4 swarms of bats and/or giant bats in any combination, plus one swarm of bats or giant bat for each level in your party's average level.

Boar. Your party spots 1d4 wild boar rooting around the forest floor for food. Boar are popular targets for hunters. They'll fight back if attacked — indeed, the challenge they present is part of the appeal of hunting them. But they have also developed a fight-or-flight instinct, and if your party wishes to avoid a fight, have them make a DC 15 Wisdom (Survival) or Intelligence (Nature) group check to scare the boar off.

Scaling the Encounter: If you wish to make the encounter more challenging, use an encounter group consisting of one giant boar for each multiple of 3 in your party's average level. Giant boar are even more aggressive than their smaller cousins and they charge anyone who disturbs them.

Treasure: Boar meat is good eating for many folk. Perhaps a nearby butcher will pay 2 gp or thereabouts for a fresh carcass. The price might go up to 5 gp for a giant boar.

Centaur. Your party crosses paths with a lone figure, half-human and half-equine. It is a centaur, and like all too many of its kind, it became irrevocably separated from its tribe during a migration and now wanders the world alone. A centaur in the forest keeps company from time to time with elves, in which case it would have knowledge of their settlements. It may have encountered hunters and explorers, such as described in Table 3.4. It could be persuaded to share what it knows. A centaur might also offer your party the chance to take on a sidequest, asking for their help in finding its long-lost tribe.

Scaling the Encounter: It is up to you whether or not to scale up an encounter with centaurs. Though most often encountered alone, it is possible that three or four centaurs might have split off from their tribe as a group. However, if you anticipate a hostile encounter, throwing more than one centaur at your party would provide a stiff challenge if their average level is less than 4.

Treasure: Centaurs carry their valuables with them. Roll once on the Individual Treasure: Challenge 0-4 table for each centaur present.

Centipede. Have your party make a DC 15 Intelligence (Nature) or Wisdom (Survival) check. Failure means that no one notices the giant centipede wending its way across their path — its dark color blends in too well with the forest floor — and someone in the front of the march order comes dangerously close to stepping on it. It responds by attacking that character. Success means that they notice the giant centipede in time to avoid provoking it, thus making a hostile encounter purely optional.

Cockatrice. Your party comes across one cockatrice poking around for fallen nuts and berries, or chasing its next meal across the forest floor. If your party wishes to avoid a fight, require a DC 15 Intelligence (Nature) or Wisdom (Survival) check. Failure means that someone in your party has made a false move that sets off the beast, and it attacks.

Scaling the Encounter: If you wish to make the encounter more challenging, use an encounter group that consists of 1d4 cockatrices plus one cockatrice for each level in your party's average level.

Not all creatures carry their treasure on their person.

Deer. Your party spots 1d8 bucks and 2d6 does grazing among the trees. If your party attacks, only the male fights, covering the females while they flee.

Even if your party does not behave in a threatening manner, there is a chance that the males mistake their actions and attack anyway. Have your party make a DC 10 Intelligence (Nature) or Wisdom (Survival) check. Failure means that someone has made a false move that sets off the males and they charge.

Treasure: Anyone for venison? Perhaps a nearby butcher will pay 2 gp or thereabouts for a fresh carcass.

Dragon. Your party notices a shadow in the sky through the forest canopy. It's a dragon on the prowl. To determine what kind of dragon roll on Table 3.3.1:

TABLE 3.3.1
Dragon – Forest

d12	ENCOUNTER
1	Black
2	Blue
3-5	Green
6	Red
7	White
8	Brass
9	Bronze
10	Copper
11	Gold
12	Silver

To determine its age, see Scaling the Encounter.

To be clear, this need not be a hostile encounter. The dragon is not defending its lair, so it may just be curious about your party. It may have more important things to do and decline to take notice of them at all. Or it may be hungry and on the hunt, or it's angry because your party has intruded on territory it claims as its own.

Alternately, you may present your party with a scenario that you can weave into the larger story of the campaign. Your party finds a dragon wyrmling propped up with its back against a tree. It's obviously in a bad way — gashed open, bleeding profusely, barely conscious. Assume that it has stabilized after being reduced to 0 hp, and that it now has 1 hp. How it got that way is up to you, and it may depend on how dragons fit into your campaign world. Perhaps it fled from a fight in which it was badly wounded. Who would its enemies be, and why were they fighting? Were any of its relatives or companions killed?

How your party decides to deal with this dragon child in distress could open up possibilities for later in your campaign. If they rescue it, will its kin reward them, or will its enemies confront them on the principle that, "The friends of my enemy must also be my enemy?" Conversely, what are the consequences if they put it out of its misery, like scavengers roaming a medieval battlefield? Will its kin seek retribution, or will its enemies treat your party as allies?

➤

Scaling the Encounter: Because dragons get tougher with age, the age of the dragon encountered should depend on your party's average level — especially if you decide that this is going to be a hostile encounter.

If your party's average level is 10 or lower, it encounters a wyrmling. If it's average level is 11-18, it encounters a young dragon. If it's average level is 19-25, it encounters an adult dragon. If its average level is higher than 25, it encounters an ancient dragon.

Fey. For the most part, these magical beings of the deep forest mean no harm. But they have agendas of their own that can work at cross-purposes with that of adventurers pursuing fortune and glory. To determine which fey creature your party comes across, roll on Table 3.3.2:

TABLE 3.3.2
Fey – Forest

d8	ENCOUNTER
1-2	Dryad
3-4	Pixies
5	Satyr
6-8	Sprite

Dryad. One dryad spots your party and develops an instant crush on the party member with the highest Charisma. It uses its *Tree Stride* ability to move among the trees without being detected and waits for a moment when the object of its affection separates from the rest of the party. If necessary, it uses its *Speak With Beasts and Plants* ability to create a distraction and its *entangle* innate spell to trap that character. Then it uses *Fey Charm* to turn him or her into its prisoner of love.

Pixies. Your party crosses paths with 1d4 pixies, but most likely only the pixies know this at first. Shy around strangers but curious all the same, they remain invisible while taking your party's measure by playing (mostly) harmless pranks on them and judging their reaction. Exactly what pranks they pull is up to you as DM, but it makes the most sense that they should use their *Innate Spellcasting* abilities somehow.

It's also up to you whether your party wins over the pixies because of (or in spite of) their reactions. They may decide that these strangers are too dangerous to deal with, in which case they use their abilities to ➤

disable your party and cover their own retreat. If they decide they like your party, they reveal themselves and offer to share their local knowledge and provide material assistance — though what material assistance tiny-sized creatures can offer is an open question.

Satyr. Your party comes upon one bored satyr looking to party. Everyone hears a melody created by its *Panpipes* ability coming from the trees. Anyone affected by the *Charming Melody* forgets his or her purpose and joins the satyr, who now emerges into view, in dancing and drinking to the exclusion of any other activity.

If anyone in your party turns hostile, the satyr switches from *Charming Melody* to *Gentle Lullaby*. If that does not pacify them sufficiently, it switches to *Frightening Strain* and retreats.

Sprites. Your party stumbles into territory claimed by a colony of sprites. Out of nowhere, a guard post of 1d4 sprites challenges them. One appears and demands that your party state their business, while the others (if present) remain invisible until combat starts or they decide your party is friendly.

Scaling the Encounter: Dryads and satyrs work alone. If you wish to make a hostile encounter with sprites more challenging, they raise an alarm to summon reinforcements. The reinforcement pool consists of 1d4 sprites for each level in your party's average level. 1d6 arrive on scene each turn after combat begins until the reinforcement pool has been exhausted.

Treasure: Dryads take those who have succumbed to their charms back to their lair, where they keep souvenirs of their previous paramours. Treasure may also be a factor in sprite encounters, since their colony is bound to have a central repository of its belongings. In both cases, roll on the Treasure Hoard: Challenge 0-4 table.

Fey have agendas of their own that can work cross-purposes to yours.

Fire Beetles. Your party comes across 1d8 giant fire beetles scuttling along the forest floor. Fire beetles are not aggressive, but they defend themselves if threatened — if they're hunted for their luminous glands, for instance.

Hyenas. Hyenas are clever predators, and they know well enough to pick their targets carefully. A hunting pack of 2d8 hyenas comes across your party, but they do not attack unless they are at least twice as numerous as your party, or unless they can isolate a party member and use their pack tactics ability — perhaps one character has gone ahead to scout the lay of the land, or separated him or herself to answer the call of nature. Otherwise, they hover about on the flank of the party, looking for an opportunity to strike. If they find none, they eventually tire of the hunt and move off.

Scaling the Encounter: If you wish to make the encounter more challenging, the encounter group consists of two giant hyenas for each multiple of 3 in your party's average level.

Lizards. Your party crosses paths with 1d4 giant lizards foraging for insects and small animals. They are not aggressive and they can be wrangled and trained to serve as pack animals or mounts. To wrangle a giant lizard, it must be successfully grappled and kept in grappled condition for 10 consecutive rounds. At that point, it becomes docile and submits to whomever grappled it. Because of its size, two medium-size creatures may grapple with the same giant lizard simultaneously, and as long as one of them maintains its grappled condition, this counts toward the requirement for wrangling it.

Mules. Mules are domestic creatures. So when your party sees 1d8 mules mulling about for no apparent purpose, it is highly likely that they have escaped someone, such as hunters or woodcutters, who brought them into the forest. Their owners will pay a reward for their return – or your party could claim them as their own without anyone (possibly) being the wiser.

Mules do not attack. But they may be skittish around strangers, especially if they have been out in the wild for a while. If your party tries to take possession of them, have them make a DC 10 Intelligence (Nature) check to avoid a hostile reaction. Remember, these creatures have a kick like a mule.

Pseudodragon. If someone in your party is looking for a familiar, here is a chance. They pass a tree that has a pseudodragon hiding in a hollow. It would like to remain hidden, but it's hard to miss a pair of yellow reptilian eyes glinting in the darkness. It is reluctant to fight, but it is cornered in this tree hollow and it defends itself if

attacked. Before that point, however, it uses its limited telepathic ability to communicate its fear and anxiety.

How the pseudodragon responds if the party tries to befriend it is up to you. You may require a Charisma (Persuasion) check with a DC of anywhere between 10-20, depending on how difficult you want to make it. Pseudodragons are picky in choosing the company they keep, but you may decide that DC 20 is a bit steep, especially for a lower-level party.

Rats. You find rats everywhere they can find food, and they can find plenty in a forest. Roll on Table 3.3.3 to determine the nature of the rat encounter:

TABLE 3.3.3
Rats – Forest

d6	ENCOUNTER
1	Lone Rat
2-4	Swarm of Rats
5-6	Giant Rats

Lone Rat. A single rat, perhaps foraging by itself or lost from its nest, approaches your party while they take a rest. It's not much of a threat, but if someone in your party is looking for a familiar or even just a pet, this is an opportunity. Interacting with the rat — especially earning its trust with food — and making a successful DC 10 Intelligence (Nature) check earns its loyalty as a pet.

Swarm of Rats. Without being aware of it, your party has stopped to rest near a nest of rats. Drawn by the party's rations, a swarm of rats makes for the nearest source of food. They don't attack party members who don't interfere with their basic mission of acquiring food. But unless the rats are stopped, they eventually account for all of your party's rations, making off with what they don't eat on the spot.

Giant Rats. In this case, the rats drawn by your party's food are giant rats. There are 2d6 of them.

Unicorn. One of these celestials has staked out an unsullied corner of the forest for itself and defends the place's sanctity against all comers. It uses its innate spell casting to *detect evil and good,* and it marks down anyone who registers as good as a probable friend and anyone who registers as evil as a probable enemy. However, even good characters who appear to be harming the forest in some way — chopping down a tree, or starting a campfire — rouse its suspicion. A successful DC 15 Intelligence (Nature) check by a good character who tries to interact with it, or a successful DC 15 Charisma (Persuasion) check by someone who speaks one of its known languages, helps turn the unicorn to your party's side. It may even join a predominantly lawful good party as an ally for a short time, but it refuses to leave the forest.

If your party can't defuse the unicorn's hostility, it may come down to a fight. If killing a unicorn is a horrific act in your campaign world, then your party will just have to deal with the consequences.

Scaling the Encounter: If your party's average level is 10 or higher and you suspect that a meeting with a unicorn will turn hostile, consider adding one unicorn to the encounter to make it more challenging.

Raven. Ravens are not particularly dangerous, but they are natural mimics. Your party hears a noise that is easily mistaken for something that demands attention — perhaps it sounds like a child's cries, a scream of distress, or noises made by a predator. If they investigate — and it's ultimately up to you as DM how far out of their way this takes them — they find it is a raven, nothing more.

Vultures. It's part of the circle of life: Creatures die in the forest, and carrion eaters swoop in to take care of the remains. Your party comes across 1d6+2 vultures picking at a deer carcass. How they respond depends on how they interpret your party's actions. You may have your party make a DC 10 Intelligence (Nature) or Wisdom (Survival) check. Failure means that a party member has made a false move that persuades the vultures to attack, thinking that they need to defend their food source.

Scaling the Encounter: If you wish to make the encounter more challenging, consider substituting giant vultures for the vultures. The encounter group then consists of two giant vultures for each multiple of 3 in your party's average level. Giant vultures may be hunting instead of feeding. Perhaps they — mistakenly or not — spotted your party as hapless travelers on their last legs, in which case they swoop down to try to hasten their demise.

Weasels. Someone at the front of your party's march order accidentally steps into a burrow housing enough weasels to cause trouble when they get angry and defend their home. You may allow your party a DC 10 Wisdom (Perception) or Wisdom (Survival) check to spot the burrow in time to avoid it or give warning to whomever is about to disturb it. The burrow houses a pack of 3d6 weasels.

Scaling the Encounter: If you wish to make the encounter more challenging, substitute giant weasels for normal-sized weasels.

Treasure: There is a 10% chance that they are actually mink, and their pelts would be of some value to furriers — 1 gp for normal-sized mink, and 5 gp for a giant mink. You may require a successful DC 15 Intelligence (Nature) check for your party to tell the difference between mink and weasels.

Elephant. Your party comes across one elephant and it is always the case with elephants in the wild that avoiding a stampede requires some care. If they want to avoid a hostile encounter, require a DC 15 Wisdom (Survival) or Intelligence (Nature) check. Failure means that someone has made a false move, triggering an attack.

Scaling the Encounter: If your party's average level is lower than 4, a hostile elephant encounter may be more than you want to throw at them. Feel free to re-roll for a different encounter. Conversely, if you want to run a more challenging encounter, the encounter group is a small herd of elephants, consisting of one for each multiple of 5 in your party's average level.

Forest Nuisances
Fey encounters are more about annoyance and flavor than anything else. Even if your players get a kick out of slaughtering sprites or kicking a satyr in the pan pipes, fey are not designed to put up a fight. Their special abilities do not mask predatory intent. They're entirely about the entertainment value of a situation that creates hindrance without much hazard, and how do your players cope with that? If you don't want that sort of action in your campaign, feel free to re-roll for another encounter.

Apes. Apes are not aggressive, but they are intensely territorial. 1d4 apes consider your party intruders, so they leap down from the trees and make a loud and angry display to establish their dominance. They do not fight unless attacked. However, you may have your party make a DC 15 Intelligence (Nature) or Wisdom (Survival) check. Failure means that someone has made a false move that the apes interpret as attack, which in turn causes them to attack.

Scaling the Encounter. If you wish to make the encounter more challenging, use an encounter group consisting of 1d4 apes for each multiple of 2 in your party's average level. If your party's average level is 8 or higher you may substitute one giant ape, which comes crashing through the jungle to confront your party.

Rhinoceros. Your party interrupts one rhinoceros as it grazes on jungle foliage. It is not aggressive — as a herbivore, it does not hunt for food. But if it feels threatened. it becomes a dangerous foe. Have your party make a DC 15 Intelligence (Nature) or Wisdom (Survival) check. Failure means that someone has made a false move that the rhinoceros interprets as a threat. It charges.

Scaling the Encounter: If you wish to make the encounter more challenging, your party faces a herd of potentially angry rhinoceros, one for each multiple of 3 in your party's average level.

Flying Snake. As your party picks its way through the jungle, they see a small, brightly-colored winged serpent zip past them at eye level. It's quite possible that this is a domesticated flying snake running an errand for its master, and it doesn't have time to bother with your party. Perhaps it has a connection to someone who is already a part of your campaign?

Whatever its purpose, however, it has no time to deal with your party's interference. If they try to capture or harm it, it tries to escape, or it fights back with its venomous bite.

TABLE 3.4
Humanoids - Forest

d20	ENCOUNTER
1-3	Drow
4-5	Bugbear
6-9	Elves
10-11	Gnolls
12-13	Gnomes
14-15	Goblins
16-17	Hobgoblins
18	Lycanthrope
19-20	Orcs
21-22	Lizardfolk

+2 to the die roll if in a tropical forest.

Drow. Drow are out of their element on the surface world and they don't come up here just to take a pleasant stroll. Most likely, they are here to take slaves or to kill elves (or both). Your party comes across a group of drow, either at night or in a gloomy part of the forest. A small group is most likely a scouting party out to identify targets for slaving raids. They could also be looking for stray targets of opportunity, such as lone hunters or gatherers, to capture and take back to their subterranean civilization.

A large group is probably an actual raiding party headed for the nearest elf settlement in the forest. Or they may be on their way back from a successful raid. In any of the above scenarios, they size up your party as possible

captives and unless your party outnumbers them they use their poison to subdue and capture and add to their haul.

Scaling the Encounter: Use an encounter group of 1d4 drow for each level in your party's average level. If your party's average level is 10-14 add one drow elite warrior to the group as its leader. If your party's average level is 15-19 use a drow mage as the group's leader instead. If you don't want to run a mass encounter, feel free to substitute one drow elite warrior for 20 drow as much as you like.

Treasure: If the encounter group is a returning raiding party, determine the total CR and roll on the appropriate Treasure Hoard table.

Bugbear. Your party crosses paths with one or more bugbears (see Scaling the Encounter). They could be mercenaries on their way to join a larger goblinoid army mobilizing for war. Conversely, they could be heading home after a victorious campaign — or straggling in the wake of a catastrophic defeat. Their exact circumstances and motivation should depend on what else is going on in your campaign world. If there is no such war in which they could take part, they're out for some casual plunder, or perhaps on their way to shake down a hobgoblin tribe that once employed them.

Their interest in fighting your party should vary according to the reason why they're here. For instance, mobilizing for war means they have a larger purpose in mind than victimizing your party. If they're looking to strong-arm some hobgoblins, they may even offer your party a cut of the take in exchange for adding to their strength in numbers.

Scaling the Encounter: A beginning-level party should only have to cope with one bugbear. If you wish to make the encounter more challenging, the encounter group consists of two bugbears for each multiple of 3 in your party's average level. If your party's average level is 10 or higher, add one bugbear chief as the group's leader.

Elves. If there is a substantial elven population in this forest, crossing paths with some of them should come as no surprise, even if it comes without warning. Your party encounters a group of elves from a nearby elven community. A wide range of plausible possibilities covers their reason for being here. Perhaps they are just hunting or gathering. Perhaps they're patrolling, on the lookout for possible threats to their community. Perhaps they're a war party, acting on information that a hostile group of one of their traditional enemies — like orcs or drow — is about. Perhaps they are pursuing a criminal, or looking for one of their own who has gone missing. Much should depend on what else is going on in this corner of your campaign world. Make it fit as closely as you like.

How the elves react to your party depends a lot on their mission and your party's composition. Obviously, a party with elves in it is more likely than not to receive friendly treatment. Conversely, they regard a party with traditional enemies of the elves with suspicion or even hostility. However, if your party establishes a rapport with this group, they may be willing to provide local lore. They may even ask for your party's help with their mission.

Scaling the Encounter: The encounter group consists of one elf scout and one elf spy for each multiple of 2 in your party's average level. You may substitute one spy for two scouts to keep the size of the encounter group manageable, if you wish. If your party's average level is higher than 5, substitute one elf priest or one elf veteran for one spy as the group's leader.

Gnolls. Your party comes across a small band of gnolls moving swiftly through the forest. They seem to have a purpose in mind, as they barely take notice of your party. In fact, they are here to scout out a nearby settlement of elves as preparation for raiding and plundering it. If there are human woodcutters or hunters working in the area, they may be the gnolls' target, as they are weak enough for a small band of gnolls to slaughter them without much trouble.

In fact, if the gnoll group is relatively large (see Scaling the Encounter) this may be the actual raiding party, headed for the nearest elf settlement in the forest. Or they may be on their way back from a successful raid, spattered with elf blood and taking with them captives whom they will sacrifice to their evil deity. In either case, they ignore anyone who declines to interfere with them, guided as they are by their primary purpose.

Scaling the Encounter: The baseline encounter group should consist of two gnolls for each multiple of 3 in your party's average level. If your party's average level is 7-9, add a gnoll pack lord to the mix as the group's leader. Feel free to substitute one gnoll pack lord for four gnolls as much as you like if you don't want to run a mass encounter.

Treasure: If the gnolls are coming back from a successful raid, you may roll on the Treasure Hoard: Challenge 0-4 table to determine the fruits of their labor. This is in addition to the individual treasure they carry.

Gnomes. Your party crosses paths with a small party of gnomes, consisting of 2d6 commoners and one priest. They may be freelance mechanics who travel between settlements, looking to sell their services. Or they may be

traders traveling to or from elven settlements. In either case, they have brought along a priest of one of their patron deities as their sole protection.

The gnomes are not aggressive. It won't take much prompting to get them to trade with your party and share local knowledge. They probably hail from a gnome settlements in the forest, one that is well concealed using their genius for artifice and illusion. Their priest may be willing to help your party with spells if they are willing to pay the going rate for such services.

Treasure: If these gnomes are traveling merchants, they should carry trade goods and/or coins in addition to their personal treasure. Roll on the Treasure Hoard: Challenge 0-4 table.

Humanoids may ignore anyone who declines to interfere with them, guided as they are by their primary purpose.

Goblins. Goblins tend to make their lairs elsewhere, but they come to the forest as a good place to find isolated victims that they can slaughter and loot, or take captive and torture for their amusement. Your party crosses paths with a such a goblin foraging party as they wend their way through the trees.

A large group of goblins is likely to be a raiding party on their way to their target. Or they may be a raiding party on their way back, with loot and 1d6 elf captives. In either case, the encounter group has more important things to do than deal with your party.

Scaling the Encounter: Use an encounter group of 1d4 goblins for each level in your party's average level. If you don't want to run a mass encounter but you still want to provide a higher-level party with a meaningful challenge, feel free to substitute one goblin boss for four goblins as much as you like.

Hobgoblins. If war plagues your campaign world, hobgoblins go about, selling their martial services to anyone willing to employ them. If your party crosses paths with a small group of hobgoblins making their way through the forest, they may have come across some mercenaries taking a shortcut on their way to their mustering point. If that's the case, they have business to take care of and they'll ignore your party as long as they don't try to interfere.

On the other hand, the hobgoblins might initiate a fight with your party if peace has prevailed for so long that they have had no work — in which case they're bored and looking for practice. Or they're broke and as long as they properly challenge your party to a fight, killing them for their belongings is not mere robbery but taking spoils of war. Alternately, these hobgoblins may be fleeing a lost battle and, like many mercenaries in such a situation, they can rationalize killing and looting your party in any number of ways — perhaps they won't get paid because their employer was killed; or they need to settle for what they can get now that the battle won't yield any spoils; or perhaps they're just hungry and desperate after separating from the army.

Scaling the Encounter: The baseline encounter group should consist of 1d4 hobgoblins for each multiple of 2 in your party's average level. If your party's average level is 10-19, add a hobgoblin captain as the group's leader, accompanied by two goblin servants or one bugbear aide. If your party's average level is 20 or higher, add instead one hobgoblin warlord with two bugbear aides.

Lycanthrope. To determine what manner of werebeast your party encounters, roll on Table 3.4.1:

TABLE 3.4.1
Lycanthrope – Forest

d8	WERECREATURE
1	Werebear
2-3	Wereboar
4	Weretiger
5-8	Werewolf

All lycanthropes assume their animal form if the encounter comes down to combat, although they may choose their hybrid form instead if they have access to a weapon.

Werebear. Your party comes across a werebear that
➤

has claimed this corner of the forest as its domain. Perhaps it was once a druid, or a wandering ranger, or a hermit of some sort who volunteered for this fate to protect the forest. It is not automatically hostile to your party, especially if there are no evil characters present, and it may be willing to provide them with useful information about the surrounding area.

On the other hand, an encounter could create difficulties for your party if the werebear decides that one of the player characters would make a good apprentice (and successor to its self-appointed duties as the local guardian). Once it realizes that there is a druid or a ranger in your party, a light goes on in its head — and it won't take "No" for an answer.

Wereboar. A wereboar met by chance in the forest was most likely an unfortunate hunter who didn't realize that the boar at which he aimed his bow was really a lycanthrope. It goes about looking for victims to share its fate, hoping that a lone boar will lure an unwary hunter. A party of adventurers could offer it an even more attractive target — confident in its ability to take at least one of them and drive the others off, it attacks.

Weretiger. Your party comes across a weretiger on the hunt, or just traveling from one place to another. If it's hungry, it may stalk and attack your party, though it is more likely to focus on driving off the party members and taking the pack animals than on hunting the party members themselves. Otherwise, it may assume human form and treat your party as fellow travelers, content to barter with them and exchange information about unknown places.

Werewolf. A werewolf spots your party and cannot turn down the opportunity to claim more victims. However, it is clever enough to approach them in its human form, pretending to be a lost traveler, or a hunter or woodcutter in distress. Once your party gets close and drops its guard, it attacks.

Scaling the Encounter: A single lycanthrope can offer a stiff challenge to a low-level party. If your party's average level is 3 or less, feel free to re-roll the encounter. Alternately, if you want to make a werewolf encounter more challenging for a higher-level party, use a pack of them consisting of one werewolf for each multiple of 5 in your party's average level, rounded up.

Treasure: It is assumed that all of these encounters take place away from the lycanthrope's base of
➤

operations, so roll on the Individual Treasure table of the appropriate CR to determine what valuables it carries.

Werebears may be an exception to this rule. Because they are territorial, your party may encounter a werebear in or near its lair. In that case, roll on the Treasure Hoard: Challenge 0-4 table to determine its treasure.

Orcs. If there are orcs in a forest, it's reasonable bet (though it's not the only possibility) that they're looking for elves and they carry bad intentions with them. A small group could be a scout party out to get the lay of the land, while a larger group would be an actual raiding party on its way to — or on its way back from — its target.

Your party crosses paths with these orcs, but if they have such a purpose in mind, they may not give your party much attention. Their leader may look your party over and decide that they're not worth the bother. But the orcs may also decide to interrogate them for information about the surrounding area, and they'll get violent if your party is too slow to cooperate. They'll make elf characters a special focus of their hostility.

Scaling the Encounter: The baseline encounter group should consist of 1d4 orcs for each multiple of 2 in your party's average level. If your party's average level is 5-9, add an orog as the group's leader. If your party's average level is 10 or higher, use an orc war chief as its leader. If you don't want to run a mass encounter but you still want to provide a higher-level party with a meaningful challenge, feel free to substitute one orog for four orcs as much as you like.

Treasure: If the orcs are coming back from a successful raid, you may roll on the Treasure Hoard: Challenge 0-4 table to determine the fruits of their labor. This is in addition to the individual treasure they carry.

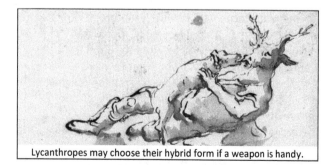
Lycanthropes may choose their hybrid form if a weapon is handy.

Lizardfolk. It's hard to to notice these things in the middle of a jungle, but your party enters a swampy patch that a lizardfolk tribe claims as their sphere of influence. They cross paths with a group of lizardfolk who are most likely either hunting or patrolling. In the first case, your party might qualify as the main course in the tribe's next feast, and in the second case the patrol are bound to be suspicious of strangers in their territory. In both cases, they may be willing to give your party the chance to convince them not to attack. Or they may decide to throw javelins first and ask questions later, if at all. It's up to you as DM.

Scaling the Encounter: The baseline encounter group should consist of 1d4 lizardfolk for each multiple of 2 in your party's average level. Most likely, this is a small patrol or a sentry post. If your party's average level is 6-9, add a lizardfolk shaman as the group's leader. If your party's average level is 10 or higher, use a lizard king/queen as the leader.

TABLE 3.5
Humans - Forest

d20	ENCOUNTER
1	Adventurers
2-3	Bandits
4	Druid
5	Exiles
7	Explorers
8	Foresters
9	Fugitives
10-11	Gatherers
12	Hermit
13-15	Hunters
16-17	Trapper
18-20	Woodsman

Adventurers. Unless your party contains all of the adventurers in your campaign world, it's at least theoretically possible that they'll run into another adventuring party roaming this forest. Perhaps they're pursuing the same objective as your party. Perhaps they have a different mission, such as chasing down a rogue band of evil humanoids, or they're headed for a site that your party knows nothing about (like a dragon's lair or ancient ruins said to hold lost treasures). Perhaps they're lost and starving, or wounded, or cursed.

How they react to your party depends on a variety of factors. Are they rivals pursuing the same goal? If not, perhaps this party is willing to share useful information. In fact, if your party is stuck and having a hard time advancing the storyline of your campaign, a friendly encounter like this can help steer them in the right direction. Differences in alignment may also shape how the two parties react to each other.

Composition of this adventuring party is up to you and can vary widely according to circumstance. A party plunging into the depths of a forest would be well-advised to have a ranger or a druid with them. An elf or half-elf would also make sense, for his or her forest lore. Conversely, a party that is struggling may be in a bad way precisely it lacks the skill or knowledge that such characters possess.

Scaling the Encounter: Unless there is some possibility that this encounter turns hostile, the relative level of the party is mainly a matter of affect. A higher-level party might project self-confidence (or arrogance), while beginning-level party might stumble about, unsure of themselves. If you're leaning towards a hostile encounter, however, consider that the total CR of the party should be roughly two-thirds of your party's average level.

Bandits. A wilderness is not the most target-rich environment in which bandits can operate, but the forest offers them a place to hide. They may be able to get by picking on the locals, but doing so feels like scraping the bottom of the barrel to self-respecting brigands. In any event, an encounter with bandits in a sparsely inhabited forest likely means that your party finds them not far from their hiding place, and either on their way to or coming back from the nearest road or settled area (although a small group may simply be lookouts protecting the hideout).

They may not target your party, as adventurers are usually too well-armed and too hard to bully. But they'll make an exception if your party carries a conspicuous and obviously valuable treasure, or they outnumber your party by at least three to two. It's also possible that they assume that your party is a posse sent out after them — or that your party intends to rob them of what they took from others by force.

Scaling the Encounter: As a rough guideline, the encounter group should contain 1d8 bandits for each level in your party's average level. If your party's average level is 4 or higher, add a bandit captain as their leader. If you don't want to run a mass encounter but you still want these criminals to provide a higher-level party with a meaningful challenge, feel free to substitute one thug for four bandits as much as you like.

Treasure: If your party finds the bandits' hideout, roll on the Treasure Hoard table appropriate to the total CR of the encounter. Do so also if you decide that the bandits encountered are on their way back from a successful raid. Consider that there is also a 20% chance that the bandits have with them a high-value captive whom they intend to ransom. The identity of this captive is left to you as DM, as it should depend on local circumstances and fit into your campaign world.

Druid. Your party crosses paths with one druid in his or her element. Druids in the wild may wander, with no fixed abode, but it's at least as likely that they choose to protect a patch of forest with fierce devotion. How druids react to your party depends almost entirely on whether or not they think your party represents a menace to the forest. A druid who is persuaded that your party's intentions are benign may be willing to provide local lore, cast spells to help them, or even join them as a friendly NPC as long as it does not involve leaving the forest.

Druids may choose to protect their patch of forest with fierce devotion.

Scaling the Encounter: If you wish to make this a hostile encounter, consider increasing the CR to make it more of a fight for a higher-level party. In this case, the encounter group is a veritable coven of druids devoted to protecting the same territory, and it consists of one druid for each multiple of 3 in your party's average level.

Exiles. Your party encounters 1d6 people who could serve as a source of adventure hooks. From their appearance, they have obviously seen better days. They have fled their home for any of a variety of reasons: perhaps they are royalty or nobility who have been usurped; perhaps the opposite is the case and they are failed usurpers on the run. Or perhaps they have gotten caught up in a blood feud in their homeland and that's why they fear for their lives. Whatever the circumstance, they have come to the deep forest because they need a place to hide.

No matter their reason for being here, they should offer your party an adventure hook of some sort. It may involve protecting the exiles from their real (or imagined) pursuers. It may involve returning to their former home and securing an important item that was left behind (a family heirloom, a badge of office), perhaps even helping them return home and force their way back into their former position of prominence. At the very least, exiles can provide your party with information about their former home territory, which in turn could be a key location in your campaign.

Use any NPC template you like for the exiles, depending on the backstory you assign them.

Explorers. Your party bumps into a small party driven by curiosity to discover the heretofore unknown — in this case, a forest wilderness mostly untouched by humans. The group consists of 1d4 scholars (treat them as commoners) and 1d4 scouts (you may substitute one druid for the scouts) who act as bodyguards. Perhaps they are here thanks to the sponsorship of an academy or a ruler eager to know more about the world, or perhaps the explorer is a wealthy eccentric who undertook this expedition on his or her own.

Perhaps they are here thanks to the sponsorship of an eager ruler.

This encounter is not likely to be hostile. Explorers are open and curious, despite the fact that the forest offers any number of ways to doom them. Instead, you may treat this as an opportunity for your party to receive some help from a knowledgeable stranger — the explorer is likely to have excellent maps of nearby areas (and knowledge of those areas) and is willing to share them. Conversely, an expedition that has been in the field for a while may be running short on cartography supplies and other necessaries and may be willing to pay well if your party can help supply them. Also, if your party is in the mood for a sidequest, an explorer want to hire them for additional security in dangerous territory.

Foresters. Perhaps it turns out that this forest is owned by someone — it's royal land, or it belongs to local nobility. If this is the case, they employ these armed caretakers to deal with poachers and trespassers and generally keep an eye on things.

Your party comes across 1d4 foresters on patrol. You may have your party make a DC 15 Wisdom (Perception) check. Success means that they spot the foresters picking their way through the trees, glancing about them and keeping their longbows handy. Failure means that the foresters, who know their way around the forest, are in a position to get the drop on them. In any event, the foresters draw down on your party and demand that they state their business. A successful DC 15 Charisma (Persuasion) check calms them down, in which case the foresters could provide information and material help. Treat foresters as scouts.

Fugitives. Your party crosses paths with 1d6 bedraggled people stumbling through the forest. They look to be in less-than-optimal shape, but they're moving as fast as they can manage. Most, if not all of them have a manacle around one wrist, with the other manacle dangling on its chain. They're escaped prisoners who have fled into the deep forest. From whom they are fleeing and why they were imprisoned in the first place is up to you, and ought to depend on where in your campaign world this encounter takes place.

How the encounter plays out depends not only on how your party reacts, but on the state of mind you assign to the fugitives. On the one hand, it's hard to imagine that they went to the trouble of a jailbreak just to allow a bunch of strangers to take their freedom back from them. On the other hand, they might be desperate with hunger and exhaustion and ready to give up. Each of them has learned whip their freed manacle by the chain and wield it as a club.

Treat the fugitives as bandits, but without weapons or armor.

Treasure: Fugitives have no treasure.

Gatherers. Your party comes across 1d4 gatherers collecting useful plants or fungi, either for food or medicine. Your party may surprise them, as they spend a lot of their time hunched over the forest floor or reaching up for leaves or tree fungi. However, they are not hostile — they're just laborers with specialized knowledge out doing their job. However, they may be persuaded to help your party with local lore and/or therapeutic concoctions made from whatever it is they're gathering (see Treasure). You may require a DC 15 Charisma (Persuasion) check to win them over. They may also ask your party to help them if they have reason to believe that they are in danger (perhaps they had a close brush with monsters recently).

Treat the gatherers as commoners armed with sickles or daggers.

Treasure: In addition to treasure from the Individual Treasure: Challenge 0-4 table, the gatherers have a small stash of helpful non-magical items made from herbs or fungi. One such item could be a poultice that heals hit points equal to 1d4+ the Wisdom (Medicine) bonus of whomever applies it after it is kept in place for 24 hours. But that is just one possibility. Use any such items that already exist in your campaign world. You can also consult "Narl's Herbal Remedies" in Ramen Sandwich Press' collection of new items, *Tome of the Utility Drawer, Volume I.*

Hermit. The deep forest is as good a destination as any for someone who has decided to withdraw from worldly cares, but that doesn't mean you can't be found. Your party stumbles upon a hermit in his or her abode — perhaps a bower in the lower limbs of a large tree, or a lean-to in a small clearing. One hermit lives here, devoted to a pure and simple life of contemplation. The hermit may be a divine spellcaster, for whom seclusion and meditation is a form of service to a deity. It may take a successful DC 15 Charisma (Persuasion) check to get past the fact that your party has broken this seclusion, but the hermit may be willing to use divine spells to aid them.

No matter their reason for being there, they should contribute to the adventure in some way.

Alternately, your party may have found a secular hermit — someone who, having been wounded by failure or grown weary of success, decided to retire completely from the world. Such a person won't have spells, but may have magic items, local lore, or even knowledge and personal connections from his or her former life that might help your party.

Yet another possibility is that this hermit is a retired adventurer or soldier, in the manner of knights in the Arthurian romances who became hermits to repent of lives spent fighting each other and dallying with married ladies. Hermits in this mold have discarded their fighting gear, but they may be persuaded to leave their seclusion and join your party as friendly NPCs.

Treat a religious hermit as an acolyte, priest or cult fanatic, but feel free to generate a higher-level divine spellcaster if you want to create a more spectacular

effect with this encounter. Treat a secular hermit as a commoner, or use a character class and level of your choice.

Treasure: Roll on the Treasure Hoard: Challenge 0-4 to determine if the hermit has any magic items and/or valuable devotional items.

Hunters. Your party comes across 2d4 hunters picking their way through the trees, looking for game. They may have set up a nearby encampment as a base of operations, but in any event they have come here from the nearest village or town.

Depending on your party's appearance, they may act with caution, even suspicion at first. Despite the fact that they are armed with bows, they know that they are operating in wilderness away from home, and there are always strange folk about. However, if your party is not hostile to them they are willing to help by trading goods and supplying food and local knowledge. You may have your party make a DC 15 Charisma (Persuasion) check to get on their good side.

Treat hunters as scouts.

There's an Elemental in My Soup
Elementals originate in and belong to their own planes. So what brings them to the Material Plane? Why are they here? There are mechanics for bringing them here through arcane summoning, but they're only allowed a limited time on the Material Plane.

This book assumes that elementals encountered at random have been trapped somehow away from their native planes. Perhaps they were summoned and could not find their way back — doomed like angry ghosts to wander a world where they do not belong, and in a mood to attack whatever crosses their path. Or perhaps there is a natural point of convergence between the Material Plane and one of the Elemental Planes — an idea posited in our Places by the Way location module, *Oasis of the Elementals.*

Trappers. Your party comes across 1d4 fur trappers setting out their traps. Their presence here is pretty straightforward; they have trading relationships with furriers in the nearest settlement, and they know that animals are more easily found the farther out into the wilderness you go. As long as your party does not interfere with their work, the trappers let them be.

They may provide your party with local lore, having trapped in this forest more than once, and they may even give them material aid. You may require a DC 15 Charisma (Persuasion) check to win them over. Conversely, the trappers may fear attack and try to enlist your party as bodyguards. They can pay in pelts that your party can sell at any settlement. Also, consider that the trappers are on a roll and they reckon that if they keep at it a little longer they'll have more pelts than they can carry home. In this case, they might offer your party a modest business opportunity, selling them some of their pelts at half the going rate, which would allow your party to double their money by selling them to a furrier. Treat the trappers as commoners armed with shortswords or daggers.

Woodsmen. Your party comes across 2d6 woodcutters who have ventured into the wilderness to gather raw materials for the nearest settlement. Their business here is mundane and they are likely to be more alarmed by the party interrupting them as they cut down trees than your party is startled by stumbling upon them. Perhaps the first sign of their presence is a tree falling on the party, as in Table 3.6: Falling Tree.

Aside from the uncertainty created by meeting complete strangers in a place where you don't expect to find them, an encounter with woodsmen is not necessarily hostile. You may require a DC 15 Charisma (Persuasion) check to win them over. They can give your party information about the local area and they may be willing to trade. On the other hand, they do carry axes — greataxes for hewing trees, battleaxes and handaxes for more detailed work) — and they are prepared to defend themselves in case wild animals menace them. Treat woodsmen as commoners.

TABLE 3.6
Watch Out! - Forest

d20	ENCOUNTER
1-2	Did You Hear That?
3-7	Falling Branch
8-9	Falling Tree
10-12	Hampering Web
13-14	Loose Ground
15	Quicksand
16	Tracks
17-20	Tripping Hazard

Did You Hear That? Choose a party member to make a DC 15 Wisdom (Survival) or Intelligence (Nature) check. Failure means that that character believes that he or she has heard a noise made by a nearby creature or a dangerous natural phenomenon. Perhaps it is the growl of an angry bear, the howl of wolves. Or perhaps it is a

noise made by an animal that is not present in the forest, like the howl of a yeti. A successful check means that that party member realizes that this is an illusion, and the noise is either much farther away than it seems, or it is something else entirely.

Roll on Table 3.6.1 to suggest what your party hears:

TABLE 3.6.1
Did You Hear That? – Forest

d10	They Think They Hear…
1	Banshee wailing
2	Bear growling
3	Footsteps of a large group of humans or humanoids
4	Lion or other big cat growling
5	Voices speaking in Elvish
6	Voices speaking in Sylvan
7	Voices speaking in Orcish
8	Voices speaking in Undercommon
9	Wolves snarling
10	Wyvern screeching overhead

Falling Branch. Look out below! A high branch falls from a dead, diseased or injured tree as your party passes by. Whatever the cause, the branch is heavy enough, or it falls from high enough, to leave a dent. Determine the party member closest to the tree in question, or pick one at random. Treat the falling branch as a melee attack with a +0 bonus that causes 1d6 bludgeoning damage.

Falling Tree. Timber! The decayed remains of a dead tree topples over just as your party nears it. Choose the tree's position relative to the party and the angle at which it falls onto them. Or roll 1d12 to determine the tree's bearing: 12 o'clock means that it is dead ahead; 1 o'clock means that its bearing is 30 degrees to the right; 6 o'clock means that it falls onto the party from directly behind, etc. The tree falls onto the party from that bearing. The trunk — the part heavy enough to cause damage — is 20 feet long. Anyone in the path of the trunk must make a successful DC 10 Strength (Athletics) or Dexterity (Acrobatics) check to get out of the way. Anyone who fails takes 2d8 bludgeoning damage. Anyone who succeeds must move out of the spaces into which the tree falls; if this means moving into a space occupied by someone else, that character must make a successful DC 15 Strength (Athletics) or Dexterity (Acrobatics) check to avoid a collision, or else take 1 bludgeoning damage and fall prone.

Hampering Web. There is a finely-woven spider's web between two trees right in your party's path, but there is no spider present. Your party may make a DC 15 Wisdom (Perception) check to spot the web before someone at the front of the march order walks right into it and becomes restrained.

The restrained character may attempt to escape by making a DC 20 Strength (Athletics) or DC 20 Dexterity (Acrobatics) check. Other party members may try to free their restrained colleague by making a total of three successful attack rolls with a slashing weapon against the web, which has AC 15. But for each attempt, there is a 10% chance, cumulative with each new attempt, that one giant spider appears enters the web from an overhanging branch to see what it caught this time. Each attack roll counts as an attempt.

Loose Ground. Your party reaches the crest of a rise from which they can get a good view of the surrounding area. However, a party member — choose one, or a character who wants to get a good look around may literally step forward as the best candidate — steps onto a patch of loose soil. It gives way and the character takes a tumble, suffering 1d6 falling damage. A successful DC 15 Strength (Athletics) or Dexterity (Acrobatics) halves the damage. Whee!

Quicksand. In parts of the forest, so little sunlight penetrates that the ground soaked by rain or natural flow never has a chance to dry out and the soil is so swampy that it behaves like quicksand — step into it, and you may never step back out. Your party stumbles into such a patch. Have your party make a DC 15 Intelligence (Nature) or Wisdom (Survival) check to spot the quicksand before one party member in the front of the march order steps right into it.

Tracks. Your party spots tracks that look like tracks that belong to a monster associated with treasure hoards. You may allow them a successful DC 15 Wisdom (Survival) check to realize that they are very old, and they will not lead to anything useful. Failure means that the believe the tracks to be fresh, perhaps leading to an amusing (for you as DM, anyway) wild goose chase.

Tripping Hazard. Pick a party member at the front of the march order. That character trips over an unseen obstacle — a tree root, or a half-buried log or rock, a thick growth of vines on the forest floor. He or she must make a successful DC 10 Strength (Athletics) or Dexterity (Acrobatics) check to avoid a hard fall that causes 1d4 damage — and perhaps no small embarrassment in the eyes of the other party members.

Hearing Things?
The auditory illusions in Table 3.6.1 (and elsewhere in the book), as well as the raven encounter in Table 3.3, give you the opportunity to throw a shaggy dog story at your players. They're about messing with their heads, as opposed to messing them up. They're inspired by elements in our Places by the Way location module, *The Paladin Queen's Forest*, which challenges a party with serious disorientation as it tries to navigate a dense forest. Whether or not you want to throw a challenge of this sort at your party is ultimately up to you as DM.

Into the Woods

Among the environments described in this book, forests come in second only to caverns (see Chapter 1) as projections of the hidden corners of the human mind. Some of those corners are not that fearful — unless you *really* hate unicorns and pixies — but forest encounters at their most impactful feel like they take place in a space closed off from the rest of the world.

GRASSLANDS

CHAPTER FOUR

Grasslands

What are Grasslands?

Grasslands occur at almost every latitude. Think of the Eurasian steppe, the prairies of North America, the savannas of equatorial Africa, the veldt of southern Africa. For that matter, The Shire would qualify as grasslands. What all of these places share is that they're mostly flat, and they're semi-arid — a technical term meaning that they're not as dry as deserts, but they also don't get enough rainfall to support forests. Hence, grasses and shrubs are the dominant forms of vegetation, and it's wet enough to support agriculture and plenty of farm animals.

However, the grasslands in this chapter are wilderness. Your party may find an isolated farmstead here and there. They may encounter a herd of livestock. They may travel roads that link proper towns and villages. But a countryside uncluttered by signs of civilization separates those settlements, and here there is plenty of room for monsters and other hazards. Sure, it looks all serene and grassy now — just wait until you see what's hiding in the dip in the ground over there.

Note that some tables in this chapter require a die-roll modifier depending on climate zone.

TABLE 4.1

Encounter Type - Grasslands

d20	CATEGORY
1-6	Aggressive Creatures (Table 4.2)
7-12	Neutral Creatures (Table 4.3)
13-16	Humanoids (Table 4.4)
17-18	Humans (Table 4.5)
19-20	Watch Out! (Table 4.6)

Then, roll on the appropriate table to determine the creature, person or thing encountered.

Grasslands tend to provide broad vistas with open sight lines. There may be undulations that block line of sight into a dip or hollow. But as a general rule, encounters begin with both sides spotting each other from a distance (unless otherwise specified). This requires that either or both sides deliberately closes the range before combat begins, which probably allows either or both sides the chance to try to avoid a fight, if so desired.

TABLE 4.2

Aggressive Creatures - Grasslands

d100	ENCOUNTER
1-3	Gorgon
4-7	Ankheg
8-9	Basilisk
10-15	Bird of Prey
16-17	Bulette
18-19	Chimera
20-22	Death Dog
23-24	Ettin
25-26	Gargoyle
27-30	Griffon
31	Hell Hound
32-33	Hill Giant
34-41	Insects
42-44	Lion
45-46	Manticore
47	Medusa
48	Nightmare
49-52	Ogre
53-54	Oni
55-57	Owlbear
58	Roc
59-64	Scorpions
65-70	Spiders
71-73	Tiger
74-76	Toad
77-84	Undead
85-86	Will-o'-Wisp
87-92	Wolves
93-94	Worgs
95-96	Wyvern
97-101	Snakes
102-103	Cheetahs

+3 to die roll if in tropical grasslands

Gorgon. Gorgons are most at home in temperate grasslands and the arid cold of montane plateaus. The hotter the climate, the less comfortable it gets for a creature constantly encased in iron plates.

Your party approaches a gorgon's lair — perhaps it is a cluster of rocks, or a small cave hollowed out of the side of a deep swale or a rocky outcropping. Petrified chunks lie scattered about outside the lair; you may allow your party a DC 15 Wisdom (Survival) check to realize that they're crumbs leftover from the gorgon's previous meals. The monster is, of course, quite happy to prey on your party, saving them for later if it isn't hungry at the moment.

Scaling the Encounter: If your party's average level is lower than 6, a gorgon may be more than you want to throw at them. Feel free to re-roll for a different encounter.

Ankheg. As your party passes overhead, one ankheg in its tunnel mistakes your party for a herd of deer. It breaches the surface and attacks.

Scaling the Encounter: If you wish to make the encounter more challenging, the encounter group consists of one ankheg for each multiple of 3 in your party's average level. Each ankheg emerges from a point no closer than 20-40 feet to any other attacking ankheg.

Treasure: Ankhegs leave a lot of wild animal bones behind them, but in the wilderness they find few targets that leave behind treasure. You may roll once on the Individual Treasure: Challenge 0-4 table for each ankheg present, if you wish.

Basilisk. Your party comes across a cluster of rocks or a deep swale that a basilisk has chosen for its lair. You may allow a DC 15 Wisdom (Perception) or Wisdom (Survival) check to hear something stirring behind the rocks, or at least to intuit that something is there.

Scaling the Encounter: A basilisk may be a bit too much for a beginning-level party. Feel free to re-roll for another encounter. Conversely, if you want to run a more challenging encounter for a higher-level party, consider that your party has encountered two basilisks sharing a lair.

Treasure: The lair contains scattered valuables belonging to the basilisk's previous victims. Roll on the appropriate Treasure Hoard table, according to the total CR of the encounter. If there is more than one basilisk in the encounter, consider that basilisk eggs may also be present for the taking.

Bird of Prey. A bird of prey — or a flock of them — wheels overhead, then strikes at your party. Keen-eyed, but bird-brained all the same, the bird has spotted something in your party as food — a familiar or small summoned creature is an obvious choice, but it could just be travelers rations, like strips of cured meat left in the open. To determine which species, roll on Table 4.2.1:

TABLE 4.2.1
Birds of Prey - Grasslands

d10	ENCOUNTER
1-2	Eagle
3	Giant Eagle
4-5	Blood Hawks
6-7	Hawks
8-9	Owl
10	Giant Owl

Eagle. One eagle swoops down on your party, aiming itself at something it has identified as food.

Giant Eagle. A giant eagle has spotted your party. Giant eagles are intelligent and may respond if your party tries to flag them down. Though it cannot speak when spoken to, a successful DC 15 Charisma (Persuasion) check by someone who speaks Common or Auran persuades it to do your party a service, if it is within its power to accomplish it. This may involve delivering a written message or token, or guiding your party to a place that it knows, or even traveling with them for a while as an airborne lookout.

Blood Hawks. A flock of 2d6 blood hawks swoops down on your party. They concentrate on a single target — most likely a pack animal, but they may settle for a small humanoid as the next best thing.

Hawks. A flocks of 2d10 hawks targets your party. They're probably going after the party's rations, but they may also have spotted rodents or small reptiles that are scurrying along the ground at your party's feet. To the extent that your party is in their way, the hawks attack them.

Owl. Owls hunt at night, so you should re-roll this encounter if it takes place during the day. Otherwise, one owl has spotted food among your party's belongings. Most likely, it has spotted a small animal companion or familiar, or rations left out in the open.

Giant Owl. Likewise, a giant owl encounter is most suitable for night, so you should re-roll this encounter if it takes place during the day. One giant owl spots food in your party's camp.

Bulette. Bad luck — a land shark senses your party walking overhead and figures they're its next meal. To create a little drama, you may require a successful DC 15 Wisdom (Perception) check to sense the ground rumbling; you may then allow a DC 15 Intelligence

(Nature) check to identify it as a bulette before it breaches the surface.

Scaling the Encounter: A bulette may be a bit much for a lower-level party to handle, so if your party's average level is less than 5, feel free to re-roll for a different encounter. Conversely, if your average party level is higher than 10, you may add another bulette to make it more challenging.

Treasure: Bulettes hunt on the move, so treasure that belonged to its previous victims is scattered far and wide. However, you may allow your party a DC 10 Wisdom (Survival) check to follow the trail back to its last kill. If successful, roll on the Individual Treasure: Challenge 0-4 table to determine what they find.

Chimera. Your party spots a winged monstrosity with three different animal heads circling above them. This can only mean one thing: A chimera has spotted them as potential prey. You may allow your party a DC 15 Wisdom (Perception) check. If successful, they notice the chimera at a range of about 200 feet, allowing them a little time to react before they are within range of its attacks. If not, they first become aware of the chimera at a range of only 100 feet.

Scaling the Encounter: If your party's average level is lower than 6, a chimera may be more than you want to throw at them. Feel free to re-roll for a different encounter.

Alternately, you may consider that your party comes upon a chimera that has been injured in a fight with a manticore or a wyvern — and that your party witnesses the dazzling air-to-air combat from a safe distance. The chimera is reduced to half of its hit points by the time it drives off its enemy and turns on your party, deep gashes or embedded manticore spikes are still visible. It's wounded, but it's still hungry — in fact, perhaps it needs to feed in order to heal and your party looks like an easier target than one of its monstrous rivals.

Giant Eagles may respond if your party flags them down.

Death Dog. One death dog roaming the wilderness stalks your party, looking to sate its unthinking bloodlust even if it means attacking a target that outnumbers it. It may not attack immediately upon being spotted by your party, but it will attack sooner or later. It may be waiting

for an opening. Will one party member break formation for whatever reason and wander just far enough from the support of the others?

Scaling the Encounter: If you wish to make the encounter more challenging, the encounter group consists of a pack of death dogs with bad intentions, two for each multiple of 3 in your party's average level.

Ettin. Your party hears two loud voices coming from below a dip in the ground, or from way in the distance. Your party must make a successful DC 15 Intelligence (Nature) check to recognize that it's an ettin arguing with itself. If they choose not to avoid the ettin, it calls out to your party and demands that they help settle a dispute. It should be something that your party would find awkward or at least pointless to answer — for instance, which meat is more tender, the leg of the chicken or the leg of the chicken farmer? No matter what answer your party gives, one or both heads accuses them of unfairly favoring the other and the ettin attacks.

Alternately, the ettin stops short when it spots the party. It realizes that it's hungry after arguing with itself for such a long time, and your party looks tasty.

Treasure: The ettin carries some coins in a pouch looped around its loincloth. Roll twice on the Individual Treasure: Challenge 0-4 table.

Gargoyle. Your party crosses paths with one gargoyle. If your party comes across an abandoned structure (even a broken-down shack would do), it makes its lair there. Otherwise, it's bored and wandering afield, looking for someone or something to torment for amusement. If there is no cover or elevated vantage point (like a boulder) handy, it remains perfectly still until your party comes close enough to ambush. You may allow your party a DC 15 Wisdom (Perception) check to spot the gargoyle before it attacks.

Scaling the Encounter: If you wish to make the encounter more challenging, the encounter group consists of one gargoyle for each multiple of 3 in your party's average level.

Treasure: If your party encounters gargoyles in their lair, roll on the Treasure Hoard table appropriate to the CR of the encounter.

Griffon. A griffon, roaming afield from its eyrie in the nearby hills, spots your party and goes for one of their mounts or pack animals — or at least, it thinks it has spotted a mount or a pack animal.

Scaling the Encounter: If you wish to make the encounter more challenging, your party encounters a flock (or pack?) of griffons hunting together. There is one for each multiple of 3 in your party's average level.

Hell Hound. Your party crosses paths with one hell hound in a mean and paranoid mood. Most likely, it came to the Material Plane as a companion of a devil and somehow got separated from its master. Or perhaps it was part of a pack kept by a fire giant up in the hills not far from here and it became hopelessly separated from them. In any event, it is none too pleased about wandering this plane alone and it takes out its separation anxiety on your party.

Scaling the Encounter: A hell hound breathing fire may be a bit too much for a beginning-level party. Feel free to re-roll for another encounter. Conversely, if you wish to make the encounter more challenging, the encounter group consists of one hell hound for each multiple of 5 in your party's average level.

Hill Giant. Your party crosses paths with one hill giant that has come down into the plains in search of someone else's belongings. A lone giant is probably looking for a small village that it can terrorize and rob by itself, but a group of adventurers presents a good target of opportunity. It tries to bully your party into giving over all of their possessions, and if they refuse the giant is quite willing to bash as many heads as it must.

Scaling the Encounter: If your party's average level is lower than 5, a hill giant may be more than you want to throw at them. Feel free to re-roll for a different encounter. Conversely, if you want to run a more challenging encounter for a higher-level party, use an encounter group of one hill giant for each multiple of 6 in your party's average level.

Insects. You may not think of insects as predatory, but they have a way of attacking without giving it much thought and they cause trouble in their own way. Some are viciously aggressive when they feel threatened. Roll on Table 4.2.2 to determine the insects encountered:

TABLE 4.2.2
Insects - Grasslands

d4	ENCOUNTER
1-3	Swarm of Insects
4	Giant Wasps

Swarm of Insects. One swarm of insects — call them gnats, midges, mosquitos, whatever you will — descends upon your party and makes their lives decidedly unpleasant. ➤

Giant Wasps. Your party comes upon two giant wasps guarding a nest hanging from a lone tree or the crumbling eaves of an abandoned structure. They are in a sufficiently bad temper to attack anything that comes close to the nest.

Scaling the Encounter: If you wish to make the encounter more challenging (or more of a nuisance, depending on how you look at it), the encounter group consists of 1d4 giant wasps for each multiple of 2 in your party's average level, or 1d4 swarms of insects plus one additional swarm for each level in your party's average level.

Lion. Your party sees a lion feeding on a fresh kill. Perhaps it is a game animal — or perhaps the lion has hunted an unfortunate human or humanoid. You may allow your party a DC 15 Wisdom (Perception) check to determine if they make out what's happening at a sufficient distance to steer clear, if they choose. Otherwise, the lion looks up at them with suspicion, not only unhappy that they have interrupted its meal, but determined that no one steals a kill from a top predator.

Scaling the Encounter: If you wish to make the encounter more challenging, your party comes upon a pride of lions feeding on a carcass, with two lions for each multiple of 3 in your party's average level.

Manticore. Your party spots a large winged beast in the sky. You may require a successful DC 15 Intelligence (Nature) check to recognize it as a manticore on the hunt before it gets close enough to attack. Once it gets close enough to launch its spikes, it may choose to toy with its prey just to watch them squirm. In this case, it demands some kind of bribe in exchange for sparing them — a bargain it will keep, if your party makes the right offer. A suitable offer might take the form of treasure or humiliating servitude that amuses the manticore. However, if there is war brewing in this part of your campaign world, perhaps the manticore is working for one of the combatants as a scout — in which case, useful information about enemy dispositions would satisfy it.

Scaling the Encounter: If you wish to make the encounter more challenging, consider that there are multiple manticores working as a team. This is especially plausible if they are on a scouting mission for an army. In such a case, the encounter group consists of one manticore for each multiple of 5 in your party's average level.

Medusa. It may be inconspicuous enough so that you have your party make a successful DC 10 Wisdom (Perception) check to notice it, but they pass by what appears to be a realistic statue of a small animal. In fact, a medusa has made its lair in a nearby abandoned structure or cluster of rocks, where it surrounds itself with the petrified remains of its victims. It decides that your party would supplement its existing collection nicely. If your party investigates, they'll find more and more such statues as they approach the actual lair.

Scaling the Encounter: If your party's average level is lower than 6, a medusa may be more than you want to throw at them. Feel free to re-roll for a different encounter.

Treasure: The medusa's gaze petrifies flesh, but not valuables. To total up the bits and pieces that once belonged to her humanoid victims, roll on the Treasure Hoard: Challenge 5-10 table.

No one steals a kill from a top predator.

Nightmare. It's not unusual to come across wild horses in grasslands, but it is decidedly less common to find one that is jet black with a mane and tail of fire. This is, of course, one of those mutilated and transmogrified pegasi known as nightmares. It may have been created on the Material Plane by someone now unknown, or it may have been summoned and then abandoned when its rider was killed. Whatever the case, it charges your party, driven by madness and rage at its fate.

Scaling the Encounter: A nightmare may be a bit too much for a beginning-level party. Feel free to re-roll for another encounter. Conversely, if you want to run a more challenging encounter for a higher-level party, the

encounter group consists of one nightmare for each multiple of 5 in your party's average level.

Ogre. Your party crosses paths with a foraging party of ogres. Whether you want to stage any meaningful interaction with these undersized giants is up to you, but it should surprise no one if they decide that your party is as good a target as any they are likely to find in the near future, whether they are looking for things or food (or both).

Scaling the Encounter: The encounter group consists of two ogres for each multiple of 3 in your party's average level. If your party is only 1st Level, consider that one half-ogre confronts them.

Treasure: These ogres are away from their lair. The treasure for this encounter includes whatever they carry on them, nothing more. Total up the CR of all ogres killed and roll on the appropriate Individual Treasure table.

Oni. Once an ogre mage has had its way in a community, it's only sensible to find another hunting ground before the locals rally and figure out what to do about it. Traveling the uninhabited lands between settlements, it tries to befriend your party while using its *Change Shape* ability to disguise itself as someone trustworthy and inoffensive; use a form that is unlikely to arouse your party's suspicions. If they allow the oni to travel with them, it bides its time until they make camp for the night. It volunteers to take the first watch, then it strikes once everyone else is asleep.

If you wish, you may allow your party a DC 20 Intelligence (Arcana) check to suspect that this apparently friendly stranger might be using magic to alter its appearance.

Scaling the Encounter: An oni may be a bit too much for a low-level party. Feel free to re-roll for another encounter. Conversely, if you want to run a more challenging encounter for a higher-level party, use an encounter group consisting of two oni if your party's average level is 10 or higher.

Owlbear. This encounter is most likely to take place at night, when owlbears hunt. Your party hears its terrible shriek in the distance; you may require a DC 15 Intelligence (Nature) check to recognize it. If it is daytime, you can either re-roll for a different encounter or consider that your party has stumbled onto a deep swale or a cave carved into a rocky outcropping that serves as its lair. If hunting, it attacks; if disturbed in its lair it fights.

Scaling the Encounter: An owlbear may be a bit too much for a beginning-level party. Feel free to re-roll for another encounter. Conversely, if you want to run a more challenging encounter for a higher-level party, consider that your party has encountered a mated pair of owlbears.

Treasure: If the encounter takes place in the owlbear lair, roll on the Treasure Hoard: Challenge 0-4 table to determine what it has taken from its previous victims. If it involves a pair of owlbears, roll twice.

Roc. A roc has roamed far afield from its mountain or hilltop eyrie in search of food. It's a long way to travel if you're just going out for lunch, but it has learned that this fertile land supports a veritable buffet from which it can choose. It spots your party and decides that they're good for at least a snack.

Scaling the Encounter: Rocs are fearsome opponents. If your party's average level is lower than 11, a roc may be more than you want to throw at them. Feel free to re-roll for a different encounter.

Scorpions. Your party takes a rest halt by some rocks, disturbing the scorpions that live among and under them. 1d8 scorpions attack your party. They have stingers, and they don't hesitate to use them.

Scaling the Encounter: If your party's average level is 5 or higher, consider that they have taken some shade from a large rock, or a rock formation, and in so doing they have disturbed one or more giant scorpions. In this case, the encounter group consists of one giant scorpion for each multiple of 5 in the party's average level.

Spiders. In a mostly flat and wide-open environment like grasslands, there aren't many places for spiders to build the large webs that make them so hazardous in forests and underground spaces. But that's not to say that you won't find them here. Instead, they'll come at you from under a rock or a burrow when you have stopped to take a breather. Roll on Table 4.2.3 to determine what kind of spider could bite you when you're not looking:

TABLE 4.2.3
Spiders - Grasslands

d8	ENCOUNTER
1-4	Spiders
5-7	Giant Wolf Spiders
8	Phase Spider

Spiders. These spiders are small, but their venom packs a punch. During a rest stop, someone in your
➤

party sits or leans against the rock under which they are hiding and disturbs them. 2d8 spiders come out in a mood to bite whomever bothered them. They spread out and attack a single target from various angles.

Giant Wolf Spider. Wolf spiders do not weave webs; they burrow into the ground and they either take whatever stumbles into their lair, or they emerge to ambush prey. As your party approaches, vibrations in the ground tell them that something juicy has come to their doorstep, and 1d4 giant wolf spiders attack. You may allow your party a DC 15 Wisdom (Perception) check to notice a hole in the ground large enough to fit a big spider, and if successful, a DC 15 Intelligence (Nature) check to realize that it's a wolf spider burrow.

Phase Spider. Phase spiders are quite fearless, and they use their ability to jump back and forth between planes to conduct hit-and-run attacks, wearing the party down until they are all incapacitated or dead.

Scaling the Encounter: If you want to create a more challenging encounter with ordinary spiders, you may add another 2d8 to the encounter group — having too many, however, not only creates an unwieldy encounter, but it assumes an awfully large population of spiders for a single web. To create a more challenging encounter with giant wolf spiders, use an encounter group consisting of 1d4 plus a number of additional giant wolf spiders equal to your party's average level.

A phase spider may be a bit too much for a beginning-level party. Feel free to re-roll for another encounter in that case. However, if you wish to make the encounter more challenging, the encounter group consists of one phase spider for each multiple of 5 in the party's average level.

Tiger. Your party draws the attention of a hunting tiger, most likely for either of two reasons. Perhaps they have startled prey it was stalking — in which case, they see the prey animal dart across its path, and they hear an angry snarl off to one side. Either that, or the tiger has targeted one of the party's pack animals as its prey.

Toad. These amphibians are not naturally aggressive, but they need to eat — and when they get this big a lot of different creatures look like food. One giant toad has wandered inland from the pond or stream where it lives and it is hungry enough to eat anything it can swallow. Assuming that at least someone in your party can be swallowed by a giant toad, the toad attacks.

Scaling the Encounter: If you wish to make the encounter more challenging, the encounter group consists of two giant toads for each multiple of 3 in your party's average level.

Undead. The natural beauty of verdant grasslands and rolling plains can be deceptive; the undead can haunt any wilderness regardless of its scenic qualities. They may come from barrows and cairns that dot the landscape; or from the fallen in past battles both great and small; or those who perished far from home at the hand of beasts, monsters, or murderers and never received the proper rites. Roll on Table 4.2.5 to determine the undead abomination that greets your party:

TABLE 4.2.5
Undead - Grasslands

d12	ENCOUNTER
1	Ghost
2-3	Ghouls/Ghasts
4-7	Skeletons
8	Wight
9	Wraith
10-12	Zombies

Ghost. That is no optical illusion; the ethereal form flitting across the plain really is a ghost. It is most likely the remnant of someone who died a miserable death in the wilderness. Whatever the case, you may make this into a hostile encounter by having the ghost try to possess a member of your party so that it may resolve unfinished business from its former life.

Ghouls/Ghasts. An encounter with ghouls is most likely to take place at night. Two ghouls (or one ghast) approach your party, driven by mindless hunger for their flesh.

Skeletons. Your party comes across the undead remnants of an ancient conflict: 1d4 skeletons carrying broken weapons and draped with fragments of the armor they wore in life. Perhaps they were soldiers killed in a skirmish. Perhaps they were adventurers or explorers ambushed by brigands — or perhaps they were bandits themselves, who were hunted down in the name of justice or revenge, or who fell out among themselves. Driven by necromantic echoes of the end of their lives, they're looking for a fight.

Wight. Your party makes camp not far from a cluster of burial sites. Whether they are mounds, cairns or barrows improvised out here in the wilderness is ➤

up to you as DM and arbiter of what makes the most sense for your campaign world. Unfortunately for your party, at least one of the occupants has become a wight, and it rises from its tomb to attack them while they are most vulnerable.

Wraith. Monumental burial sites like mounds, cairns or barrows — even if they're hastily improvised — can house a wraith. As your party passes by, they can see that the site is ringed by barren and blasted ground with only withered grass to show that it once supported life. A cold, charcoal-gray mist emerges and resolves itself into a wraith, which then attacks your party, acting out the resentment that it bore at the end of its natural life.

Zombies. Your party come across 1d4 zombies who have been programmed to kill every living thing they encounter. The source of the necromancy that created these zombies we leave to you. Perhaps they slipped the leash of their creator and they now wander the land mindlessly looking for victims.

Scaling the Encounter: Ghosts and wraiths always work alone. Also, if your party's average level is lower than 5, a wraith may be more than you want to throw at them. Feel free to re-roll for a different encounter.

Ghoul/Ghast: If you wish to make the encounter more challenging, the encounter group consists of two ghouls (for or one ghast) each multiple of 3 in your party's average level. Feel free to mix and match ghouls and ghasts as long as you maintain the right proportion of total CR to average party level.

Skeletons: If you wish to make the encounter more challenging, the encounter group consists of 1d4 skeletons plus one additional skeleton for each level in your party's average level. You may substitute one warhorse skeleton for two skeletons.

Wights: A wight may be a bit too much for a beginning-level party. Feel free to re-roll for another encounter. Conversely, if you want to run a more challenging encounter for a higher-level party, add one zombie minion for each level in your party's average level above 3.

Zombies: If you wish to make the encounter more challenging, the encounter group consists of 1d4 zombies plus one additional zombie for each level in your party's average level. If the average party level is 3 or higher, you may use an encounter group consisting of one ogre zombie for each multiple of 3 in the party's average level. ➤

Treasure: Most likely, ghosts are encountered in or near what passes for a lair with them and you may consider that there they keep possessions that they had in life. Roll on the Treasure Hoard: Challenge 0-4 table for the contents of their stash. You may require a successful DC 15 Wisdom (Perception) check to find its exact location.

Likewise, wights and wraiths do not stray far from their place of burial, which are usually constructed as monuments to the dead. Therefore, their location should be self-apparent. Roll on the Treasure Hoard table appropriate to the total CR of the encounter.

With ghouls, ghasts, skeletons and zombies, they may have with them some remains of what they had on their person at the time of their death. Roll on the Individual Treasure table appropriate to the total CR of the encounter.

Will-o'-Wisp. The modest undulations in the terrain reveal a depression where the lack of natural drainage has created a small bog. Here, your party sees a luminous globe dancing and bobbing above the mire. It's a will-o'-wisp, the remnant of an unquiet soul that perished here.

(Relatively) Flat Earth

Perhaps the most important thing to keep in mind about grasslands, as defined here, is that they are not hills or mountains. Some grasslands, like the Great Plains of North America, are quite flat, presenting you with vast planes of earth and sky that spread out all around you. On the other hand, the grasslands of Central Europe undulate — read enough accounts of Napoleonic Era battles, and one thing that strikes is how dips in the ground could hide whole units of soldiers from view, even from observers fairly close by. This chapter applies to both, and it is up to you to decide how much elevation changes apply to this part of your campaign world.

If you want to add some spice to the encounter, consider that this evil spirit tries to lure victims into a patch of quicksand to render them helpless. In this case, the will-o'-wisp restricts itself to a 50-foot diameter area at the center of the clearing. At the center of this area, the swamp turns into a 20-foot diameter pit of quicksand. If the will-o'-wisp is not already directly above the quicksand when it is engaged in melee combat, it retreats until it is above the quicksand, thus forcing its attacker to step into it in order to continue the melee.

Scaling the Encounter: If you wish to make the encounter more challenging, the encounter group consists of one will-o'-wisp for each multiple of 3 in the party's average level.

Treasure: Belongings from the will-o'-wisp's previous victims have been piling up here, with various valuables scattered in the muck. To determine the treasure, roll once on the Treasure Hoard: Challenge 0-4 table for each will-o'-wisp present.

Wolves. Wolves freely roam the wilderness in lands fertile enough to support the animals on which they prey, so it should come as no surprise if your party meets a pack on the prowl. Roll on Table 4.2.6 to determine whether your party encounters wolves or dire wolves:

TABLE 4.2.6
Wolves - Grasslands

d4	ENCOUNTER
1	Dire Wolf
2-4	Wolves

Dire Wolves. One dire wolf sets upon your party from amongst the trees. As their name suggests, dire wolves are vicious and fearless and they attack regardless of the numerical odds.

Wolves. Your party meets a pack of 1d4+1 wolves on the prowl. They split into two groups and maneuver to attack your party from the flanks.

Scaling the Encounter: If you wish to make the encounter more challenging, the encounter group consists of two dire wolves for each multiple of 3 in your party's average level, or 1d4 wolves plus one additional wolf for each level in your party's average level.

Treasure: Furriers in your world may be willing to pay for wolf pelts. How much is ultimately up to you, but 2 gp is a reasonable baseline price for a normal wolf pelt and 3 gp for a dire wolf pelt. Dire wolf pelts are not necessarily more desirable, but they are larger and offer more fur to work with.

Worgs. Your party crosses paths with 1d4 worgs. It's possible that they are wild. But it is also possible that they were domesticated, but escaped or lost their goblinoid masters — in which case, the presence of worgs could indicate that there are goblins or hobgoblins nearby. In fact, a large group of worgs without their riders could indicate that a whole goblinoid tribe was wiped out, and their mounts are now wandering without anyone to keep them. In any event, they are feeling hungry and mean, and your party looks like a good target regardless of the numerical odds.

Scaling the Encounter: If you wish to make the encounter more challenging, the encounter group consists of a pack of escaped or abandoned worgs, 1d4 for each multiple of 2 in your party's average level.

Wyvern. A wyvern has emerged from its lair in nearby hills to hunt and it spots your party from above. It is either very hungry or very aggressive, so it swoops down to attack despite the odds.

Scaling the Encounter: If your party's average level is lower than 6, a wyvern with its blood up may be more than you want to throw at them. Feel free to re-roll for a different encounter.

Snakes. As the old expression goes, a snake in the grass is dangerous indeed. It's so easy for them to hide in the ground cover that you may not see them until it's too late to avoid them, and if they're venomous, well, that's just an extra serving of trouble heaped high on your plate. You may allow your party to make a DC 15 Wisdom (Perception) or Wisdom (Survival) check to realize that someone in the front of the march order is about to step on a snake. This should give them enough time to take evasive action, although you may consider that this simply means they aren't surprised when the snake lashes out.

Roll on Table 4.2.7 to determine the size of the snake(s) encountered:

TABLE 4.2.7
Snakes - Grasslands

d10	ENCOUNTER
1-5	Swarm of Poisonous Snakes
6-9	Poisonous Snake
10	Giant Poisonous Snake
11	Constrictor Snake

+1 to die roll if in tropical grasslands

Swarm of Poisonous Snakes. Your party comes across a shallow depression which is, literally, a snake pit with one swarm of poisonous snakes present. You may decrease the DC to notice the snakes to 5, to reflect the facts that there are more snakes present and the terrain feature is relatively easy to notice.

Poisonous Snake. Your party comes close to stepping on one poisonous snake. ➤

Giant Poisonous Snake. Your party comes across one giant poisonous snake. You may decrease the DC to notice the snakes to 10 to reflect its size.

Constrictor Snake. Constrictor snakes are found only in tropical regions, where it's hot and humid enough for such a large cold-blooded creature to survive. But where they do occur, they are awe-inspiring predators. A constrictor tries to sneak up on your party and make a meal of one of its members.

Cheetahs. A small coalition of 1d6 of these sleek, fast predators spots your party. They're hungry, and your party looks as good as anything else they are likely to find at the moment. They hear the cheetahs make sharp, high noises like birds chirping as they circle your party and prepare to attack.

Treat cheetahs as panthers, except their speed is 60 ft.

Scaling the Encounter: If you wish to make the encounter more challenging, the encounter group consists of a large coalition of 2d6 cheetahs.

TABLE 4.3
Neutral Creatures - Grasslands

d100	ENCOUNTER
1-3	Brown Bear
4-7	Elk
8-10	Black Bear
11-14	Awakened Shrub
15-18	Axe Beaks
19-23	Badgers
24-32	Boar
33	Centaur
34-39	Centipede
40-41	Cockatrice
42-49	Deer
50	Dragon
51-54	Goats
55-57	Hippogriff
58-63	Horses
64-68	Hyenas
69-72	Jackals
73-76	Lizard
77-78	Mastiff
79-82	Mules
83-84	Pegasus ➤

85-90	Rats
91-95	Vultures
96-101	Weasels
102-106	Elephant
107-110	Rhinocerous

+2 to die roll if in temperate grasslands.
+10 to die roll if in tropical grasslands.

Brown Bear. Your party spots a brown bear prowling around for food. If they are resting, the bear comes sniffing around, drawn by whatever rations they are carrying. If your party just wants to scare it off, require a DC 15 Intelligence (Nature) or Wisdom (Survival) check. Success means that the bear takes the hint and lumbers away. Failure means that the bear charges them.

Elk. Your party spots a herd of 1d6 bulls and 3d6 cows grazing. If your party attacks them, only the males fight, covering the fleeing females.

Even if your party does not behave in a threatening manner, you may consider that there is a chance that the bulls mistake their actions and attack anyway. Have your party make a DC 15 Intelligence (Nature) or Wisdom (Survival) check. Failure means that someone has made a false move that sets off the males and they charge.

Scaling the Encounter: If you wish to make the encounter more challenging, your party sees a lone (and rare) giant elk at a distance. As they approach it they realize that it's larger than it seemed. Confident in its power as an alpha of its kind, it attacks your party if it senses any hostile intent (remember that giant elk have the ability to understand certain languages).

Perhaps it is bad luck in your campaign world to hunt a giant elk. If your party kills it, each party member is cursed as if affected by the spell *bane*, except that the effect lasts until it is magically dispelled, or until those who did the deed atone for it.

Treasure: Elk are hunted for food wherever they share territory with humans. Perhaps a nearby butcher will pay 2 gp or thereabouts for a fresh carcass.

Black Bear. Your party spots a black bear prowling around for food. If they are resting, the bear comes around, drawn by their rations. If your party just wants to scare it off, require a DC 15 Intelligence (Nature) or Wisdom (Survival) check. Success means that the bear takes the hint and lumbers away. Failure does not necessarily mean that the bear attacks, but it does stand its ground. If they attack it, the bear defends itself. At that point, require another DC 15 Intelligence (Nature) or Wisdom (Survival) check. Failure means that someone

has made a false move, provoking the bear to attack. Otherwise, it eventually takes the hint and retreats.

Awakened Shrub. Just as trees in pristine forests can become sentient through mysterious enchantments, more humble plants that dot the wilderness can also awaken. Your party comes into contact with one or more such awakened shrubs. Perhaps a party member takes advantage of it to answer the call of nature. Perhaps it produces berries that look appetizing. These or similar actions cause the shrub to express alarm.

Even your party has done mischief to it, an encounter with an awakened shrub is not necessarily hostile. If your party asks it for help, a successful DC 10 Charisma (Persuasion) check wins it over, but the DC is 15 if your party has harmed it in some way. Help from an awakened shrub includes providing knowledge of the surrounding area.

Scaling the Encounter: If you wish to make the encounter more challenging, the encounter group consists of one awakened shrub for each multiple of 3 in your party's average level, rounded up.

It is possible that as many as three or four centaurs might have split off from their tribe as a group.

Axe Beaks. Your party comes across a hunting pack of 1d4+2 of these odd-looking, bad-tempered flightless birds. They don't like having their hunt interrupted, but it's not a sure thing that they'll attack. You may have your party make a DC 15 Intelligence (Nature) or Wisdom (Survival) check. Failure means that a party member has made a false move that angers the axe beaks, which then attack.

Badgers. Your party comes across two badgers out in the open. They spot your party, then dart for their nearby burrow. If your party investigates, they see two pairs of eyes like black marbles glinting in the shadows. Have your party make a DC 15 Intelligence (Nature) or Wisdom (Survival) check. Failure means that a party member has made a false move that activates the badgers' fight-or-flight response. Their burrow only has one opening, so they feel cornered and fight like badgers.

Scaling the Encounter: If you wish to make the encounter more challenging, use an encounter group of two giant badgers.

Boar. Your party spots 1d4 wild boar rooting around in the grass for food. Boar are popular targets for hunters. They'll fight back if attacked — indeed, the challenge they present is part of the appeal of hunting them. But they have also developed a fight-or-flight instinct, and if your party wishes to avoid a fight, you may have them make a DC 15 Wisdom (Survival) or Intelligence (Nature) group check to scare the boar off, or at least avoid provoking it until they break contact.

Scaling the Encounter: If you wish to make the encounter more challenging, use an encounter group consisting of one giant boar for each multiple of 3 in your party's average level. Giant boar are even more aggressive than their smaller cousins and they charge anyone who disturbs them.

Treasure: Boar meat is good eating for many folk. Perhaps a nearby butcher will pay 2 gp or thereabouts for a fresh carcass. The price might go up to 5 gp for a giant boar.

Centaur. Your party spots in the distance a lone figure, half-human and half-equine. It is a centaur, and like all too many of its kind, it became irrevocably separated from its tribe during a migration and now wanders the world alone. A centaur roaming the plains may have knowledge of nearby settlements and roads that would help your party, and it could be persuaded to share it. A centaur might also offer your party a sidequest, asking for their help in finding its long-lost tribe.

Scaling the Encounter: It is up to you whether or not to scale up an encounter with centaurs. Though most often encountered alone, it is possible that as many as three or four centaurs might have split off from their tribe as a group. If you anticipate a hostile encounter, throwing more than one centaur at your party would provide a stiff challenge if their average level is less than 4.

Treasure: Centaurs carry their valuables with them. Roll once on the Individual Treasure: Challenge 0-4 table for each centaur present.

Centipede. Have your party make a DC 15 Intelligence (Nature) or Wisdom (Survival) check. Failure means that no one notices the giant centipede making ripples in the grass as it crosses their path and someone in the front of the march order comes dangerously close to stepping on it. It responds by attacking that character. Success means that they notice the giant centipede in time to avoid provoking it, thus making a hostile encounter purely optional.

Cockatrice. Your party comes across one cockatrice poking around for fallen nuts and berries, or chasing a small animal for its next meal. If your party wishes to avoid a fight, require a DC 15 Intelligence (Nature) or Wisdom (Survival) check. Failure means that someone in your party has made a false move that sets off the beast, and it attacks.

Scaling the Encounter: If you wish to make the encounter more challenging, use an encounter group that consists of 1d4 cockatrices plus one additional cockatrice for each level in your party's average level.

Deer. Your party spots 1d8 bucks and 2d6 does grazing. If your party attacks, only the males fight, covering the females while they flee.

Even if your party does not behave in a threatening manner, there is a chance that the males mistake their actions and attack anyway. Have your party make a DC 10 Intelligence (Nature) or Wisdom (Survival) check. Failure means that someone has made a false move that sets off the males and they charge.

Treasure: Anyone for venison? Perhaps a nearby butcher will pay 2 gp or thereabouts for a fresh carcass.

These encounters are surprising but not necessarily fatal.

Dragon. Your party notices a shadow in the sky. It's a dragon on the prowl. To determine what kind of dragon roll on Table 4.3.1:

TABLE 4.3.1
Dragon - Grasslands

d12	ENCOUNTER
1	Black
2-3	Blue
4	Green
5	Red
6	White
7	Brass
8-9	Bronze
10	Copper
11	Gold
12	Silver

To determine its age, see Scaling the Encounter.

To be clear, this need not be a hostile encounter. The dragon is not defending its lair, so it may just be curious about your party. It may have more important things to do and decline to take notice of them at all. Or it may be hungry and on the hunt, or it's angry because your party has intruded on territory it claims as its own.

Alternately, you may present your party with a scenario that you can weave into the larger story of the campaign. Your party finds a dragon wyrmling propped up with its back against a tree. It's obviously in a bad way — gashed open, bleeding profusely, barely conscious. Assume that it has stabilized after being reduced to 0 hp, and that it now has 1 hp. How it got that way is up to you, and it may depend on how dragons fit into your campaign world. Perhaps it fled from a fight in which it was badly wounded. Who would its enemies be, and why were they fighting? Were any of its relatives or companions killed?

How your party decides to deal with this dragon child in distress could open up possibilities for later in your campaign. If they rescue it, will its kin reward them, or will its enemies confront them on the principle that, "The friends of my enemy must also be my enemy?" Conversely, what are the consequences if they put it out of its misery, like scavengers roaming a medieval battlefield? Will its kin seek retribution, or will its enemies treat your party as allies? ➤

Scaling the Encounter: Because dragons get tougher with age, the age of the dragon encountered should depend on your party's average level — especially if you decide that this is going to be a hostile encounter.

If your party's average level is 10 or lower, they encounters a wyrmling. If their average level is 11-18, they encounter a young dragon. If their average level is 19-25, they encounter an adult dragon. If their average level is higher than 25, they encounter an ancient dragon.

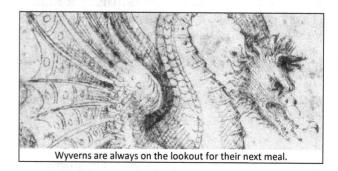
Wyverns are always on the lookout for their next meal.

Goats. Your party comes across a small herd of 1d8 billies and 2d8 nannies grazing. Perhaps they are wild goats — or perhaps they have gotten separated from a larger herd, and somewhere nearby there is a goatherd who would give a reward for their safe return. In any event, billies can be ornery beasts and if your party approaches them, you may require your party to make a DC 15 Intelligence (Nature) check to avoid setting off an attack in which the males charge to cover the fleeing females.

Scaling the Encounter: If you wish to make the encounter more challenging, use a herd of wild (and potentially irritated) giant goats instead. The encounter group should consist of 1d4 giant goats for each multiple of 2 in your party's average level with the same 1:2 ratio of males to females. Giant goats are quite wild; there is no chance that they are being kept by someone else.

Hippogriff. Your party sees a hippogriff circling overhead, looking for its next meal, or on the ground dealing with its prey. Hippogriffs are not as aggressive as birds of prey, and it is no sure bet that they would attack your party on the hope that it could make off with a pack animal or their stash of rations. Whether or not this is a hostile encounter is up to you.

Hippogriffs may be a kind of prey as well as predators. If hippogriffs are used as mounts in your world, it must follow that captive adults have value as breeding stock, and chicks captured from the wild also have value because they are still young enough to be tamed. To that end, you may allow your party a DC 20 Wisdom (Survival) check to trace a path to the hippogriff's lair (likely to be sited atop a large rock or on a hilltop) after observing it for a while. If your party has someone capable of flight, reduce the DC to 15. To subdue an adult hippogriff to the point where it can be bound and held captive, it must be successfully grappled and kept in grappled condition for 10 consecutive rounds.

Scaling the Encounter: If you want to stage a hostile encounter with hippogriffs and you need to make it more of a challenge for a higher-level party, consider that the encounter group consists of one hippogriff for each multiple of 3 in your party's average level.

Horses. Horses are very much at home in the open spaces of grasslands, so it should come as no surprise if your party comes across a small herd of them. They only questions are, how many of them are there, and do they belong to someone else? Horse encounters are unlikely to be hostile, although they may put up a fight if you try to wrangle them before they've been broken. Roll on Table 4.3.2 to determine the nature of the horse encounter:

If you don't approach them right, they'll take you for an enemy.

TABLE 4.3.2
Horses - Grasslands

d6	ENCOUNTER
1-2	Pony
3-5	Riding Horse
6	Warhorse

Pony. Your party comes across a small herd of 2d8 ponies grazing, or moving across the landscape at a walk. It's up to you to decide whether they're wild, or if they belong to someone — and if the latter, have they escaped from someone who would pay a reward for their return?

If they are wild, they can be wrangled. To wrangle a pony, it must be successfully grappled and kept in grappled condition for 3 consecutive rounds. At that point, it becomes docile and whomever grappled it may ride it or use it as a pack animal. Only one medium-size creature may try to grapple a pony at any given time. ➤

Riding Horse. Your party comes across a small herd of 2d6 riding horses grazing, or moving across the landscape at a walk. It's up to you to decide whether they're wild, or if they belong to someone — and if the latter, have they escaped from someone who would pay a reward for their return?

If they are wild, they can be wrangled. To wrangle a riding horse, it must be successfully grappled and kept in grappled condition for 6 consecutive rounds. At that point, it becomes docile and whomever grappled it may ride it or use it as a pack animal. Because of its size, two medium-size creatures may grapple with the same riding horse simultaneously, and as long as one of them maintains its grappled condition, this counts toward the requirement for wrangling it.

Warhorse. Your party comes across 1d4 warhorses. Whether their owners were killed in battle, or they just escaped from the stable, is not clear at first glance. Warhorses do not need to be wrangled; they have been broken and disciplined, so they're used to working with humans. However, they're also trained fighters and if you don't approach them just right in a situation like this, they'll take you for the enemy and attack. If your party approaches the warhorses, have them make a DC 15 Intelligence (Nature) check to avoid setting them off.

Insignia on their barding should give some hints as to whom the warhorses belong (or belonged). A good warhorse is highly prized, and its owner would pay dearly for its return.

Treasure: If your party encounters riding horses that have escaped from their owners, they may be saddled and their saddlebags contain valuables equal to one roll on the Individual Treasure: Challenge 0-4 table. Warhorses, of course, have their barding.

Hyenas. Hyenas are clever predators, and they know well enough to pick their targets carefully. A hunting pack of 2d8 hyenas comes across your party, but they do not attack unless they are at least twice as numerous as your party, or unless they can isolate a party member and use their pack tactics ability — perhaps one character has gone ahead to scout the lay of the land, or separated him or herself to answer the call of nature. Otherwise, they hover about on the flank of the party, looking for an opportunity to strike. If they find none, they eventually tire of the hunt and move off.

Scaling the Encounter: If you wish to make the encounter more challenging, the encounter group consists of two giant hyenas for each multiple of 3 in your party's average level.

Jackals. Your party comes across a small pack of 2d4 jackals scavenging a carcass. It's a feast compared to nosing through the tall grass for small animals, so they're keen to protect their find. If your party wishes to avoid a fight, have them make a DC 15 Wisdom (Survival) check. Failure means that someone has made a move that the jackals take as a threat, and they attack.

Lizards. Your party crosses paths with 1d4 giant lizards foraging for large insects and smaller lizards. They are not aggressive and they can be wrangled and trained to serve as pack animals or mounts. To wrangle a giant lizard, it must be successfully grappled and kept in grappled condition for 10 consecutive rounds. At that point, it becomes docile and submits to whomever grappled it. Because of its size, two medium-size creatures may grapple with the same giant lizard simultaneously, and as long as one of them maintains its grappled condition, this counts toward the requirement for wrangling it.

Mastiff. Your party comes across one hunting dog that has, evidently, slipped its leash. It may be anxious because it's separated from its pack and its master, or it may be perfectly content to wander on its own. Either way, it's conditioned to attack. If your party approaches it, require a DC 15 Intelligence (Nature) check. Failure means that someone has made a false move, and the mastiff charges the nearest character.

It's a big, aggressive dog — but on the other hand, the fact that it's a hunting dog means that it belongs to someone. That someone probably lives in the area, and is probably a person of substance (i.e., someone who can afford to keep hunting dogs). Returning the lost dog could lead to a hefty reward.

Scaling the Encounter: If you wish to make the encounter more challenging, the encounter group consists of an entire hunting pack of 1d4+2 mastiffs.

If you want to make the encounter downright vicious, consider that the mastiff is rabid. You may have your party make a DC 15 Wisdom (Perception) check to notice that it is foaming at the mouth, but there is no way to dissuade it from attacking the nearest character.

14 days after the encounter, have everyone who was bitten by the rabid mastiff make a DC 20 Constitution saving throw to avoid developing rabies themselves. Those who fail begin to feel feverish. 1-3 days later, those affected become agitated and may start to hallucinate. Treat this as short-term madness. 1-3 days later, affected characters become paralyzed. 1-2 days

later, they become unconscious. 1-2 days after that, they die. This disease is always fatal if left untreated, but it responds normally to magical cures and any non-magical cures for serious diseases.

Even if you could subdue it somehow, a rabid hunting dog dies of the disease before you can return it to its owner. And, come to think of it, who would want a rabid dog returned to them, anyway?

> **Bad Dog!**
> An encounter with a rabid dog is another idea lifted from Places by the Way #9: *The Paladin Queen's Forest.* It seemed like an interesting niche encounter, but one that was bound to be unique — the royal forest is not overrun with rabid lost hunting dogs. The module suggests ignoring it if rolled again.
>
> Similarly, this encounter receives a low probability of occurring here — although, if your campaign world really is overrun with rabid dogs, feel free to change that.

Mules. Mules are domestic creatures. So when your party sees 1d8 mules mulling about for no apparent purpose, it is highly likely that they have escaped from the nearest farm or village. Their owners will pay a reward for their return — or your party could claim them as their own without anyone (possibly) being the wiser.

Mules do not attack. But they may be skittish around strangers, especially if they have been out in the wild for a while. If your party tries to take possession of them, have them make a DC 10 Intelligence (Nature) check to avoid a hostile reaction. Remember, these creatures have a kick like a mule.

Pegasus. Your party sees one pegasus wheeling overhead. It does not attack, even if it sees evil creatures. However, it may be flagged down by signaling or calling to it and making a successful DC 15 Charisma (Persuasion) check. If your party can get the pegasus' attention, they may persuade it to render some kind of aid — such as taking a party member to a nearby location — with a successful DC 20 Charisma (Persuasion) check. For good-aligned characters who can speak Celestial, Elvish or Sylvan the DC is 15.

Scaling the Encounter: If you wish to make the encounter more challenging, the encounter group consists of one pegasus for each multiple of 3 in your party's average level.

Rats. Rats find plenty to eat in fertile land like this, but they won't turn up their noses if they sniff out your party's travelers' rations. Roll on Table 4.3.3 to determine the nature of the rat encounter:

TABLE 4.3.3
Rats - Grasslands

d6	ENCOUNTER
1	Lone Rat
2-4	Swarm of Rats
5-6	Giant Rats

Lone Rat. A single rat, perhaps foraging by itself or perhaps lost from its nest, approaches your party while they take a rest. It's not much of a threat, but if someone in your party is looking for a familiar or even just a pet, this is an opportunity. Interacting with the rat — especially earning its trust with food — and making a successful DC 10 Intelligence (Nature) check earns its loyalty as a pet.

Swarm of Rats. Without being aware of it, your party has stopped to rest near a nest of rats. Drawn by the party's rations, a swarm of rats makes for the nearest source of food. They don't attack party members who don't interfere with their basic mission of acquiring food. But unless they are stopped, they eventually account for all of your party's rations, making off with what they don't eat on the spot.

Giant Rats. In this case, the rats drawn by the food your party carries are giant rats. There are 2d6 of them.

Vultures. Your party comes across 1d6+2 vultures picking at a carcass. It could be an animal — or it could be a humanoid or a human. How they respond depends on how they interpret your party's actions. You may have your party make a DC 10 Intelligence (Nature) or Wisdom (Survival) check. Failure means that a party member has made a false move that persuades the vultures to attack, thinking that they need to defend their food source.

Scaling the Encounter: If you wish to make the encounter more challenging, consider substituting giant vultures for the vultures. The encounter group then consists of two giant vultures for each multiple of 3 in your party's average level. Giant vultures may be hunting instead of feeding. Perhaps they — mistakenly or not — spotted your party as hapless travelers on their last legs, in which case they swoop down to try to hasten their demise.

Weasels. Someone at the front of your party's march order accidentally steps into a burrow housing enough weasels to cause trouble when they get angry and defend their home. You may allow your party a DC 10 Wisdom (Perception) or Wisdom (Survival) check to spot the burrow in time to avoid it or give warning to whomever is about to disturb it. The burrow houses a pack of 3d6 weasels.

Scaling the Encounter: If you wish to make the encounter more challenging, substitute giant weasels for normal-sized weasels.

Treasure: There is a 10% chance that they are actually mink, and their pelts would be of some value to furriers — 1 gp for normal-sized mink, and 5 gp for a giant mink. You may require a successful DC 15 Intelligence (Nature) check for your party to tell the difference between mink and weasels.

Elephant. Your party comes across one of these behemoths wandering across the savanna. If it is not part of a herd, it is very likely that it escaped from captivity — perhaps after rampaging and killing its handler and who knows who else. At the moment, it is not aggressive. But your party has come close enough so that a false move could persuade it to rampage again. Have your party make a DC 15 Wisdom (Survival) check. Failure triggers elephant, and it charges.

On the other hand, if your party succeeds, your party may tap into its specialized knowledge to persuade the elephant to follow it. This requires a party member who has ranks in Intelligence (Nature) and a successful DC 20 check using that skill, or some magical means of controlling the beast. Success means that the elephant becomes obedient to that party member, and allows itself to be used as a pack animal. Failure incites the elephant to charge your party.

If this encounter occurs in a sub-arctic climate, you may substitute a mammoth for an elephant.

Scaling the Encounter: An elephant (or a mammoth) may be a bit too much for a beginning-level party. Feel free to re-roll for another encounter. Conversely, if you want to run a more challenging encounter for a higher-level party, use an encounter group that consists of one elephant for every multiple of 5, or one mammoth for every multiple of 7, in your party's average level.

Rhinoceros. Your party comes across one rhinoceros grazing peacefully. Rhinos are not carnivores, but they are potentially aggressive and their horn can leave a mark. It's too late to pretend that the rhino hasn't noticed your party. Have your party make a DC 15

Wisdom (Survival) check to avoid making a false move that angers it enough to charge.

Scaling the Encounter: If you wish to make the encounter more challenging, use a herd of rhinos consisting of one for each multiple of 3 in your party's average level as the encounter group.

TABLE 4.4

Humanoids - Grasslands

d20	ENCOUNTER
1-2	Bugbear
3-5	Gnolls
6-7	Gnomes
8-10	Goblins
11-13	Halflings
14-15	Hobgoblins
16	Lycanthrope
17-20	Orcs

Bugbear. Your party crosses paths with one or more bugbears (see Scaling the Encounter). They could be mercenaries on their way to join a larger goblinoid army mobilizing for war. Conversely, they could be heading home after a victorious campaign — or straggling in the wake of a catastrophic defeat. Their exact circumstances and motivation should depend on what else is going on in your campaign world. If there is no such war in which they could take part, they're out for some casual plunder, or perhaps on their way to shake down a hobgoblin tribe that once employed them.

Their interest in fighting your party should vary according to the reason why they're here. For instance, mobilizing for war means they have a larger purpose in mind than victimizing your party. If they're looking to strong-arm some hobgoblins, they may even offer your party a cut of the take in exchange for adding to their strength in numbers.

Scaling the Encounter: A beginning-level party should only have to cope with one bugbear. If you wish to make the encounter more challenging, the encounter group consists of two bugbears for each multiple of 3 in your party's average level. If your party's average level is 10 or higher, add one bugbear chief as the group's leader.

Gnolls. Your party comes across a small band of gnolls moving swiftly across the plain. They seem to have a purpose in mind, as they barely take notice of your party. In fact, they are here to scout out a nearby settlement as preparation for raiding and plundering it. If the gnoll group is relatively large (see Scaling the Encounter) this may be the actual raiding party, headed for the nearest

settlement. Or they may be on their way back from a successful raid, spattered with blood and taking with them captives to sacrifice to their . In either case, they ignore your party if your party declines to interfere with them, guided as they are by their primary purpose.

Scaling the Encounter: The baseline encounter group should consist of two gnolls for each multiple of 3 in your party's average level. If your party's average level is 7-9, add a gnoll pack lord to the mix as the group's leader. If your party's average level is 10 or higher, feel free to substitute one gnoll pack lord for four gnolls as much as you like if you don't want to run a mass encounter.

Treasure: If the gnolls are coming back from a successful raid, you may roll on the Treasure Hoard: Challenge 0-4 table to determine the fruits of their labor. This is in addition to the individual treasure they carry.

Gnomes. Your party crosses paths with a small party of gnomes, consisting of 2d6 commoners and one priest. They may be freelance mechanics who travel between towns and villages, looking to sell their services. Or they may be traders. In either case, they have brought along a priest of one of their patron deities as their sole protection.

The gnomes are not aggressive. It won't take much prompting to get them to trade with your party and share local knowledge. They probably hail from a nearby gnome village, although it's rare for them to feel safe where the terrain will not do much to supplement their skill at artifice in keeping them safe. Their priest may be willing to help your party with spells if they are willing to pay the going rate for such services.

Treasure: If these gnomes are traveling merchants, they should carry trade goods and/or coins in addition to their personal treasure. Roll on the Treasure Hoard: Challenge 0-4 table.

Goblins. Unless they can find a burrow large enough to hold a tribe, goblins tend to make their lairs elsewhere. But they come to the flatlands as a good place to find farms, herders and small settlements to plunder and take captives. Your party crosses paths with a such a goblin raiding party crossing the plain. They spot each other a distance; the goblins see your party as a target of opportunity and they fan out to attack from multiple angles, using undulations in the ground (if any) to conceal their movements as much as possible.

Scaling the Encounter: Use an encounter group of 1d4 goblins for each level in your party's average level. If you don't want to run a mass encounter but you still want to provide a higher-level party with a meaningful challenge, feel free to substitute one goblin boss for four goblins as much as you like.

Also, consider that flat, open terrain offers the perfect environment for employing cavalry — in other words, worg mounts. Feel free to substitute one worg for two goblins, as long as there are not more worgs present than goblins to ride them.

Halflings. Your party crosses paths with a group of 1d10+2 halflings. They may be farmers from homesteads scattered in the wilderness, who have joined together to share a wagon and take their produce to market. It's up to you whether they're on their way to market, or on their way back, with their pony-drawn wagon being either full of foodstuffs or half-full of trade goods. In this case, treat one or two of the halflings as guards and the rest as commoners. There's no reason why they wouldn't be willing to trade with your party and share knowledge of the area. In fact, they might be willing to hire your party to escort them wherever they're going if they think that there are dangerous monsters about.

It's also possible that they're an adventuring party, 1d6+2 in number. In this case, treat one of them as an acolyte and the rest as scouts. Treat them, too, as a potential source of useful information for your party. They're a good-natured lot, but if the subject of what they're up to arises, it should be clear to your party that these bold, but naive halflings have bitten off more than they can chew. If your party decides to tag along to keep them out of trouble, this creates a nice little sidequest for them.

Scaling the Encounter: If you want to run a more robust encounter with halfling adventurers, treat them as thugs and spies instead of guards and scouts.

Hobgoblins. If war plagues your campaign world, hobgoblins go about, selling their martial services to anyone willing to employ them. If your party meets a small group of hobgoblins marching across country, they may have come across mercenaries taking a shortcut on their way to their mustering point. If that's the case, they have business to take care of and they'll ignore your party as long as they don't try to interfere.

On the other hand, the hobgoblins might initiate a fight with your party if peace has prevailed for so long that they have had no work — in which case they're bored and looking for practice. Or they're broke and as long as they properly challenge your party to a fight, killing them for their belongings is not mere robbery but taking spoils of war. Alternately, these hobgoblins may be fleeing a lost battle and, like many mercenaries in such a situation, they can rationalize killing and looting your party in any number of ways — perhaps they won't get paid because

their employer was killed; or they need to settle for what they can get now that the battle won't yield any spoils; or perhaps they're just hungry and desperate after separating from the army.

Scaling the Encounter: The baseline encounter group should consist of 1d4 hobgoblins for each multiple of 2 in your party's average level. If your party's average level is 10-19, add a hobgoblin captain as the group's leader. If your party's average level is 20 or higher, add instead one hobgoblin warlord with two bugbear aides.

Also, consider that flat, open terrain offers the perfect environment for employing cavalry — in other words, worg mounts. Feel free to substitute one worg for one hobgoblin as long as you maintain the correct CR for the encounter.

Lycanthrope. To determine what manner of werebeast your party encounters, roll on Table 4.4.1:

TABLE 4.4.1
Lycanthrope - Grasslands

d8	ENCOUNTER
1	Werebear
2-3	Wereboar
4-5	Wererat
6-8	Werewolf

All lycanthropes assume their animal form if the encounter comes down to combat, although they may choose their hybrid form instead if they have access to a weapon.

Werebear. Your party comes across a werebear that has staked out this patch of wilderness as its domain. Perhaps it was once a druid, or a wandering ranger, or a religious hermit of some sort, who volunteered for this fate as a way of protecting the land. It is not automatically hostile to your party, especially if there are no evil characters present, and it may be willing to provide your party with useful information about the surrounding area.

On the other hand, an encounter could create difficulties for your party if the werebear decides that someone in your party would make a good apprentice (and successor to its self-appointed duties as the local guardian). Once it realizes that there is a druid or a ranger in your party, a light goes on in its head — and it won't take "No" for an answer.

➤

Wereboar. A wereboar met by chance was most likely an unfortunate hunter who didn't realize that the boar at which he aimed his bow was really a lycanthrope.

Or it might have been a herder who presented an isolated target. The wereboar goes about looking for victims to share its fate, hoping that a lone boar will lure someone into engaging with it. A party of adventurers could offer it an attractive target — confident in its ability to take at least one of them and drive the others off, it attacks.

Wererat. Rats are not much welcome in farm country. Your party comes across a wererat driven into the wilderness along with the rats with whom it kept company. Now, it dreams of revenge on the farmers or millers who defeated its companions. It hopes to create a party of wererats who will give them more than they can handle — and your party looks like it will make nice lycanthropes. It appears to your party in its human form, pretending to be a traveler in distress who hopes to travel with your party for protection. It tries to slip toward the back of the march order and waits for a time when everyone's back is turned to it.

Werewolf. A werewolf spots your party and cannot turn down the opportunity to claim more victims. However, it is clever enough to approach them in its human form, pretending to be a lost traveler in distress. Once your party gets close and drops its guard, it attacks.

Scaling the Encounter: A single lycanthrope can offer a stiff challenge to a low-level party. If your party's average level is 3 or less, feel free to re-roll the encounter. Alternately, if you want to make a werewolf encounter more challenging for a higher-level party, use a pack of them consisting of one werewolf for each multiple of 5 in your party's average level, rounded up.

Treasure: It is assumed that all of these encounters take place away from the lycanthrope's base of operations, so roll on the Individual Treasure table of the appropriate CR to determine what valuables it carries.

Werebears may be an exception to this rule. Because they are territorial, your party may encounter a werebear in or near its lair. In that case, roll on the Treasure Hoard: Challenge 0-4 table to determine its treasure.

Orcs. You may add orcs to the list of humanoids who know that grasslands are dotted with ripe raiding targets — not just villages, but isolated farms and herders who roam the plains as well. A small group of orcs could be a scout party out to get the lay of the land, while a larger group would be an actual raiding party on its way to — or on its way back from — its target.

Your party crosses paths with these orcs, but if they have such a purpose in mind, they may not give pay your party much attention. Their leader may look your party over and decide that they're not worth the bother. But they may also decide to interrogate your party for information about the surrounding area, and they'll get violent if your party is too slow to cooperate. They'll make elf characters a special focus of hostility.

Scaling the Encounter: The baseline encounter group should consist of 1d4 orcs for each multiple of 2 in your party's average level. If your party's average level is 5-9, add an orog as the group's leader. If your party's average level is 10 or higher, use an orc war chief as its leader. If you don't want to run a mass encounter but you still want to provide a higher-level party with a meaningful challenge, feel free to substitute one orog for four orcs as much as you like.

Treasure: If the orcs are coming back from a successful raid, you may roll on the Treasure Hoard: Challenge 0-4 table to determine the fruits of their labor. This is in addition to the individual treasure they carry.

TABLE 4.5
Humans - Grasslands

d20	ENCOUNTER
1	Adventurers
2-4	Bandits
5-7	Farmers
8	Gatherers
9-10	Herders
11	Hunters
12-14	Merchants
15-16	Military
17-18	Nomads
19-20	Pilgrims

Adventurers. Unless your party contains all of the adventurers in your campaign world, it's at least theoretically possible that they'll run into another adventuring party crossing the plains. Perhaps they're pursuing the same objective as your party. Perhaps they have a different mission; perhaps they're headed for a site that your party knows nothing about (like ancient ruins said to hold lost treasures). Perhaps they're lost and starving, or wounded, or cursed.

How they react to your party depends on a variety of factors. Are they rivals pursuing the same goal? If not, perhaps this party is willing to share useful information. In fact, if your party is stuck and having a hard time advancing the storyline of your campaign, a friendly encounter like this can help steer them in the right direction. Differences in alignment may also shape how the two parties react to each other.

Composition of this rival party is up to you and can vary according to circumstance. Any party in the wilderness would be well-advised to have someone accomplished in Survival, such as a ranger, with them. Conversely, a party that is struggling may be in a bad way precisely no one is well-versed in Survival or Nature.

Scaling the Encounter: Unless there is some possibility that this encounter turns hostile, the relative level of the party is mainly a matter of affect. A higher-level party might project self-confidence and calm (or arrogance), while beginning-level party might stumble about, unsure of themselves. If you're leaning towards a hostile encounter, however, consider that the total CR of the party should be roughly two-thirds of your party's average level.

Bandits. Grasslands don't offer many places for a gang of bandits to shelter, but small caves and abandoned buildings may be found here and there. They can also get away with camping in the open, as long as they don't stay in any one spot for too long. Besides, merchants and other travelers taking isolated country roads offer easy targets.

Even though a party of adventurers like yours is better-armed than their typical target, it's not out of the question that they'll attack. They see travelers coming and going all the time, and some of them are armed and look tougher than they turn out if it comes to a fight. It's also possible that they view your party as a threat; they assume that your party is a posse sent out after them — or that your party intends to rob them of what they robbed from others.

Scaling the Encounter: As a rough guideline, the encounter group should contain 1d8 bandits for each level in your party's average level. If your party's average level is 4 or higher, add a bandit captain as their leader. If you don't want to run a mass encounter but you still want these criminals to provide a higher-level party with a meaningful challenge, feel free to substitute one thug for four bandits as much as you like.

Treasure: If your party finds the bandits' hideout, roll on the Treasure Hoard table appropriate to the total CR of the encounter. Do so also if you decide that the bandits encountered are on their way back from a successful raid. Consider that there is also a 20% chance that the bandits have with them a high-value captive whom they intend to ransom. The identity of this captive is left to you as DM, as it should depend on local circumstances and fit into your campaign world.

No Constructs?

Constructs like golems and homunculi present a problem similar to that posed by angels, demons and devils: They don't occur naturally in the Material Plane, so it's hard to make a case for them appearing in a particular type of terrain. They have to be created by someone in order to exist at all. Without any sort of connection to the natural world, they just don't have a role to play in a book about random wilderness encounters. If you want your party to run into a golem while tramping through the plains, you'll have to put it there yourself.

Farmers. Your party crosses paths with 1d8 farmers and farm hands from a nearby village or isolated farmstead traveling to or from market. They have a horse-drawn wagon; if they are going to market it's full of the fruits of their labor, and if they're returning from market they'll have household goods, tools and some extra coin with them.

The farmers are not hostile. They're used to seeing strangers as they travel on business. They're willing to trade as long as the exchange is fair; if your party wants to shortchange them it will take a successful DC 20 Charisma (Persuasion) check. They may be rubes, but they're no fools. If your party has horses or mules available, they may even be interested in buying one on account of theirs being on its last legs, or just because they need another.

Treat the farmers as commoners.

Gatherers. Your party comes across 1d4 gatherers collecting herbs and wild grasses, either for food or medicine. It's possible that your party surprises them, as they work hunched over and close to the ground. However, they are not hostile — they're just laborers with specialized knowledge out doing their job. They may be persuaded to help your party with local lore and/or therapeutic concoctions made from whatever it is they're gathering (see Treasure). They may also ask your party to help them if they have reason to believe that they are in danger (perhaps they had a close brush with monsters recently).

Treat the gatherers as commoners armed with sickles or daggers.

Treasure: In addition to treasure from the Individual Treasure: Challenge 0-4 table, the gatherers have a small stash of helpful non-magical items made from herbs. One such item could be a poultice that heals hit points equal to 1d4+ the Wisdom (Medicine) bonus of whomever applies it after it is kept in place for 24 hours. But that is just one possibility. Mix in any such items that already exist in your campaign world. You can also consult "Narl's Herbal Remedies" in Ramen Sandwich Press' collection of new items, *Tome of the Utility Drawer, Volume I.*

Herders. Your party spots in the distance a herd of sheep, or goats, or some other livestock. There are 2d6 herders in their midst. They may be grazing the animals, or driving them to market. They are not hostile, and since they range far and wide by the nature of their work, they can provide your party with helpful local knowledge. They know all the nearby sources of water, the places where monsters are reputed to reside, gossip from any settlements in the area. They may even have specific knowledge that can help your party get where they want to go.

Treat herders as commoners. They carry crooks or staves that they can wield two-handed as clubs, but they wear no armor.

Hunters. Your party comes across a group of 2d4 hunters mounted on riding horses looking for game among the herd animals that roam the grasslands. Unlike nomads (see below), they are settled people, and they live in the nearest village or town. This is just a short trip for them, not a way of life.

Depending on your party's appearance, they may act with caution, even suspicion at first. Despite the fact that they are armed with bows, they know that they are operating in wilderness away from home, and there are always strange folk about. However, if your party is not hostile to them they are willing to help by trading goods and supplying food and local knowledge. If your wish, have your party make a DC 10 Charisma (Persuasion) check to get on their good side.

Treat hunters as scouts.

Merchants. If your party is playing it safe and sticking to roads or major trails, it's a reasonable bet that they share that route at some point with a caravan consisting of 2d6 merchants and 2d8 guards accompanying a string of horses, mules or giant lizards carrying trade goods.

As a natural first reaction to armed strangers, the caravan guards interpose themselves between your party and the pack animals. You may require a DC 15 Charisma (Persuasion) check to convince them that your party means no harm. In turn, traveling merchants could help your party by selling them necessary items, exchanging hard money for treasure items or providing knowledge of just about anywhere in your campaign world (where is this caravan going, and where did it originate?). A caravan that is low on guards might offer to hire your party as additional security.

Treat the merchants as commoners. Treat the guards as guards, although you may freely substitute veterans for guards if you want the caravan to have more capable escort.

Treasure: Roll once on the Individual Treasure: Challenge 0-4 table for each merchant or guard. In addition, roll once on the Treasure Hoard: Challenge 0-4 table for each merchant present to determine the value of goods and/or hard money in the caravan. You may substitute valuable goods — spices, fine cloth, expensive hardwood, etc. — for art objects or coin as you wish.

Military. Flat, open ground and a relatively comfortable climate create a friendly environment for armies armed with pre-gunpowder weapons — especially armies with mounted soldiers. So if war is a part of your campaign world, your party could encounter an army or part of an army on its way to meet the enemy — or running away from the enemy.

An entire army on the march, or deployed for battle, can be seen from a long ways away in open terrain. However, they're certain to have more important things on their mind than dealing with a party of adventurers, so they're more useful for spectacle and flavor than a meaningful encounter.

A small group of soldiers is most likely a patrol, tasked with scouting ahead of the main army, or on its flanks. Their job is to locate the enemy and, conversely, to prevent enemy scouts from spotting their main force. They won't attack your party without reason to believe that your party is somehow connected to their enemy. However, they do stop your party to grill them for information, and possibly enlist their help with their mission. A larger group is most likely a unit of soldiers hurrying to join the main army — or running away from the fight.

Treat a typical, rank-and-file soldier as a guard. If mounted, the horse is a riding horse. Leaders should qualify as veterans or knights, and they get to ride warhorses if you want them on horseback.

Scaling the Encounter: As a rough guideline, the encounter group should consist of 1d8 guards for each level in your party's average level. If your party's average level is 6 or higher, add a veteran or a knight as the group's leader. If you don't want to run a mass encounter, feel free to substitute one veteran for 12 guards as much as you like. Veterans who are not officers could be rank-and-file soldiers from an elite unit, or bodyguards for the leader.

Goliath

The history of warfare is replete with stories — accurate or not — of individuals who stepped up and performed prodigious deeds in this battle or that. It's not even a matter of courage, necessarily. It's just that, in that particular moment, a lone soldier proves himself very, very good at war and killing.

If your party is high-level so that the guidelines in Scaling the Encounter would create a huge, ungovernable mass of common soldiers, you may replace 40 of them with one gladiator. He's not a leader, just one of the rank-and-file who can fight like 40 men.

Nomads. The open spaces of the plains or steppes are the ideal environment for nomadic peoples who center their lives on herd animals. Whether such peoples live in your campaign world is up to you, but if they do your party comes across a group of 2d6 of them mounted on riding horses. Despite having no fixed abode, they consider a wide stretch of the grasslands to be their territory and treat outsiders with suspicion. You may require a DC 15 Charisma (Persuasion) check, ratcheted down to DC 10 if your party offers them gifts, to win over the nomads, who may then help your party by trading animals suitable as mounts or pack animals, or providing useful local knowledge about nearby settlements (settled peoples being their longstanding enemies), monster lairs, etc.

Treat nomads as tribal warriors who carry shortbows in addition to spears.

Scaling the Encounter: As a rough guideline, the encounter group should contain 1d8 nomads multiplied by your party's average level. If your party's average level is 6 or higher, add a veteran as the group's leader. If you don't want to run a mass encounter, feel free to substitute one thug with a shortbow for four tribal warriors as much as you like.

Pilgrims. The pantheon and nature of religious practice in your campaign world is up to you as the designer of that world. If it makes sense in that context, consider that your party crosses paths with a group of devotees traveling to (or perhaps from) a holy site. Perhaps they have a specific request to make of their deity (ending a drought or plague, curing someone of disease, etc.). Or perhaps it's just a ritual that their religion says they must perform regularly. Depending on how religions work in your world, perhaps their mission is to vandalize a shrine to a rival deity.

Their deity and alignment should dictate how they react to meeting your party. In any event, they are lightly armed at best and they may want to travel in your party's company for safety — especially if they know of a specific hazard in the area, like bandits or monsters. If friendly, they may also be willing to share local knowledge and trade with your party, or even share what divine magic capabilities they possess for your party's benefit.

Roll on Table 4.5.1 to give the encounter a more specific character:

TABLE 4.5.1
Pilgrims - Grasslands

d6	ENCOUNTER
1-2	Acolytes
3	Cultists
4-6	Lay Followers

Acolytes. Your party crosses paths 1d4 monks or junior clerics from a religion of your choice. Treat them as acolytes.

Cultists. Your party crosses paths with 2d6 hard-core followers of an evil deity. How they react to your party is up to you, and should be influenced by the numerical odds for or against them. If their cult involves some kind of sacrifice to their deity, perhaps the cultists consider that your party would do nicely.

Treat the cultists as cultists.

Lay Followers. Your party crosses paths with 2d6 lay followers making a pilgrimage. They're just everyday folk performing an elaborate act of worship, and they're the most likely to need your party's protection as they travel through uninhabited land. Treat them as commoners.

Scaling the Encounter. If you wish to make the encounter more challenging, add one priest or cult leader to the encounter, as appropriate.
➤

Treasure: In addition to whatever treasure they carry on their person, pilgrims may carry with them an offering to their deity. At your discretion, roll on the Treasure Hoard: Challenge 0-4 table to determine its value.

TABLE 4.6

Watch Out! - Grasslands

d10	ENCOUNTER
1	Did You Hear That?
2-4	Hidden Hole
5-6	Loose Ground
7	Marshy Ground
8	Tracks
9	Tripping Hazard
10	Wind Gust

Did You Hear That? Choose a party member to make a DC 15 Wisdom (Survival) or Intelligence (Nature) check. Failure means that that character believes that he or she has heard a noise made by a nearby creature or a dangerous natural phenomenon carried on the wind. It can be as consequential as a dragon's roar in the distance, or as eerily intimate as a rattlesnake's rattle close by. A successful check means that that party member realizes that this is an illusion; either it's not as close as it seems or it isn't real at all. If you wish, roll on Table 4.6.1 for guidance on what your party thinks it hears:

TABLE 4.6.1

Did you Hear That? - Grasslands

d10	They Think They Hear...
1	Clash of Weapons
2	Dragon roaring overhead
3	Footsteps of a large group of humans of humanoids
4	Giant insects buzzing
5	Hoofbeats of horses or other herd animals
6	Rumbling from underground
7	Snake slithering through high grass
8	Voices speaking in Common
9	Voices speaking in Goblin
10	Wolves howling

Hidden Hole. Any given stretch of grasslands may be dotted with animal burrows. They're hard to spot, and it's easy to put your foot in one by accident. Too much weight on a burrow causes it to collapse underfoot. Have your party make a DC 15 Wisdom (Perception) check to spot one that is right in their path in time to avoid it. Failure means that a party member of your choice in the front of march order steps into it, with all of the hazards that come with an unexpected tumble. That party members suffers 1d6 falling damage, with a successful DC 15 Dexterity (Acrobatics) check to halve the damage.

Loose Ground. The terrain undulates where your party is currently located, and they near the crest of a rise from which they can get a good view of the surrounding area. However, a party member — choose one, or a character who wants to get a good look around may literally step forward as the best candidate — steps onto a patch of loose soil. It gives way and the character takes a tumble, suffering 1d6 falling damage. A successful DC 15 Strength (Athletics) or Dexterity (Acrobatics) halves the damage. Whee!

Marshy Ground. Your party comes upon a patch of ground where, for whatever reason, natural drainage patterns allow rainwater to pool, saturating the soil and turning it into muck. Have your party make a DC 15 Wisdom (Survival) check to spot the quagmire before one party member in the front of the march order steps right into it. This doesn't behave like quicksand — there's no danger of drowning in it. But someone who steps into it cannot get out without help. Pulling that character out requires a successful DC 15 Strength (Athletics) check.

Tracks. Your party spots tracks that look like tracks that belong to a monster associated with treasure hoards. They may make a successful DC 15 Wisdom (Survival) check to realize that they are very old, and they will not lead to anything useful. If no one makes a successful check, this may be the start of an amusing (for you as DM, anyway) wild goose chase.

Tripping Hazard. Pick a party member at the front of the march order. That character trips over an unseen obstacle — a rock sticking up out of the ground or a half-buried abandoned weapon or farm implement, for instance. He or she must make a successful DC 10 Strength (Athletics) or Dexterity (Acrobatics) check to avoid a hard fall that causes 1d4 damage — and perhaps no small embarrassment in the eyes of the other party members.

Wind Gust. A sudden gust of wind blows up and catches your party by surprise. If they have made camp for the night, their campfire is extinguished, forcing them to light another one. If they've already used all their wood and kindling, they'll have to go hunting in the dark for more.

If they're carrying torches, they go out. If they're using lanterns, they may lose their grip (see below).

Regardless of whether it's day or night, any party member who is standing must make a DC 5 Strength check to avoid being knocked down. Anyone who is knocked down by the wind immediately loses grasp of anything held in hand. Fragile objects break when they are dropped. In addition, anyone who is knocked down while wearing his or her pack must make a DC 5 Dexterity (Acrobatics) check to avoid the pack falling heavily so that anything containing liquid, such as canteens and potions, breaks and spills.

Clear Terrain

It's easy to think of grasslands as a kind of default setting. In a wargame, you'd probably call it clear terrain, the type that shows up blank on the map and costs the least movement points to cross. But grasslands are anything but boring, and you'll find as broad a range of beasts, humanoids and humans to encounter here as anywhere else. In that sense, they're anything but clear.

HILLS

CHAPTER FIVE

Hills

What are Hills?

It feels odd to try to answer that question too closely. Instinctively, we all understand what hills are: They don't rise as high or as steeply as mountains, but they're anything but flat in the way that plains are flat. They're… you know… *hilly*. But pinning it down as a term of science with a precise definition gets tricky. Different authorities have different ideas about the point at which a hill becomes a mountain, and geographers have even used altitude above sea level instead of relative height to quantify the difference. Again, the most you can say for certain is that hills is that they're not plains, and they're not mountains.

For better or worse, that's pretty much how this book defines hill country. Hills occur in every climate zone. There are hills fertile enough to support livestock and farming at at least subsistence level, as well as barren hills where the only wealth you'll find is of the mineral kind.

Regardless, you'll know you're in hill country from the pull in your legs when you're walking up a hillside and the pull of gravity when you're going down the other side. Certain creatures favor hill country, and that also makes it distinctive. Many winged predators like to nest in the hills, both to gain vantage over the surrounding country, and to make their homes harder to find. Caves and hollows carved out of hillsides provide plenty of shelter for creatures that want it — as well as bandits, fugitives, hermits and other humans who don't want to be found. You can certainly find adventure if you head for the hills.

What Do You Find in Hills?

When you determine that a random encounter is in order, roll on Table 5.1 to determine the category:

TABLE 5.1

Encounter Type - Hills

d20	CATEGORY
1-5	Aggressive Creatures (Table 5.2)
6-11	Neutral Creatures (Table 5.3)
12-15	Humanoids (Table 5.4)
16-17	Humans (Table 5.5)
18-20	Watch Out! (Table 5.6)

Then, roll on the appropriate table to determine the creature, person or thing encountered.

The range at which an encounter starts should vary depending on local conditions. High ground, such as a hilltop or ridge, should give a commanding view of the surrounding area. Your party can spot potential foes from a distance up there. On the other hand, undulations in the terrain and obstacles like boulders obstruct line of sight, so that your party may not see what they're up against until it's right up against them. This is especially true if someone or something is observing your party from higher ground without being seen itself, and it can remain concealed while closing the range.

TABLE 5.2

Aggressive Creatures - Hills

d100	ENCOUNTER
1-3	Ankheg
4-5	Basilisk
6-12	Bird of Prey
13-14	Bulette
15-16	Chimera
17-20	Cougar
21-23	Cyclops
24-25	Earth Elemental
26-28	Ettin
29-30	Gargoyle
31-33	Gorgon
34-38	Griffon
39-41	Harpy
42-49	Insects
50-51	Manticore
52-53	Medusa
54-56	Mud Mephits
57-60	Ogres
61-62	Oni
63	Purple Worm
64	Roc
65-69	Scorpions
70-74	Snakes
75-79	Spiders
80-81	Troll
82-88	Undead
89-94	Wolf
95-96	Worgs
97-98	Wyvern
99-100	Xorn

Ankheg. These burrowing monstrosities are drawn to the more fertile hills and vales, where they can prey on wild herd animals that taste just as good as livestock. As your party passes overhead, an ankheg in its tunnel mistakes your party for a herd of goats. It breaches the surface and attacks.

Scaling the Encounter: If you wish to make the encounter more challenging, the encounter group consists of one ankheg for each multiple of 3 in your party's average level. Each ankheg emerges from a point no closer than 20-40 feet to any other attacking ankheg.

Treasure: Ankhegs leave a lot of wild animal bones behind them in their tunnels, but in the wilderness they find few targets that leave behind treasure. You may roll once on the Individual Treasure: Challenge 0-4 table for each ankheg present, if you wish.

A basilisk may be too much for a beginner-level party..

Basilisk. Your party passes a hollow in a hillside. Unfortunately for hapless creatures that pass by it — or even worse, that try to shelter inside — it houses a basilisk. As your party passes, have your party make a DC 15 Wisdom (Perception) or Wisdom (Survival) check to hear something stirring inside this little cave, or at least to intuit that something is there.

Scaling the Encounter: A basilisk may be a bit too much for a beginning-level party. Feel free to re-roll for another encounter. Conversely, if you want to run a more challenging encounter for a higher-level party, your party encounters two basilisks sharing a lair.

Treasure: The lair contains scattered valuables belonging to the basilisk's previous victims. Roll on the appropriate Treasure Hoard table, according to the total CR of the encounter. If there is more than one basilisk in the encounter, consider that basilisk eggs may also be present for the taking.

Bird of Prey. A bird of prey, or a flock of them, wheels overhead, then swoops down on your party. Keen-eyed,

but bird-brained all the same, the bird has spotted something in your party as food — a familiar or small summoned creature is an obvious choice, but it could just be travelers rations, like strips of cured meat left in the open. To determine which species, roll on Table 5.2.1:

TABLE 5.2.1
Birds of Prey - Hills

d10	ENCOUNTER
1-2	Eagle
3	Giant Eagle
4-5	Blood Hawks
6-7	Hawks
8-9	Owl
10	Giant Owl

Eagle. One eagle swoops down on your party, aiming itself at something it has identified as food.

Giant Eagle. A giant eagle has spotted your party. Giant eagles are intelligent and may respond if your party tries to flag them down. Though it cannot speak when spoken to, a successful DC 15 Charisma (Persuasion) check by someone who speaks Common or Auran persuades it to do your party a service, if it is within its power to accomplish it. This may involve delivering a written message or token, or guiding your party to a place that it knows, or even traveling with them for a while as an airborne lookout.

Blood Hawks. A flock of 2d6 blood hawks swoop down on your party. They concentrate on a single target — most likely a pack animal, but they may settle for a small humanoid as the next best thing.

Hawks. A flock of 2d10 hawks targets your party. They're probably going after the party's rations, but they may also have spotted rodents or small reptiles who are literally scurrying along the ground at your party's feet. To the extent that your party is in their way, the hawks attack them.

Owl. Owls hunt at night, so you should re-roll this encounter if it takes place during the day. Otherwise, one owl has spotted food as your party rests outdoors overnight. Most likely, it has spotted a small animal companion or familiar, or rations left out in the open.

Giant Owl. Likewise, a giant owl encounter is most suitable for night, so you should re-roll this encounter if it takes place during the day. One giant owl spots food in your party's camp.

Bulette. Bad luck — a land shark senses your party walking overhead and figures they're its next meal. To create a little drama, you may require a successful DC 15 Wisdom (Perception) check to sense the ground rumbling; you may then allow a DC 15 Intelligence (Nature) check to identify it as a bulette before it breaches the surface.

Scaling the Encounter: A bulette may be a bit much for a lower-level party to handle, so if your party's average level is less than 5, feel free to re-roll for a different encounter. Conversely, if your average party level is higher than 10, you may add another bulette to make it more challenging.

Treasure: Bulettes hunt on the move, so treasure that belonged to its previous victims is scattered far and wide. However, you may allow your party a DC 10 Wisdom (Survival) check to follow the trail back to its last kill. If successful, roll on the Individual Treasure: Challenge 0-4 table to determine what they find.

Chimera. Your party spots a winged monstrosity with three different animal heads circling above them. This can only mean one thing: A chimera has spotted them as potential prey. You may allow your party a DC 15 Wisdom (Perception) check. If successful, they notice the chimera at a range of about 200 feet, allowing them a little time to react before they are within range of its attacks. If not, they first become aware of the chimera at a range of only 100 feet.

Scaling the Encounter: If your party's average level is lower than 6, a chimera may be more than you want to throw at them. Feel free to re-roll for a different encounter.

Alternately, consider that your party comes upon a chimera that has been injured in a fight with a manticore or a wyvern. Your party may get to watch the dazzling air-to-air combat from a safe distance. The chimera is reduced to half of its hit points by the time it drives off its enemy and turns on your party. Deep gashes and embedded manticore spikes are still visible. It's wounded, but it's still hungry — in fact, perhaps it needs to feed in order to heal and your party looks like an easier target than one of its monstrous rivals.

Cougar. As your party passes a boulder, a rocky outcropping, or some other kind of elevated ground, require a DC 15 Wisdom (Perception) check to notice a lone cougar crouched and ready to pounce. It's used to hunting deer and goats here in the hills, but your party will do. Failure means that they don't spot it before it springs its ambush.

Treat cougars as panthers.

Wait... That's a Panther?
Looking into the taxonomy of large cats reveals that the name "panther" covers a range of predatory felines that you wouldn't want to face down when they're hungry. The black panther is related to jaguars and leopards, as is the less famous white panther. The Florida panther, however, is a subspecies of cougar (or mountain lion), which in turn is a separate species from black and white panthers. But it all seems to tie together well enough so that it makes sense to treat cougars as panthers.

Cyclops. Your party sees a cyclops roaming the countryside, unconcerned about its lack of depth perception. It may be on its way to meet with another cyclops living on the next hill over, or it may be out to rustle herd animals to add to its flock. If you wish, it could be out grazing its flock or herd, in which case it's accompanied by 3d6 goats or sheep (treat sheep as deer). In any event, it sees your party as prey — a delicacy, compared to eating goat or mutton all the time — and it attacks.

Scaling the Encounter: If your party's average level is lower than 6, a cyclops may be more than you want to throw at them. Feel free to re-roll for a different encounter.

Earth Elemental. An earth elemental found on the Material Plane was most likely summoned here, and it found itself unable to return to the Elemental Plane of Earth after its summoner was done with it. It is also possible that it has crossed over via a natural portal with the Plane of Earth. A rugged hillside dotted with boulders and natural caves burrowed into its natural element could house such a crossing point.

Your party may feel the tremors before it sees one earth elemental approach them. You may allow them to interact with it if someone knows Terran or has the capability to control elementals. Otherwise, it's likely that the elemental will treat your party as an enemy; it either hears echoes of its original summoner, who brought it to this plane to attack enemies, or it bears an uncontrollable grudge against the Material Plane, whose residents are always trying to dominate elementals.

Scaling the Encounter: If your party's average level is lower than 5 an earth elemental may be more than you want to throw at them. Feel free to re-roll for a different encounter. Conversely, if you want to run a more challenging encounter for a higher-level party, consider that your party has encountered two earth elementals.

Ettin. Your party hears two loud voices coming from beyond a slope that blocks line of sight, or they see two giant heads cheek-by-jowl poking up above it. Have your party make a DC 15 Intelligence (Nature) check to recognize that it's an ettin arguing with itself. If they choose not to avoid the ettin, it calls out to your party and demands that they help settle a dispute. It should be something that the party would find awkward or at least pointless to answer — for instance, whether or not kobold legs are too salty to eat. No matter what answer the party gives, one or both heads accuses them of unfairly favoring the other and the ettin attacks.

Alternately, the ettin stops short when it spots the party and realizes that it's hungry after arguing with itself for such a long time.

Scaling the Encounter: As amusing as ettins can be if you run the encounter with the right sense of humor, one is a bit much for a party with an average level of less than 4.

Treasure: The ettin carries some coins in a pouch looped around its loincloth. Roll twice on the Individual Treasure: Challenge 0-4 table.

Gargoyle. Gargoyles that live up in the hills have probably found an abandoned house or some other structure in which to make their lair. If they're lucky, they found a ruined fortification on strategic (or at least, it used to be strategically located) high ground. Your party crosses paths with one gargoyle that is just bored and looking for someone or something to torment for amusement. It uses an elevated vantage point like a boulder or a rocky outcropping to observe its prey. It remains perfectly still until your party comes close enough to ambush. You may allow your party a DC 15 Wisdom (Perception) check to notice the gargoyle moving just a bit and identify it as a living thing before it attacks.

Some gargoyles are just looking to torment someone for amusement.

Scaling the Encounter: If you wish to make the encounter more challenging, the encounter group consists of one gargoyle for each multiple of 3 in your party's average level.

Treasure: If your party encounters gargoyles in their lair, roll on the Treasure Hoard table appropriate to the CR of the encounter.

Gorgon. Your party approaches a gorgon's lair — perhaps it is a cluster of rocks, or a small hollow carved out of a hillside. Petrified chunks lie scattered about outside the lair; you may allow your party a DC 15 Wisdom (Survival) check to realize that they're crumbs leftover from the gorgon's previous meals. The monster is, of course, quite happy to prey on your party, saving them for later if it isn't hungry at the moment.

Scaling the Encounter: If your party's average level is lower than 6, a gorgon may be more than you want to throw at them. Feel free to re-roll for a different encounter.

Treasure: The lair contains scattered valuables belonging to the gorgon's previous victims. Roll on the Treasure Hoard: Challenge 0-4 table to determine the total haul.

Griffon. Griffons enjoy hunting in forests and flatlands but they nest in elevated places, and hill country offers them places to do just that. A griffon spots your party and, pleased that it hasn't had to range far afield to hunt, it goes for one of their mounts or pack animals — or at least, it thinks it has spotted a mount or a pack animal.

Scaling the Encounter: If you wish to make the encounter more challenging, your party encounters a flock (or pack?) of griffons hunting together. There is one for each multiple of 3 in your party's average level.

Harpy. It is a thoroughly unsettling thing to hear a harpy's song echoing through the hills and vales, but strangely hard to resist it all the same. Harpies are not as common in hill country as they are in littoral areas, where they prey on sailors seduced by their siren call. But they still manage to find victims among herders and hapless travelers who come within the sound of their voice. Your party comes within range of a harpy's bewitching voice, which emanates from nearby high ground. Whether or not they can resist its dangerous charm is up to them and their saving throws.

Scaling the Encounter: If you wish to make the encounter more challenging, use a veritable harpy choir as the encounter group, consisting of two harpies for each multiple of 3 in your party's average level.

Treasure: By definition, a harpy's perch is its lair, so it's unlikely that this encounter takes place far from its home. Roll on the Treasure Hoard table appropriate to the CR of the encounter to determine the accumulated belongings from its earlier victims.

Insects. You may not think of insects as predatory, but they feed without giving it much thought to who might be put out by their actions and they cause trouble in their own way. Some are viciously aggressive when they feel threatened. Roll on Table 5.2.2 to determine the insects encountered:

TABLE 5.2.2
Insects - Hills

d4	ENCOUNTER
1-3	Swarm of Insects
4	Giant Wasps

Swarm of Insects. One swarm of insects — call them gnats, midges, mosquitos, whatever you will — descends upon your party and makes their lives decidedly unpleasant.

Giant Wasps. Your party comes upon two giant wasps guarding a nest hanging from a rocky outcropping or the crumbling eaves of an abandoned structure. They are in a sufficiently bad temper to attack anything that comes close to the nest.

Scaling the Encounter: If you wish to make the encounter more challenging (or more of a nuisance, depending on how you look at it), the encounter group consists of 1d4 giant wasps for each multiple of 2 in your party's average level, or 1d4 swarms of insects one additional swarm for each level in your party's average level.

Manticore. Your party spots a large winged beast in the sky. You may require a successful DC 15 Intelligence (Nature) check to recognize it as a manticore on the hunt before it gets close enough to attack. Once it gets close enough to launch its spikes, it may choose to toy with its prey just to watch them squirm. In this case, it demands some kind of bribe in exchange for sparing them — a bargain it will keep, if your party makes the right offer. A suitable offer might take the form of treasure or humiliating servitude that amuses the manticore. However, if there is war brewing in this part of your campaign world, perhaps the manticore is working for one of the combatants as a scout — in which case, useful information about enemy dispositions would satisfy it.

Scaling the Encounter: If you wish to make the encounter more challenging, consider that there are multiple manticores working as a team. This is especially plausible

if they are on a scouting mission for an army. In such a case, the encounter group consists of one manticore for each multiple of 5 in your party's average level, rounded up.

Medusa. It may be inconspicuous enough so that you have your party make a successful DC 10 Wisdom (Perception) check to notice it, but they pass by what appears to be a realistic statue of a small animal. In fact, a medusa has made its lair in a nearby hillside cave where it surrounds itself with the petrified remains of its victims. From within its lair, it spots your party and decides that they would supplement its existing collection nicely. If your party investigates, they'll find more and more such statues as they approach the actual lair.

Scaling the Encounter: If your party's average level is lower than 6, a medusa may be more than you want to throw at them. Feel free to re-roll for a different encounter.

Treasure: The medusa's gaze petrifies flesh, but not valuables. To total up the bits and pieces that once belonged to her humanoid victims, roll on the Treasure Hoard: Challenge 5-10 table.

Mud Mephits. Your party comes across 1d4+1 mud mephits lounging by a stream, a pool, or even just a muddy patch of hillside. They're droning on and on to each other about petty complaints — the weather, physical discomfort, being picked on by larger elementals, anything. When they notice your party, they turn on them, whining and begging them in their native tongues for valuable items like coins and gems. If your party ignores them, the mephits pursue, continuing to drone and whine until your party drives them off.

Scaling the Encounter: If you wish to make the encounter more challenging, the encounter group consists of 1d4 mud mephits for each plus one mud mephit for each level in your party's average level — it's a mud mephit pity party!

Ogres. Your party crosses paths with a foraging party of ogres. Whether you want to stage any meaningful interaction with these undersized giants is up to you, but it should surprise no one if they decide that your party is as good a target as any they are likely to find in the near future, whether they are looking for things or food (or both).

Scaling the Encounter: The encounter group consists of two ogres for each multiple of 3 in your party's average level. If your party is only 1st Level, consider that one half-ogre confronts them.

Treasure: These ogres are away from their lair. The treasure for this encounter includes whatever they carry on them, nothing more. Assuming your party remains in possession of the field, total up the CR of all ogres killed and roll on the appropriate Individual Treasure table.

A medusa decorates it's lair with the remains of it's petrified victims.

Oni. Once an ogre mage has had its way in a community, it's only sensible to find another hunting ground before the locals rally and figure out what to do about it. Traveling the uninhabited lands between settlements, it tries to befriend your party while using its *Change Shape* ability to disguise itself as someone trustworthy and inoffensive; use a form that is unlikely to arouse your party's suspicions. If they allow the oni to travel with them, it bides its time until they make camp for the night. It volunteers to take the first watch, then it strikes once everyone else is asleep.

If you wish, you may allow your party a DC 20 Intelligence (Arcana) check to suspect that this apparently friendly stranger might be using magic to alter its appearance.

Scaling the Encounter: An oni may be a bit too much for a low-level party. Feel free to re-roll for another encounter. Conversely, if you want to run a more challenging encounter for a higher-level party, use an encounter group consisting of two oni if your party's average level is 10 or higher.

Purple Worm. It's never a good sign when the hillside beneath your feet rumbles, quivers and buckles. In this case, a purple worm, using its tremorsense, has spotted your party as its next meal. The worm's approach should give them enough time to sense that something is amiss and do something about it; you may allow them a DC 15 Intelligence (Nature) check to realize that it's a purple worm causing the disturbance underfoot. Combat begins when it breaches the surface within striking distance of your party.

Scaling the Encounter: If your party's average level is lower than 15, a purple worm may be more than you want to throw at them. Feel free to re-roll for a different encounter.

Treasure: Cutting open and gutting a purple worm is quite a chore, but it should reveal valuables that belonged to its previous prey — and purple worms eat a lot. Roll on the Treasure Hoard: Challenge 11-16 table to determine total haul.

Roc. The sky darkens for a moment. Your party looks up and sees a roc wheeling overhead. Even at such a height, it's large enough to block out the sun while it hunts. As to whether or not it tries to make your party into its next meal, see Scaling the Encounter.

Scaling the Encounter: Rocs are fearsome opponents. If your party's average level is lower than 11, a roc may be more than you want to throw at them. Feel free to re-roll for a different encounter.

Or you may choose to give your party a scare, just for effect. Since the roc probably makes its lair in nearby mountains, it has just begun its hunt and it feels that it can still pick and choose at this point. It swoops down on your party from a great height — close enough for them to look in the eyes of this gargantuan avian predator. Then it decides that your party is not worth its bother, and flies off.

Scorpions. Your party takes a rest halt by some rocks, disturbing the scorpions that live among and under them. 1d8 scorpions attack your party. They have stingers, and they don't hesitate to use them.

Scaling the Encounter: If your party's average level is 5 or higher, consider that they have taken some shade from a large rock, or a rock formation, and in so doing they have disturbed one or more giant scorpions. In this case, the encounter group consists of one giant scorpion for each multiple of 5 in the party's average level, rounded up.

Snakes. Whether they're slithering along a grassy hillside or among some rocks, snakes tend to disappear into the ground cover and you may not see them until it's too late to avoid them. You may allow your party to make a DC 15 Wisdom (Perception) or Wisdom (Survival) check to realize that the front of the march order is about to have a close encounter with a snake. This should give them enough time to take evasive action, although you may consider that this simply means they aren't surprised when the snake lashes out.

Roll on Table 5.2.3 to determine the size of the snake(s) encountered:

TABLE 5.2.3
Snakes - Hills

d10	ENCOUNTER
1-4	Swarm of Poisonous Snakes
5-9	Poisonous Snake
10	Giant Poisonous Snake

Swarm of Poisonous Snakes. Your party comes across a shallow depression which is, literally, a snake pit with one swarm of poisonous snakes present. You may decrease the DC to notice the snakes to 5, to reflect the facts that there are more snakes present and the terrain feature is relatively easy to notice.

Poisonous Snake. Your party comes close to stepping on one poisonous snake.

Giant Poisonous Snake. Your party comes across one giant poisonous snake. You may decrease the DC to notice the snakes to 10 to reflect its size.

Spiders. On a hillside where there are not a lot of trees, there aren't many places for spiders to build the large webs that make them so hazardous in forests and underground spaces. But that's not to say that you won't find them here. Instead, they'll come at you from under a rock or a burrow when you have stopped to take a breather. If it's a rocky hillside, it's also possible that two boulders are close enough together that spiders can build their web between them and offer a hazard similar to (though easier to spot than) a spider web that spans two tree trunks in a dense forest. Roll on Table 5.2.4 to determine what kind of spider could bite you when you're not looking:

TABLE 5.2.4
Spiders - Hills

d8	ENCOUNTER
1-3	Spiders
4-7	Giant Wolf Spider
8	Phase Spider

Spiders. These spiders are small, but their venom packs a punch. During a rest stop, someone in your party sits or leans against the rock under which they are hiding and disturbs them. 2d8 spiders come out in a mood to bite whomever bothered them. They spread out and attack a single target from various angles.

Alternately, if your party is picking their way through a rocky hillside, someone brushes a web stretched between two boulders. When your party gets close enough, the spiders attack.

Giant Wolf Spider. Wolf spiders do not weave webs; they burrow into the ground and they either take whatever stumbles into their lair, or they emerge to ambush prey. As your party approaches, vibrations in the ground tell them that something juicy has come to their doorstep, and 1d4 giant wolf spiders attack. You may allow your party a DC 15 Wisdom (Perception) check to notice a hole in the ground large enough to fit a big spider, and if successful, a DC 15 Intelligence (Nature) check to realize that it's a wolf spider burrow.

Phase Spider. Phase spiders are quite fearless, and they use their ability to jump back and forth between planes to conduct hit-and-run attacks, wearing the party down until they are all incapacitated or dead.

Scaling the Encounter: If you want to create a more challenging encounter with ordinary spiders, you may add another 2d8 to the encounter group — having too many, however, not only creates an unwieldy encounter, but it assumes an awfully large population of spiders for a single web. To create a more challenging encounter with giant wolf spiders, use an encounter group consisting of 1d4 plus a number of additional giant wolf spiders equal to your party's average level.

A phase spider may be a bit too much for a beginning-level party. Feel free to re-roll for another encounter in that case. However, if you wish to make the encounter more challenging, the encounter group consists of one phase spider for each multiple of 5 in the party's average level.

Troll. A troll haunts this hillside, preying on stray livestock and other animals. It also extracts a toll from intelligent creatures that enter into this territory that it claims for itself, and it doesn't mind killing and eating anyone who refuses. Your party passes a large rock that it uses for shelter. It steps out and confronts them and demands something from them before it lets them pass — perhaps one of the party's pack animals as its toll, or a suitable amount of coins. It fights rather than let anyone pass for free.

Scaling the Encounter: If your party's average level is lower than 5, a troll may be more than you want to throw at them. Feel free to re-roll for a different encounter. Conversely, if your party's average level is 10 or higher, feel free to add one troll to the encounter — a tag-team of trolls.

Treasure: The troll's racket has worked well enough in the past: Its victims pay one way or another, and it has accumulated a decent hoard. Searching the area turns up its stash, thrown in to a pile, on a successful DC 10 Wisdom (Perception) check. Roll on the Treasure Hoard: Challenge 5-10 table to determine the contents.

Undead. Whether the hills through which your party tramps are barren or verdant matters little to the undead; they may haunt any wilderness regardless of its scenic qualities. They may come from barrows and cairns that dot the landscape; or from the fallen in battles both great and small; or those who perished far from home at the hand of beasts, monsters, or murderers and never received the proper rites. Roll on Table 5.2.5 to determine the undead abomination that greets your party:

TABLE 5.2.5
Undead - Hills

d12	ENCOUNTER
1	Ghost
2-3	Ghouls/Ghasts
4	Shadows
5-7	Skeletons
8	Specter
9	Wight
10	Wraith
11-12	Zombies

Ghost. That is no optical illusion; the ethereal form flitting across the hillside really is a ghost. It is most likely the remnant of someone who died a
➤

miserable death in the wilderness. Whatever the case, you may make this into a hostile encounter by having the ghost try to possess a member of your party so that it may resolve unfinished business from its former life.

Ghouls/Ghasts. An encounter with ghouls is most likely to take place at night, although the gloom at the bottom of a vale as the sun disappears behind the hills may work well enough for that purpose. Two ghouls (or one ghast) approach your party, driven by mindless hunger for their flesh.

Shadows. In the gloom caused by higher ground blocking out the rising or setting sun, the dark shape flitting toward your party may seem like a trick that the mind plays with what the corner of the eye glimpses. But it's not an illusion, it's undead! Without thinking or feeling, two shadows attack the nearest party member, eager to drain the life from another victim and create one more of their own kind.

Skeletons. Your party comes across the undead remnants of an ancient conflict: 1d6 skeletons carrying broken weapons and draped with fragments of the armor they wore in life. Perhaps they were soldiers killed in a skirmish, or part of an army that made its last stand on this hilltop. Perhaps they were adventurers or explorers ambushed by brigands — or perhaps they were bandits themselves, who were hunted down in the name of justice or revenge, or who fell out among themselves. Driven by necromantic echoes of the end of their lives, they're looking for a fight.

Specter. Specters prefer to come out at night, when it is completely dark; but in deep vales where the surrounding hills cast their shadows, they may appear at dusk and dawn as well. It isn't darkness, but it's close enough. Your party comes upon one specter that was once someone who perished in the wilderness, but all connections to who and what it was in life no longer exist. Only blind hatred of the living drives it to attack your party on sight.

Wight. Your party makes camp not far from a cluster of burial sites. Whether they are hollows dug out of the hillside or cairns or barrows improvised out here in the wilderness is up to you as DM and arbiter of what makes the most sense for your campaign world. Unfortunately for your party, at least one of the occupants has become a wight, and it rises from its tomb to attack them while they are most vulnerable.

Wraith. Monumental burial sites — even if they're hastily improvised — can house a wraith. As your ➤

party passes by, they can see that the site is ringed by barren and blasted ground with only withered grass to show that it once supported life. A cold, charcoal-gray mist emerges and resolves itself into a wraith, which then attacks your party, acting out the resentment that it bore at the end of its natural life.

Zombies. Your party come across 1d4 zombies who have been programmed to kill every living thing they encounter. The source of the necromancy that created these zombies we leave to you. Perhaps they slipped the leash of their creator and they now wander the land mindlessly looking for victims.

Scaling the Encounter: Ghosts and wraiths always work alone. The base encounter group for specters also consists of only one of its kind.

A wraith may be too much for a beginning-level party, so feel free to re-roll the encounter in that case. With specters, you may create a more challenging encounter by using two for each multiple of 3 in your party's average level, with all of them being part of a group that perished *en masse*.

Ghouls/Ghasts: If you wish to make the encounter more challenging, the encounter group consists of two ghouls (or one ghast) each multiple of 4 in your party's average level. Feel free to mix and match ghouls and ghasts as long as you maintain the right proportion of total CR to average party level.

Shadows: The encounter group consists of two shadows for each multiple of 3 in your party's average level.

Skeletons: If you wish to make the encounter more challenging, the encounter group consists of 1d4 skeletons plus one additional skeleton for each level in your party's average level. You may substitute one warhorse skeleton for two skeletons.

Wights: A wight may be a bit too much for a beginning-level party. Feel free to re-roll for another encounter. Conversely, if you want to run a more challenging encounter for a higher-level party, add one zombie minion for each level in your party's average level above 3.

Zombies: If you wish to make the encounter more challenging, the encounter group consists of 1d4 zombies plus one additional zombie for each level of your party's average level. If the average party level is 3 or higher, you may use an encounter group consisting of one ogre zombie for each multiple of 3 ➤

In the party's average level.

Treasure: Most likely, ghosts are encountered in or near what passes for a lair with them and you may consider that there they keep possessions that they had in life. Roll on the Treasure Hoard: Challenge 0-4 table for the contents of their stash. You may require a successful DC 15 Wisdom (Perception) check to find its exact location.

Likewise, wights and wraiths do not stray far from their place of burial, which are usually constructed as monuments to the dead. Therefore, their location should be self-apparent. Roll on the Treasure Hoard table appropriate to the total CR of the encounter

With ghouls, ghasts, skeletons and zombies, they may have with them some remains of what they had on their person at the time of their death. Roll on the Individual Treasure table appropriate to the total CR of the encounter (rounded up to the nearest whole number).

Wolves. Your party meets a pack of wolves on the prowl. Roll on Table 5.2.6 to determine whether your party encounters wolves or dire wolves:

TABLE 5.2.6
Wolves - Hills

d6	ENCOUNTER
1-2	Dire Wolf
4-6	Wolves

Dire Wolves. One dire wolf sets upon your party, leaping from a boulder or charging down from higher ground. As their name suggests, dire wolves are vicious and fearless and the attack regardless of the numerical odds.

Wolves. Your party meets a pack of 1d4+1 wolves on the prowl. They split into two groups and maneuver to attack your party from the flanks.

Scaling the Encounter: If you wish to make the encounter more challenging, the encounter group consists of two dire wolves for each multiple of 3 in your party's average level, or 1d4 wolves plus one additional wolf for each level in your party's average level.

Treasure: Furriers in your world may be willing to ➤

pay for wolf pelts. How much is ultimately up to you, but 2 gp is a reasonable baseline price for a normal wolf pelt and 3 gp for a dire wolf pelt. Dire wolf pelts are not necessarily more desirable, but they are larger and offer more fur to work with.

Furriers in your world may be willing to pay for wolf pelts.

Worgs. Your party crosses paths with one or more worgs. It's possible that they are wild. But it is also possible that they were domesticated, but escaped or lost their goblinoid masters — in which case, the presence of worgs could indicate that there are goblins or hobgoblins nearby. In fact, a large group of worgs without their riders could indicate that a whole goblinoid tribe was wiped out, and their mounts are now wandering without anyone to keep them. In any event, they are feeling hungry and mean, and your party looks like a good target regardless of the numerical odds.

Scaling the Encounter: If you wish to make the encounter more challenging, the encounter group consists of a pack of escaped or abandoned worgs, 1d4 for each multiple of 2 in your party's average level. A pack of worgs might have defected *en masse*, or been left to their own devices after an entire tribe of goblins was slaughtered.

Wyvern. A wyvern has emerged from its nearby lair to hunt and it spots your party from above. It is either very hungry or very aggressive, so it swoops down to attack despite the odds.

Scaling the Encounter: If your party's average level is lower than 6, a wyvern with its blood up may be more than you want to throw at them. Feel free to re-roll for a different encounter.

Xorn. It's one of the last things you'd expect to meet among verdant hills: a weird tripodal beast with its maw and three arms emerging from the top of its head. But here it is, all the same. Your party comes across a xorn burrowing into the hillside in search of food. It is convinced that it has located a vein of precious metal or raw gems. It could be a small fortune to your party, but to the xorn, it's digging for its all-important next meal — and it's willing to fight for possession of what it regards as its kill. As soon as it realizes that your party is there, combat begins.

Scaling the Encounter: If your party's average level is lower than 5, a xorn may be more than you want to throw at them. Feel free to re-roll for a different encounter.

TABLE 5.3
Neutral Creatures - Hills

d100	ENCOUNTER
1-5	Brown Bear
6-10	Elk
11-13	Awakened Shrub
14-18	Axe Beaks
19-24	Badgers
25-28	Black Bear
29-36	Boar
37-39	Centipede
40-41	Cockatrice
42-50	Deer
51	Dragon
52-54	Giant
55-64	Goats
65-69	Hippogriff
70-78	Horses
79-84	Mules
85-87	Pegasus
88-94	Rats
85-100	Weasels
101-105	Bats
106-110	Vultures

+10 to die roll in temperate and tropical hills

Brown Bear. Your party spots a brown bear prowling around for food. If they are resting, the bear comes sniffing around, drawn by whatever rations they are carrying. If your party just wants to scare it off, require a DC 15 Intelligence (Nature) or Wisdom (Survival) check. Success means that the bear takes the hint and lumbers away. Failure means that the bear charges them.

Elk. Your party spots a herd of 1d6 bulls and 3d6 cows grazing among the trees. If your party attacks them, only the males fight, covering the fleeing females.

Even if your party does not behave in a threatening manner, the bulls may mistake their actions and attack anyway. Have your party make a DC 15 Intelligence (Nature) or Wisdom (Survival) check. Failure means that someone has made a false move that sets off the males and they charge.

Scaling the Encounter: If you wish to make the encounter more challenging, your party sees a lone (and rare) giant elk at a distance. As they approach it they realize that it's larger than it seemed. Confident in its power as an alpha of its kind, it attacks your party if it senses any hostile intent (remember that giant elk have the ability to understand certain languages).

Perhaps it is bad luck in your campaign world to hunt a giant elk. If your party kills it, each party member is cursed as if affected by the spell *bane*, except that the effect lasts until it is magically dispelled, or until those who did the deed atone for it.

Treasure: Elk are hunted for food wherever they share territory with humans. Perhaps a nearby butcher will pay 2 gp or thereabouts for a fresh carcass.

Awakened Shrub. Just as trees in pristine forests can become sentient through mysterious enchantments, more humble plants that dot the wilderness can also awaken. Your party comes into contact with one or more such awakened shrubs among the plants that dot the hillside. Perhaps a party member takes advantage of it to answer the call of nature. Perhaps it produces berries that look appetizing. These or similar actions cause the shrub to express alarm.

Even your party has done mischief to it, an encounter with an awakened shrub is not necessarily hostile. If your party asks it for help, a successful DC 10 Charisma (Persuasion) check wins it over, but the DC is 15 if your party has harmed it in some way. Help from an awakened shrub includes providing knowledge of the surrounding area.

Scaling the Encounter: If you wish to make the encounter more challenging, the encounter group consists of one awakened shrub for each multiple of 3 in your party's average level, rounded up.

Axe Beaks. Your party comes across a hunting pack of 1d4+2 of these odd-looking, bad-tempered flightless birds. They don't like having their hunt interrupted, but it's not a sure thing that they'll attack. You may have your party make a DC 15 Intelligence (Nature) or Wisdom (Survival) check. Failure means that a party member has made a false move that angers the axe beaks, which then attack the party.

Badgers. Your party comes across two badgers out in the open. They spot your party, then dart for their nearby burrow. If your party investigates, they see two pairs of eyes like black marbles glinting in the gloom. Have your party make a DC 15 Intelligence (Nature) or Wisdom (Survival) check. Failure means that a party member has made a false move that activates the badgers' fight-or-

flight response. Their burrow only has one opening, so they feel cornered and fight like badgers.

Scaling the Encounter: If you wish to make the encounter more challenging, use an encounter group of two giant badgers.

Neutral creatures always have a reason behind their attack.

Black Bear. Your party spots a black bear prowling around for food. If they are resting, the bear comes around, drawn by their rations. If your party just wants to scare it off, require a DC 15 Intelligence (Nature) or Wisdom (Survival) check. Success means that the bear takes the hint and lumbers away. Failure does not necessarily mean that the bear attacks, but it does stand its ground. If they attack it, the bear defends itself. At that point, require another DC 15 Intelligence (Nature) or Wisdom (Survival) check. Failure means that someone has made a false move, provoking the bear to attack. Otherwise, it eventually takes the hint and retreats.

Boar. Your party spots 1d4 wild boar rooting around the hillside for food. Boar are popular targets for hunters. They'll fight back if attacked — indeed, the challenge they present is part of the appeal of hunting them. But they have also developed a fight-or-flight instinct, and if your party wishes to avoid a fight, you may have them make a DC 15 Wisdom (Survival) or Intelligence (Nature) group check to scare the boar off.

Scaling the Encounter: If you wish to make the encounter more challenging, use an encounter group consisting of one giant boar for each multiple of 3 in your party's average level. Giant boar are even more aggressive than their smaller cousins and they charge anyone who disturbs them.

Treasure: Boar meat is good eating for many folk. Perhaps a nearby butcher will pay 2 gp or thereabouts for a fresh carcass. The price might go up to 5 gp for a giant boar.

Centipede. Have your party make a DC 15 Intelligence (Nature) or Wisdom (Survival) check. Failure means that no one notices the giant centipede making ripples in the grass or winding its way among the rocks and someone in the front of the march order comes dangerously close to stepping on it. It responds by attacking that character. Success means that they notice the giant centipede in time to avoid provoking it, thus making a hostile encounter purely optional.

Cockatrice. Your party comes across one cockatrice poking around the hillside for fallen nuts and berries, or chasing its next meal. If your party wishes to avoid a fight, require a DC 15 Intelligence (Nature) or Wisdom (Survival) check. Failure means that someone in your party has made a false move that sets off the beast, and it attacks.

Scaling the Encounter: If you wish to make the encounter more challenging, use an encounter group that consists of 1d4 cockatrices plus one additional cockatrice for each level in your party's average level..

Deer. Your party spots 1d4 bucks and 2d4 does grazing quietly. If your party attacks, only the males fight, covering the females while they flee.

Neutral does not mean harmless.

Even if your party does not behave in a threatening manner, there is a chance that the bucks mistake their actions and attack anyway. Have your party make a DC 10 Intelligence (Nature) or Wisdom (Survival) check. Failure means that someone has made a false move that sets off the males and they charge.

Treasure: Anyone for venison? Perhaps a nearby butcher will pay 2 gp or thereabouts for a fresh carcass.

Dragon. Your party notices a shadow in the sky. It's a dragon on the prowl. To determine what kind of dragon roll on Table 5.3.1:

D12	ENCOUNTER
	TABLE 5.3.1
	Dragon - Hills
1	Black
2	Blue
3	Green
4-5	Red
6	White
7	Brass
8	Bronze
9-10	Copper
11	Gold
12	Silver

To determine its age, see Scaling the Encounter.

To be clear, this need not be a hostile encounter. The dragon is not defending its lair, so it may just be curious about your party. It may have more important things to do and decline to take notice of them at all. Or it may be hungry and on the hunt, or it's angry because your party has intruded on territory it claims as its own.

Alternately, you may present your party with a scenario that you can weave into the larger story of the campaign. Your party finds a dragon wyrmling sprawled on the ground. It's obviously in a bad way — gashed open, bleeding profusely (or it has almost bled out), barely conscious. Assume that it has stabilized after being reduced to 0 hp, and that it now has 1 hp. How it got that way is up to you, and it may depend on how dragons fit into your campaign world. Perhaps it fled from a fight in which it was badly wounded. Who would its enemies be, and why were they fighting? Were any of this dragon's relatives or companions killed?

How your party decides to deal with this child in distress could open up possibilities for later in your campaign. If they rescue it, will its kin reward them later, or will its enemies confront them on the principle that, "The friends of my enemy must also be my enemy?" Conversely, what are the consequences if they put it out of its misery, like scavengers roaming a medieval battlefield? Will its kin seek retribution, or will its enemies treat your party as allies?

Scaling the Encounter: Because dragons get tougher with age, the age of the dragon encountered should depend on your party's average level — especially ➤

if you decide that this is going to be a hostile encounter.

If your party's average level is 10 or lower, they encounter a wyrmling. If their average level is 11-18, they encounter a young dragon. If their average level is 19-25, they encounter an adult dragon. If their average level is higher than 25, they encounter an ancient dragon.

Giant. Hill country is closer than any other environment, with possible exception of mountains, to giants' home turf. Hill giants and stone giants find plenty of caves and hollows gouged out of hillsides and fire giants find defensible high ground for their strongholds. A giant lair, where you find a group of giants who will defend their home to the death, is a significant location and should be planned, not random. However, you shouldn't be surprised to find giants, alone or in small groups, away from their lairs and going about their business. To determine the giant encountered, roll on Table 5.3.2:

TABLE 5.3.2
Giant - Hills

d8	ENCOUNTER
1	Fire Giant
2-6	Hill Giant
7	Stone Giant
8	Storm Giant

Fire Giant. Fire giants feel most at home in areas where there is volcanic activity, and that is where you will find their most imposing strongholds. However, they go forth in search of iron and raw steel from which they forge the tools of war, or to collect tribute from lands that they have conquered. Your party crosses paths with one such fire giant, who has gone abroad on an errand for its tribe.

A fire giant is not necessarily hostile to your party. If it is abroad on business, it has better things to do than pick a fight with them. However, it does judge whether or not they'd be useful as slaves — especially dwarves, whom fire giants value as miners and smiths. They also value gnomes for their mechanical skill. At your discretion, it may decide to take your party captive, forcing them to either come along quietly or fight for their freedom. If they choose the latter, the giant tries to incapacitate those it thinks useful rather than kill them. ➤

Hill Giant. Your party crosses paths with one hill giant looking for a village that it can raid, or perhaps on an errand to another lair of hill giants, or perhaps just out for a casual stroll. Your party is not its first choice for terrorizing and robbing, but they will do. It tries to bully your party into giving over all of their possessions, and if they refuse the giant is quite willing to bash as many heads as it must.

Stone Giant. Stone giants find isolated quarries and carve mines into hillsides, where they prefer going about their business in peace and quiet. Your party crosses paths with one stone giant, who has left its lair to explore for another quarry site, or to meet with clients interested in using stone giants' legendary skill for their own purposes. The stone giant is not interested in fighting, but persuading it to help your party means overcoming its decided lack of interest one way or another. Consider that it requires a successful DC 20 Charisma (Persuasion) check.

Storm Giant. Storm giants generally reside in more remote places at higher altitudes, but they may come down from their mountain from time to time for reasons of their own. Their unique gifts for taking in the big picture and looking into the future may inspire them to share their prophecies with the wider world. Your party encounters one such storm giant. This not likely to be a hostile encounter, but it is a chance for you to share important information with your party and influence their course of action.

Scaling the Encounter: A giant encounter of any kind may be a bit too much for a low-level party. Feel free to re-roll for another encounter. Conversely, if you want to run a more challenging encounter for a higher-level party, use an encounter group consisting of two hill giants if your party's average level is 10 or higher. If your party's average level is 20 or higher, use an encounter group of three hill giants.

You may also give giants companion creatures if you want to make the encounter more challenging. All giants may have ogre underlings with them. Each fire giant may have a pet hell hound — in fact, the reason it is abroad from its stronghold may be that it's walking the dog. Each stone giant may keep a black bear on a leash. Just keep the total CR of the encounter in mind and don't pile on until it's more difficult than you intended.

Goats. Your party comes across a small herd of 1d6 billies and 2d6 nannies grazing. Perhaps they are wild goats — or perhaps they have gotten separated from a larger herd, and somewhere nearby there is a goatherd who would give a reward for their safe return. In any event, billies can be ornery beasts and if your party approaches them, you may require your party to make a DC 15 Intelligence (Nature) check to avoid setting off an attack in which the males charge to cover the fleeing females.

The (Relatively) Gentle Giant

It may strike you as odd to classify giants as something other than aggressive creatures. Giants are enemies, right? We all remember Gary Gygax's classic "G" series of adventure modules; we know how it works: You fight giants as a warm-up act for the drow and eventually, Lolth herself. Seems like a logical progression.

But in fact, *Dungeons & Dragons* has always treated giants more subtly than that, and at least one species of giant has always been good-aligned. In 5th Edition, they get a relatively complex set of motivations and ways of living. Hill giants — always the lumpenproletariat of giant-kind — default to plunder and killing, but all others may have something else in mind when you approach them. They are intelligent beings who, like humans and most humanoids, are capable of a wide range of reactions to strangers like your party, including simple curiosity, social calculation, pure indifference and at least some degree of geniality, as well as violence.

Scaling the Encounter: If you wish to make the encounter more challenging, use a herd of wild (and potentially irritated) giant goats instead. The encounter group should consist of 1d4 giant goats for each multiple of 2 in your party's average level with the same 1:2 ratios of males to females. Giant goats are quite wild; there is no chance that they are being kept by someone else.

Hippogriff. Your party sees a hippogriff circling overhead, looking for its next meal, or on the ground dealing with its prey. Hippogriffs are not as aggressive as birds of prey, and it is no sure bet that they would attack your party on the hope that it could make off with a pack animal or their stash of rations. Whether or not this is a hostile encounter is up to you.

Hippogriffs may be a kind of prey as well as predators. If hippogriffs are used as mounts in your world, it must follow that captive adults have value as breeding stock, and chicks captured from the wild also have value because they are still young enough to be tamed. To that end, you may allow your party a DC 20 Wisdom (Survival) check to trace a path to the hippogriff's lair (likely to be sited atop a large rock or on a hilltop) after observing it for a while. If your party has someone capable of flight,

reduce the DC to 15. To subdue an adult hippogriff to the point where it can be bound and held captive, it must be successfully grappled and kept in grappled condition for 10 consecutive rounds.

Scaling the Encounter: If you want to stage a hostile encounter with hippogriffs and you need to make it more of a challenge for a higher-level party, consider that the encounter group consists of one hippogriff for each multiple of 3 in your party's average level.

Horses. Your party comes across a small herd of horses. They only questions are, how many of them are there, and do they belong to someone else? Horse encounters are unlikely to be hostile, although they may put up a fight if you try to wrangle them before they've been broken. Roll on Table 5.3.3 to determine the nature of the horse encounter:

TABLE 5.3.3
Horses - Hills

d6	ENCOUNTER
1-2	Pony
3-5	Riding Horse
6	Warhorse

Pony. Your party comes across a small herd of 2d8 ponies grazing, or moving across the landscape at a walk. It's up to you to decide whether they're wild, or if they belong to someone — and if the latter, have they escaped from someone who would pay a reward for their return?

If they are wild, they can be wrangled. To wrangle a pony, it must be successfully grappled and kept in grappled condition for 3 consecutive rounds. At that point, it becomes docile and whomever grappled it may ride it or use it as a pack animal. Only one medium-size creature may try to grapple a pony at any given time.

Riding Horse. Your party comes across a small herd of 2d4 riding horses grazing, or moving at a walk. It's up to you to decide whether they're wild, or if they belong to someone — and if the latter, is their herder nearby (see Table 5.5) or have they escaped from someone who would pay a reward for their return?

If they are wild, they can be wrangled. To wrangle a riding horse, it must be successfully grappled and kept in grappled condition for 6 consecutive rounds. At that point, it becomes docile and whoever grappled it may ride it or use it as a pack animal. Because of its ➤

size, two medium-size creatures may grapple with the same riding horse simultaneously, and as long as one of them maintains its grappled condition, this counts toward the requirement for wrangling it.

Warhorse. Your party comes across 1d4 warhorses. Whether their owners were killed in battle, or they just escaped from the stable, is up to you. If the former, they wear empty saddles. Warhorses do not need to be wrangled; they have been broken and disciplined, so they're used to working with humans. However, they're also trained fighters and if you don't approach them just right in a situation like this, they'll take you for the enemy and attack. If your party approaches the warhorses, require a DC 15 Intelligence (Nature) check to avoid setting the horses off.

Insignia on their barding should give some hints as to whom the warhorses belong (or belonged). A good warhorse is highly prized, and its owner would pay dearly for its return.

Treasure: If your party encounters riding horses that have escaped from their owners, they may be saddled and their saddlebags contain valuables equal to one roll on the Individual Treasure: Challenge 0-4 table. Warhorses, of course, have their barding.

Mules. Mules are domestic creatures. So when your party sees 1d6 mules mulling about for no apparent purpose, it is highly likely that they have escaped from the nearest farm or someone using them as pack animals, such as miners. Their owners will pay a reward for their return — or your party could claim them as their own without anyone (possibly) being the wiser.

Mules do not attack. But they may be skittish around strangers, especially if they have been out in the wild for a while. If your party tries to take possession of them, have them make a DC 10 Intelligence (Nature) check to avoid a hostile reaction. Remember, these creatures have a kick like a mule.

Pegasus. Your party sees one pegasus wheeling overhead. It does not attack, even if it sees evil creatures. However, it may be flagged down by signaling or calling to it and making a successful DC 15 Charisma (Persuasion) check. If your party can get the pegasus' attention, it may be persuaded to render some kind of aid to your party — such as taking a party member to a nearby location — with a successful DC 20 Charisma (Persuasion) check. For good-aligned characters who can speak Celestial, Elvish or Sylvan the DC is 15.

Scaling the Encounter: If you wish to make the encounter more challenging, the encounter group consists of one pegasus for each multiple of 3 in the party's average level, rounded up.

Rats. Even on relatively barren hillsides, rats can find enough food to justify living here. That's how they roll. But your party's presence gives them a welcome opportunity to feast. Roll on Table 5.3.4 to determine the nature of the rat encounter:

TABLE 5.3.4
Rats - Hills

d6	ENCOUNTER
1-2	Lone Rat
3-4	Swarm of Rats
5-6	Giant Rats

Lone Rat. A single rat, perhaps foraging by itself or perhaps lost from its nest, approaches your party while they take a rest. It's not much of a threat, but if someone in your party is looking for a familiar or even just a pet, this is an opportunity. Interacting with the rat — especially earning its trust with food — and making a successful DC 10 Intelligence (Nature) check earns its loyalty as a pet.

Swarm of Rats. Without being aware of it, your party has stopped to rest near a nest of rats. Drawn by the party's rations, a swarm of rats makes for the nearest source of food. They don't attack party members who don't interfere with their basic mission of acquiring food. But unless they are stopped, they eventually account for all of your party's rations, making off with what they don't eat on the spot.

Giant Rats. In this case, the rats drawn by the food your party carries are giant rats. There are 2d6 of them.

Weasels. Someone at the front of your party's march order accidentally steps into a burrow housing enough weasels to cause trouble when they get angry and defend their home. You may allow your party a DC 10 Wisdom (Perception) or Wisdom (Survival) check to spot the burrow in time to avoid it or give warning to whomever is about to disturb it. The burrow houses a pack of 2d8 weasels.

Scaling the Encounter: If you wish to make the encounter more challenging, substitute giant weasels for normal-sized weasels.

Treasure: There is a 10% chance that they are actually mink, and their pelts would be of some value to furriers — 1 gp for normal-sized mink, and 5 gp for a giant mink. You may require a successful DC 15 Intelligence (Nature) check for your party to tell the difference between mink and weasels.

Bats. Even a small cave carved into a hillside provides an agreeable home to bats. If your party enters, they find a colony consisting of a 1d4+1 swarms of bats However, even though they're uncomfortably close to the bats' lair, it's possible to avoid setting them off. You may have your party make a DC 15 Wisdom (Survival) or Intelligence (Nature) check. Failure means that someone makes a false move that triggers the bats to attack.

Scaling the Encounter: If you want to make the encounter more challenging for a higher-level party, use an encounter group consisting of 1d4 swarm of bats and/or giant bats in any combination, plus one swarm of bats or giant bat for each level in your party's average level.

Vultures. Your party comes across 1d4+1 vultures picking at a carcass. It could be an animal — or it could be a humanoid or a human. How they respond depends on how they interpret your party's actions. You may have your party make a DC 10 Intelligence (Nature) or Wisdom (Survival) check. Failure means that a party member has made a false move that persuades the vultures to attack, thinking that they need to defend their food source.

Scaling the Encounter: If you wish to make the encounter more challenging, consider substituting giant vultures for the vultures. The encounter group then consists of two giant vultures for each multiple of 3 in your party's average level. Perhaps they — mistakenly or not — spotted your party as hapless travelers on their last legs, in which case they swoop down to try to hasten their demise.

TABLE 5.4

Humanoids - Hills

d20	ENCOUNTER
1	Bugbear
2-5	Dwarves
6	Gnolls
7-8	Gnomes
9-12	Goblins
13	Halflings
14	Hobgoblins
15	Kobolds
16-17	Lycanthrope
18-20	Orcs

Bugbear. Your party crosses paths with one or more bugbears (see Scaling the Encounter). They could be mercenaries on their way to join a larger goblinoid army that is mobilizing for war. Conversely, they could be heading home after a victorious campaign — or straggling in the wake of a catastrophic defeat. Their exact circumstances and motivation should depend on what else is going on in your campaign world. If there is no such war in which they could take part, they're out for some casual plunder, or perhaps on their way to shake down a hobgoblin tribe that once employed them.

Their interest in fighting your party should vary according to the reason why they're here. For instance, mobilizing for war means they have a larger purpose in mind than victimizing your party. If they're looking to strongarm some hobgoblins, they may even offer your party a cut of the take in exchange for adding to their strength in numbers.

Scaling the Encounter: A beginning-level party should only have to cope with one bugbear. If you wish to make the encounter more challenging, the encounter group consists of two bugbears for each multiple of 3 in your party's average level. If your party's average level is 10 or higher, add one bugbear chief as the group's leader.

Dwarves. Hill country is home turf for dwarves, especially if there are veins of precious or industrial metal running through the hillsides. Mining and metalworking is what dwarves do; it's their thing. The possibilities for why you would run into a small group of dwarves in hill country while they are abroad from one of their mining or industrial settlements vary according to the full range of the activities and functions of those settlements.

They might be miners exploring for new veins, or workers shuttling from one mine to another. Or they might be out looking for firewood to keep the forges working. In such cases, treat them as commoners armed with battleaxes and war picks, and the weapon proficiency to use them. Or they might be taking loads of ore from a nearby mine for smelting — in which case, treat them as commoners leading an equal number of mules. Or they might be a war party on the alert because there are orcs or other enemies about — in which case, treat them as guards armed with battleaxes.

Unless your party includes any such enemies, dwarves are unlikely to treat them with hostility. It's much more likely that they freely share their local knowledge and even material help — you may require the party to make a successful DC 10 Charisma (Persuasion) check in the latter case. You may also use an encounter with dwarves to provide your party with a sidequest, with the dwarves trying to enlist them in defending their colony against external threats.

Scaling the Encounter: The encounter group consists of 1d8 guards (armed with battle-axes instead of spears) plus two guards for each level in your party's average level for a war party. A work group consists of 2d6 commoners armed with pickaxes (treat as spears that cannot be thrown) plus two guards for each level in your party's average level. If you don't want to run a mass encounter, feel free to substitute one priest for 16 guards or one veteran for 24 guards as freely as you like.

Heigh Ho, Heigh Ho?

As the guidelines for scaling the encounter suggest, you are more likely to find large populations of dwarves in the hills (and also in the mountains, but that is a matter for Chapter 7). Mines and other settlements should be fixed locations, not random encounters, of course. But it's more likely than not that dwarves that your party meets by chance are affiliated with one such population center.

However, population density brings certain hazards in a dangerous world. You have more to defend, and it becomes more worthwhile for someone to try to take it from you. Plus, your enemies have little doubt about where to find you. There is security in numbers, but also insecurity. So the dwarves your party meets in hill country might actually need their help more urgently than those they meet in areas where dwarves blend into the background. If anything, they are more likely to offer your party a sidequest, promising weapons or even ingots of precious metal in exchange for their help in dealing with monsters or other enemies.

Gnolls. Your party comes across a small band of gnolls moving across the hillside. They seem to have a purpose in mind, as they barely take notice of your party. In fact, they are here to scout out a nearby settlement as preparation for raiding and plundering it. If the gnoll group is relatively large (see Scaling the Encounter) this may be the actual raiding party, headed for the nearest settlement. Or they may be on their way back from a successful raid, spattered with blood and taking with them captives to sacrifice to their deity. In either case, they ignore your party if your party declines to interfere with them, guided as they are by their primary purpose.

Scaling the Encounter: The baseline encounter group should consist of two gnolls for each multiple of 3 in your party's average level. If your party's average level is 7-9, add a gnoll pack lord to the mix as the group's leader. If

your party's average level is 10 or higher feel free to substitute one gnoll pack lord for four gnolls as much as you like if you don't want to run a mass encounter.

Treasure: If the gnolls are coming back from a successful raid, you may roll on the Treasure Hoard: Challenge 0-4 table to determine the fruits of their labor. This is in addition to the individual treasure they carry.

Gnomes. Gnomes live in small settlements nestled among hills and fertile valleys. They also live in towns and villages among dwarves, humans and halflings where their skills as mechanics and craftsmen make them valuable specialists. Your party crosses paths with a group of 2d6 gnomes accompanied by one gnome priest. They are traveling to a community where they expect to take up work, such as a dwarf mining settlement or a human or halfling farming village, or even a market town or big city. Or perhaps they are traveling back to their home village. Or they may be traders. In any case, they have brought along a priest of one of their patron deities as their sole protection.

Whatever the case, they know the area well enough to provide your party with local knowledge. Perhaps they know of a specific threat from a particular creature — that there are worgs or a roc haunting these hills, or they're worried about getting jumped by goblins or orcs. In this case, they'll pay your party what they can for their protection (perhaps they know where their potential enemies make their lair). Their priest may be willing to help your party with spells if they are willing to pay the going rate for such services.

Treasure: If these gnomes are traveling merchants, they should carry trade goods and/or coins in addition to their personal treasure. Roll on the Treasure Hoard: Challenge 0-4 table to determine their total value.

Goblins. Your party crosses paths with goblin raiders on their way to or from their target. They see your party as a target of opportunity and they fan out to attack from multiple angles, using changes in elevation and obstacles like rocks and boulders to conceal their movements as much as possible.

Scaling the Encounter: Use an encounter group of 1d4 goblins for each level in your party's average level. If you don't want to run a mass encounter but you still want to provide a higher-level party with a meaningful challenge, feel free to substitute one goblin boss for four goblins as much as you like. It is also possible that the goblins use worg mounts. Feel free to substitute one worg for two goblins, as long as there are not more worgs present than goblins to ride them.

Halflings. Your party crosses paths with a group of 1d10+2 halflings. They may be farmers from homesteads scattered among the verdant hills who have joined together to share a wagon and take their produce to market. It's up to you whether they're on their way to market, or on their way back, with their pony-drawn wagon being either full of foodstuffs or half-full of trade goods. In this case, treat one or two of the halflings as guards and the rest as commoners. There's no reason why they wouldn't be willing to trade with your party and share knowledge of the area. In fact, they might be willing to hire your party to escort them wherever they're going if they think that there are dangerous monsters about.

Gnomes live in small settlements hidden among the hills and valleys.

It's also possible that they're an adventuring party, 1d6+2 in number. In this case, treat half of them as guards and half of them as scouts; if there is an odd number, treat the odd halfling as a priest. Treat them, too, as a potential source of useful information for your party. They're a good-natured lot, but if the subject of what they're up to arises, it should be clear to your party that these bold, but naive folk have bitten off more than they can chew. If your party decides to tag along to keep

them out of trouble, this creates a nice little sidequest for them.

Scaling the Encounter: If you want to run a more robust encounter with halfling adventurers, treat them as thugs and spies instead of guards and scouts.

Hobgoblins. If war plagues your campaign world, hobgoblins go about, selling their martial services to anyone willing to employ them. Your party comes across a small group of hobgoblins marching across country. They may be mercenaries taking a shortcut on their way to their mustering point — in which case, they have business to take care of and they'll ignore your party as long as they don't try to interfere.

On the other hand, the hobgoblins might initiate a fight with your party if peace has prevailed for so long that they have had no work — in which case they're bored and looking for practice. Or they're broke and as long as they properly challenge your party to a fight, killing them for their belongings is not mere robbery but taking spoils of war. Alternately, these hobgoblins may be fleeing a lost battle, scuttling back to their stronghold in the hills. Like many mercenaries in such a situation, they can rationalize killing and looting your party in any number of ways — perhaps they won't get paid because their employer was killed; or they need to settle for what they can get now that the campaign won't yield any spoils; or perhaps they're just hungry and desperate after separating from the army.

Scaling the Encounter: The baseline encounter group should consist of 1d4 hobgoblins for each multiple of 2 in your party's average level. If your party's average level is 10-19, add a hobgoblin captain as the group's leader, accompanied by two goblin servants or one bugbear aide. If your party's average level is 20 or higher, add instead one hobgoblin warlord with two bugbear aides.

Kobolds. These nasty little reptilian humanoids prefer to live underground, but they can get by in hillside caves. They subsist in hill country through the usual way — raiding and plundering anyone weaker than them. Interestingly enough, they are at best beta predators in the more familiar (to them) ecosystem of underground caverns, but out in the open they find settled communities of folk who offer soft targets in that they aren't hardened by constant fighting with their neighbors.

Since kobolds react poorly to sunlight, your party most likely encounters them at night, or by entering a cave that they occupy (in which case, there is a trap of your choice guarding the entrance). To them, your party looks like a suitable target of opportunity — a relatively small group that has stuff worth taking. They fan out to try to surround your party and attack from more than one angle.

Scaling the Encounter: Use an encounter group of 2d4 kobolds plus 1d4 kobolds for each level in your party's average level. If you'd rather not run a mass encounter, you may cut down on the kobold's numbers by substituting one winged kobold for two kobolds as much as you like.

Lycanthrope. To determine what manner of werebeast your party encounters, roll on Table 5.4.1:

TABLE 5.4.1
Lycanthrope - Hills

d8	ENCOUNTER
1	Werebear
2-3	Wereboar
4-5	Wererat
6-8	Werewolf

All lycanthropes assume their animal form if the encounter comes down to combat, although they may choose their hybrid form instead if they have access to a weapon.

Werebear. Your party comes across a werebear that has staked out a hill in the wilderness. It makes its lair on the hilltop behind a ring of stones — a modest fortress from which it can observe its domain. Perhaps it was once a druid, or a wandering ranger, or a religious hermit of some sort, who volunteered for this fate as a way of protecting the land. It is not automatically hostile to your party, especially if there are no evil characters present, and it may be willing to provide your party with useful information about the surrounding area.

On the other hand, an encounter could create difficulties for your party if the werebear decides that someone in your party would make a good apprentice (and successor to its self-appointed duties as the local guardian). Once it realizes that there is a druid or a ranger in your party, a light goes on in its head — and it won't take "No" for an answer.

Wereboar. It's most likely that a wereboar met by chance was at some point an unfortunate hunter who didn't realize that the boar at which he aimed his bow was really a lycanthrope. Or it might have been a herder who presented an isolated target. The wereboar goes about looking for victims to share its fate, hoping that a lone boar will lure someone into ➤

engaging with it. A party of adventurers could offer it an attractive target — confident in its ability to take at least one of them and drive the others off, it attacks.

Wererat. Your party comes across a wererat driven out of a nearby settlement, along with the rats with whom it kept company. Now, it dreams of revenge on the folk who defeated its companions. It hopes to create a party of wererats who will give them more than they can handle — and your party looks like it will make nice lycanthropes. It appears to your party in its humanoid form, pretending to be a traveler in distress, having gotten separated from its companions and hoping to travel with your party for protection. It tries to slip toward the back of the march order and waits for a time when everyone's back is turned to it.

Werewolf. A werewolf spots your party and cannot turn down the opportunity to claim more victims. However, it is clever enough to approach them in its human form, pretending to be a herder or farmer in distress — injured while looking for a lost animal, for instance. Once your party gets close and drops its guard, it attacks.

Scaling the Encounter: A single lycanthrope can offer a stiff challenge to a low-level party. If your party's average level is 3 or less, feel free to re-roll the encounter. Alternately, if you want to make a werewolf encounter more challenging for a higher-level party, use a pack of them consisting of one werewolf for each multiple of 5 in your party's average level.

Treasure: Werebears are territorial, so your party may encounter it in or near its lair. In that case, roll on the Treasure Hoard: Challenge 0-4 table to determine its treasure.

Orcs. You may add orcs to the list of evil humanoid races who make their lairs up in the hills, where they can find isolated caves and ridges and hilltops that allow them a good view of the surrounding area. A small group orcs could be a scout party on their way to the plains and forests below, while a larger group would be an actual raiding party on its way to — or on its way back from — its target.

Your party crosses paths with these orcs, but if they have such a fixed purpose in mind, they may not give your party much attention. Their leader may look your party over and decide that they're not worth the bother. But they may also decide to interrogate your party for information about places rumored to be lucrative targets for raiding, and they'll resort to violence without hesitation if your party is too slow to cooperate. They are less likely to give your party a break if there are dwarves in it, and they'll make dwarf characters a special focus of hostility in any interactions with them.

Scaling the Encounter: The baseline encounter group should consist of 1d4 orcs for each multiple of 2 in your party's average level. If your party's average level is 5-9, add an orog as the group's leader. If your party's average level is 10 or higher, use an orc war chief as its leader. If you don't want to run a mass encounter but you still want to provide a higher-level party with a meaningful challenge, feel free to substitute one orog for four orcs as much as you like.

Treasure: If the orcs are coming back from a successful raid, you may roll on the Treasure Hoard: Challenge 0-4 table to determine the fruits of their labor. This is in addition to the individual treasure they carry.

TABLE 5.5
Humans - Hills

d20	ENCOUNTER
1	Adventurers
2-4	Bandits
5	Exiles
6	Explorers
7-8	Farmers
9	Fugitives
10	Gatherers
11-12	Herders
13	Hermit
14	Hunters
15	Military
16-17	Miners
18	Pilgrims
19-20	Traders

Adventurers. Unless your party contains all of the adventurers in your campaign world, it's at least theoretically possible that they'll run into another adventuring party as they work their way through the hills. Perhaps they're pursuing the same objective as your party. Perhaps they have a different mission; perhaps they're headed for a site that your party knows nothing about (like ancient ruins said to hold lost treasures). Perhaps they're lost and starving, or wounded, or cursed.

How they react to your party depends on a variety of factors. Are they rivals pursuing the same goal? If not, perhaps this party is willing to share useful information. In fact, if your party is stuck and having a hard time

advancing the storyline of your campaign, a friendly encounter like this can help steer them in the right direction. Differences in alignment may also shape how the two parties react to each other.

Composition of this rival party is up to you and can vary according to circumstance. Any party in the wilderness would be well-advised to have someone accomplished in Survival, such as a ranger, with them. Conversely, a party that is struggling may be in a bad way precisely no one is well-versed in Survival or Nature.

Scaling the Encounter: Unless there is some possibility that this encounter turns hostile, the relative level of the party is mainly a matter of affect. A higher-level party might project self-confidence and calm (or arrogance), while beginning-level party might stumble about, unsure of themselves. If you're leaning towards a hostile encounter, however, consider that the total CR of the party should be roughly two-thirds of your party's average level.

Bandits. Hill country offers bandits hillside caves in which to hide and ridge lines and hilltops where they can put up strongholds and observe the surrounding country. Your party crosses paths with a group of bandits coming down from the hills, or on their way back up after successfully hitting a merchant caravan in the flatlands below. Alternately, they may have spotted your party from the high ground and they come down to confront them, fanning out among rocks and vegetation to conceal their movements and get the drop. Even though a party of adventurers like yours is better-armed than their typical target, it's not out of the question that the bandits attack. It's possible that they assume that your party is a posse sent out after them — or that your party intends to rob them of what they took from others by force.

Scaling the Encounter: As a rough guideline, the encounter group should contain 1d8 bandits for each level in your party's average level. If your party's average level is 4 or higher, add a bandit captain as their leader. If you don't want to run a mass encounter but you still want these criminals to provide a higher-level party with a meaningful challenge, feel free to substitute one thug for four bandits as much as you like.

Treasure: If your party finds the bandits' hideout, roll on the Treasure Hoard table appropriate to the total CR of the encounter. Do so also if you decide that the bandits encountered are on their way back from a successful raid. Consider that there is also a 20% chance that the bandits have with them a high-value captive whom they intend to ransom. The identity of this captive is left to you as DM, as it should depend on local circumstances and fit into your campaign world.

Exiles. Your party encounters 1d6 people who could serve as a source of adventure hooks. From their appearance, they have obviously seen better days. They have fled up into these uninhabited hills for any of a variety of reasons: perhaps they are royalty or nobility who have been usurped; perhaps the opposite is the case and they are failed usurpers on the run. Or perhaps they have gotten caught up in a blood feud in their homeland and that's why they fear for their lives. Whatever the circumstance, they left their home to head for the hills because they need to hide.

Such an encounter does not need to be hostile.

No matter their reason for being here, they should offer your party an adventure hook of some sort. It may involve protecting the exiles from their real (or imagined) pursuers. It may involve returning to their former home and securing an important item that was left behind (a family heirloom, a badge of office), perhaps even helping them return home and force their way back into their former position of prominence. At the very least, exiles can provide your party with information about their former home territory, which in turn could be a key location in your campaign.

Use any NPC template you like for the exiles, depending on the backstory you assign them.

Explorers. Your party bumps into a small party driven by human curiosity to explore and map these forbidding hills. The group consists of 1d4 scholars (treat them as commoners) and 1d4 scouts who act as bodyguards. Perhaps they are here thanks to the sponsorship of a ruler or noble who has heard rumors that precious metals and gemstones can be found out here, or an academy looking for a lost civilization. Perhaps the explorer is a wealthy eccentric who undertook this expedition on his or her own.

Such an encounter is not likely to be hostile. Explorers are open and curious, despite the fact that the hills hide any number of hazards. Instead, you may treat this as an opportunity for your party to receive some help from a knowledgeable stranger — the explorer is likely to have excellent maps of nearby areas (and knowledge of those areas) and is willing to share them. Conversely, an expedition that has been in the field for a while may be running short on cartography supplies and other necessaries and may be willing to pay well if your party can help supply what they lack. Also, if your party is in the mood for a sidequest, an explorer may offer one: If the expedition is headed into particularly dangerous territory, it may need additional guards to keep it safe.

Farmers. Your party cross paths with 1d8 farmers and farm hands from a nearby isolated farmstead traveling to or from market. They have a horse-drawn wagon; if they are going to market it's full of the fruits of their labor, and if they're returning from market they'll have household goods, tools and some extra coin with them.

The farmers are not hostile. They're used to seeing strangers as they travel on business. They're willing to trade as long as the exchange is fair; if your party wants to shortchange them it will take a successful DC 20 Charisma (Persuasion check). If your party has horses or mules available, they may even be interested in buying one on account of theirs being on its last legs, or just because they need another.

Treat the farmers as commoners.

Fugitives. Your party crosses paths with 1d6 bedraggled people stumbling along the hillside. They look to be in less-than-optimal shape, but they're moving as fast as they can manage. Most, if not all of them have a manacle around one wrist, with the other manacle dangling on its chain. They're escaped prisoners who have fled into the hills. From whom they are fleeing and why they were imprisoned is up to you, and ought to depend on where in your campaign world this encounter takes place.

How the encounter plays out depends entirely on how your party reacts, but one thing on which you may rely is that these fugitives did not go to the trouble of a jailbreak just to allow a bunch of strangers to take their freedom back from them. Each of them has learned whip their freed manacle by the chain and wield it as a club.

Treat the fugitives as bandits, but without weapons or armor.

Treasure: Fugitives have no treasure.

Gatherers. Your party comes across 1d4 gatherers collecting herbs and wild grasses, either for food or medicine. It's possible that your party surprises them, as they work hunched over and close to the ground. However, they are not hostile — they're just laborers with specialized knowledge out doing their job. They may be persuaded to help your party with local lore and/or therapeutic concoctions made from whatever it is they're gathering (see Treasure). They may also ask your party to help them if they have reason to believe that they are in danger (perhaps they had a close brush with monsters recently).

Treat the gatherers as commoners armed with sickles or daggers.

Treasure: In addition to treasure from the Individual Treasure: Challenge 0-4 table, the gatherers have a small stash of helpful non-magical items made from herbs. One such item could be a poultice that heals hit points equal to 1d4+ the Wisdom (Medicine) bonus of whomever applies it after it is kept in place for 24 hours. But that is just one possibility. Mix in any such items that already exist in your campaign world. You can also consult "Narl's Herbal Remedies" in Ramen Sandwich Press' collection of new items, *Tome of the Utility Drawer, Volume I.*

Herders. Your party spots a herd of sheep, or goats, or some other domesticated herd animal on the hillside. There are 2d4 herders in their midst. They may be grazing the animals, or driving them to market. They are not hostile, and since they range far and wide by the nature of their work, they can provide your party with helpful local knowledge. They know all the nearby sources of water and the places where monsters are reputed to reside. They may even have specific knowledge that can help your party get where they want to go.

Treat herders as commoners. They carry crooks or staves that they can wield two-handed as clubs, but they wear no armor.

Hermit. Remote hill country — and the more rugged, the better — makes convivial surroundings for someone who has decided to withdraw from worldly cares. But that doesn't mean you can't be found. Your party stumbles upon a hermit in his or her abode — a small cave, or a lean-to or abandoned building on hilltop. One hermit lives here, devoted to a pure and simple life of contemplation. The hermit may be a divine spellcaster, for whom seclusion and meditation is a form of service to a deity. It may take a successful DC 15 Charisma (Persuasion) check to get past the fact that your party has broken this seclusion, but the hermit may be willing to use divine spells to aid them.

Alternately, your party may have found a secular hermit — someone who, having been wounded by failure or grown weary of success, decided to retire completely from the world. Such a person won't have divine spells, but may have magic items, local lore, or even knowledge and personal connections from his or her past life that might help your party.

Yet another possibility is that this hermit is a retired adventurer or soldier, in the manner of knights in the Arthurian romances who became hermits to repent of lives spent fighting each other and dallying with married women. Hermits in this mold have discarded their fighting gear, but they may be persuaded to leave their seclusion and join your party as friendly NPCs.

Treat a religious hermit as an acolyte or a priest, but feel free to generate a higher-level divine spellcaster if you want to create a more spectacular effect with this encounter. Treat a secular hermit as a commoner, or use a character class and level of your choice.

These encounters can be opportunities for non-combat role-play.

Treasure: Roll on the Treasure Hoard: Challenge 0-4 to determine if the hermit has any magic items and/or valuable devotional items.

Hunters. Your party comes across 1d4 hunters looking for game. Depending on your party's appearance, they may act with caution, even suspicion at first. Despite the fact that they are armed with bows, they know that they are operating in wilderness away from home, and there are always strange folk about. However, if your party is not hostile to them they are willing to help by trading goods and supplying food and local knowledge. If your wish, have your party make a DC 10 (Charisma) Persuasion check to get on their good side.

Treat hunters as scouts.

Military. Hill country is not as conducive to maneuvering armies as open plains, but by no means is it safe from war. A hilltop or a ridge line is perfect place to put up a fortress; the high ground ideal for making a stand; and rugged, remote hillsides dotted with caves shelter irregular warriors. If war is a part of your campaign world, your party could encounter an army or part of an army on its way to meet the enemy — or running away from the enemy.

An entire army is certain to have more important things on their mind than dealing with a party of adventurers, so they're more useful for spectacle and flavor than a challenging encounter. For an actual encounter, a small group of soldiers is most likely a patrol, tasked with scouting ahead of the main army, or on its flanks. Their job is to locate the enemy and, conversely, to prevent enemy scouts from spotting their main force. They won't attack your party without reason to believe that your party is somehow connected to their enemy. However, they do stop your party to grill them for information, and possibly enlist their help with their mission. A larger group is most likely a unit of soldiers hurrying to join the main army.

Scaling the Encounter: As a rough guideline, the encounter group should contain 1d8 guards for each level in your party's average level. If your party's average level is 6 or higher, add a veteran or a knight as the group's leader. If you don't want to run a mass encounter, feel free to substitute one veteran for 12 guards as much as you like. Veterans who are not officers could be rank-and-file soldiers from an elite unit, or bodyguards for the leader.

Miners. Your party crosses paths with a small group of 1d10 miners looking for a fresh source of metals or raw gemstones. If there is a mining colony nearby, they might well be an offshoot from it.

This is not likely a hostile encounter. Instead, the miners could have local knowledge that your party finds useful, as well as torches, lamp oil, rope and other supplies for exploring underground. They might also want your party to serve as armed escort, having realized a little too late that the hills shelter dangerous creatures. In fact, if you want to stage a situation in which your party has the chance to rescue them from their foolhardiness, roll for an additional encounter.

Treat the miners as commoners armed with pickaxes (treat as spears that cannot be thrown).

Pilgrims. The pantheon and nature of religious practice in your campaign world is up to you as the designer of that world. If it makes sense in that context, consider that your party crosses paths with a group of devotees traveling to or from a holy site up in the hills. Perhaps they have a specific request to make of their deity (ending a drought or plague, curing someone of disease, etc.) and they bring an offering. Or perhaps it's just a ritual that their religion says they must perform regularly. Depending on how religions work in your world, perhaps their mission is to vandalize a shrine to a rival deity.

Their deity and alignment should dictate how they react to meeting your party. In any event, they are lightly armed at best and they may want to travel in your party's company for safety — especially if they know of a specific hazard in the area, like bandits or monsters. If friendly, they may also be willing to share local knowledge and trade with your party, or even share what divine magic capabilities they possess for your party's benefit.

Roll on Table 5.5.1 to give the encounter a more specific character:

TABLE 5.5.1
Pilgrims - Hills

d6	ENCOUNTER
1-2	Acolytes
3	Cultists
4-6	Lay Followers

Acolytes. Your party crosses paths 1d4 monks or junior clerics from a religion of your choice. Treat them as acolytes.

Cultists. Your party crosses paths with 2d6 hard-core followers of an evil deity. How they react to your party is up to you, and should be influenced by the numerical odds for or against them. If their cult involves some kind of sacrifice to their deity, perhaps the cultists consider that your party would do nicely. Treat the cultists as cultists.

Lay Followers. Your party crosses paths with 2d6 lay followers making a pilgrimage. They're just everyday folk performing an elaborate act of worship, and they're the most likely to need your party's protection as they travel through uninhabited land. Treat them as commoners.

Scaling the Encounter. If you wish to make the encounter more challenging, add one priest or cult leader to the encounter, as appropriate.

Treasure: In addition to whatever treasure they carry on their person, pilgrims may carry with them an offering to their deity. At your discretion, roll on the Treasure Hoard: Challenge 0-4 table to determine its value.

Traders. Hill country is too rugged for large merchant caravans. However, your party may cross paths with small-time merchants who go from village to village with a modest selection of basic goods — 1d4 of them with a horse-drawn cart or a giant lizard harnessed to carry cargo. They're happy to do business with your party. Consider that full range of basic items described in the

Player's Handbook could be available; assortment and quantity at your discretion as DM.

Peddlers are naturally sociable, and as travelers they are willing to share lore and stories picked up during their wanderings. They're a good device for providing your party with information about distant places as well as nearby locations. They may also be interested in traveling with your party for as long as they can, wanting protection from monsters and/or bandits.

Treat traders as commoners.

Treasure: Traveling merchants carry their worldly belongings with them. Roll on the Individual Treasure: Challenge 0-4 table once for each peddler present, and once on the Treasure Hoard: Challenge 0-4 table to determine the value of their wares.

TABLE 5.6
Watch Out! - Hills

d20	ENCOUNTER
1-2	Falling Rocks
3	Flash Flood
4-5	Hidden Hole
6-8	Loose Ground
9	The Hills are Alive
10	Tracks
11	Tripping Hazard
12	Wind Gust

Falling Rocks. A large rock higher up the hillside comes loose. Gravity does the rest. It tumbles onto a random party member. The rock causes 1d8 bludgeoning damage, but a successful DC 15 Dexterity (Acrobatics) check halves the damage, rounded down.

Flash Flood. A sudden rain storm provides the water, and gravity does the rest. Unless your players make it a point that their characters are keeping to higher ground, they pass by a gully or creek that serves as a natural channel for rainwater flowing downhill. The rush of water may sweep up one or more party member. In this situation, swimming is not possible and drowning becomes a possibility.

Anyone caught in the path of the flood can make a DC 15 Wisdom (Perception) or Wisdom (Survival) check to sense it in time to get out. Failure, however, means that they are caught in the torrent and carried downhill. Every 30 seconds, they are carried 30 feet downstream, but they may make a DC 20 Strength (Athletics) or Wisdom (Survival) check to catch hold of something and haul themselves out of the water to safety.

Hidden Hole. The hillside may be dotted with animal burrows. They may also weaken the ground above them. Have your party make a DC 15 Wisdom (Perception) check to spot one that is right in their path in time to avoid it. Failure means that a party member of your choice in the front of the march order steps into one, with all of the hazards that come with an unexpected fall. That party members suffers 1d6 falling damage, with a successful DC 15 Dexterity (Acrobatics) check to halve the damage.

Loose Ground. Your party reaches the crest of a rise from which they can get a good view of the surrounding area. However, a party member — choose one, or a character who wants to get a good look around may literally step forward as the best candidate — steps onto a patch of loose soil. It gives way and the character takes a tumble downhill, suffering 1d8 falling damage. A successful DC 15 Strength (Athletics) or Dexterity (Acrobatics) results in only half damage. Whee!

The Hills Are Alive. Choose a party member to make a DC 15 Wisdom (Survival) or Intelligence (Nature) check. Failure means that that character believes that he or she has heard a noise made by creature or a dangerous natural phenomenon. It can be as consequential as a dragon's roar in the distance, or as eerily intimate as a rattlesnake's rattle close by. A successful check means that that party member realizes that this is an illusion; either it's not as close as it seems or it isn't real at all.

If you wish, roll on Table 5.6.1 for guidance on what your party thinks it hears:

TABLE 5.6.1
The Hills Are Alive - Hills

d10	ENCOUNTER
1	Crash of rocks tumbling down the hillside
2	Dragon roaring overhead
3	Ettin arguing with itself
4	Griffon screeching
5	Hoofbeats of horses or other herd animals
6	Human or humanoid cry of distress
7	Picks smashing against rock
8	Voices speaking in Dwarven
9	Voices speaking in Giant
10	Wolves howling

Tracks. Your party spots tracks that look like tracks that belong to a monster associated with treasure hoards. They may make a successful DC 15 Wisdom (Survival) check to realize that they are very old, and they will not lead to anything useful. If no one makes a successful check, this may be the start of an amusing (for you as DM, anyway) wild goose chase.

Tripping Hazard. Pick a party member at the front of the march order. That character trips over an unseen obstacle — a rock sticking up out of the ground or a half-buried abandoned weapon, for instance. He or she must make a successful DC 10 Strength (Athletics) or Dexterity (Acrobatics) check to avoid a hard fall that causes 1d6 damage — and perhaps no small embarrassment in the eyes of the other party members.

Wind Gust. The winds that whip around in hilly country blow up and catch your party by surprise. If they have made camp for the night, their campfire is extinguished, forcing them to light another one. If they've already used all their wood and kindling, they'll have to go hunting in the dark for more. If they're carrying torches, they go out. If they're using lanterns, they may lose their grip (see below).

Regardless of whether it's day or night, any party member who is standing must make a DC 5 Strength check to avoid being knocked down. Anyone who is knocked down by the wind immediately loses grasp of anything held in hand. Fragile objects break when they are dropped. In addition, anyone who is knocked down while wearing his or her pack must make a DC 5 Dexterity (Acrobatics) check to avoid the pack falling heavily so that anything containing liquid, such as canteens and potions, breaking and spilling.

Up One Side and Down the Other

Hill country can offer places to graze a herd as well as mine for mithral. It can offer places to make a homestead as well as places to hide from enemies. But all such places share creatures (and folk) who can adapt to the uneven ground and rough terrain — a characteristic that creates a distinctive range of possible encounters.

LITTORAL

CHAPTER SIX

Littoral

What is Littoral?

You can think of littoral as a transitional space between dry land and a large body of water — the ocean, a major river, a major lake. It's shoreline or a riverbank and the adjacent area. This may seem limited in extent; it's not a vast desert or plain, or a deep forest. But littoral is an environment unto itself. It is here that you find creatures who are comfortable both on land and in water. The transition between dry land and deep water — where the water is shallow enough so that you can wade into it — makes this the only place where you can encounter aquatic creatures while remaining within a quick sprint of land.

This chapter assumes that your party is traveling at or in the vicinity of the water's edge, or along a river. The terrain is mostly flat, except where the land slopes down to the water, and how steep is the gradient depends on local conditions. Therefore, line of sight varies according to differences in elevation and possible blocking terrain features, but for the most part it should be possible to spot other creatures at a distance. In humanoid and human encounters (Tables 6.4 and 6.5) the encounter group may be aboard some kind of vessel when your party spots them, or not, at your discretion as DM.

What Do You Find in Littoral?

When you determine that a random encounter is in order, roll on Table 6.1 to determine the category:

TABLE 6.1
Encounter Type - Littoral

d20	CATEGORY
1-6	Aggressive Creatures (Table 6.2)
7-12	Neutral Creatures (Table 6.3)
13-15	Humanoids (Table 6.4)
16-17	Humans (Table 6.5)
18-20	Watch Out (Table 6.6)

Then, roll on the appropriate table to determine the creature, person or thing encountered.

TABLE 6.2
Aggressive Creatures - Littoral

d100	CATEGORY
1	Aboleth
2-4	Basilisk
5-10	Bird of Prey
11-12	Chuul
13-16	Crocodile
17	Dragon Turtle
18-19	Elemental
20-22	Gargoyle
23-26	Griffon
27-29	Harpy
30-31	Hill Giant
32-33	Hydra
34-42	Insects
43	Kraken
44-45	Medusa
46-49	Mephits
50-52	Merrow
53-56	Mimic
57-60	Ogres
61-62	Oni
63-66	Quippers
67-70	Reef Shark
71	Roc
72-77	Scorpions
78-79	Sea Hag
80-85	Snakes
86-88	Toad
89-91	Troll
92-97	Undead
98-100	Will-o'-Wisp

Aboleth. Your party sees one of these ancient monstrosities rear up at the water's edge as 2d4 robed and hooded cultists prostrate themselves or wail and gyrate before it. This is not the aboleth itself, but an illusory image that it has created to receive its followers. This means, of course, that it's very likely that an aboleth lair is located within one mile from here. If your party draws the cultists' attention, they become enraged that their moment of sacred communion has been interrupted, and they attack.

If your party's average level is higher than 10, consider that the aboleth is not an illusion, but an actual aboleth that has hauled itself onto the shore to receive worship. It tries to enslave as many of your party as it can into allying with the cultists as they attack the party members who cannot be enslaved. In this case, treat one of the cultists as a cult fanatic.

Basilisk. Your party passes a small cave or hollow carved into the ground that rises from the shoreline. A basilisk makes its lair here — as your party finds out if they so much as poke their heads inside. You may allow them a DC 15 Wisdom (Perception) or Wisdom (Survival) check to hear something stirring from within, or at least to intuit that something is there.

Scaling the Encounter: A basilisk may be a bit too much for a beginning-level party. Feel free to re-roll for another encounter. Conversely, if you want to run a more challenging encounter for a higher-level party, your party encounters two basilisks sharing a lair.

Treasure: The lair contains scattered valuables belonging to the basilisk's previous victims. Roll on the appropriate Treasure Hoard table, according to the total CR of the encounter. If there is more than one basilisk in the encounter, basilisk eggs may also be present for the taking.

Bird of Prey. A bird of prey — or a flock of them — wheels overhead, then strikes at your party. Keen-eyed, but bird-brained all the same, the bird has spotted something in your party as food — a familiar or small summoned creature is an obvious choice, but it could just be travelers rations, like strips of cured meat left in the open. To determine which species, roll on Table 6.2.1:

TABLE 6.2.1
Birds of Prey - Littoral

d4	ENCOUNTER
1-2	Eagle
3	Giant Eagle
4-5	Blood Hawks
6-7	Hawks
8-9	Owl
10	Giant Owl

Eagle. One eagle swoops down on your party, aiming itself at something it has identified as food.

Giant Eagle. A giant eagle has spotted your party. Giant eagles are intelligent and may respond if your party tries to flag them down. Though it cannot speak when spoken to, a successful DC 15 Charisma (Persuasion) check by someone who speaks ▸

Common or Auran persuades it to do your party a service, if it is within its power to accomplish it. This may involve delivering a written message or token, or guiding your party to a place that it knows, or even traveling with them for a while as an airborne lookout.

Blood Hawks. A flock of 2d6 blood hawks swoop down on your party. They concentrate on a single target — most likely a pack animal, but they may settle for a small humanoid as the next best thing.

Hawks. A flock of 2d10 hawks targets your party. They're probably going after the party's rations, but they may also have spotted rodents or small reptiles who are literally scurrying along the ground at your party's feet. To the extent that your party is in their way, the hawks attack them.

Owl. Owls hunt at night, so you should re-roll this encounter if it takes place during the day. Otherwise, one owl has spotted food as your party rests outdoors overnight. Most likely, it has spotted a small animal companion or familiar, or rations left out in the open, or a frog or other amphibian that has gotten in among your party.

Giant Owl. Likewise, a giant owl encounter is most suitable for night, so you should re-roll this encounter if it takes place during the day. One giant owl spots food in your party's camp.

Chuul. Walking along or near the shore, your party comes across one chuul, until very recently wandering and without purpose. By chance — or perhaps by some deeply-hidden instinct, it has come to the edge of a body of water and come back in contact with one of its old aboleth masters. This activated its ancient sense of purpose, and it attacks your party for their treasure. The presence of such an aggressive chuul near a body of water suggests that an aboleth lair is nearby.

Scaling the Encounter: A chuul may be more than you want to throw at a beginning-level party. Feel free to re-roll for another encounter. Conversely, if you want to run a more challenging encounter for a higher-level party, consider that the encounter group consists of one chuul for each multiple of 5 in your party's average level.

Crocodile. Traveling along the shore, your party has the misfortune to come across one crocodile. It may just be sunning itself on land, or it may be prowling for food. Either way, as soon as it spots your party, it realizes that it's hungry and it attacks. They're simple creatures, so it's as simple as that.

Scaling the Encounter: If you wish to make the encounter more challenging, consider that your party comes across a bask of crocodiles, all of whom are hungry enough to eat your party. The encounter group consists of 1d4 crocodiles for each multiple of 2 in your party's average level. You may freely substitute one giant crocodile for six crocodiles.

Dragon Turtle. A dragon turtle that makes its lair in a reef or a coastal cave hunts close to shore, and it may even come onto land to hunt. It's amphibious and it's really, really large, so standing back from the water's edge is no guarantee of safety from this beast. It spots your party as a possible source of treasure as well as food, so it rises from the water to attack them.

It is possible to bribe a dragon turtle to spare your life. If your party can communicate with it, they may make a DC 20 Charisma (Persuasion) check to convince it to do so. Make the DC 25 or even 30 if they're stupid enough to insult a dragon turtle by lowballing it; the beast knows that it can crush a small party with barely any effort. It's willing to parlay to some extent, but the dragon turtle's intention is essentially aggressive.

Scaling the Encounter: A close encounter with a dragon turtle may be too much for a lower-level party. If your party's average level is less than 20, feel free to re-roll for another encounter.

Either Fish, or Fowl, or Both

Visualizing littoral encounters presents a challenge in that not every creature described here is land-based. Some are aquatic or amphibious, and an encounter may require that your party be in the water, or at least by the water's edge. A reef shark isn't going to take a chunk out of you as long as you stay on dry land. Also, amphibious capability is a matter of degree. For instance: Yes, both crocodiles and octopi can leave the water. But an octopus won't go nearly as far up the beach to have at your party as a croc.

As the DM, it's up to you how to handle these fine distinctions, whether you want to hold aquatic or amphibious encounters for when your party puts themselves in the right position for them; or decide, in the absence of any contrary declarations from your players, that they have put themselves in an appropriate situation; or to re-roll for a more realistic encounter. You may also decide to ram it through regardless of plausibility and have that octopus climb a palm tree to get at a party member, or they meet an ogre frolicking in the water while fording a river. It's your world and your campaign.

Elemental. If most or all of your party is in the water, a water elemental rears up next to them. If most of all of your party is on land, the ground beside them resolves itself into an earth elemental. In either case, the elemental being is disturbed by its proximity to an alien element. It's an unhappy camper, and it lashes out at your party.

Scaling the Encounter: If your party's average level is lower than 5, an elemental may be more than you want to throw at them. Feel free to re-roll for a different encounter. Conversely, if your party's average level is 10 or higher, feel free to add one elemental to the encounter group.

Gargoyle. Promontories overlooking the sea and bends in a river are popular locations for fortifications. Castles whose builders want to get showy sometimes use gargoyles to decorate them — and when those castles are destroyed or abandoned, real gargoyles use them as their lair. Even more bizarrely, evil magic could infuse sculpted gargoyles that lie among ruins and turn them into real gargoyles.

Your party crosses paths with one gargoyle. Unless your party comes across a ruined fortress or some other place where it would make its lair, it's bored and looking for someone or something to torment for amusement. It uses convenient cover, like a large rock or a hollow in a riverbank or the base of a seaside cliff, or perches on high ground so it can attack from ambush. You may allow your party a DC 15 Wisdom (Perception) check to spot the gargoyle before it begins its attack run.

Scaling the Encounter: If you wish to make the encounter more challenging, the encounter group consists of one gargoyle for each multiple of 3 in your party's average level.

Treasure: If your party encounters gargoyles in their lair, roll on the Treasure Hoard table appropriate to the CR of the encounter.

Griffon. A griffon, roaming afield from its eyrie in higher ground, spots your party and goes for one of their mounts or pack animals — or at least, it thinks it has spotted a mount or a pack animal.

Scaling the Encounter: If you wish to make the encounter more challenging, your party encounters a flock (or pack?) of griffons hunting together. There is one for each multiple of 3 in your party's average level, rounded up.

Harpy. Harpies like to perch on coastal cliffs that overlook rocks, jagged reefs and other such hazards close to shore. They enjoy luring in hapless sailors with their songs and watching them crash and founder, and then preying on them when they're helpless. Your party approaches a harpy's perch and hears its siren song.

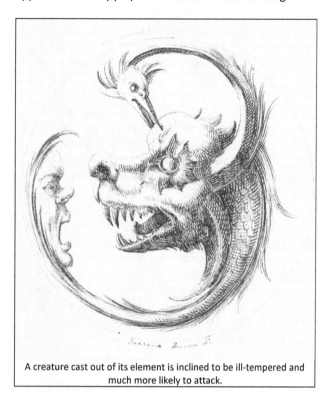

A creature cast out of its element is inclined to be ill-tempered and much more likely to attack.

Scaling the Encounter: If you wish to make the encounter more challenging, use a veritable harpy choir as the encounter group, consisting of two harpies for each multiple of 3 in your party's average level.

Treasure: By definition, a harpy's perch is its lair, so it's unlikely that this encounter takes place far from home. Roll on the Treasure Hoard table appropriate to the CR of the encounter.

Hydra. As your party takes a relaxing stroll by the shore, they see monstrous reptilian heads rear up out of the water. They have come across one hydra that has come close to shore to hunt — perhaps it has hunted out its normal territory. Your party looks as edible to it as any aquatic creature.

Scaling the Encounter: A hydra is probably too much for a low-level party. Feel free to re-roll for another encounter. Conversely, if you want to run a more challenging encounter for a high-level party, consider that your party has encountered a pair of hydras hunting together — 18 heads are better than nine, after all.

Insects. You may not think of insects as predatory, but they have a way of attacking without giving it much thought and they cause trouble in their own way. Your party should not be surprised if one swarm of insects — call them gnats, midges, mosquitos, whatever you will — descends upon them and makes life unpleasant. In

particular, mosquitos are bound to be a problem wherever there is stagnant fresh water.

Scaling the Encounter: If you wish to make the encounter more challenging (or more of a nuisance, depending on how you look at it), the encounter group consists of 1d4 swarms of insects plus one additional swarm for each level in your party's average level.

Kraken. When you're out for a relaxing stroll by the water's edge, the last thing you want to see is an enormous tentacled leviathan looming up before you. But kraken are known to come ashore and even make their lairs on land. Today is your party's lucky day: They get to meet one.

At least they will have some warning of the kraken's presence, as the sky and the surrounding water darken ominously before they actually see it. You may allow your party a DC 15 Intelligence (Nature) check to read the portents and figure out what is going on. The kraken, as always, is in a predatory mood; even if isn't looking to feed on your party, it feels like destroying them just for the sake of doing so.

Scaling the Encounter: A close encounter with a kraken may be too much for a lower-level party. If your party's average level is less than 20, feel free to re-roll for another encounter.

Medusa. Your party approaches the mouth of a seaside cave or a hollow in the riverbank. As they get closer, they notice that the opening is decorated by stone statues. In fact, a medusa makes its lair here and the statues are the petrified remains of its victims who got a little too curious. It decides that your party would supplement its existing collection nicely.

Scaling the Encounter: If your party's average level is lower than 6, a medusa may be more than you want to throw at them. Feel free to re-roll for a different encounter.

Treasure: The medusa's gaze petrifies flesh, but not valuables. To total up the bits and pieces that once belonged to its humanoid victims, roll on the Treasure Hoard: Challenge 5-10 table.

Mephits. These annoying little elementals have a habit of crossing over into the Material Plane, like ink bleeding through paper, and making nuisances of themselves. They are not predatory, but they are very annoying and they interpret any attempt to brush them aside as an attack. Roll on Table 6.2.2 to determine the kind of mephit your party encounters:

TABLE 6.2.2
Mephits - Littoral

d4	ENCOUNTER
1	Ice Mephit
2	Dust Mephit
3-5	Mud Mephits

+1 to the die roll if in temperate or tropical littoral

Ice Mephit. Even large bodies of water freeze over if it gets cold enough, and ice mephits find such conditions hospitable. One ice mephit perches on high ground like the top of a riverbank and pelts your party with small rocks, and it cackles contemptuously at someone who would intrude on its realm. This isn't enough to cause damage, but it refuses to stop. If it knows of a place where the ice is thin, it tries to get your party to chase it onto that place (whether or not it knows enough about local conditions to set up that sort of trap is up to you as DM).

Dust Mephit. Dust mephits lurk in seaside caves and hollows in riverbanks. Remains of living things that drift by or wash up on land fascinate them. Your party finds one dust mephit gazing out over the water. When it notices your party it fixes them with a piercing gaze, but it won't make the first move (unless there is a group of them and they outnumber your party; see Scaling the Encounter). When dust mephits attack, they concentrate on one target to the extent possible. They want to make sure of at least one kill, and if the rest run off they're okay with that; their goal is to satisfy their morbid curiosity about death.

Mud Mephits. As your party traverses or passes by a muddy riverbank or a tide pool at low tide, two mud mephits spot them. They mephits have slowly been driving each other mad with incessant and pointless complaints about everything and nothing, and they see your party as a diversion. They're lounging in the mud and too lazy to move, so they yell out to your party and start complaining about how the ocean or the river is too wet, or how they're poor, or bored, or exhausted. They start to beg your party for handouts. All of this is in Aquan or Terran, of course. If your party ignores them, the mephits chase after them and eventually become exasperated enough to attack. If your party confronts them, they become agitated and attack.

Scaling the Encounter: If you wish to make the encounter more challenging, the encounter group consists of 1d4 dust mephits or ice mephits for each multiple of 2 in your party's average level, or 1d4 mud

mephits plus a number of additional mud mephits equal to your party's average level.

Merrow. One of these monstrous descendants of warped merfolk comes ashore, intent on finding prey. Your party crosses paths with it, and it decides that taking them on will be less trouble than trying to snatch someone from a coastal settlement, where it might have to face down an entire village if caught in the act.

Scaling the Encounter: If you wish to make the encounter more challenging, the encounter group consists of one merrow for each multiple of 3 in your party's average level.

Mimic. Your party sees a chest sitting on the shore or riverbank. Is it a treasure chest abandoned by pirates or washed ashore from a shipwreck? Why, no! It's a mimic! The wilderness may seem like an odd place for a mimic to find victims, but has seen enough merchant traffic (consisting of intelligent creatures interested in money and things) passing by to give it a shot. If your party inspects it up close, it attacks. You may allow your party a DC 15 Wisdom (Perception) to notice a twitch or some other movement that gives it away.

Scaling the Encounter: If you wish to make the encounter more challenging, your party finds a veritable hoard of fake treasure chests — one for each multiple of 3 in your party's average level.

Ogres. Your party crosses paths with a party of ogres that has come to the riverside or seaside looking for merchants or other travelers to plunder. Whether you want to stage any meaningful interaction with these undersized giants is up to you, but it should surprise no one if they decide that your party is as good a target as any they are likely to find in the near future, whether they are looking for things or food (or both).

Scaling the Encounter: The encounter group consists of one ogre for each multiple of 3 in the party's average level. If your party is only 1st Level, consider that one half-ogre confronts them.

Treasure: These ogres are away from their lair. Total up the CR of all ogres killed and roll on the appropriate Individual Treasure table.

Oni. Once an ogre mage has had its way in a community, it may consider it sensible to find another hunting ground before the locals rally and figure out what to do about it. Your party crosses paths with an oni traveling between coastal or riverside settlements using its *Change Shape* ability to disguise itself as someone harmless. Maybe it has a raft or a boat that will help your party get where they want to go. If they allow the oni to travel with them, it bides its time until they make camp for the night. It volunteers to take the first watch, then it strikes once everyone else is asleep.

If you wish, you may allow your party a DC 20 Intelligence (Arcana) check to suspect that this apparently friendly stranger might be using magic to alter its appearance.

Scaling the Encounter: An oni may be a bit too much for a low-level party. Feel free to re-roll for another encounter. Conversely, if your party's average level is 10 or higher, consider that they have encountered two oni working together.

Quippers. If some or all of your party wades into a river or large lake, one swarm of quippers sees their next meal and attacks. You may allow your party a DC 15 Wisdom (Perception) or Wisdom (Survival) check to notice a school of fish with sharp teeth close to shore.

Scaling the Encounter: If you wish to make the encounter more challenging, the encounter group consists of two swarms of quippers for each multiple of 3 in your party's average level, rounded up. That's a whole lot of nasty little fish, but then again, this is the wilderness.

Reef Shark. These sharks are small enough to come close inshore, even into tide pools when the tide is in. They are comfortable in both salt and fresh water. When some or all of your party wades into shallow water, one reef shark sees them as tasty shanks of meat and attacks.

Scaling the Encounter: If you wish to make the encounter more challenging, the encounter group consists of 1d4 reef sharks plus one additional reef shark for each level in your party's average level.

It's Nessie!
You will have noticed by now that this chapter allows for encounters with some very large aquatic monsters even if you're on still on dry land. This accords with the canonical descriptions of these monsters, so there's nothing fishy going on here. In fact, there are parallels in our own world — and that's whether or not you give credence to the Loch Ness Monster and other such tales. The beluga sturgeon — the largest known freshwater fish — would qualify as huge or even gargantuan when fully grown.

Roc. A roc has roamed far afield from its mountain or hilltop eyrie in search of food. It's no pelican and it's out for bigger prey than fish, but coasts and rivers offer plenty of suitable targets. If anything, the roc has learned that someone on a boat or a raft has nowhere to run and nowhere to hide from a powerful aerial predator, so riverine merchants and other such travelers are easy pickings. When it spots your party, they look pretty tasty, too, so it attacks.

Scaling the Encounter: Rocs are fearsome opponents. If your party's average level is lower than 11, a roc may be more than you want to throw at them. Feel free to re-roll for a different encounter.

Scorpions. Your party takes a rest halt by some rocks, disturbing the scorpions that live among and under them. 1d8 scorpions attack your party. They have stingers, and they don't hesitate to use them.

Alternately, you may use this encounter to allow your party to witness a riverside encounter between one giant scorpion and one giant frog. They see the two creatures go to the water's edge. The scorpion gets up on the frog's back and the frog jumps into the water, keeping the scorpion above the surface. Halfway across the river, the scorpion stings the frog and they both sink, never to be seen again — unless your party intercedes. If they somehow rescue the giant frog, it follows them out of gratitude; treat it as a familiar or friendly NPC.

Scaling the Encounter: If your party's average level is 5 or higher, they see one giant scorpion scuttling along the beach or shore. Its size makes it quite fearless, so it attacks them. In this case, the encounter group consists of one giant scorpion for each multiple of 5 in the party's average level.

Sea Hag. Your party sees what appears to be one human — haggard and misshapen, but human nonetheless — walking inland from the water's edge. It's actually a sea hag that has come onto land looking for a child to steal so it can propagate. You may allow your party a DC 15 Intelligence (Arcana) check to realize it's using some kind of ability to conceal its true nature. You may also have the sea hag make a Wisdom check for each party member with a Charisma of 13 or higher, with the DC equal to the Charisma score. If it fails so much as once, its hatred of beauty drives it to attack that party member, despite knowing that this will blow its cover.

Scaling the Encounter: If you wish to make the encounter more challenging, your party encounters a coven of sea hags consisting of one for each multiple of 3 in your party's average level.

Snakes. There are poisonous snake species that live in salt water or fresh water, so leaving the land is no guarantee that you'll escape them. Whether your party is ashore or in shallow water, you may allow them a DC 15 Wisdom (Perception) or Wisdom (Survival) check to realize that they're about to disturb a snake or swarm of snakes. This should give them enough time to take evasive action, although you may consider that this simply means they aren't surprised when the snake lashes out.

In the tropics, your party may have the dubious pleasure of meeting a constrictor instead of a poisonous snake. Roll on Table 6.2.3 to determine the snake(s) encountered:

TABLE 6.2.3
Snakes - Littoral

d10	ENCOUNTER
1-4	Swarm of Poisonous Snakes
5-9	Poisonous Snake
10	Giant Poisonous Snake
11-12	Constrictor Snake
13	Giant Constrictor Snake

+3 to the die roll if in tropical littoral

Swarm of Poisonous Snakes. Your party comes across a shallow depression which is, literally, a snake pit with one swarm of poisonous snakes present. You may decrease the DC to notice the snakes to 5, to reflect the facts that there are more snakes present and the terrain feature is relatively easy to notice.

Poisonous Snake. Your party comes close to stepping on one poisonous snake.

Giant Poisonous Snake. Your party comes across one giant poisonous snake. You may decrease the DC to notice the snake to 10 to reflect its size.

Constrictor Snake. Constrictor snakes are found only in tropical regions where it's hot and humid enough for such a large cold-blooded creature to survive. But where they do occur, they are awe-inspiring predators. A constrictor tries to sneak up on your party and make a meal of one of its members.

Giant Constrictor Snake. If there is anything more daunting than running afoul of a constrictor snake, it is being targeted by a giant constrictor snake. One of these beasts targets one of your party members, confident that the rest won't be able to harm it.

Treasure: It's quite possible that a giant constrictor snake has fed on humans or humanoids before and that the less perishable possessions remain in its

➤

digestive tract. If your party bothers to slit the giant snake open and root around inside, roll on the Individual Treasure: Challenge 0-4 table to determine what they find.

Toad. These amphibians are not naturally aggressive, but they need to eat — and when they get this big a lot of different creatures look like food. Near a lake or a river (note that toads are not much fond of salt water), your party comes across one giant toad that is hungry enough to eat anything it can swallow. Assuming that at least someone in your party can be swallowed by a giant toad, the toad attacks.

Scaling the Encounter: If you wish to make the encounter more challenging, the encounter group consists of two giant toads for each multiple of 3 in your party's average level.

Troll. It's less common to find a troll by the ocean or a lake, but the river's edge is its natural domain. If there is no bridge nearby for the troll to guard, consider that your party has found a natural ford that the monster has staked out as its own. It demands one of the party's pack animals as its toll, or a suitable amount of coins. It fights rather than let anyone pass for free. It refuses to believe that your party is not interested in crossing, so it attacks them even if they do not want to get to the other side.

Scaling the Encounter: If your party's average level is lower than 5, a troll may be more than you want to throw at them. Feel free to re-roll for a different encounter. Conversely, if your party's average level is 10 or higher, feel free to add one troll to the encounter — a tag-team of trolls.

Treasure: The troll's racket has worked well enough in the past: Its victims pay one way or another, and it has accumulated a decent hoard. Searching the area turns up its stash, thrown in to a pile, on a successful DC 10 Wisdom (Perception) check. Roll on the Treasure Hoard: Challenge 5-10 table to determine the contents

Undead. Littoral areas are by no means immune to haunting by the undead. Water gives life, but it can also take life and receive the dead. Roll on Table 6.2.4 to determine the undead abomination that greets your party:

Wherever there is untimely death, there are undead.

TABLE 6.2.4
Undead - Littoral

d10	ENCOUNTER
1	Ghosts
2-3	Ghouls/Ghasts
4	Shadows
5-7	Skeletons
8	Wraith
9-10	Zombies

Ghost. That is no optical illusion; the ethereal form floating in the air at the water's edge really is a ghost. It is most likely the remnant of someone who drowned or died some other miserable death far from home. Whatever the case, you may make this into a hostile encounter by having the ghost try to possess a member of your party so that it may resolve unfinished business from its former life.

Ghouls/Ghasts. An encounter with ghouls is most likely to take place at night. Two ghouls (or one ghast) approach your party, driven by mindless hunger for their flesh.

Shadows. Walking in the shadow of a riverbank or passing by a coastal cave, your party glimpses a shadow in the gloom out of the corner of the eye. But it's not an illusion, it's undead! Without thinking or feeling, two shadows attack the nearest party member, eager to drain the life from another victim and create one more of their own kind.

Skeletons. Your party comes across the undead remnants of an ancient conflict: 1d6 skeletons carrying broken weapons and draped with fragments of the armor they wore in life. Perhaps they were soldiers killed defending a river crossing (or trying to force one), or storming ashore. Perhaps they were adventurers or explorers ambushed by brigands — or perhaps they were pirates themselves, who were hunted down in the name of justice or revenge, or who fell out among themselves. Driven by necromantic echoes of the end of their lives, they're looking for a fight.

Wraith. Your party chances upon an improvised burial site. Who knows how and why someone came to be buried here? What is certain is that that person came to an unhappy end, and its restless spirit became a wraith. As your party passes by, they can see that the site is ringed by barren and blasted ground with only withered grass to show that it once supported life. ➤

A cold, charcoal-gray mist emerges and resolves itself into a wraith, which then attacks your party.

Zombies. Your party come across 1d4 zombies, created from unfortunates who have drowned or otherwise met a bad end. Like all zombies, they have been programmed to kill every living thing they encounter. The source of the necromancy that created these zombies we leave to you. Perhaps they slipped the leash of their creator and they now wander the land mindlessly looking for victims.

Scaling the Encounter: Ghosts and wraiths always work alone. Also, if your party's average level is lower than 5, a wraith may be more than you want to throw at them. Feel free to re-roll for a different encounter.

Ghouls/Ghasts: If you wish to make the encounter more challenging, the encounter group consists of two ghouls (for or one ghast) each multiple of 4 in your party's average level. Feel free to mix and match ghouls and ghasts as long as you maintain the right proportion of total CR to average party level.

Shadows: The encounter group consists of two shadows for each multiple of 3 in your party's average level.

Skeletons: If you wish to make the encounter more challenging, the encounter group consists of 1d4 skeletons plus one additional skeleton for each level in your party's average level. You may substitute one warhorse skeleton for two skeletons.

Zombies: If you wish to make the encounter more challenging, the encounter group consists of 1d4 zombies plus one additional zombie for each level in your party's average level. If the average party level is 3 or higher, you may use an encounter group consisting of one ogre zombie for each multiple of 3 in the party's average level.

Treasure: Most likely, ghosts are encountered in or near what passes for a lair with them and you may consider that there they keep possessions that they had in life. Roll on the Treasure Hoard: Challenge 0-4 table for the contents of their stash. You may require a successful DC 15 Wisdom (Perception) check to find its exact location.

With ghouls, ghasts, skeletons and zombies, they may have with them some remains of what they had on their person when they died. Roll on the Individual Treasure table appropriate to the total CR of the encounter (rounded up to the nearest whole number).

Will-o'-Wisp. Will-o'-wisps can be found at or near places where someone has drowned. It could be the site of a murder, or a point in a river where soldiers fleeing a battle drowned, or a popular site for suicides. Whatever the case, a will-o'-wisp appears out of the fog rolling in from lake, river or the ocean and tries to draw your party into water deep enough to drown them.

Scaling the Encounter: If you wish to make the encounter more challenging, the encounter group consists of one will-o'-wisp for each multiple of 3 in your party's average level.

TABLE 6.3
Neutral Creatures - Littoral

d100	ENCOUNTER
1-5	Brown Bear
6-9	Awakened Shrub
10-14	Axe Beak
15-20	Boar
21-22	Centaur
23-27	Crabs
28-36	Deer
37-38	Dragon
39-44	Frogs
45-52	Goats
53-57	Hippogriff
58-65	Horses
66-70	Mules
71-74	Octopus
75-77	Pegasus
78-85	Rats
86-87	Storm Giant
88-95	Vultures
96-100	Water Weird
101-105	Lizards

+3 to the die roll if in temperate littoral
+10 to the die roll if in tropical littoral

Brown Bear. This is only something you will see by fresh water — a rapidly flowing river, or a lake — but brown bears have a taste for fish, and they know how to bat them out of the water. It's quite a sight even in a world filled with magic and monsters, but brown bears don't like to be interrupted when they're acquiring food. Catching fish requires concentration, and the distraction throws their *chi*. If your party wants to avoid a confrontation with an irritated brown bear, require a DC 15 Intelligence (Nature) or Wisdom (Survival) check. Success means that the bear ignores them; failure means that it charges them.

Awakened Shrub. Just as trees in pristine forests can become sentient through mysterious enchantments, more humble plants that dot the wilderness can also awaken. Your party comes into contact with one or more such awakened shrubs growing by a riverbank or in sandy soil near the beach. Perhaps it produces berries that look appetizing and someone in your party picks them. Perhaps your party is looking for kindling for the campfire. These or similar actions cause the shrub to express alarm.

Awakened shrubs are feistier than awakened trees, but less intimidating — not unlike the bark of a small dog compared to that of a large dog. An encounter with them is not necessarily hostile, even your party has done mischief to it. If your party asks it for help, a successful DC 10 Charisma (Persuasion) check wins it over, but the DC is 15 if your party has harmed it in some way. Help from an awakened shrub includes providing knowledge of the surrounding area.

Scaling the Encounter: If you wish to make the encounter more challenging, the encounter group consists of one awakened shrub for each multiple of 3 in your party's average level.

Axe Beaks. Your party comes across 1d4+2 of these odd-looking, bad-tempered flightless birds hunting by the shore. They don't like having their hunt interrupted, but it's not a sure thing that they'll attack. You may have your party make a DC 15 Intelligence (Nature) or Wisdom (Survival) check. Failure means that a party member has made a false move that angers the axe beaks, which then attack the party.

Boar. Your party spots 1d4 wild boar rooting around near the water's edge. Boar are popular targets for hunters. They'll fight back if attacked — indeed, the challenge they present is part of the appeal of hunting them. But they have also developed a fight-or-flight instinct, and if your party wishes to avoid a fight, you may have them make a DC 15 Wisdom (Survival) or Intelligence (Nature) group check to scare the boar off.

Scaling the Encounter: If you wish to make the encounter more challenging, use an encounter group consisting of one giant boar for each multiple of 3 in your party's average level. Giant boar are even more aggressive than their smaller cousins and they charge anyone who disturbs them.

Treasure: Boar meat is good eating for many folk. Perhaps a nearby butcher will pay 2 gp or thereabouts for a fresh carcass. The price might go up to 5 gp for a giant boar.

There is a chance that wild creatures mistake your actions for a threat.

Centaur. Your party spots a lone figure, half-human and half-equine following the shoreline or the course of the river. It is a centaur, and like all too many of its kind, it became irrevocably separated from its tribe during a migration. Now it uses the coastline or the river as a navigational aide as it searches for its tribe, staying a little while at settlements along the way to collect information. As such, it may have knowledge of nearby settlements and roads that would help your party, and it could be persuaded to share it. A centaur might also offer your party the chance to take on a sidequest, asking for their help in finding its long-lost tribe.

Scaling the Encounter: It is up to you whether or not to scale up an encounter with centaurs. Though most often encountered alone, it is possible that as many as three or four centaurs might have split off from their tribe as a group. However, if you anticipate a hostile encounter, throwing more than one centaur at your party would provide a stiff challenge if their average level is less than 4.

Treasure: Centaurs carry their valuables with them. Roll once on the Individual Treasure: Challenge 0-4 table for each centaur present.

Crabs. While dipping their toes into the water, or even strolling at the water's edge, your party runs afoul of 2d6 giant crabs. They attack only if they feel threatened, so have your party make a DC 15 Intelligence (Nature) or Wisdom (Survival) check. Failure means that a party member has made a false move that sets the crabs' pincers snapping.

Treasure: If crab meat is a delicacy in your campaign world, live giant crabs could fetch 2-5 gp each at a seafood market, but they would have to be sold live and they cannot survive out of water for very long. The easiest way to trap a crab is to lure it into a container. Grappling is much more difficult; it requires someone to maintain a grapple on the crab while someone else binds its claws, which requires an action and a successful DC 15 Strength check.

Deer. Your party spots 1d8 bucks and 2d6 does and grazing quietly. If your party attacks, only the males fight, covering the females while they flee.

Even if the party does not behave in a threatening manner, you may consider that there is a chance that the bucks mistake their actions for a threat and attack anyway. Have your party make a DC 10 Intelligence (Nature) or Wisdom (Survival) check. Failure means that someone has made a false move that sets off the males and they charge.

Treasure: Anyone for venison? Perhaps a nearby butcher will pay 2 gp or thereabouts for a fresh carcass.

Dragon. Your party notices a shadow on the water. It's made by something looming in the sky above: a dragon on the prowl. To determine what kind of dragon roll on Table 6.3.1:

TABLE 6.3.1
Dragon - Littoral

d12	ENCOUNTER
1-2	Black
3	Blue
4	Green
5	Red
6	White
7	Brass
8-9	Bronze
10	Copper
11	Gold
12	Silver

To determine its age, see Scaling the Encounter.

To be clear, this need not be a hostile encounter. The dragon is not defending its lair, so it may just be curious about your party. It may have more important things to do and decline to take notice of them at all. Or it may be hungry and on the hunt, or it's angry because your party has intruded on territory it claims as its own.

Alternately, you may present your party with a scenario that you can weave into the larger story of the campaign. It may even serve as the main thrust of the campaign. Your party finds a dragon wyrmling sprawled on the beach or laying against the riverbank. It's obviously in a bad way — gashed open, bleeding profusely (or it has almost bled out), barely conscious. Assume that it has stabilized after being reduced to 0 hp, and that it now has 1 hp. How it got that way is up to you, and it may depend on how dragons fit into your campaign world. Perhaps it fled from a fight in which it was badly wounded. Who would its enemies be, and why were they fighting? Were any of its relatives or companions killed?

How your party decides to deal with this child in distress could open up possibilities for later in your campaign. If they rescue it, will its kin reward them later, or will its enemies confront them on the principle that, "The friends of my enemy must also be my enemy?" Conversely, what are the consequences if they put it out of its misery, like scavengers roaming a medieval battlefield? Will its kin seek retribution, or will its enemies treat your party as allies?

Scaling the Encounter: Because dragons get tougher with age, the age of the dragon encountered should depend on your party's average level — especially if you decide that this is going to be a hostile encounter. If your party's average level is 10 or lower, they encounter a wyrmling. If their average level is 11-18, they encounter a young dragon. If their average level is 19-25, they encounter an adult dragon. If their average level is higher than 25, they encounter an ancient dragon.

Frogs. Frogs are not aggressive predators, but even so an amphibian's got to eat. When your party wanders along the lake shore or riverbank, they draw the attention of 1d4 giant frogs. If any party member is small or smaller, or there is a familiar or other animal companion present, the frogs lash out instinctively and the first frog to stick out its tongue tries to swallow it. They leave alone anyone of medium or larger size.

Scaling the Encounter: If you wish to make the encounter more challenging, add one giant frog for each level in your party's average level. That is a lot of humanoid-sized frogs to be gathered in one place, and it is bound to make things awfully crowded on the lily pads.

Goats. Your party comes across a small herd of 1d8 billies and 2d8 nannies grazing near the water. Perhaps they are wild goats — or perhaps they have gotten separated from a larger herd, and somewhere nearby there is a goatherd who would give a reward for their safe return. In any event, billies can be ornery beasts and if your party approaches them, you may require your party to make a DC 15 Intelligence (Nature) check to avoid setting off an attack.

Scaling the Encounter: If you wish to make the encounter more challenging, use a herd of wild (and potentially irritated) giant goats instead. The encounter group should consist of 1d4 giant goats for each multiple of 2 in your party's average level with the same 1:2 ratio of males to females. Giant goats are quite wild; there is no chance that they are being kept by someone else.

Hippogriff. Your party sees a hippogriff circling overhead, looking for its next meal, or on the ground dealing with its prey. Hippogriffs are not as aggressive as birds of prey, and it is no sure bet that they would attack your party on the hope that it could make off with a pack animal or their stash of rations. Whether or not this is a hostile encounter is a matter of your discretion.

Hippogriffs may be a kind of prey as well as predators. If hippogriffs are used as mounts in your world, it must follow that captive adults have value as breeding stock, and chicks captured from the wild also have value because they are still young enough to be tamed. To that end, you may allow your party a DC 20 Wisdom (Survival) check to trace a path to the hippogriff's lair (likely to be sited atop a cliff overlooking the water or some other elevated point, or in nearby hills) after observing it for a while. If your party has someone capable of flight, reduce the DC to 15. To subdue an adult hippogriff to the point where it can be bound and held captive, it must be successfully grappled and kept in grappled condition for 10 consecutive rounds.

Scaling the Encounter: If you want to stage a hostile encounter with hippogriffs and you need to make it more of a challenge for a higher-level party, consider that the encounter group consists of one hippogriff for each multiple of 3 in your party's average level.

Horses may put up a fight if they don't want to be caught.

Horses. Your party comes across a small herd of horses that have wandered down to the riverbank or shoreline. It's only natural that they should go to a source of water, regardless of whether or not you could make them drink it. The only questions are, how many of them are there, and do they belong to someone else? Horse encounters are unlikely to be hostile, although they may put up a fight if you try to wrangle them before they've been broken. Roll on Table 6.3.2 to determine the nature of the horse encounter:

TABLE 6.3.2
Horses - Littoral

d6	ENCOUNTER
1-2	Pony
3-5	Riding Horse
6	Warhorse

Pony. Your party comes across a small herd of 2d8 ponies grazing, or moving across the landscape at a walk. It's up to you to decide whether they're wild, or if they belong to someone — and if the latter, is their owner nearby (see Table 5.5) or have they escaped from someone who would pay a reward for their return?

If they are wild, they can be wrangled. To wrangle a pony, it must be successfully grappled and kept in grappled condition for 3 consecutive rounds. At that point, it becomes docile and whomever grappled it may ride it or use it as a pack animal. Only one medium-size creature may try to grapple a pony at any given time.

Riding Horse. Your party comes across a small herd of 2d6 riding horses grazing, or moving across the landscape at a walk. It's up to you to decide whether they're wild, or if they belong to someone — and if the latter, have they escaped from someone who would pay a reward for their return?

If they are wild, they can be wrangled. To wrangle a riding horse, it must be successfully grappled and kept in grappled condition for 6 consecutive rounds. At ▶

that point, it becomes docile and whomever grappled it may ride it or use it as a pack animal. Because of its size, two medium-size creatures may grapple with the same riding horse simultaneously, and as long as one of them maintains its grappled condition, this counts toward the requirement for wrangling it.

Warhorse. Your party comes across 1d4 warhorses. Whether their owners were killed in battle, or they just escaped from the stable, is not clear at first glance. Warhorses do not need to be wrangled; they have been broken and disciplined, so they're used to working with humans. However, they're also trained fighters and if you don't approach them just right in a situation like this, they'll take you for the enemy and attack. If your party approaches the warhorses, have them make a DC 15 Intelligence (Nature) check to avoid setting the horses off.

Insignia on their barding should give some hints as to whom the warhorses belong (or belonged). A good warhorse is highly prized, and its owner would pay dearly for its return.

Treasure: If your party encounters riding horses that have escaped from their owners, they may be saddled and their saddlebags contain valuables equal to one roll on the Individual Treasure: Challenge 0-4 table. Warhorses, of course, have their barding.

Mules. Mules are domestic creatures. So when your party sees 1d8 mules mulling about for no apparent purpose, it is highly likely that they have escaped from their owners — probably traveling merchants or smugglers. It's also possible that they came from a farm located inland. Their owners will pay a reward for their return — or your party could claim them as their own without anyone (possibly) being the wiser.

Mules do not attack. But they may be skittish around strangers, especially if they have been out in the wild for a while. If your party tries to take possession of them, have them make a DC 10 Intelligence (Nature) check to avoid a hostile reaction. Remember, these creatures have a kick like a mule.

Octopus. Octopi are not aggressive, but they are curious and they express it ways that can be uncomfortable for the object of their interest. While wading into a tide pool, river or lake, your party catches the attention of 1d6 octopi. You may have your party make a DC 15 Intelligence (Nature) or Wisdom (Survival) check to somehow convince the octopi that they are uninteresting and better left alone. Otherwise, they swarm one party member, making melee attacks until they have grappled their target.

Scaling the Encounter: If you wish to make the encounter more challenging, substitute one giant octopus for the normal-sized octopi. However, giant octopi prefer deep water and rarely come onto land.

Pegasus. Your party sees one pegasus wheeling overhead. It does not attack, even if it sees evil creatures. However, it may be flagged down by signaling or calling to it and making a successful DC 15 Charisma (Persuasion) check. If your party can get the pegasus' attention, they may persuade it to render some kind of aid — such as taking a party member to a nearby location — with a successful DC 20 Charisma (Persuasion) check. For good-aligned characters who can speak Celestial, Elvish or Sylvan the DC is 15.

Scaling the Encounter: If you wish to make the encounter more challenging, the encounter group consists of one pegasus for each multiple of 3 in the party's average level, rounded up.

Rats. Even if they haven't just fled a sinking ship, you find rats in coastal areas and riversides. Some species of rats spend enough time in freshwater so that they're practically amphibious, so even if you go out onto the water you won't escape them; they'll find a way to get at your food. Roll on Table 6.3.3 to determine the nature of the rat encounter:

TABLE 6.3.3
Rats - Littoral

d6	ENCOUNTER
1	Lone Rat
2-4	Swarm of Rats
5-6	Giant Rats

Lone Rat. A single rat, perhaps foraging by itself or perhaps lost from its nest, approaches your party while they take a rest. It's not much of a threat, but if someone in your party is looking for a familiar or even just a pet, this is an opportunity. Interacting with the rat — especially earning its trust with food — and making a successful DC 10 Intelligence (Nature) check earns its loyalty as a pet.

Swarm of Rats. Without being aware of it, your party has stopped to rest near a nest of rats. Drawn by the party's rations, a swarm of rats makes for the nearest source of food. They don't attack party members who don't interfere with their basic mission of acquiring ➤

food. But unless they are stopped, they eventually account for all of your party's rations, making off with what they don't eat on the spot.

Giant Rats. In this case, the rats drawn by the food your party carries are giant rats. There are 2d6 of them.

Storm Giant. A storm giant cuts an imposing figure in any setting, but somehow it looks all the more impressive rising above the flat planes of sea and shore and all but touching the sky. It may be on its way to visit another storm giant's underwater palace, or on its way from beneath the waters to visit a storm giant living in the mountains. Or it may have come onto land simply to meditate on an isolated stretch of shore.

It greets your party with courtesy and gives them a chance to demonstrate their intentions before it reacts to them. Unless your party would rather fight than chat, you can use the storm giant as a conduit for information that would move your campaign forward. As beings who have lived long and seen much, and who strive to read omens and see into the future, they are bound to know things that your party does not and could not know. It may even be persuaded to use its innate spell casting to aid your party, though it should take a successful DC 15 or 20 Charisma (Persuasion) check, depending on how respectfully your party has treated it.

Treasure: Good luck trying to separate a storm giant from its possessions. But be that as it may, roll on the Individual Treasure level 11-20 table to determine what it carries on its person.

Vultures. Your party comes across 1d6+2 vultures drawn by dead fish or the remains of a larger aquatic creature washed ashore. How they respond depends on how they interpret your party's actions. You may have your party make a DC 10 Intelligence (Nature) or Wisdom (Survival) check. Failure means that a party member has made a false move that persuades the vultures to attack, thinking that they need to defend their food source.

Scaling the Encounter: If you wish to make the encounter more challenging, consider substituting giant vultures for the vultures. The encounter group then consists of two giant vultures for each multiple of 3 in your party's average level. Giant vultures may be hunting instead of feeding. Perhaps they — mistakenly or not — spotted your party as hapless travelers on their last legs, in which case they swoop down to try to hasten their demise.

Vultures would much rather you be dead.
But it's too much work to kill a party by themselves.

Water Weird. Your party comes upon a place that is guarded by a water weird — an elemental tasked with safeguarding a specific location. As an elemental, it acts instinctively and treats your party as intruders. However, its actions vary according to the alignment it has absorbed from its surroundings, so consider that there is a 50% chance that it is neutral good and guarding a sacred site and 50% that it is neutral evil and bound to a befouled site.

Scaling the Encounter: If you wish to make the encounter more challenging, consider that more than one water weird has been bound to this place. The encounter group consists of one water weird for each multiple of 5 in the party's average level, rounded up. At your discretion, you may require your players to say, "one weird water weird" three time fast.

Treasure: Since the water weird is bound to the spot, it stands to reason that belongings from others who have run afoul of it would be located here. Roll on the Individual Treasure table appropriate for the total CR of the encounter.

Lizards. Your party crosses paths with 1d4 giant lizards foraging for large insects and smaller lizards near the shore. They may be wild, or they may be pack animals left at the water's edge by smugglers or legitimate merchants who transferred their goods to a vessel and

found they didn't have room for the beasts. In this case, it may be possible to track down the former owners and return them.

If they're wild lizards, they can be wrangled and trained to serve as pack animals or mounts. To wrangle a giant lizard, it must be successfully grappled and kept in grappled condition for 10 consecutive rounds. At that point, it becomes docile and submits to whomever grappled it. Because of its size, two medium-size creatures may grapple with the same giant lizard simultaneously, and as long as one of them maintains its grappled condition, this counts toward the requirement for wrangling it.

TABLE 6.4
Humanoids - Littoral

d20	ENCOUNTER
1	Bugbear
2-5	Elves
6-7	Goblins
8	Hobgoblins
9-12	Lizardfolk
13	Lycanthrope
14-16	Merfolk
17-18	Orcs
19-20	Sahuagin

Bugbear. Your party crosses paths with one or more bugbears (see Scaling the Encounter). They could be mercenaries on their way to join a larger goblinoid army mobilizing for war. Conversely, they could be heading home after a victorious campaign — or straggling in the wake of a catastrophic defeat. Their exact circumstances and motivation should depend on what else is going on in your campaign world. If there is no such war in which they could take part, they're out for some casual plunder, or perhaps on their way to shake down a hobgoblin tribe that once employed them.

Their interest in fighting your party should vary according to the reason why they're here. For instance, mobilizing for war means they have a larger purpose in mind than victimizing your party. If they're looking to strongarm some hobgoblins, they may even offer your party a cut of the take in exchange for adding to their strength in numbers.

Scaling the Encounter: A beginning-level party should only have to cope with one bugbear. If you wish to make the encounter more challenging, the encounter group consists of two bugbears for each multiple of 3 in your party's average level. If your party's average level is 10 or higher, add one bugbear chief as the group's leader.

Elves. Your party encounters 2d6 elves from a nearby settlement of mariners. This close to land, they are traveling in boats or on rafts. If your party is by a river or lake, they may be traders going about their business. Or they may be explorers familiarizing themselves with the river system. By the ocean, your party may find mariners making a short hop along the sea coast — or they may be survivors of a wreck crawling ashore!

Seafaring elves are more open to outsiders than their kin who live deep in the forest. But even still, they'll feel more comfortable with a party with fellow elves in it. Conversely, they regard a party with traditional enemies of the elves in it with suspicion or even hostility. If your party establishes a rapport with this group, they may be willing to provide local lore and trade. Shipwreck victims may have a tale to tell of nearby danger, whether there be jagged reefs, storms or monsters. They may also offer your party a sidequest by asking for protection against the hazards of the wild, or specific enemies that they know to be about.

Treat the elves as commoners, although you may add one priest for flavor.

Goblins. Goblins may make their lairs in seaside caves, and certainly they find coastal riverside communities suitable targets for raiding. Your party crosses paths with a goblin raiding party. They may stop to pry information out of them about the local area, or they may just spot a target of opportunity and attack.

Scaling the Encounter: Use an encounter group of 1d4 goblins for each level in your party's average level. If you don't want to run a mass encounter but you still want to provide a higher-level party with a meaningful challenge, feel free to substitute one goblin boss for four goblins as much as you like.

Also, littoral offers a suitable environment for employing cavalry — in other words, worg mounts. Feel free to substitute one worg for two goblins, as long as there are not more worgs present than goblins to ride them.

Hobgoblins. If there is a war going on in this corner of your campaign world, consider that one side or another has hired hobgoblin mercenaries, so that your party may cross paths with a small group of them. In a littoral setting, perhaps they have been ordered to guard a river crossing, or they have come ashore on a seacoast as a scout party. In either case, they inquire closely into your party's identity to see if you're friend or foe. Or they may be following the river while marching to their mustering point, in which case, they have business to take care of and they'll ignore your party as long as they don't try to interfere.

Scaling the Encounter: The baseline encounter group should consist of 1d4 hobgoblins for each multiple of 2 in your party's average level. If your party's average level is 10-19, add a hobgoblin captain as the group's leader, accompanied by two goblin servants or one bugbear aide. If your party's average level is 20 or higher, add instead one hobgoblin warlord with two bugbear aides.

Also, littoral offers a suitable environment for employing cavalry — in other words, worg mounts. Feel free to substitute one worg for two goblins, as long as there are not more worgs present than hobgoblins to ride them.

Lizardfolk. Your party has entered the territory of a lizardfolk tribe based in a nearby seaside cave or patch of swampy ground by a lake or river. A patrol or war party from that tribe spots your party. In their overdeveloped reptilian brains, they identify your party first as intruders, then as possible captives to be sacrificed or eaten later. So they attack.

Scaling the Encounter: The encounter group consists of 1d4 lizardfolk for each multiple of 2 in your party's average level. You may substitute one lizardfolk shaman for four lizardfolk. If you party's average level is 10 or higher, add one lizardfolk king/queen to the group as its leader.

Lycanthrope. To determine what manner of werebeast your party encounters, roll on Table 6.4.1:

TABLE 6.4.1
Lycanthropes - Littoral

d6	ENCOUNTER
1	Wereboar
2-4	Wererat
5-6	Werewolf

All lycanthropes assume their animal form if the encounter comes down to combat, although they may choose their hybrid form instead if they have access to a weapon.

Wereboar. It's most likely that a wereboar met by chance was at some point an unfortunate hunter who didn't realize that the boar at which he aimed his bow was really a lycanthrope. Or it might have been a herder who presented an isolated target. The wereboar goes about looking for victims to share its fate, hoping that a lone boar will provide a lure someone into engaging with it. A party of ➤

adventurers could offer it an even more attractive target — confident in its ability to take at least one of them and drive the others off, it attacks.

Wererat. It's not hard to find rats in littoral areas, but they're not much welcome where people live. Your party comes across a wererat driven into the wilderness along with the rats with whom it kept company. Now, it hopes to create a party of wererats and take revenge on its former persecutors — and your party looks like it will make nice lycanthropes. It appears to your party in its human form, pretending to be a shipwreck victim washed ashore, or a distressed traveler who hopes to travel with your party for protection. It tries to slip toward the back of the march order and waits for a time when everyone's back is turned to it.

Werewolf. A werewolf spots your party and cannot turn down the opportunity to claim more victims. However, it is clever enough to approach them in its human form, pretending that it washed ashore after a shipwreck. Or perhaps it really is a victim of a shipwreck, or perhaps it caused the loss of the ship by attacking the crew, who were helpless before it. In any event, once your party gets close and drops its guard, the werewolf attacks.

Scaling the Encounter: A single lycanthrope can offer a stiff challenge to a low-level party. If your party's average level is 3 or less, feel free to re-roll the encounter. Alternately, if you want to make a werewolf encounter more challenging for a higher-level party, use a pack of them consisting of one werewolf for each multiple of 5 in your party's average level, rounded up.

Treasure: It is assumed that all of these encounters take place away from the lycanthrope's base of operations, so roll on the Individual Treasure table of the appropriate CR to determine what valuables it carries.

Merfolk. Merfolk don't come onto land in large numbers, but there are various reasons why your party might run into a small band of 2d8 merfolk in a littoral area. You won't find a massive army of merfolk storming ashore, or an imposing procession of merfolk royalty. But they may come onto land to explore or to trade, knowing that many land-dwellers have a strange aesthetic fascination with coral (which is as mundane to them as lumber to land dwellers), and that some would rather buy fish and other aquatic food sources from them than catch their own. They're as happy to trade with your party as any other land-dweller. They might also ask for directions to

the nearest settlement, or general information about the lay of the land.

Or perhaps they're emissaries from a tribe threatened by merrow or other aquatic monsters, and they're looking for help in dealing with them. In this case, they offer your party a sidequest, albeit one that requires breathing underwater.

Orcs. You may add orcs to the list of humanoid races who know that ripe raiding targets dot coastlines and rivers. A small group orcs could be a scout party out to get the lay of the land, while a larger group would be an actual raiding party on its way to — or on its way back from — its target.

Your party crosses paths with these orcs, but if they have such a fixed purpose in mind, it's no guarantee that they'll pay your party much attention. Their leader may look your party over and decide that they're not worth the bother. But they may also decide to interrogate your party for information about the surrounding area, and they'll resort to violence without hesitation if your party is too slow to cooperate. They are less likely to give your party a break if there are elves in it, and they'll make elf characters a special focus of hostility.

Scaling the Encounter: The baseline encounter group should consist of 1d4 orcs for each multiple of 2 in your party's average level. If your party's average level is 5-9, add an orog as the group's leader. If your party's average level is 10 or higher, use an orc war chief as its leader. If you don't want to run a mass encounter but you still want to provide a higher-level party with a meaningful challenge, feel free to substitute one orog for four orcs as much as you like.

Treasure: If the orcs are coming back from a successful raid, you may roll on the Treasure Hoard: Challenge 0-4 table to determine the fruits of their labor. This is in addition to the individual treasure they carry.

Sahuagin. Sahuagin make their lairs deep beneath the surface of the waters, so when they come ashore to raid costal and riverside settlements, it inevitably seems to their victims that they arrive from out of nowhere. So it seems to your party also when they see sahuagin raiders rise out of the water and come ashore. A small group may just be a scouting party, but a larger group has a target and plunder in mind. It's entirely possible that they view your party as a good target of opportunity. *Scaling the Encounter:* The encounter group consists of two sahuagin for each multiple of 3 in your party's average level. You may substitute one sahuagin priestess for four sahuagin. If you party's average level is 10 or higher, add one sahuagin baron to the group as its leader.

TABLE 6.5

Humans - Littoral

d20	ENCOUNTER
1	Adventurers
2-3	Divers
4	Exiles
5	Explorers
6-7	Fishermen
8	Fugitives
9-10	Merchants
11-12	Military
13	Pilgrims
14-16	Pirates
17-18	Sailors
19-20	Smugglers

Adventurers. Unless your party contains all of the adventurers in your campaign world, it's at least theoretically possible that they'll run into another adventuring party following the river course or shoreline. Perhaps they're pursuing the same objective as your party. Perhaps they have a different mission; perhaps they're headed for a site that your party knows nothing about (like ancient ruins said to hold lost treasures). Perhaps they're lost and starving, or wounded, or cursed.

How they react to your party depends on a variety of factors. Are they rivals pursuing the same goal? If not, perhaps this party is willing to share useful information. In fact, if your party is stuck and having a hard time advancing the storyline of your campaign, a friendly encounter like this can help steer them in the right direction. Differences in alignment may also shape how the two parties react to each other.

Composition of this rival party is up to you and can vary according to circumstance. Any party in the wilderness would be well-advised to have someone accomplished in Survival, such as a ranger, with them. Conversely, a party that is struggling may be in a bad way precisely no one is well-versed in Survival or Nature.

Scaling the Encounter: Unless there is some possibility that this encounter turns hostile, the relative level of the party is mainly a matter of affect. A higher-level party might project self-confidence and calm (or arrogance), while beginning-level party might stumble about, unsure of themselves. If you're leaning towards a hostile encounter, however, consider that the total CR of the party should be roughly two-thirds of your party's average level.

Divers. Your party comes across 1d4 gatherers who dive for shellfish or gather them in tide pools or shallows. They work this spot regularly, so they can provide your party with local knowledge. They may ask your party to protect them if there are monsters, bandits or personal enemies about. At your discretion, these divers may be collecting raw pearls — in which case they have more than their own lives to protect. They can reward your party with pearls, and in any event they can also sell them at half one-fourth the price that a finished pearl would command in your campaign world.

Treat divers as commoners who carry long knives (treat as shortswords) for prying open shellfish.

Exiles. Your party encounters 1d6 people who could serve as a source of adventure hooks. From their appearance, they have obviously seen better days. They have come to the river's edge looking for transportation to someplace safer, or to the coast because the ocean blocks them from fleeing any further from their troubles. They can have any one a variety of backstories: perhaps they are royalty or nobility who have been usurped; perhaps the opposite is the case and they are failed usurpers on the run. Or perhaps they have gotten caught up in a blood feud in their homeland and that's why they fear for their lives.

No matter their reason for being here, they should offer your party an adventure hook of some sort. It may involve protecting the exiles from their real (or imagined) pursuers. It may involve returning to their former home and securing an important item that was left behind (a family heirloom, a badge of office), perhaps even helping them return home and force their way back into their former position of prominence. At the very least, exiles can provide your party with information about their former home territory, which in turn could be a key location in your campaign.

Use any NPC template you like for the exiles, depending on the backstory you assign them.

Explorers. Your party bumps into a small human party, driven by the curiosity that characterizes their kind, to map and describe a seacoast or river system that has been mostly untouched by human hands. The group consists of 1d4 scholars (treat them as commoners) and 1d4 scouts who act as bodyguards. Perhaps they are here thanks to the sponsorship of an academy or a ruler eager to know more about the world, or perhaps the explorer is a wealthy eccentric who undertook this expedition on his or her own.

Such an encounter is not likely to be hostile. Explorers are open and curious. Instead, you may treat this as an opportunity for your party to receive some help from a knowledgeable stranger — the explorer is likely to have excellent maps of nearby areas (and knowledge of those areas) and is willing to share them. Conversely, an expedition that has been in the field for a while may be running short on cartography supplies and other necessaries and may be willing to pay well if your party can provide what they lack. Also, if your party is in the mood for a sidequest, an explorer may offer one: If the expedition is headed into particularly dangerous territory, it may need additional guards to keep it safe.

Fishermen. Your party comes across 1d6 anglers engaged in their occupation. If by a river, they're set on the bank with their lines in the water. If by the ocean or a large lake, they're by their boats and either on the way out onto the water or returning with their catch. If returning with fish in hand, they're willing to sell fish from their catch for half of what a tavern meal would cost — the hitch being, of course, that you have to clean and smoke or cook it yourself before it goes bad. With just bit of coaxing, they're also happy to provide your party with local knowledge, including tales of monsters in the water nearby and of course, stories of the one that got away.

Treat fishermen as commoners.

No Tarrasque?

That's *the* tarrasque, thank you very much, and it insists on being addressed as such. Because the tarrasque is unique and there is only supposed to be one in any given campaign world, I assume that any encounter with it should be planned, not conjured out of a random encounter table.

Fugitives. Your party crosses paths with 1d6 bedraggled people stumbling along the shore or riverbank. They look to be in less-than-optimal shape, but they're moving as fast as they can manage. Most, if not all of them have a manacle around one wrist, with the other manacle dangling on its chain. They're escaped prisoners who have fled into the forest. From whom they are fleeing and why they were imprisoned in the first place is up to you, and ought to depend on where in your campaign world this encounter takes place.

How the encounter plays out depends entirely on how your party reacts, but one thing on which you may rely is that these fugitives did not go to the trouble of a jailbreak just to allow a bunch of strangers to take their freedom back from them. Each of them has learned to whip their freed manacle by the chain and wield it as a club. Treat the fugitives as bandits, but without weapons or armor.

Treasure: Fugitives have no treasure.

Merchants. Your party spots some merchants moving their goods by raft or boat (if on a river or lake) or by ship (if on the ocean). If the latter, they would only come within hailing distance of your party while ashore looking for fresh water or provisions. The group consists of 1d8 merchants and 2d4 guards. Traveling merchants could help your party by selling them necessary items, exchanging hard money for treasure items or providing knowledge of just about anywhere in your campaign world (where are they going, and where did they come from?). They may also be interested in hiring your party as additional guards if they fear pirates.

Treat the merchants as commoners. Treat the guards as guards, although you may substitute veterans for as many guards as you wish.

Treasure: Roll once on the Individual Treasure: Challenge 0-4 table for each merchant or guard. In addition, roll once on the Treasure Hoard: Challenge 0-4 table for each merchant present to determine the value of goods and/or hard money in the caravan. You may substitute valuable goods — spices, fine cloth, expensive hardwood, etc. — for art objects or coin as you wish.

Military. Littoral areas are bound to play an important role in a world plagued by war. Rivers are useful lines of defense, and for invaders and defenders alike control of rivers and river crossings are crucial for moving armies and their supplies. An army marching along a river that it controls can be supplied by accompanying boats and rafts. An enemy with ships can invade from across the ocean, making it important to defend seacoasts. So if war is a part of your campaign world, your party could encounter an army or part of an army.

An entire army on the march, or deployed for battle, can be seen from a long ways away in open terrain. However, they're certain to have more important things on their mind than dealing with a party of adventurers, so they're more useful for spectacle and flavor than a challenging encounter.

For an actual encounter, a small group of soldiers is most likely a patrol, tasked with scouting ahead of the main army, or on its flanks. Their job is to locate the enemy and, conversely, to prevent enemy scouts from spotting their main force. They might also be a detachment guarding a ford, a bridge or a coastal lookout. They won't attack your party without reason to believe that your party is somehow connected to their enemy. However, they do stop your party to grill them for information, and possibly enlist their help with their mission.

Scaling the Encounter: As a rough guideline, the encounter group should contain 1d8 guards for each level in your party's average level. If your party's average level is 6 or higher, add a veteran or a knight as the group's leader. If you don't want to run a mass encounter, feel free to substitute one veteran for 12 guards as much as you like. Veterans who are not officers could be rank-and-file soldiers from an elite unit, or bodyguards for the leader.

Pilgrims. The pantheon and nature of religious practice in your campaign world is up to you as the designer of that world. If it makes sense in that context, consider that your party crosses paths with a group of devotees traveling to (or perhaps from) a holy site, whether the site is associated with a body of water or they're just using the river or coastline for navigation. Perhaps they have a specific request to make of their deity (ending a drought or plague, curing someone of disease, etc.) and they bring an offering, or perhaps it's just a ritual that their religion says they must perform regularly. Depending on how religions work in your world, perhaps their mission is to vandalize a shrine to a rival deity.

A pilgrim's definition of treasure may be different from your party's.

Their deity and alignment should dictate how they react to meeting your party. Cultists in a littoral area may be aboleth worshippers who see your party as potential captives whom they can offer to the aboleth for enslavement. In any event, pilgrims are lightly armed and they may want to travel in your party's company for safety — especially if they know of a specific hazard in the area, like bandits or monsters. If friendly, they may also be willing to share local knowledge and trade with your party, or even share what divine magic capabilities they possess for your party's benefit.

Roll on Table 6.5.1 to give the encounter a more specific character:

TABLE 6.5.1
Pilgrims – Littoral

d6	ENCOUNTER
1-2	Acolytes
3-4	Cultists
5-6	Lay Followers

Acolytes. Your party crosses paths 1d4 monks or junior clerics. Treat them as acolytes.

Cultists. Your party crosses paths with 2d6 hard-core followers of an evil deity. How they react to your party is up to you, and should be influenced by the numerical odds for or against them. If their cult involves some kind of sacrifice to their deity, perhaps the cultists consider that your party would do nicely.

Treat the cultists as cultists.

Lay Followers. Your party crosses paths with 2d6 lay followers making a pilgrimage. They're just everyday folk performing an elaborate act of worship, and they're the most likely to need your party's protection as they travel through uninhabited land.

Treat them as commoners.

Scaling the Encounter. If you wish to make the encounter more challenging, add one priest or cult leader to the encounter, as appropriate.

Treasure: In addition to whatever treasure they carry on their person, pilgrims may carry with them an offering to their deity. At your discretion, roll on the Treasure Hoard: Challenge 0-4 table to determine its value.

Pirates. Your party comes across a band of pirates, working the river or coast, or come ashore to sort through their ill-gotten gains. Seaside caves and other obscure places near a large body of water make excellent bases of operation for them, so it's possible that they'll have their lair nearby. Even though a party of adventurers like yours is better-armed than their typical target, it's not out of the question that they'll attack. They're bound to be suspicious of strangers, especially if they have plunder with them. They may think that your party is a posse sent out after them — or that they're out to rob them of what they robbed from others.

Treat pirates as bandits; they're essentially bandits with boats. Add peg legs, eyepatches, parrots on the shoulder and exclamations of "Aarrgh, mateys!" at your discretion.

Scaling the Encounter: As a rough guideline, the encounter group should contain 1d8 pirates for each level in your party's average level. If your party's average level is 4 or higher, add a bandit captain as their leader. If you don't want to run a mass encounter but you still want these criminals to provide a higher-level party with a meaningful challenge, feel free to substitute one thug for four pirates as much as you like.

Treasure: If your party finds the pirates' hideout, roll on the Treasure Hoard table appropriate to the total CR of the encounter. Do so also if you decide that the pirates encountered are laden with booty from a successful raid. Consider that there is also a 20% chance that the bandits have with them a high-value captive whom they intend to ransom. The identity of this captive is left to you as DM, as it should depend on local circumstances and fit into your campaign world.

Heavy Traffic Leaving Town

It may seem like this chapter describes a lot of human activity, considering that it's supposed to be talking about wilderness. That's a fair point. But areas close to water, even if it's saltwater, offer places to go and things to do even away from settlements. As with grasslands, people want to live here, so even between population centers you find them traveling between towns and villages, and engaging in activities that support those settlements. Note how many of the human activities described in Table 6.5 involve gathering food or wealth, or transporting it — or preying on the people engaged in these activities.

Sailors. Your party comes across 2d6 sailors come ashore. Why they have chosen to come ashore far from port is another question. Perhaps they're a shore party looking for food and fresh water. Or perhaps they were kicked off their ship by mutineers or pirates. Perhaps they survived a shipwreck and they barely made it to shore, half-drowned but still alive.

In any case, they could have a reason to deal with your party, perhaps even hand them a sidequest. Being mariners, of course they have a tale to tell of adventures in faraway places, and it might even have some truth to it. If they're a shore party, they'd be willing to trade for supplies and local knowledge — at the very least they offer a free ride to a port on their ship's itinerary. If they're victims of mutiny or piracy, your party has the choice of hunting down the villains for a reward or a

finder's fee on recovered treasure. If they're shipwreck survivors, they're grateful for any aid they receive and give your party the chance to salvage the wreck and earn even more gratitude if there are more survivors still fighting for their lives at the wreck site.

Treat sailors as commoners.

Smugglers. Working in the wilderness requires smugglers to balance the pros and the cons. On one hand, they're far from any place they could fence their contraband goods. But on the other hand, they can count on doing business unobserved. Unfortunately for them, your party discovers a gang of 2d6 smugglers in the process of loading or unloading their boats.

The smugglers draw their weapons in alarm at having been made, but it's not a given that they attack your party on sight. They may try to play it off and pretend that they're not doing anything illegal. They may try to bribe your party into forgetting what they just saw. They may try to bully your party into silence. In any event, if your party decides to leave them alone, the smugglers may still try to tail your party until they are well out of the area, to make sure that the keep silent — thus setting up possible encounters for later in the campaign.

Treat smugglers as bandits equipped only with shortswords.

Scaling the Encounter: If you wish to make the encounter more challenging, add one bandit captain to the encounter group. You may also substitute thugs for bandits freely.

TABLE 6.6
Watch Out! - Littoral

d12	ENCOUNTER
1	Did You Hear That?
2-3	Loose Ground
4-5	Message in a Bottle
6-7	Quicksand
8	Surf is Up
9	Tracks
10-11	Tripping Hazard
12	Wind Gust

Did You Hear That? Choose a party member to make a DC 15 Wisdom (Survival) or Intelligence (Nature) check. Failure means that that character believes that he or she has heard a noise made by creature or a dangerous natural phenomenon. It can be as consequential as a kraken's roar in the distance, or as eerily intimate as muttering in Orcish coming from behind those rocks. A successful check means that that party member realizes that this is an illusion, and the noise is either much farther away than it seems, or it is something else entirely.

If you wish, roll on Table 6.6.1 for guidance on what your party thinks it hears:

TABLE 6.6.1
Did You Hear That? – Littoral

d10	ENCOUNTER
1	Boat or raft's timbers creaking
2	Harpy's song
3	Hoofbeats or horses or other herd animals
4	Human or humanoid screaming, water splashing
5	Large toad croaking
6	Loud crash of something breaching the surface of the water
7	Roc screeching overhead
8	Voices speaking in Aquan
9	Voices speaking in Common
10	Voices speaking in Sahuagin

Loose Ground. Your party reaches the crest of a riverbank or other steep slope. However, a party member — choose one, or a character who wants to get a good look around may literally step forward as the best candidate — steps onto a patch of loose soil. It gives way and the character takes a tumble, suffering 1d8 falling damage. A successful DC 15 Strength (Athletics) or Dexterity (Acrobatics) results in only half damage. Whee!

Anyone can make a misstep, even your party's pack animals.

Message in a Bottle. It need not be a literal message in a bottle, but it is an item washed ashore that can lead your party into a sidequest, or advance the narrative of the campaign. Table 6.6.2 suggests some possibilities, but feel free to gin up something that makes sense for that place and point in time in your campaign:

TABLE 6.6.2
Message in a Bottle - Littoral

d8	ENCOUNTER
1-2	Debris
3	Magic!
4-5	News from Abroad
6	Personal Message
7	Plea for Help
8	Remains

Debris. Not a message in a bottle *per se*, but some kind of object that has washed up on shore. Maybe it is something that would fetch a reward or be resold for a handsome price in the nearest settlement, like the decorative figurehead from a wrecked ship. Or it could be as mundane as the trunk of a tree knocked over in the last storm.

Magic! Shazam! The water-tight bottle contains a potion or scroll, intact and ready to use. Roll on the Individual Treasure table appropriate to your party's average level to determine the treasure table the potion or scroll comes from, and go from there. Of course, in order to remain absolutely water-tight, the bottle should be stoppered so that it's hard to get open again. Require a DC 10 Strength (Athletics) check to open it. Smashing the bottle will ruin the item inside.

News From Abroad. You could use this as a chance to convey information about what's going on elsewhere in your campaign world. The reason why someone would put it on a scrap of paper, put it in a bottle and cast it adrift may remain obscure; the information itself is what's important.

Personal Message. An authentic message in a bottle, one that is personal and sentimental in nature. It was sent from someone far away to someone also far away — or perhaps, to no one in particular. It might have some significance to someone in a nearby settlement, or it might be a red herring.

Plea for Help. An authentic message in a bottle, cast upon the waters by a shipwreck victim stranded too far from the mainland to just swim for it. It could be a sidequest for your party — it's up to you as DM whether or not it provides a good idea of where it came from.

Remains. Your party discovers what is left of a human or humanoid gone missing from a nearby settlement.
➤

The news is a big deal there, and it could earn gratitude from the locals — or make your party as welcome as tends to be the case with bearers of bad news. If you don't want to present your party with moldering remains, an identifying personal item, like an engraved ring, will suffice.

Quicksand. By the water's edge, the ocean, or the river, or the lake washes over the shore and leaves more water behind that you see at first glance. In patches, the soil is so saturated that it behaves like quicksand — step into it, and you may never step back out. Your party stumbles into such a patch. Have your party make a DC 15 Intelligence (Nature) or Wisdom (Survival) check to spot the quicksand before one party member in the front of the formation steps right into it.

Surf is Up. It's not a tidal wave, but water crashing forcefully against the shore catches your party by surprise at the water's edge. Have each party member make a DC 10 Dexterity (Acrobatics) check to avoid getting soaked. For anyone who fails, all sources of illumination held in hand, like torches or lanterns, are snuffed out. Water damage may, at your discretion, ruin documents like maps and letters, and other items that don't appreciate being doused (like rations).

Tracks. Your party spots tracks that look like tracks that belong to a monster associated with treasure hoards. They may make a successful DC 15 Wisdom (Survival) check to realize that they are very old, and they will not lead to anything useful. If no one makes a successful check, this may be the start of an amusing (for you as DM, anyway) wild goose chase.

Tripping Hazard. Pick a party member at the front of the march order. That character trips over an unseen obstacle — a root protruding from sandy soil, a half-buried log or some half-hidden driftwood. He or she must make a successful DC 10 Strength (Athletics) or Dexterity (Acrobatics) check to avoid a hard fall that causes 1d6 damage — and perhaps no small embarrassment in the eyes of the other party members.

Wind Gust. As your party walks along the shore, a sudden gust of wind catches them by surprise. Whether it blows onshore or offshore is up to you. Any party member who is standing must make a DC 5 Strength check to avoid being knocked down. Anyone who is knocked down by the wind immediately loses grasp of anything held in hand. Fragile objects break when they are dropped. In addition, anyone who is knocked down while wearing a pack must make a DC 5 Dexterity (Acrobatics) check to avoid the pack falling heavily so that at least some of its contents spill out. If it's an

offshore wind (i.e., coming from inland), there is a chance that anything dropped can get carried into the water and drift away. At your discretion, this may be an object of some importance, like a map, or simply a useful mundane item, like rations.

A Tale of a Fateful Trip...

When running your party through a littoral environment, keep in mind whether it's saltwater or freshwater nearby, because that can affect whether or not it makes sense for some creatures to show up.

Also, littoral includes the proverbial deserted island as well as long ocean coastlines, lakeshores and the banks of rivers. If your campaign involves your party washing up on such a place, treat it as littoral, at least until they get well inland. Just remember that the water they just came from is not fit to drink — they'll have to go inland to find some.

MOUNTAINS

CHAPTER SEVEN

Mountains

What are Mountains?

Chapter 5 took you up into the hills, so what makes Chapter 7 different? What distinguishes mountains from hills? Apparently, not even geographers can agree on a universal set of distinctions that separate the mountains from the hills. For the purposes of this book, it's a matter of relative elevation and the effect of elevation on terrain and wildlife. Hills and mountains may be contiguous, but mountains rise above the hills and the higher elevation creates an environment that is colder, windier and overall more hostile to life. Caradhras and the Misty Mountains in Middle Earth are mountains; they are not hills. You have to be hardy to live here, hence the relatively slender selection of creatures that your party is likely to encounter.

What Do You Find in Mountains?

When you determine that a random encounter is in order, roll on Table 7.1 to determine the category:

TABLE 7.1

Encounter Type - Mountains

d20	CATEGORY
1-8	Aggressive Creatures (Table 7.2)
9-14	Neutral Creatures (Table 7.3)
15-16	Humanoids (Table 7.4)
17	Humans (Table 7.5)
18-20	Watch Out! (Table 7.6)

Then, roll on the appropriate table to determine the creature, person or thing encountered.

The distance at which an encounter takes place varies in the mountains. You can have a nice, clear line of sight to the other end of a mountain pass or a clear view of whatever is coming up the mountainside behind you. On the other hand, a sharp turn in a pass, or a large boulder, or a crag on the mountain above you can hide an encounter group until the last moment.

Steep slopes and rugged terrain characterize mountains, so encounters usually take place with one side or the other having some advantage from occupying higher ground. It's relatively easy to strike from ambush if you're above your target and you can hide from their view. Even where the ground is relatively flat, there are

bound to be obstructions that restrict line of sight, such as mountainsides rising on either side of a pass.

TABLE 7.2

Aggressive Creatures - Mountains

d100	ENCOUNTER
1-6	Bird of Prey
7-9	Chimera
10-13	Cyclops
14-16	Elemental
17-20	Ettin
21-23	Grick
24-29	Griffon
30-32	Hell Hound
33-42	Insects
43-46	Manticore
47-50	Mephits
51-57	Mountain Lion
58-61	Ogres
62-63	Oni
64	Purple Worm
65-67	Remorhaz
68	Roc
69-70	Salamanders
71-75	Spiders
76-79	Troll
80-85	Undead
86-89	Wolves
90-93	Wyvern
94-95	Xorn
96-100	Yeti

Bird of Prey. A bird of prey — or a flock of them — wheels overhead, then strikes at your party. Keen-eyed, but bird-brained all the same, the bird has spotted something in your party as food — a familiar or small summoned creature is an obvious choice, but it could just be travelers rations, like strips of cured meat left in the open. To determine which species, roll on Table 7.2.1:

Hawks will only attack if you are between them and their prey

TABLE 7.2.1

Birds of Prey - Mountains

d12	ENCOUNTER
1-2	Eagle
3	Giant Eagle
4-5	Blood Hawks
6-7	Hawks
8-9	Owl
10	Giant Owl

Eagle. One eagle swoops down on your party, aiming itself at something it has identified as food.

Giant Eagle. A giant eagle has spotted your party. Giant eagles are intelligent and may respond if your party tries to flag them down. Though it cannot speak when spoken to, a successful DC 15 Charisma (Persuasion) check by someone who speaks Common or Auran persuades it to do your party a service, if it is within its power to accomplish it. This may involve delivering a written message or token, or guiding your party to a place that it knows, or even traveling with them for a while as an airborne lookout.

Blood Hawks. A flock of 2d4 blood hawks swoops down on your party. They concentrate on a single target — most likely a pack animal, but they may settle for a small humanoid as the next best thing.

Hawks. A flock of 2d6 hawks targets your party. They're probably going after the party's rations, but they may also have spotted rodents or small reptiles who are literally scurrying along the ground at your party's feet. To the extent that your party is in their way, the hawks attack them.

Owl. Owls hunt at night, so you should re-roll this encounter if it takes place during the day. Otherwise, one owl has spotted food as your party rests outdoors overnight. Most likely, it has spotted a small animal companion or familiar, or rations left out in the open, or a frog or other amphibian that has gotten in among your party.

Giant Owl. Likewise, a giant owl encounter is most suitable for night, so you should re-roll this encounter if it takes place during the day. One giant owl spots food in your party's camp.

Chimera. Your party spots a winged monstrosity with three different animal heads circling above them. This can only mean one thing: A chimera has spotted them as

potential prey. You may allow your party a DC 15 Wisdom (Perception) check. If successful, they notice the chimera at a range of about 200 feet, allowing them a little time to react before they are within range of its attacks. If not, they first become aware of the chimera at a range of only 100 feet.

Scaling the Encounter: If your party's average level is lower than 6, a chimera may be more than you want to throw at them. Feel free to re-roll for a different encounter.

Alternately, you may consider that your party comes upon a chimera that has been injured in a fight with a manticore or a wyvern — and that your party witnesses the dazzling air-to-air combat from a safe distance. In this case, the chimera is reduced to half of its hit points by the time it drives off its enemy and turns on your party, deep gashes or embedded manticore spikes are still visible. It's wounded, but it's still hungry — in fact, perhaps it needs to feed in order to heal and your party looks like an easier target than one of its monstrous rivals.

Cyclops. Your party sees a cyclops roaming the mountainside, unconcerned about its lack of depth perception. It may be on its way to meet with another cyclops, or it may be collecting goats to add to its herd. It could be out grazing its herd, in which case it's accompanied by 3d6 goats. In any event, it sees your party as prey — a delicacy, compared to eating goat all the time — and it attacks.

Scaling the Encounter: If your party's average level is lower than 6, a cyclops may be more than you want to throw at them. Feel free to re-roll for a different encounter.

Elemental. Your party crosses paths with an elemental — either because it was summoned to the Material Plane and then abandoned or because, here in the remote mountains, a natural portal between its native plane and the Material Plane exists. Use the local terrain to guide you in choosing the elemental, or roll on Table 7.2.2:

A chimera may be a bit tough for a low-level party.

TABLE 7.2.2
Elemental -Mountains

d10	ENCOUNTER
1-4	Air Elemental
5-8	Earth Elemental
9-10	Fire Elemental

Elementals attack anything and anyone they encounter, without thinking or caring about the why's and wherefores. They are not thinking beings, but they are angry about having to wander an alien plane.

Air Elemental. The wind whips through a mountain pass, or down a mountainside. As your party presses on, however, they see that an elemental whirlwind is the source of all this motion.

Earth Elemental. A shower of rocks and dirt pelts your party. Unfortunately for them, it is caused by an earth elemental rearing up from the mountainside.

Fire Elemental. If there is volcanic activity nearby — a lava flow, an active caldera, a crevasse with bubbling magma at the bottom — it's possible that a fire elemental uses it as a gateway into the Material Plane. As your party passes by, a fire elemental rears up from it.

Scaling the Encounter: If your party's average level is lower than 5, an elemental may be more than you want to throw at them. Feel free to re-roll for a different encounter. On the other hand, if your party's average level is 10 or higher, feel free to add another elemental to the encounter.

Ettin. Your party hears two loud voices resonating in a mountain pass or bouncing off the mountainside. Have your party make a DC 15 Intelligence (Nature) check to recognize that it's an ettin arguing with itself. If they choose not to avoid the ettin, it calls out to your party and demands that they help settle a dispute. It should be something that the party would find awkward or at least pointless to answer — for instance, whether or not cloud giants are more ticklish under the chin or under the arms. No matter what answer the party gives, one or both heads accuses them of unfairly favoring the other and the ettin attacks.

Alternately, the ettin stops short when it spots the party and realizes that it's hungry after arguing with itself for such a long time.

Scaling the Encounter: As amusing as ettins can be if you run the encounter with the right sense of humor, one is a bit much for a party with an average level of less than 4.

Treasure: The ettin carries some coins in a pouch looped around its loincloth. Roll twice on the Individual Treasure: Challenge 0-4 table.

Grick. A grick tries to hide, coiled into a crevice or just inside the mouth of a mountain cave waiting for a target such as your party to come along. If it fails, they notice that one oversized worm-like thing with a maw surrounded by four tentacles instead of a face is trying to cloak itself in shadow or squeeze down behind some rocks. When your party comes within striking distance, it attacks.

Scaling the Encounter: If you wish to make the encounter more challenging, the encounter group consists of one grick for each multiple of 3 in your party's average level, rounded up. If your party's average level is 15 or higher, consider adding one grick alpha to the encounter as the group's leader. Alternately, you may use an encounter group that consists of one grick alpha for each multiple of 10 in your party's average level, rounded up.

Treasure: Since gricks are opportunity predators rather than hunters, your party may find treasure that has piled up from the belongings of former victims. Roll once on the Treasure Hoard: Challenge 0-4 table for each grick in the encounter group, and once on the Treasure Hoard: Challenge 5-10 table for each grick alpha.

Gambling with Cloud Giants is Legal in Most States
The precise form that a wager with a cloud giant should take is one of those things best left to you as DM. It can take virtually any form. It could be as simple as dicing for it — the giant just happens to have 2d6 in its pocket. Or it may have a deck of cards and it suggests playing a hand of whatever game is well known in your campaign world. It could be a riddle. It could be a physical challenge — a standing jump onto a nearby rock or climbing onto a tall ledge — that requires a Strength (Athletics) or Dexterity (Acrobatics) check from your party. Or — if it's an evil cloud giant — it could be a proposition that is rigged so that the giant is sure to win, no matter what.

Griffon. A griffon spots your party and goes for one of their mounts or pack animals — or at least, it thinks it has spotted a mount or a pack animal.

Scaling the Encounter: If you wish to make the encounter more challenging, your party encounters a flock (or pack?) of griffons hunting together. There is one for each multiple of 3 in your party's average level.

Treasure: Your party won't be able to find a griffon's lair by tracking in the conventional sense, but it probably isn't that far away and they may be able to intuit its location. You may allow them a DC 20 Wisdom (Survival) check to figure out it out. If they find it, they also find belongings from the griffon's victims, equalling one roll on the Treasure Hoard table appropriate to the CR of the encounter.

Hell Hound. Your party crosses paths with one hell hound that has gotten loose from a fire giant stronghold. Bored with what it perceived as inactivity, it escaped; now it hunts just for the sheer pleasure of the kill. And guess whom it has found?

As a side note, you may allow your party a DC 15 Wisdom (Survival) check to track the hell hound's path from the fire giant stronghold. If your party can somehow subdue the beast and return it to its former masters, the giants may look favorably upon them.

Scaling the Encounter: A hell hound may be a bit too much for a beginning-level party. Feel free to re-roll for another encounter. Conversely, If you wish to make the encounter more challenging, the encounter group consists of one hell hound for each multiple of 4 in your party's average level.

Insects. You may not think of insects as predatory, but they feed without giving it much thought and they cause trouble in their own way. Some are viciously aggressive when they feel threatened. Roll on Table 7.2.3 to determine the insects encountered:

TABLE 7.2.3
Insects -Mountains

d4	ENCOUNTER
1-3	Swarm of Insects
4	Giant Wasps

Swarm of Insects. One swarm of insects — call them gnats, midges, mosquitos, whatever you will — descends upon your party and makes their lives decidedly unpleasant.

Giant Wasps. Your party comes upon two giant wasps guarding a nest hanging from a rocky outcropping or a lone tree. They are in a sufficiently bad temper to attack anything that comes close to the nest. ➤

Scaling the Encounter: If you wish to make the encounter more challenging (or more of a nuisance, depending on how you look at it), the encounter group consists of 1d4 giant wasps for each multiple of 2 in your party's average level, or 1d4 swarms of insects plus one additional swarm for each level in your party's average level.

Manticore. Your party spots a large winged beast in the sky. You may insist that they make a successful DC 15 Intelligence (Nature) check to recognize it as a manticore on the hunt before it gets close enough to attack. Once it gets close enough to launch its spikes, it may choose to toy with its prey just to watch them squirm. In this case, it demands some kind of bribe in exchange for sparing them — a bargain it will keep, if your party makes the right offer. A suitable offer might take the form of treasure or humiliating servitude that amuses the manticore.

Scaling the Encounter: If you wish to make the encounter more challenging, consider that there are multiple manticores working as a team. In such a case, the encounter group consists of one manticore for each multiple of 5 in your party's average level.

Mephits. Just as the mountains can accommodate a surprising range of elementals, different kinds of mephits can feel at home here. Use the local terrain to guide in choosing the elemental, or roll on Table 7.2.4:

TABLE 7.2.4
Mephits -Mountains

d6	ENCOUNTER
1-4	Ice
5	Magma
6	Steam

Ice Mephits. Frigid temperatures at high altitude create a friendly environment for ice mephits that slip over from the Elemental Plane of Water. Your party sees one ice mephit perched atop a rock, poking up out of a snow drift, or lounging atop glacial ice. It glares at them and pelts them with small rocks or chunks of ice — not enough to cause any damage, but it refuses to stop.

Magma Mephits. Magma mephits can emerge into the Material Plane wherever there is the slightest indication of volcanism. It doesn't have to be an eruption, it can be something as modest as a hot ➤

spring or magma bubbling at the very bottom of a crevasse. One magma mephit blocks your party's path. It ignores all attempts to brush it aside and it interprets any attempt to step over it or aside from it as an attack.

Steam Mephits. Like magma mephits, steam mephits can be found where there is volcanic activity. For obvious reasons, they have a particular affinity for hot springs, where the elemental steam that they give off blends with the natural steam from the springs. 1d4+1 steam mephits pop out at your party from within a cloud of steam and they accuse them of some perceived — even wholly imaginary — insult or offense. Perhaps a bit of debris kicked aside by a party member landed a little too close to them, or they overhear a passing remark and interpret it as an insult. They do not attack, but they refuse to stop pestering your party. Ignoring them just makes them more indignant.

Scaling the Encounter: The encounter group consists of 1d4 ice mephits or magma mephits for each multiple of 2 in your party's average level, or 1d4 steam mephits plus one additional steam mephitis for each level in your party's average level.

Ogres. Your party crosses paths with a foraging party of ogres. Whether you want to stage any meaningful interaction with these undersized giants is up to you, but it should surprise no one if they decide that your party is as good a target as any they are likely to find in the near future, whether they are looking for things or food (or both).

Scaling the Encounter: The encounter group consists of one ogre for each multiple of 3 in your party's average level, rounded up. If your party is only 1st Level, consider that one half-ogre confronts them.

Treasure. These ogres are away from their lair. Add the CR of all ogres killed and roll on the appropriate Individual Treasure table.

Oni. Your party crosses paths with an ogre mage that has fled up into the mountains after being driven out of the community it victimized. Here, it intends to regroup before looking for new victims. When it spots your party, it tries to befriend them while using its *Change Shape* ability to disguise itself as someone trustworthy; use a form that is unlikely to arouse your party's suspicions. If they allow the oni to travel with them, it bides its time until they make camp for the night. It volunteers to take the first watch, then it strikes once everyone else is asleep.

If you wish, you may allow your party a DC 20 Intelligence (Arcana) check to suspect that this apparently friendly stranger might be using magic to alter its appearance.

Scaling the Encounter: An oni may be a bit too much for a low-level party. Feel free to re-roll for another encounter. Conversely, if you want to run a more challenging encounter for a higher-level party, use an encounter group consisting of two oni if your party's average level is 10 or higher.

Purple Worm. When you're picking your way up or down a mountainside and suddenly, the ground beneath your feet starts rumbling and quivering, it is seldom — if ever — a good sign. This is especially true if a purple worm burrowing through the rock underfoot is the cause. The worm has detected your party as prey and emerges to attack them. The worm's approach should give them enough time to sense that something is amiss and do something about it; you may allow them a DC 15 Intelligence (Nature) check to realize that it's a purple worm causing the disturbance. Combat begins when it breaches the surface within striking distance of your party.

Scaling the Encounter: If your party's average level is lower than 15, a purple worm may be more than you want to throw at them. Feel free to re-roll for a different encounter.

Treasure: Cutting open and gutting a purple worm is quite a chore, but it should reveal valuables that belonged to its previous prey — and purple worms eat a lot. Roll on the Treasure Hoard: Challenge 11-16 table to determine the total hoard.

Remorhaz. These weird creatures of snow and ice are more commonly found in arctic regions, but some make their way to high altitudes, where they find the cold hospitable. They feast on hapless travelers in the mountains. One remorhaz takes your party for such a group as they pass a snow drift into which it has burrowed, and it leaps out to attack as they pass.

Scaling the Encounter: If your party's average level is 5-10, a young remorhaz is most suitable for the encounter. If it is higher than 10, feel free to use a fully grown remorhaz. If your party's average level is lower than 5, however, a remorhaz of any age may be more than you want to throw at them. Feel free to re-roll for a different encounter.

Treasure: Since remorhazes swallow their prey whole, cutting open and gutting one should reveal undigested valuables that it consumed. Roll on the Treasure Hoard table appropriate to the CR of the encounter. You may also allow your party a DC 15 Wisdom (Survival) check to find a trail back to the remorhaz' nest and find 1d4 eggs.

Ow, My Eye!
Book IX of *The Odyssey* tells us rather vaguely that cyclops are creatures of the hills and mountains. But Polyphemus, Odysseus' good buddy whose fate suggests that having only one eye is something of an evolutionary disadvantage, lives in a seaside cave — at sea level, pretty much, and in what this book would call littoral.

However, the notion that cyclops live up in the hills and mountains took root in the Greek tradition. Later writers — including Euripides — link cyclops with Mt. Etna and the volcanic Aeolian Islands. So this book follows this particular strand of Greek literary tradition. After all, if you can't trust Euripides, who can you trust?

Roc. Your party spots — or perhaps more accurately, it has been spotted by — a roc on the hunt. It's quite at home up here in the mountains and it knows the ins and outs of the terrain, so there is no hiding from it. One of these enormous aerial predators swoops down, blotting out the sky as it descends. Its first target is the largest party member, but any creature of medium size or larger will do.

Scaling the Encounter: Rocs are fearsome opponents. If your party's average level is lower than 11, a roc may be more than you want to throw at them. Feel free to re-roll for a different encounter.

Treasure: Rocs are most at home at higher elevations, so its lair may not be far away. Your party won't be able to find it by tracking in the conventional sense, but they may be able to intuit its location. You may allow your party a DC 20 Wisdom (Survival) check to figure out it out. If they find it, they also find belongings from the roc's victims, equalling one roll on the Treasure Hoard level 11-16 table.

Salamanders. These creatures of elemental fire are drawn to any trace of volcanic activity, so your party may encounter them up in the mountains if there is even just a stirring of magma beneath the ground. Your party comes across one fire snake at its ease in or near a steaming crater or flow of lava. It decides to set fire to them just for amusement.

Scaling the Encounter: To make the encounter more challenging, use an encounter group of two fire snakes

for each multiple of 3 in your party's average level. You may substitute one salamander for five fire snakes.

Spiders. It gets a little chilly up in the mountains for the comfort of most spiders, but they cope with it by taking shelter, weaving their webs between rocks or inside caves where they are sheltered from the wind. Wolf spiders, which burrow into the ground, make themselves at home here, even with the effort required to dig into the rocky soil. Roll on Table 7.2.5 to determine what kind of spider your party encounters:

TABLE 7.2.5
Spiders -Mountains

d10	ENCOUNTER
1-4	Spiders
5-7	Giant Spider
8-9	Giant Wolf Spiders
10	Phase Spider

Spiders. These spiders are small, but their venom packs a punch. They won't leave their web, but if someone in your party gets close enough, they'll attack. Perhaps your party disturbs them by resting against some rocks under which they are hiding. 2d8 spiders live here.

Giant Spider. Giant spiders prefer the seclusion of mountain caves. They live alone, so your party encounters one in its web.

Giant Wolf Spiders. Wolf spiders do not weave webs; they burrow into the ground and they either take whatever stumbles into their lair, or they emerge to ambush prey. As your party approaches, vibrations in the ground tell them that something juicy has come to their doorstep, and 1d4 giant wolf spiders attack. You may allow your party a DC 15 Wisdom (Perception) check to notice a hole in the ground large enough to fit a big spider, and if successful, a DC 15 Intelligence (Nature) check to realize that it's a wolf spider burrow.

Phase Spider. Phase spiders are quite fearless, and they use their ability to jump back and forth between planes to conduct hit-and-run attacks, wearing the party down until they are all incapacitated or dead.

Scaling the Encounter: Giant spiders live alone, as too much weight would drag down their web. If you want to create a more challenging encounter with ordinary spiders, you may add another 2d8 to the encounter group — having too many, however, not only creates an unwieldy encounter, but it assumes an awfully

➤

large population of spiders for a single web. To create a more challenging encounter with giant wolf spiders,

use an encounter group consisting of 1d4 plus a number of additional giant wolf spiders equal to your party's average level.

A phase spider may be a bit too much for a beginning-level party. Feel free to re-roll for another encounter. Conversely, if you want to run a more challenging encounter for a higher-level party, use an encounter group consisting of one phase spider for each multiple of 4 in your party's average level.

Treasure. With larger spiders, they may have trapped humanoid-sized victims in the past and left some of their valuables caught in their web. You may roll on the Individual Treasure: Challenge 0-4 table if you wish.

Troll. It gets a little cold at this elevation for a troll's liking, but a narrow pass or trail up the mountain presents the perfect opportunity to extort struggling travelers. One troll confronts your party and demands something from them before it lets them pass — perhaps one of their pack animals is its toll, or a suitable amount of coins. It fights rather than let anyone pass for free.

Scaling the Encounter: If your party's average level is lower than 5, a troll may be more than you want to throw at them. Feel free to re-roll for a different encounter. Conversely, if your party's average level is 10 or higher, feel free to add one troll to the encounter — a tag-team of trolls.

Treasure: The troll's racket has worked well enough in the past: Its victims pay one way or another, and it has accumulated a decent hoard. Searching the area turns up its stash, thrown in to a pile, on a successful DC 10 Wisdom (Perception) check. Roll on the Treasure Hoard: Challenge 5-10 table to determine the contents.

Undead. Spend enough time in the mountains, and you will find evidence of those who died without proper rites and may be kept restless by necromantic forces: travelers who perished in the cold or were buried by avalanches, soldiers killed in skirmishes in remote mountain passes, those who were killed by monsters and other predators that haunt these perilous heights. Roll on Table 7.2.6 to determine the undead abomination that greets your party:

Driven by necromantic echoes, undead are looking for a fight.

TABLE 7.2.6
Undead- Mountains

d12	ENCOUNTER
1	Ghost
2-3	Ghouls/Ghasts
4	Shadow
5-6	Skeletons
7	Specter
8-9	Wight
10	Wraith
11-12	Zombies

Ghost. That is no optical illusion; the ethereal form flitting across the mountainside really is a ghost. It is most likely the remnant of someone who died a miserable death in the wilderness. Whatever the case, you may make this into a hostile encounter by having the ghost try to possess a member of your party so that it may resolve unfinished business from its former life.

Ghouls/Ghasts. An encounter with ghouls is most likely to take place at night. Two ghouls (or one ghast) approach your party, driven by mindless hunger for their flesh.

Shadows. In the gloom caused by a mountain snowstorm or sharply rising ground blocking out the rising or setting sun, the dark shape flitting toward your party may seem like a trick that the mind plays with what the corner of the eye glimpses. But it's not an illusion, it's undead! Without thinking or feeling, the shadow attacks the nearest party member, eager to drain the life from another victim and create one more of its own kind.

Skeletons. Your party comes across the undead remnants of an ancient skirmish or armed travelers who perished in a hostile wilderness: 1d6 skeletons carrying broken weapons and draped with fragments of the armor they wore in life. Driven by necromantic echoes of the end of their lives, they're looking for a fight.

Specter. Specters prefer to come out at night, when it is completely dark; but where mountains rise high into

➤

the sky all around you and cast their shadows, they may appear at dusk and dawn as well. It isn't darkness, but it's close enough. Your party comes upon one specter that was once someone who perished in the mountains, but all connections to who and what it was in life no longer exist. Only blind hatred of the living drives it to attack your party on sight.

Wight. Your party makes camp for the night not far from a burial site, like an improvised cairn or a cave. Unfortunately for your party, at least one of the occupants has become a wight, and it rises from its tomb to attack them while they are most vulnerable.

Wraith. As your party passes a pile of rocks, a cold, charcoal-gray mist emerges and resolves itself into a wraith, which then attacks them, acting out the resentment that it bore at the end of its natural life. Perhaps it bears a grudge against companions who abandoned it in this forsaken place, or against the particular event that ended its life. You may allow your party a DC 15 Intelligence (Nature) or Wisdom (Survival) check to realize that this is not a natural formation; it looks more like an improvised cairn.

Zombies. Your party come across 1d6 zombies who have been programmed to kill every living thing they encounter. The source of the necromancy that created these zombies we leave to you. Perhaps they slipped the leash of their creator and they now wander the mountain mindlessly looking for victims.

Scaling the Encounter: Ghosts and wraiths always work alone. The base encounter group for specters also consists of only one of its kind.

A wraith may be too much for a beginning-level party, so feel free to re-roll the encounter in that case. With specters, you may create a more challenging encounter by using two for each multiple of 3 in your party's average level, with all of them being part of a group that perished *en masse*.

Ghouls/Ghasts: If you wish to make the encounter more challenging, the encounter group consists of two ghouls (for or one ghast) each multiple of 4 in your party's average level. Feel free to mix and match ghouls and ghasts as long as you maintain the right proportion of total CR to average party level.

Shadows: The encounter group consists of two shadows for each multiple of 3 in your party's average level.

➤

Skeletons: If you wish to make the encounter more challenging, the encounter group consists of 1d4 skeletons plus one additional skeleton for each level in your party's average level. You may substitute one warhorse skeleton for two skeletons.

Wights: A wight may be a bit too much for a beginning-level party. Feel free to re-roll for another encounter. Conversely, if you want to run a more challenging encounter for a higher-level party, add one zombie minion for each level in your party's average level above 3.

Zombies: If you wish to make the encounter more challenging, the encounter group consists of 1d4 zombies plus one additional zombie for each level in your party's average level. If your party's average level is 3 or higher, you may use an encounter group consisting of one ogre zombie for each multiple of 3 in your party's average level.

Treasure: Most likely, ghosts are encountered in or near what passes for a lair with them and you may consider that there they keep possessions that they had in life. Roll on the Treasure Hoard: Challenge 0-4 table for the contents of their stash. You may require a successful DC 15 Wisdom (Perception) check to find its exact location.

Likewise, wights and wraiths do not stray far from their place of burial, which are usually constructed as monuments to the dead. Therefore, their location should be self-apparent. Roll on the Treasure Hoard table appropriate to the total CR of the encounter.

With ghouls, ghasts, skeletons and zombies, they may have with them some remains of what they had on their person at the time of their death. Roll on the

Individual Treasure table appropriate to the total CR of the encounter (rounded up to the nearest whole number).

Wolves. Even in the mountains, wolves can find enough prey animals to keep them fed. But the cold and relative deprivation mean that the wolves you find at high altitude are going to be tougher and meaner than the ones you find at lower elevations. Roll on Table 7.2.7 to determine the wolves encountered:

Wolves are tougher in the mountains.

TABLE 7.2.7
Spiders - Mountains

d10	ENCOUNTER
1-3	Dire Wolves
4-5	Winter Wolves
6	Wolves

Wolves are confident predators in the best of times, but they are even more dangerous when prey is in relatively short supply and they become desperate. Whether the wolfpack approaches you from the other end of a mountain pass, or track you from above along a rock ledge, they attack.

Scaling the Encounter: The encounter group consists of two dire wolves for each multiple of 3 in your party's average level; or one winter wolf for each multiple of 4 in your party's average level; or 1d4 wolves plus a one additional wolf for each level in your party's average level.

Treasure: Furriers in your world may be willing to pay for wolf pelts. How much is ultimately up to you, but 2 gp is a reasonable baseline price for a normal wolf pelt; 3 gp for a dire wolf pelt; and 5 gp for a winter wolf pelt.

Wyvern. A wyvern has emerged from its nearby lair to hunt and it spots your party from above. It is either very hungry or very aggressive, so it swoops down to attack despite the odds.

Scaling the Encounter: If your party's average level is lower than 6, a wyvern with its blood up may be more than you want to throw at them. Feel free to re-roll for a different encounter.

Treasure: Wyverns are most at home at higher elevations, so its lair may not be far away. Your party won't be able to find it by tracking in the conventional sense, but they may be able to intuit its location by an extraordinary leap of intuition. You may allow your party a DC 20 Wisdom (Survival) check to figure it out. If they find it, they also find belongings from the wyvern's victims, equaling one roll on the Treasure Hoard: Challenge 5-10 table.

Xorn. Your party comes upon a mountain cave that looks like an inviting shelter. Unfortunately, a xorn has beaten them to this location on the impression — perhaps correct — that a naturally occurring vein of precious metals or gemstones may be found here. It is willing to

fight to the death for possession of the cave, which it considers, in its own extraplanar way of thinking, its kill.

Scaling the Encounter: If your party's average level is lower than 5, a xorn may be more than you want to throw at it. Feel free to re-roll for a different encounter. On the other hand, if your party's average level is higher than 6, consider adding one xorn to the encounter group to make it more challenging.

Yeti. Your party may well hear a yeti's roar well before seeing the creature itself, especially since its white fur provides excellent camouflage in snow. Yeti are ferocious when hungry and on the prowl, so they attack as soon as they identify a suitable target.

Scaling the Encounter: A yeti may be a bit too much for a beginning-level party. Feel free to re-roll for another encounter. Conversely, if you want to run a more challenging encounter, consider using an abominable yeti if your party's average level is 10 or higher.

TABLE 7.3
Neutral Creatures - Mountains

d20	ENCOUNTER
1-2	Ape
3	Awakened Plant
4	Bats
5-6	Bear
7-8	Deer
9	Dragon
10-11	Elk
12-13	Giant
14-15	Goats
16	Hippogriff
17	Mule
18-19	Pegasus
20	Rats

Ape. Your party crosses paths with one mountain ape, spotted at the opposite end of a mountain pass, or perhaps perched on a ledge above your party. It is not necessarily hostile, but it does make an aggressive display to try to warn them off. You may have your party make a DC 15 Intelligence (Nature) or Wisdom (Survival) check. Failure means that a party member has made a false move that provokes the ape, and it attacks.

Scaling the Encounter: If you wish to make the encounter more challenging, the encounter group consists of one ape for each level In your party's average level. If your party's average level is 10 or higher, substitute one giant ape for ten apes, as desired.

Awakened Plant. Roll on Table 7.3.1 to determine whether your party comes across an awakened shrub or an awakened tree:

TABLE 7.3.1
Awakened Plant - Mountains

d10	ENCOUNTER
1-3	Awakened Shrub
4	Awakened Tree

Awakened Shrub. Your party comes into contact with one awakened shrub. Perhaps a party member takes advantage of it to answer the call of nature. Perhaps it produces berries that look appetizing. Perhaps your party is looking for kindling for the campfire. These or similar actions cause the shrub to express alarm. An encounter with them is not necessarily hostile, even your party has done mischief to it. If your party asks it for help, a successful DC 10 Charisma (Persuasion) check wins it over, but the DC is 15 if your party has harmed it in some way. Help from an awakened shrub includes providing knowledge of the surrounding area.

Awakened Tree. Your party has some sort of physical contact with a tree that stands alone among the rugged mountain landscape. Perhaps someone stumbles over a root. Perhaps someone just leans against it to rest. Perhaps someone breaks off a branch, or carves a sigil into the trunk, or does some other casual mischief. Perhaps a dog or some other animal companion uses the tree for its own purposes. Whatever it is, the tree expresses its alarm.

An awakened tree is not necessarily hostile. If your party asks it for help, a successful DC 10 Charisma (Persuasion) check wins it over. If your party includes someone visibly carrying an axe of some sort, the DC is 15. If the party has harmed the tree in any way, the DC is 20. Help from an awakened tree includes providing knowledge about the immediate area, or even accompanying your party as an ally as long as this doesn't involve going very far.

However, an awakened tree instinctively reacts to open flame with hostility. Lighting a torch or starting campfire causes it to attack.

Scaling the Encounter: If you wish to make the encounter more challenging, the encounter group consists of one awakened shrub for each multiple of 3 in your party's average level or one awakened tree for each multiple of 4 in your party's average level.

Bats. If you think that climbing a mountain will get you away from bats, guess again. Your party enters a mountain cave only to find a colony consisting of 1d4+1 swarms of bats, all of them hanging from the ceiling and walls. However, even though they have intruded on the bats' lair, it's possible to avoid setting them off. You may have your party make a DC 15 Wisdom (Survival) or Intelligence (Nature) check. Failure means that someone makes a false move that triggers the bats' fight-or-flight response, and having nowhere to flee, they fight.

Scaling the Encounter: If you want to make the encounter more challenging for a higher-level party, use an encounter group consisting of 1d4 swarm of bats and/or giant bats in any combination, plus one swarm of bats or giant bat for each level in your party's average level.

Bear. Your party takes shelter in a mountain cave, only to find that a bear has beaten them to it. Roll on Table 7.3.2 to determine whether it's a black bear or a brown bear:

TABLE 7.3.2
Bear - Mountains

d6	ENCOUNTER
1-4	Black Bear
5-6	Brown Bear

Either way, if it is winter, the bear is hibernating and sleeps on as long as your party makes a successful DC 15 Dexterity (Stealth) check to avoid disturbing it. If it wakes up, it awakens in a foul mood and attacks.

Alternately, the bear is abroad from its cave lair and hunting for food. The smell of your party's travelers' rations draw its attention. To scare it off, have your party make a DC 15 Intelligence (Nature) or Wisdom (Survival) check. Success means that the bear takes the hint and lumbers away. Failure means that the bear stands its ground, and if the party does not retreat it charges them.

Deer. Your party spots 1d4 bucks and 2d4 does grazing. If your party attacks, only the males fight, covering the females while they flee. Even if your party does not behave in a threatening manner, there is a chance that the bucks mistake their actions and attack anyway. Have your party make a DC 10 Intelligence (Nature) or Wisdom (Survival) check. Failure means that someone has made a false move that sets off the males and they charge.

Treasure: Anyone for venison? Perhaps a nearby butcher will pay 2 gp or thereabouts for a fresh carcass

Dragon. Your party notices a shadow in the sky. It's a dragon on the prowl. To determine what kind of dragon roll on Table 7.3.3:

TABLE 7.3.3
Dragon - Mountains

d12	ENCOUNTER
1	Black
2	Blue
3	Green
4-5	Red
6	White
7	Brass
8	Bronze
9	Copper
10	Gold
11-12	Silver

To determine its age, see Scaling the Encounter, below.

To be clear, this need not be a hostile encounter. The dragon is not defending its lair, so — being a highly intelligent creature — it may just be curious about your party. It may have more important things to do and decline to take notice of them at all. Or it may be hungry and on the hunt, or it's angry because your party has intruded on territory it claims as its own.

Alternately, you may present your party with a scenario that you can weave into the larger story of the campaign. It may even serve as the main thrust of the campaign. Your party finds a dragon wyrmling sprawled on the ground. It's obviously in a bad way — gashed open, bleeding profusely (or it has almost bled out), barely conscious. Assume that it has stabilized after being reduced to 0 hp, and that it now has 1 hp.

How it got that way is up to you, and it may depend on how dragons fit into your campaign world. Perhaps it fled from a fight in which it was badly wounded.

Who would its enemies be, and why were they fighting? Were any of this dragon's relatives or companions killed?

How your party decides to deal with this child in distress could open up possibilities for later in your campaign. If they rescue it, will its kin reward them ➤

later, or will its enemies confront them on the principle that, "The friends of my enemy must also be my enemy?" Conversely, what are the consequences if they put it out of its misery, like scavengers roaming a medieval battlefield? Will its kin seek retribution, or will its enemies treat your party as allies?

Scaling the Encounter: Because dragons get tougher with age, the age of the dragon encountered should depend on your party's average level — especially if you decide that this is going to be a hostile encounter. If your party's average level is 10 or lower, they encounter a wyrmling. If their average level is 11-18, they encounter a young dragon. If their average level is 19-25, they encounter an adult dragon. If their average level is higher than 25, they encounter an ancient dragon.

Elk. Your party spots a herd of 1d4 bulls and 2d6 cows grazing a grassy patch of mountainside. If your party attacks them, only the males fight, covering the fleeing females.

Even if your party does not behave in a threatening manner, the bulls may mistake their actions and attack anyway. Have your party make a DC 15 Intelligence (Nature) or Wisdom (Survival) check. Failure means that someone has made a false move that sets off the males and they charge.

Scaling the Encounter: If you wish to make the encounter more challenging, your party sees a lone (and rare) giant elk at a distance. As they approach it they realize that it's larger than it seemed. Confident in its power as an alpha of its kind, it attacks your party if it senses any hostile intent (remember that giant elk have the ability to understand certain languages).

Perhaps it is bad luck in your campaign world to hunt a giant elk. If your party kills it, each party member is cursed as if affected by the spell *bane*, except that the effect lasts until it is magically dispelled, or until those who did the deed atone for it.

Treasure: Elk are hunted for food wherever they share territory with humans. Perhaps a butcher in a mountain village will pay 2 gp or thereabouts for a fresh carcass.

Giant. It may seem odd to classify giants as "neutral" rather than "aggressive," but the fact is that giants cover a wide range of attitudes and behaviors, and some are quite intelligent. And mountains are giants' home turf, so one may find the full range of giant-kind on display here. To determine the giant(s) encountered, roll on Table 7.3.4:

TABLE 7.3.4

Giants - Mountains

d10	ENCOUNTER
1	Cloud Giant
2	Fire Giant
3-5	Frost Giant
6-7	Hill Giant
8-9	Stone Giant
10	Storm Giant

Cloud Giant. Your party crosses paths with a cloud giant out for a casual stroll, or on its way to visit other giants whom it regards as its vassals. Regardless of whether its alignment is good or evil, it is not instinctively hostile, just condescending. It treats your party with a mixture of curiosity and haughty amusement; it may even invite them to pass some time at its mountain palace. If your party possesses a valuable item of some kind — it could be jewelry or artwork as easily as a magical artifact — this catches the cloud giant's eye. Instead of trying to take it by force, it proposes a wager, putting up something of roughly comparable worth in return: perhaps coins and gems, perhaps a pet wyvern, or even the services of one of its hill giant lackeys.

Fire Giant. Fire giants are most likely found where there is volcanic activity, but they are also hired by other giants to forge tools and weapons. They like their forges powered by heat directly from the earth, but they can work with created fires, too. Your party crosses paths with one fire giant, heavily bundled up against the cold, and traveling to a giant stronghold where it and its kin are employed — or to one of its own strongholds lower down the mountain, or near a volcano.

It may view your party as a target of opportunity — not to kill for plunder, but as potential servants. It tries to intimidate your party into swearing fealty and coming along quietly until its fellow fire giants can put them to some form of backbreaking and uncomfortably hot work.

Frost Giant. Frost giants are the warriors of the mountains, even as giants go. When they venture forth from their mountain strongholds in search of conquest and plunder, they mean business. Your party crosses paths with one frost giant acting as a scout for its clan, or as a messenger on its way to another frost giant clan. Unless your party can persuade it that they mean no harm, it takes them as a potential enemy

➤

that must be eliminated, even it's just to be on the safe side. Consider that your party needs a successful DC 20 Charisma (Persuasion) check to talk their way out of a fight.

Hill Giant. Your party crosses paths with one hill giant lumping its way across the mountainside. It may be part of a clan that lives at a higher altitude than most hill giants, or it may be a thrall of a cloud giant lord that lives in the area. In the latter case, it is out hunting or running some petty errand for its master, and it reverts to a surly mood when out of its lord's earshot. It tries to bully your party into giving over all of their possessions, and if they refuse the giant is quite willing to bash as many heads as it must.

Stone Giant. Stone giants are very much at home in the mountains, where a clan of them can work a mine or a quarry without being disturbed. However, other stone giants work for cloud giants and fire giants as servants or hired help, wanted for their grasp of mining and masonry. Your party crosses paths with one stone giant, who has left its lair to explore for another quarry site, or to meet with clients interested in using the stone giants' legendary skill for their own purposes. The stone giant is not interested in fighting your party, but persuading it to help your party means overcoming its lack of interest one way or another. Consider that it requires a successful DC 20 Charisma (Persuasion) check.

Storm Giant. Your party comes upon one storm giant in a contemplative mood, posed dramatically atop a boulder or rock ledge, surveying the world spread out below it as the mountain wind strokes its great beard. It greets your party with good cheer; this is a storm giant's home turf and its palace is probably nearby, so it feels comfortable here. Storm giants have a unique gift for taking in the big picture and looking into the future, and this one is in a mood where it would share its wisdom with your party. Think of it as a chance to share important information with your party and influence their course of action.

Scaling the Encounter: Even the lowliest giant is formidable foe for a low-level party. Feel free to re-roll for a different encounter.

Otherwise, you may add to the encounter group if you have a high-level party and want to increase the challenge. As a rough guideline, the total CR of the encounter group should be no higher than equal to your party's average level. You can tinker with the CR by adding more of the same giant, or by adding companions. All giants may have ogre underlings

➤

with them. Fire giants may have pet hell hounds. A stone giant may be accompanied by a black bear on a leash. Cloud giants may have hill giant and/or frost giant servants; they may also have a pet wyvern in tow.

Treasure: Giants always have some personal possessions of note on them. If encountered away from their lair, roll on the appropriate Individual Treasure table for each giant present.

Goats. Your party comes across a small herd of 1d8 billies and 2d8 nannies grazing. Perhaps they are wild goats — or perhaps they have gotten separated from a larger herd, and somewhere nearby there is a goatherd who would give a reward for their safe return. In any event, billies can be ornery beasts and if your party approaches them, you may require your party to make a DC 15 Intelligence (Nature) check to avoid setting off an attack in which the males charge to cover the fleeing females.

Scaling the Encounter: If you wish to make the encounter more challenging, use a herd of wild (and potentially irritated) giant goats instead. The encounter group should consist of 1d4 giant goats for each multiple of 2 in your party's average level with the same 1:2 ratios of males to females. Giant goats are quite wild; there is no chance that they are being kept by someone else.

Hippogriff. Your party sees a hippogriff circling overhead, looking for its next meal, or on the ground dealing with its prey. Hippogriffs are not as aggressive as birds of prey, and it is no sure bet that they would attack your party on the hope that it could make off with a pack animal or their stash of rations. Whether or not this is a hostile encounter is up to you.

Hippogriffs may be a kind of prey as easily as they could be predators. If hippogriffs are used as mounts in your world, it must follow that captive adults have value as breeding stock, and chicks captured from the wild also have value because they are still young enough to be tamed. To that end, you may allow your party a DC 15 Wisdom (Survival) check to trace a path to the hippogriff's lair, which is likely to be nearby. To subdue an adult hippogriff to the point where it can be bound and held captive, it must be successfully grappled and kept in grappled condition for 10 consecutive rounds.

Scaling the Encounter: If you want to stage a hostile encounter with hippogriffs and you need to make it more of a challenge for a higher-level party, consider that the encounter group consists of one hippogriff for each multiple of 3 in your party's average level.

Mule. Mules are domestic creatures. So when your party sees 1d4 mules mulling about on a mountainside for no apparent purpose, it is highly likely that they have escaped from someone using them as pack animals, such as miners or explorers. Their owners will pay a reward for their return — or your party could claim them as their own without anyone (possibly) being the wiser.

Mules do not attack. But they may be skittish around strangers, especially if they have been out in the wild for a while. If your party tries to take possession of them, have them make a DC 10 Intelligence (Nature) check to avoid a hostile reaction. Remember, these creatures have a kick like a mule.

Pegasus. Your party sees one pegasus wheeling in the sky. It does not attack, even if it sees evil creatures. However, it may be flagged down by signaling or calling to it and making a successful DC 15 Charisma (Persuasion) check. If your party can get the pegasus' attention, it may be persuaded to render some kind of aid — such as taking a party member to a nearby location — with a successful DC 20 Charisma (Persuasion) check. For good-aligned creatures who can speak Celestial, Elvish or Sylvan the DC is 15.

Scaling the Encounter: If you wish to make the encounter more challenging, the encounter group consists of one pegasus for each multiple of 3 in the party's average level.

Rats. Even in relatively barren mountainous country, rats can find enough food to justify living here. That's how they roll. Your party's presence presents them with a welcome opportunity to feast. Roll on Table 7.3.5 to determine the nature of the rat encounter:

TABLE 7.3.5
Rats -Mountains

d6	ENCOUNTER
1	Lone Rat
2-4	Swarm of Rats
5-6	Giant Rats

Lone Rat. A single rat, perhaps foraging by itself or perhaps lost from its nest, approaches your party while they take a rest. It's not much of a threat, but if someone in your party is looking for a familiar or even just a pet, this is an opportunity. Interacting with the rat — especially earning its trust with food — and making a successful DC 10 Intelligence (Nature) check earns its loyalty as a pet.
➤

Swarm of Rats. Without being aware of it, your party has stopped to rest near a nest of rats. Drawn by the party's rations, a swarm of rats makes for the nearest source of food. They don't attack party members who don't interfere with their basic mission of acquiring food. But unless they are stopped, they eventually account for all of your party's rations, making off with what they don't eat on the spot.

Giant Rats. In this case, the rats drawn by the food your party carries are giant rats. There are 2d6 of them.

TABLE 7.4
Humanoids - Mountains

d10	ENCOUNTER
1	Bugbear
2-4	Dwarves
5	Goblins
6	Hobgoblins
7	Kobolds
8	Lycanthrope
9-10	Orcs

Bugbear. Your party crosses paths with a small group of bugbears. Left to their own devices, bugbears would shun the cold and discomfort of the mountains. But under the command of hobgoblin leaders, a squad has been entrusted with guarding a mountain pass. Or perhaps they're part of a group stationed at a mountain fort, and the hobgoblins have sent them on a high-altitude training hike. Either way, they're in a disgruntled mood and they might pick a fight with your party just to vent their aggravation.

Scaling the Encounter: A beginning-level party should only have to cope with one bugbear. If you wish to make the encounter more challenging, the encounter group consists of two bugbears for each multiple of 3 in your party's average level. If your party's average level is 10 or higher, add one bugbear chief as the group's leader.

Dwarves. One shouldn't be surprised to encounter dwarves in the mountains. They're hardy enough to survive in a cold and barren place, and they know how to build strongholds that can keep them safe up here.

Your party crosses paths with a small group of dwarves. Their purpose in going abroad from their mine or stronghold is up to you as DM. They might be exploring for new veins, or miners shuttling from one mine to another. Or they might be out looking for firewood to keep the forges working. Or they might be taking loads of ore from a nearby mine for smelting — in which case, they have with them an equal number of mules. Or they might be a war party on the alert because there are orcs or other enemy humanoids about — in which case, treat them as guards armed with battleaxes.

In any event, they could offer your party a sidequest, offering weapons or even ingots of precious metal in exchange for their help in dealing with monsters or other enemies.

Scaling the Encounter: The encounter group consists of 1d8 guards (armed with battle-axes instead of spears) plus two guards for each level in your party's average level for a war party. A work group consists of 2d6 commoners armed with pickaxes (treat as spears that cannot be thrown) plus two guards for each level in your party's average level. If you don't want to run a mass encounter, feel free to substitute one priest for 16 guards or one veteran for 24 guards as freely as you like.

Goblins. Your party crosses paths with a small group of goblins from a tribe based in a nearby mountain cave. They may be on their way to the lands below to look for raiding targets, or they may be patrolling the vicinity of their lair to make sure nobody sneaks up on them. Either way, they don't expect to find your party here and they react with suspicion. They interrogate your party about their identity and their business; you may allow your party a DC 15 Charisma (Persuasion) check to convince the goblins that they're no enemy.

Scaling the Encounter: Use an encounter group of 1d4 goblins for each level in your party's average level. If you don't want to run a mass encounter but you still want to provide a higher-level party with a meaningful challenge, feel free to substitute one goblin boss for four goblins as much as you like. Because of the steep and rough terrain, it's unlikely that goblins in the mountains will have worg mounts.

Hobgoblins. Mountainous country provides hobgoblin tribes that live by war a good place to hole up in between campaigns. Safe within their strongholds, they can refit and rebuild their strength without fear of being attacked. Your party encounters a small group of hobgoblins who have set forth from their tribe's fort, either on patrol or out on a training march down and back up the mountain. Alternately, if there is a war going on, perhaps the hobgoblins have been entrusted with guarding a mountain pass or they're scouting enemy fortifications.

In either case, they're suspicious of your party — are they friend or foe? The hobgoblins interrogate them closely. They'll let them go if they're convinced your party is not a foe, but you may require that your party make a DC 15 Charisma (Persuasion) check to make it so.

Scaling the Encounter: The baseline encounter group should consist of 1d4 hobgoblins for each multiple of 2 in your party's average level. If your party's average level is 10-19, add a hobgoblin captain as the group's leader, accompanied by two goblin servants or one bugbear aide. If your party's average level is 20 or higher, add instead one hobgoblin warlord with two bugbear aides.

Kobolds. These nasty little reptilian humanoids prefer to live underground, but mountain caves offer them a gloomy sort of shelter that they find comfortable, as well as seclusion from anyone who would pick on them. Since kobolds react poorly to sunlight, your party most likely encounters them at night, or by entering a cave that they occupy (in which case, there is a trap of your choice guarding the entrance). To them, your party looks like a suitable target of opportunity — a relatively small group that has stuff worth taking. They fan out to try to surround your party and attack from more than one angle.

Scaling the Encounter: Use an encounter group of 2d4 kobolds plus 1d4 kobolds for each level in your party's average level. If you'd rather not run a mass encounter, you may cut down on the kobolds' numbers by substituting one winged kobold for two kobolds as much as you like.

Lycanthrope. To determine what manner of werebeast your party encounters, roll on Table 7.4.1:

TABLE 7.4.1
Lycanthrope - Mountains

d6	ENCOUNTER
1-3	Werebear
4	Wererat
5-6	Werewolf

All lycanthropes assume their animal form if the encounter comes down to combat, although they may choose their hybrid form instead if they have access to a weapon.

Werebear. Your party comes across a mountain cave that houses what appears to be a bear, but it is no ordinary bear. As soon as it sees your party, it drops its hybrid form and adopts its human form. The cave is the center of its domain, a part of the mountainside that it has decided to keep safe from harm. It is not

➤

automatically hostile to your party, especially if there are no evil characters present, and it may be willing to provide them with useful information about the surrounding area.

On the other hand, an encounter could create difficulties for your party if the werebear decides that someone in your party would make a good apprentice (and successor to its self-appointed duties as the local guardian). Once it realizes that there is a druid or a ranger in your party, a light goes on in its head — and it won't take "No" for an answer.

Wererat. Your party comes across a wererat driven from its natural home into this cold and desolate place, along with the rats with whom it kept company. It hopes to create a party of wererat followers who will give it some clout next time someone tries to run it out of town — and your party looks like it will make nice lycanthropes. It appears to your party in its humanoid form, pretending to be a traveler in distress. It asks to travel with your party for protection until it can find the next village and a warm bed. It tries to slip toward the back of the march order and waits for a time when everyone's back is turned to it.

Werewolf. Werewolves haunt even the high mountains. One spots your party and cannot turn down the opportunity to claim more victims. However, it is clever enough to approach them in its human form, pretending to be a lost traveler or a hunter in distress. Once your party gets close and drops its guard, it attacks.

Scaling the Encounter: A single lycanthrope can offer a stiff challenge to a low-level party. If your party's average level is 3 or less, feel free to re-roll the encounter. Alternately, if you want to make a werewolf encounter more challenging for a higher-level party, use a pack of them consisting of one werewolf for each multiple of 5 in your party's average level.

Orcs. Your party crosses paths with a band of orcs. If it's a small group, they're probably scouts sent by their tribe to find raiding targets — or they may be stragglers from a larger group. A larger group is probably a raiding party bent on attacking the nearest mine or settlement. If there are dwarves in this part of your campaign world, the orcs make them their highest priority target. The orcs may look your party over and decide that they're not worth the bother. But they may also decide to interrogate your party for information about places rumored to be lucrative targets for raiding, and they'll resort to violence without hesitation if your party is too slow to cooperate.

Alternately, the orcs are running toward your party and away from something as yet unseen. They may stop long enough to tell you what it is, or not. It may be a fearsome monster whom they could not hope to defeat, or it could be an army that got the better of them.

Scaling the Encounter: The baseline encounter group should consist of 1d4 orcs for each multiple of 2 in your party's average level. If your party's average level is 5-9, add an orog as the group's leader. If your party's average level is 10 or higher, use an orc war chief as its leader. If you don't want to run a mass encounter but you still want to provide a higher-level party with a meaningful challenge, feel free to substitute one orog for four orcs as much as you like.

Treasure: If the orcs are coming back from a successful raid, you may roll on the Treasure Hoard: Challenge 0-4 table to determine the fruits of their labor. This is in addition to the individual treasure they carry.

If the other adventurers are after the same goal, you may need to fight

TABLE 7.5

Humans - Mountains

d12	ENCOUNTER
1	Adventurers
2-3	Bandits
4	Explorers
5	Fugitives
6	Hermit
7	Hunters
8	Military
9-10	Miners
11-12	Pilgrims

Adventurers. Unless your party contains all of the adventurers in your campaign world, it's at least theoretically possible that they'll run into another adventuring party as they cross the mountains. Perhaps they're pursuing the same objective as your party. Perhaps they have a different mission; perhaps they're headed for a site that your party knows nothing about (like ancient ruins said to hold lost treasures). Perhaps they're lost and starving, or wounded, or cursed.

How they react to your party depends on a variety of factors. Are they rivals pursuing the same goal? If not, perhaps this party is willing to share useful information. In fact, if your party is stuck and having a hard time advancing the storyline of your campaign, a friendly encounter like this can help steer them in the right direction. Differences in alignment may also shape how the two parties react to each other.

Composition of this rival party is up to you and can vary according to circumstance. Any party in the wilderness would be well-advised to have someone accomplished in Survival, such as a ranger, with them. Conversely, a party that is struggling may be in a bad way precisely no one is well-versed in Survival or Nature.

Scaling the Encounter: Unless there is some possibility that this encounter turns hostile, the relative level of the party is mainly a matter of affect. A higher-level party might project self-confidence and calm (or arrogance), while beginning-level party might stumble about, unsure of themselves. If you're leaning towards a hostile encounter, however, consider that the total CR of the party should be roughly two-thirds of your party's average level.

Bandits. As with so many other aspects of banditry, setting up a hideout high in the mountains is a matter of tradeoffs. On the one hand, bandits know that anyone chasing after them will need a lot of skill and determination to find them in such a rugged and remote place. On the other hand, there aren't a lot of targets handy, so there is a lot of travel involved. Plus, it snows a lot.

If your party runs into a group of bandits in the mountains, a small group of them may be lookouts perched on a rock ledge or boulder. A large group is probably on its way down the mountain to look for targets, or on their way back from hitting up caravans and villages below (in which case, they probably figure they're home free at this point). They're surprised to run into your party, and even though adventurers are better-armed than their typical target, it's not out of the question that they attack. It's possible that they assume that your party is a posse sent out after them, but if they're outbound from their lair they may figure that targeting your party beats a long trek to find a more lucrative target.

Scaling the Encounter: As a rough guideline, the encounter group should contain 1d8 bandits for each level in your party's average level. If your party's average level is 4 or higher, add a bandit captain as their leader. If you don't want to run a mass encounter but you still want these criminals to provide a higher-level party with a meaningful challenge, feel free to substitute one thug for four bandits as much as you like.

Treasure: If your party finds the bandits' hideout, roll on the Treasure Hoard table appropriate to the total CR of the encounter. Do so also if you decide that the bandits encountered are on their way back from a successful raid. Consider that there is also a 20% chance that the bandits have with them a high-value captive whom they intend to ransom. The identity of this captive is left to you as DM, as it should depend on local circumstances and fit into your campaign world.

Explorers. Your party crosses paths with a small human party who appear to be well-bundled up against the mountain cold and properly equipped to deal with snow, ice and difficult terrain. They may be explorers driven by curiosity to map a mountain about which little is known, or they be climbers who see themselves as conquering the mountain just for its own sake. The party consists of 1d4 scouts.

Such an encounter is not likely to be hostile. Instead, you may treat this as an opportunity for your party to receive some help from a knowledgeable stranger — the explorer is likely to have excellent maps of nearby areas (and knowledge of those areas) and is willing to share them. Conversely, an expedition that has been in the field for a while may be running short on rope, pitons, cartography supplies or other necessaries and may be willing to pay well if your party can help supply what they lack. Also, if your party is in the mood for a sidequest, an explorer may offer one: If the expedition is headed into particularly dangerous territory, it may need additional guards to keep it safe.

Fugitives. Your party crosses paths with 1d4 bedraggled people stumbling along the hillside. They're under-dressed for the weather at this altitude and they look haggard and half-starved, but they're moving quickly. Most, if not all of them have a manacle around one wrist, with the other manacle dangling on its chain. They're escaped prisoners who have fled all the way up into the mountains. From whom they are fleeing and why they were imprisoned in the first place is up to you, and ought to depend on where in your campaign world this encounter takes place, but they're probably desperate to come all the way up here.

How the encounter plays out depends entirely on how your party reacts, but one thing on which you may rely is that these fugitives did not go to the trouble of a jailbreak just to allow a bunch of strangers to take their freedom back from them. Each of them has learned whip their freed manacle by the chain and wield it as a club.

Treat the fugitives as bandits, but without weapons or armor.

Treasure: Fugitives have no treasure.

Explorers may be willing to pay well for goods they lack.

Hermit. A high mountain cave is an excellent destination (perfect, except for the weather) for someone who has decided to withdraw from worldly cares, but that doesn't mean you can't be found. Your party stumbles upon a hermit in his or her abode. One hermit lives here, devoted to a pure and simple life of contemplation. The hermit may be a divine spellcaster, for whom seclusion and meditation is a form of service to a deity. A hermit from a religious sect that embraces asceticism may have no shelter at all — perhaps devotion requires that you live on top of a boulder, naked to the elements. It may take a successful DC 15 Charisma (Persuasion) check to get past the fact that your party has broken this seclusion, but the hermit may be willing to use divine spells to aid them.

Alternately, your party may have found a secular hermit — someone who, having been wounded by failure or grown weary of success, decided to retire completely from the world. Such a person won't have divine spells, but may have magic items, local lore, or even knowledge and personal connections from his or her past life that might help your party.

Yet another possibility is that this hermit is a retired adventurer or soldier, in the manner of knights in the Arthurian romances who became hermits to repent of lives spent fighting each other and dallying with married women. Hermits in this mold have discarded their fighting gear, but they may be persuaded to leave their seclusion and join your party as friendly NPCs.

Treat a religious hermit as an acolyte or a priest, but feel free to generate a higher-level divine spellcaster if you want to create a more spectacular effect with this encounter. Treat a secular hermit as a commoner, or use a character class and level of your choice.

Treasure: Roll on the Treasure Hoard: Challenge 0-4 to determine if the hermit has any magic items and/or valuable devotional items.

Hunters. Your party comes across 1d6 hunters looking for game. They're bound to be pretty rugged — or desperate — folk to be hunting at this elevation. Most likely, they live farther down and have come up into the mountains either because they're looking for rare game, or because game is hard to find closer to home. Depending on your party's appearance, they may act with caution, even suspicion at first. Despite the fact that they are armed with bows, they know that they are operating in wilderness, and there are always strange folk about. However, if your party is not hostile to them they are willing to help by trading goods and supplying food and local knowledge. If you wish, have your party make a DC 10 (Charisma) Persuasion check to get on their good side.

Treat hunters as scouts.

Military. Rough terrain and high altitude are not conducive to military operations. But if there is a war in this corner of your campaign world, mountains make a good place to make a defensive stand — or a mountain pass could make a good route if you want to take the enemy from an unexpected direction. Your party encounters a modest force tasked to guard a pass, or a patrol based in a nearby stronghold. They are naturally suspicious. You may require your party to make a DC 15 Charisma (Persuasion) check to convince them that they are not aligned with the enemy — especially if they have nothing to identify them, such as a passport or a written guarantee of safe conduct. If persuaded that your party is

friendly, the soldiers are willing to provide them with local knowledge, as well as material assistance if the soldiers are not themselves short of supplies.

Scaling the Encounter: As a rough guideline, the encounter group should contain 1d8 guards for each level in your party's average level. If your party's average level is 6 or higher, add a veteran or a knight as the group's leader. If you don't want to run a mass encounter, feel free to substitute one veteran for 12 guards as much as you like. Veterans who are not officers could be rank-and-file soldiers from an elite unit, or bodyguards for the leader.

Miners. Your party crosses paths with a small group of 1d10 miners who are either prospecting for gems or metals, or they're headed for an established mining settlement up in the mountains. This is not in and of itself a hostile encounter. The miners could have local knowledge that your party finds useful, as well as cold weather gear, torches, lamp oil, rope and other supplies for working in a hostile environment. They might also want your party to serve as armed escort, having realized a little too late that dangerous creatures lurk even in this inhospitable land. In fact, if you want to stage a situation in which your party has the chance to rescue them from danger, roll for another encounter.

Pilgrims. Mountains often seem remote and mysterious to folk who live in the lands below, and so they have a way of becoming places of religious significance. Your party crosses paths with a group of devotees traveling to or from a holy site up in the mountains; they would have no other reason for coming to such forbidding country. Perhaps they have a specific request to make of their deity (ending a drought or plague, curing someone of disease, etc.) and they bring an offering, or perhaps it's just a ritual that their religion says they must perform regularly. Depending on how religions work in your world, perhaps their mission is to vandalize a shrine to a rival deity.

Roll on Table 7.5.1 to give the encounter a more specific character:

TABLE 7.5.1
Pilgrims -Mountains

d6	ENCOUNTER
1-3	Acolytes
4	Cultists
5-6	Lay Follwers

Acolytes. Your party crosses paths 1d4 monks or ▶

junior clerics. Treat them as acolytes.

Cultists. Your party crosses paths with 2d6 hard-core followers of an evil deity. How they react to your party is up to you, and should be influenced by the numerical odds for or against them. If their cult involves some kind of sacrifice to their deity, perhaps the cultists consider that your party would do nicely. Treat the cultists as cultists.

Lay Followers. Your party crosses paths with 2d6 lay followers making a pilgrimage. They're just everyday folk performing an elaborate act of worship, and they're the most likely to need your party's protection as they travel through uninhabited land. Treat them as commoners.

Scaling the Encounter. If you wish to make the encounter more challenging, add one priest or cult leader to the encounter, as appropriate.

Treasure: In addition to whatever treasure they carry on their person, pilgrims may carry with them an offering to their deity. At your discretion, roll on the Treasure Hoard: Challenge 0-4 table to determine its value.

The pilgrim's deity and alignment should dictate how they react to meeting your party. In any event, they are lightly armed at best and they may want to travel in your party's company for safety — especially if they know of a specific hazard in the area, like bandits or monsters. If friendly, they may also be willing to share local knowledge and trade with your party, or even share what divine magic capabilities they possess for your party's benefit.

TABLE 7.6
Watch Out! - Mountains

d12	ENCOUNTER
1	Avalanche
2	Did You Hear That?
3-5	Falling Rocks
6	Hidden Crevasse
7	Mountain Specter
8	Tracks
9-10	Treacherous Footing
11	Tripping Hazard
12	Wind Gust

Avalanche. The snow-blanketed mountainside above your party begins to rumble. That is never a good sign. An overwhelming wave of snow and debris comes downhill, right at them. Have each party member make a DC 15 Strength (Athletics) or Dexterity (Acrobatics) check to avoid getting caught by the avalanche. Failure means that that character is buried into snow; treat this like falling into quicksand.

Did You Hear That? Choose a party member to make a DC 15 Wisdom (Survival) or Intelligence (Nature) check. Failure means that that character believes that he or she has heard a noise made by creature or a dangerous natural phenomenon. It can be as consequential as a dragon's roar in the distance, or as eerily intimate as muttering in Orcish coming from behind those rocks. A successful check means that that party member realizes that this is an illusion; either it's not as close as it seems or it isn't real at all.

If you wish, roll on Table 7.6.1 for guidance on what your party thinks it hears:

TABLE 7.6.1
Did You Hear That? – Mountains

d10	ENCOUNTER
1	Crash of falling rocks
2	Dragon roaring overhead
3	Ghostly wail
4	Human or humanoid cry of distress that trails off
5	Mule braying
6	Rumble of something tunneling through rock
7	Voices speaking in Common
8	Voices speaking in Giant
9	Wolves snarling
10	Yeti howling

Falling Rocks. Rocks higher up the mountain come loose, and gravity does the rest. Pick a point in the party's march order as the center of the rockfall's area of effect. Each party member within a 10-foot radius takes 2d6 bludgeoning damage, but a successful DC 15 Dexterity (Acrobatics) check halves the damage, rounded up.

Hidden Crevasse. Snow, thin ice, an optical illusion, bad visibility — all of these things alone or working in concert can conceal a crevasse from your party's notice. You may allow your party a DC 15 Wisdom (Perception) check to notice that the ground in their path is treacherous. Failure means that someone at the front of the march order fails to spot the crevasse in time to avoid it, and plunges 1d4 x 10 feet to the bottom, suffering the appropriate falling damage.

The crevasse is narrow enough to cross with a running long jump, but this requires a successful DC 10 Strength (Athletics) or Dexterity (Acrobatics) check.

Mountain Specter. Mist has set in around the mountain, so thickly that your party can no longer see the lands below them. At their altitude, however, the sky is clear. With their backs to the sun, your party sees a dark shape form on the thick sheet of mist below them. Is it an incorporeal undead — a shadow, a wraith, a specter? Why doesn't it attack? You may allow your party a DC 15 Intelligence (Nature) or Wisdom (Survival) check to recognize that this an optical illusion caused by their own shadows being cast on the mist.

Tracks. Your party spots tracks that look like they belong to a rare monster native to the mountains, like a yeti. They may make a successful DC 15 Wisdom (Survival) check to realize that they are very old, and they will not lead to anything useful. If no one makes a successful check, this may be the start of an amusing (for you as DM, anyway) wild goose chase.

Treacherous Footing. Someone in your party steps onto loose ground, precipitating a dangerous tumble down the mountainside. Pick one party member at or near the front of the march order. That character loses his or her balance and the tumble causes 2d6 falling damage. A successful DC 15 Strength (Athletics) or Dexterity (Acrobatics) results in half damage, rounded down.

Tripping Hazard. Pick a party member at the front of the march order. That character trips over an unseen obstacle — a rock sticking up out of the ground is a good candidate here in the mountains. He or she must make a successful DC 15 Strength (Athletics) or Dexterity (Acrobatics) check to avoid a hard fall that causes 1d8 damage — and perhaps no small embarrassment in the eyes of the other party members.

Wind Gust. A biting mountain wind whips up, catching your party off guard. If they have made camp for the night, their campfire is extinguished, forcing them to light another one. If they've already used all their wood and kindling, they'll have to go hunting in the dark for more. If they're carrying torches, they go out. If they're using lanterns, they may lose their grip (see below).

Regardless of whether it's day or night, any party member who is standing must make a DC 5 Strength check to avoid being knocked down. Anyone who is knocked down by the wind immediately loses grasp of anything held in hand. Fragile objects break when they are dropped. In addition, anyone who is knocked down while wearing his or her pack must make a DC 5 Dexterity (Acrobatics) check to avoid the pack falling heavily so that anything containing liquid, such as canteens and potions, breaks and spills.

The Remorhaz Came Over the Mountain

You may note that this chapter does not comment on how game mechanics should reflect the effect of high altitude on your party or creatures. It is assumed that all player characters have done their altitude training, and that the encounters described here involve creatures that, to some degree, self-select for their ability to function in the rarefied air. Powerful aerial predators like rocs and wyverns fly at high altitude anyway, and breathing freely doesn't seem to be much of a concern to purple worms and xorns.

OCEAN

CHAPTER EIGHT

Ocean

What is an Ocean?

Among the ten wilderness environments described in this book, the open ocean is unique. Once you leave sight of land, the sea is flat and eerily featureless, with only the sun by day and the stars at night to help you get your bearings. It is also a hostile environment to most of the creatures described in the SRD, as well as all of the player character races. No doubt, you have noticed that only a distinct minority of canonical creatures are either aquatic or amphibious. Sailing on the ocean, as defined here, also means that you're farther from land than most aerial creatures care to venture. This rather limits the range of plausible encounters on the high seas.

Not only that, but the sheer vastness of the ocean, as well as the depths of the waters, puts a further limit on what you may encounter here. Giant frogs are amphibious, but you're not going to find any in salt water and this far from land. An unusually high proportion of the encounters described here involve large, high-level monsters. They're comfortable out here, with plenty of elbow (or tentacle) room and hostile working conditions for pesky bands of smaller beings who might hunt them. This chapter includes a couple of encounters that assume the presence of small stowaways on your party's ship, but many of them involve big, tough customers.

What Do You Find in an Ocean?

When you determine that a random encounter is in order, roll on Table 8.1 to determine the category:

TABLE 8.1

Encounter Type - Ocean

d20	CATEGORY
1-8	Aggressive Creatures (Table 8.2)
9-11	Neutral Creatures (Table 8.3)
12-17	Humanoids and Humans (Table 8.4)
18-20	Watch Out! (Table 8.5)

Then, roll on the appropriate table to determine the creature, person or thing encountered.

TABLE 8.2

Aggressive Creatures - Ocean

d20	CATEGORY
1	Aboleth
2	Dragon Turtle
3-4	Elemental
5-8	Hunter Shark
9	Giant Octopus
10-11	Killer Whale
12	Kraken
13-14	Merrow
15-16	Mimic
17-18	Quippers
19	Sea Hag
20	Snakes

Aboleth. Your party's ship has the misfortune to sail into the area of effect of an aboleth's undersea lair. They notice the waters around the ship darken and a stench, like the ocean itself retching, rises from the surface. Then, one of these ancient monstrosities emerges from the water right beside the ship, presenting a spectacle designed to paralyze even the most seasoned mariner. However, this is not the aboleth itself, but an illusory image that it created to persuade the crew to beg mercy and become its followers. The ploy works on 2d4 of the ship's crew, who behave from that point as cultists of the aboleth. They then turn on the remaining crew and passengers, trying to subdue them for later use as slaves or sacrificial victims.

Scaling the Encounter: If your party's average level is higher than 10, consider that the aboleth is not an illusion, but an actual aboleth that has risen from the depths. It tries to enslave as many of your party as it can as the ship's crew-turned-cultists attack the party members who cannot be enslaved. In this case, treat one of the cultists as a cult fanatic.

Dragon Turtle. The ship in which your party sails has, much to the misfortune of everyone on board, drawn the attention of a dragon turtle. One of these awesome beasts rises from the deep to attack the ship and plunder its wreckage. It is possible to bribe a dragon turtle to spare a ship and those onboard — if your party can communicate with it, they may make a Charisma (Persuasion) check to convince it to do so, with the DC dependent on how much they offer — but the dragon turtle's intention is aggressive.

If you wish to give your party the chance to run away, you may have the dragon turtle breach the surface far enough away for someone on the ship to recognize it at a distance. In this case, make a DC 15 Wisdom (Perception) check with a +1 ability bonus for the ship's lookout. If this fails, you may allow your party a DC 15 Wisdom (Perception) or Intelligence (Nature) check. If one or the other succeeds, someone has spotted the dragon turtle in time for the ship to turn and make a run for it. If both fail, everyone mistakes its gargantuan shell for the play of sunlight (or moonlight) on the water.

Scaling the Encounter: A close encounter with a dragon turtle may be too much for a lower-level party. If your party's average level is less than 20, feel free to re-roll for another encounter.

Elemental. The expanse of the open ocean provides room enough for gateways to the Elemental Planes of Air and Water, or for elementals who have escaped their summoner to wander the Material Plane. Whether your party encounters an air elemental or a water elemental is up to you, or you may roll on Table 8.2.1:

TABLE 8.2.1
Elemental - Ocean

d6	ENCOUNTER
1-2	Air Elemental
3-6	Water Elemental

Either way, the elemental reads the presence of the ship as a threat and attacks it.

Air Elemental. An air elemental takes the form of a waterspout headed right at your party's ship.

Water Elemental. A water elemental appears as a small, but powerful rogue wave headed right at your party's ship.

Scaling the Encounter: If your party's average level is lower than 5, an elemental may be more than you want to throw at them. Feel free to re-roll for a different encounter.

Hunter Shark. Though large and aggressive, a hunter shark will not attack a ship. An ocean-going vessel is obviously too much for it to take on. However, a ship's boat — and certainly, anyone who has gone into the water — is a potential target. A hunter shark attacking a boat tries to break or overturn it, thus leaving the occupants vulnerable in the water.

Scaling the Encounter: If you wish to make the encounter more challenging, you may add one hunter shark to the encounter group for each multiple of 3 in your party's

average level. Or you may use one giant shark for each multiple of 10 in your party's average level. Giant sharks are large enough to attack a ship.

Killer Whale. A killer whale has echolocated your ship. It is large and aggressive enough so that it could conceivably upend a small ship and pick off anyone thrown overboard. It will certainly try to make a meal of a ship's boat or snack on individuals in the water.

Scaling the Encounter: If you wish to make the encounter more challenging, you may add one killer whale to the encounter group for each multiple of 5 in your party's average level, rounded up.

Kraken. Here be monsters. Your party has the great misfortune of coming to the attention of a kraken. The ship's crew should have some warning of what is to come, as the sky turns darker than the darkest storm clouds before the monster breaches the surface, and the ocean takes on an inky black hue. Before it gets close enough to grapple the ship and bludgeon it to pieces, it uses its *lightning storm* ability to attack the anyone on board who tries, however ineffectually, to fight back.

Scaling the Encounter: A close encounter with a kraken may be too much for a lower-level party. If your party's average level is less than 20, feel free to re-roll for another encounter.

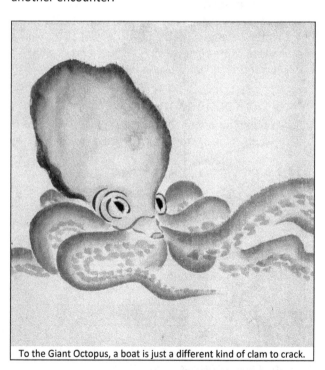

To the Giant Octopus, a boat is just a different kind of clam to crack.

Giant Octopus. Normal-sized octopi stick to shallows and coastal waters. An octopus met on the open ocean is bound to be a giant on the hunt. One giant octopus will not take on an entire ship. But it is capable of tipping over a boat to get those aboard into the water, where they are more vulnerable, and attacking individuals already in the water. You may allow the giant octopus' target a DC 15 Wisdom (Perception) or Wisdom (Survival) check to notice an alarmingly large tentacle reaching for it in time to react.

Scaling the Encounter: Octopi are intelligent creatures (though giant octopi are not proportionately more intelligent than their smaller cousins). If you wish to make the encounter more challenging, you may add one giant octopus to the encounter group for each multiple of 2 in your party's average level, to represent octopi ganging up on a target.

Merrow. Merrow prefer hunting in littoral areas and raiding land-based settlements. They're richer in lucrative targets than the open ocean. Occasionally, though, they venture into deeper water to scout and here, they sometimes skirmish with small bands of merfolk and sauhagin intent on gathering information about its tribe's surroundings.

One merrow scout comes across your party's ship or boat. It's a target of opportunity, and the merrow is not above trying its hand at piracy.

Scaling the Encounter: If you wish to make the encounter more challenging, the encounter group consists of one merrow for each multiple of 3 in your party's average level.

Mimic. This is not so much an ocean encounter as a shipboard encounter. One mimic has stowed away on the ship in which your party travels, disguising itself as a chest or a sailor's locker. No one recognizes it, but everyone assumes that it belongs onboard. It ambushes your party while they are rummaging around in the hold.

Scaling the Encounter: If you want to make the encounter more challenging, consider that more than one stowaway has found its way on board. The encounter group consists of two mimics for each multiple of 3 in your party's average level, rounded up.

Quippers. Schools of saltwater-compatible quippers roam the seas and they're always hungry. But anyone within the confines of a ship is safe from them; quippers are at least smart enough not to jump on board in search of food. However, anyone in the water, or simply dangling an arm or leg over the side, is a good enough target and has to deal with one swarm of quippers. You may allow the quippers' target a DC 15 Wisdom (Perception) or Wisdom (Survival) check to notice a school of fish with unusually sharp teeth approaching in time to pull back.

Scaling the Encounter: If you wish to make the encounter more challenging, the encounter group consists of one swarm of quippers for each multiple of 2 in your party's average level, rounded up.

Sea Hag. Sea hags are real threats, not just a popular name for a ship. One sea hag, perhaps enraged at the sight of the ship's decorative figurehead, hauls itself aboard and attacks the crew.

Scaling the Encounter: If you wish to make the encounter more challenging, it's a coven (or part of a coven) of sea hags attacking the ship. The encounter group consists of one sea hag for each multiple of 3 in your party's average level, rounded up.

Snakes. While some species of snake are aquatic, it is more likely that snakes hidden on board in the ship's cargo prove to be a hazard at sea. The problem may start as no more than a couple of small snakes who escape detection while the ship is loaded, but if they breed at sea the difficulties they present literally multiply. Either the crew or a member of your party incites a snake attack while rummaging around. 1d4 venomous snakes dart out from a crate of stores and attack the nearest party member.

Scaling the Encounter: If you wish to make the encounter more challenging, the encounter group consists of one swarm of venomous snakes.

TABLE 8.3
Neutral Creatures - Ocean

d6	CATEGORY
1-2	Rats
3-4	Sea Horse
5	Storm Giant
6	Water Weird

Rats. Presumably, the ship carrying your party has not begun to sink. So there may well be rats on board, hiding amongst the cargo, or in any hidden space they can find. Your party disturbs them while rummaging around in the hold, or opening a crate full of stores. They encounter one swarm of rats. They don't attack party members who don't interfere with their basic mission of acquiring food. But it's highly unlikely that the ship's crew want to share their valuable supplies with rats, and they'll be glad if your party gets rid of them. Perhaps the captain grants your party free passage in exchange for working as exterminators.

Sea Horse. Someone on board spots a small herd of 2d6 sea horses just beneath the surface. They are curious about the ship, even friendly. Among them is 1d4 giant sea horses, which may be wrangled and ridden as a mount by a human or humanoid that can breathe underwater.

To wrangle a giant sea horse, it must be successfully grappled and kept in grappled condition for 6 consecutive rounds. At that point, it becomes docile and whomever grappled it may ride it or use it as a pack animal. Because of its size, two medium-size creatures may grapple with the same riding horse simultaneously, and as long as one of them maintains its grappled condition, this counts toward the requirement for wrangling it. However, other giant sea horses in the herd react to what looks like an attack on another member. At your discretion, the sea horses in the herd may join in and attack the wranglers as well.

Storm Giant. A storm giant who dwells on the bottom of the sea pops up to the surface for some fresh salt air and discovers your ship. It calls out a friendly greeting. It welcomes the chance to chat, because it has been a long time since anyone has come by. It willingly supplies local knowledge, accurate predictions of the weather, advice on how to avoid hazards in the ship's path, monsters that lie ahead, and the like. Conversely, it uses its *lightning strike* ability to unleash the power of the storm on anyone it deems unfriendly.

Scaling the Encounter: If you anticipate a hostile encounter, a storm giant is a bit too much for a low-level party. Feel free to re-roll for another encounter.

Water Weird. It is exceptional, though not entirely inconceivable, that one would find a water weird bound to a patch of open ocean. Who would have bothered to summon it to guard this place? But here it is. As an elemental, it acts instinctively and treats your party as intruders. However, its actions vary according to the alignment it has absorbed from its surroundings, so consider that there is a 50% chance that it is neutral good and guarding a sacred site and 50% that it is neutral evil and bound to a befouled site.

Scaling the Encounter: If you wish to make the encounter more challenging, consider that more than one water weird has been bound to this place. The encounter group consists of one water weird for each multiple of 5 in the party's average level. At your discretion, you may require your players to say, "one weird water weird" three time fast.

Getting between a creature and its prey means serious business.

TABLE 8.4
Humanoids and Humans - Ocean

d12	CATEGORY
1	Explorer
2	Fishermen
3-4	Merchants
5	Merfolk
6	Military Vessel
7-8	Pirates
9-10	Sahuagin
11	Shipwreck
12	Smugglers

Explorer. A ship headed for unknown lands — at least, lands unknown in the place from which it set out — hails the ship carrying your party. In addition to the ship's crew, the explorers consist of one commoner — the scholar who leads the expedition — and one scout or druid acting as aide and bodyguard. Perhaps they are here thanks to the sponsorship of an academy or a ruler eager to know more about the world, or perhaps the explorer is a wealthy eccentric who undertook this expedition on his or her own.

Such an encounter is not likely to be hostile. Explorers are open and curious, and experienced ones know they may need a helping hand to survive a long ocean voyage. Instead, treat this as an opportunity for your party to receive some help from a knowledgeable stranger — the explorer is likely to have excellent maps and is willing to share them. Conversely, if they have been at sea for a while, they may be lost and short of supplies, in which case they would express gratitude for whatever help your party could provide them. Also, if your party is in the mood for a sidequest, an explorer may offer one: If the expedition is headed into particularly dangerous territory, it may need additional guards to keep it safe.

Fishermen. Someone on board spots a boat or small ship with 1d6 anglers in search of large fish that one can only catch in the open ocean. If returning with fish in hand, they're willing to sell part of their catch. This presents two challenges, however: They're after big game fish, large enough to provide 100 tavern meals (though the fishermen will sell for the cost of only 40 tavern meals); and, of course, the fish will have to be preserved, cleaned and smoked or cooked before it goes bad.

Another possibility is that your party comes upon them while they are being attacked by a monster or creature of your choice from Table 8.2. They'll be grateful for any help your party lends them.

In any event, they're happy to provide your party with local knowledge, including tales of monsters and of course, stories of the one that got away.

Treat fishermen as commoners.

Merchants. A merchant ship comes within hailing distance of the ship carrying your party. The merchant group on board consists of 2d4 merchants and 1d6 guards. They could help your party by making available necessary items, exchanging hard money for treasure items or providing knowledge of just about anywhere in your campaign world — where is this ship going, and from whence did it sail? They may also be interested in hiring the ship — more specifically, the rugged adventurers on board the ship — as an escort if they fear pirates or sea monsters.

Treat the merchants as commoners. Treat the guards as guards, although you may substitute veterans for as many guards as you wish.

Treasure: Roll once on the Individual Treasure: Challenge 0-4 table for each merchant or guard. In addition, roll once on the Treasure Hoard: Challenge 0-4 table for each merchant present to determine the value of goods and/or hard money in the ship's holds. You may substitute valuable goods — spices, fine cloth, expensive hardwood, etc. — for art objects or coin as you wish.

Merfolk. Merfolk rarely venture into the deep ocean, but regardless of your party's ship's position relative to land they may come across a small band of 2d6 merfolk. This far out from coastal waters, they are likely to be a scout party from a nearby settlement — or refugees fleeing from an enemy, such as merrow raiders or other monsters. In the former case, they may be willing to trade with your party and share local knowledge. In the latter case, they may ask your party to help them against their predatory foe, creating a sidequest.

How Well do Kobolds Swim?
Let's be honest: There just aren't enough aquatic humanoids to justify a separate table for them, so this chapter combines humanoids and the various "human" occupations into one set of possible encounters. This is not to say that humanoid races are hydrophobic and would never sail the oceans. But if you encounter them, they are likely to fit under one or more vocational descriptions set aside for humans: hobgoblin soldiers on a transport ship; orc pirates; elven merchants. And so on.

Military Vessel. Your party's ship may cross paths with one or more large transports carrying soldiers to a far-off place, but trans-oceanic invasions are rare undertakings. Or they may spot a fleet of warships on their way to battle an enemy fleet. If they get too close, they'll be ordered to stop and await a boarding party tasked with determining whether they are friend, foe or neither. Your party may find itself in a situation where they have to talk their way out of being detained.

Shipwreck survivors may allow players pick over the ruined cargo.

Much more likely, however, they come upon a small warship tasked with protecting a trade route and hunting down pirates. This ship hails your party's vessel and demands that they pull alongside. The warship's captain demands to know your party's ship's identity, destination and purpose. They want to determine, of course, whether your party's ship is involved in piracy and/or smuggling, and seize or sink it if so. If they are persuaded that everything on board is aboveboard, they'll let your party go on their way, perhaps even escort them for a while.

If you want to use a Charisma (Persuasion) check to determine if you party can talk their way out of being suspected of bad intentions, a DC of 15 is always a reasonable baseline. But the DC could (and should) vary according to the situation.

Treat all sailors on the warship as guards.

Scaling the Encounter: The size of the encounter group should depend on the size of the vessel. Whatever the size, one veteran is present as the ship's captain.

Pirates. Unless your party has taken passage on a warship bristling with weapons, their vessel presents pirates with a plausible target. The pirate ship pulls alongside and calls for everyone on board to surrender or face the consequences. Everyone can see that the pirates have a boarding party ready to go. Whether the ship's crew decides to give up or fight depends on you as DM. Treat pirates as bandits; they're essentially bandits with boats. Add peg legs, eyepatches and parrots on the shoulder at your discretion.

Scaling the Encounter: The size of the encounter group should depend on the size of the pirate vessel. Pirates prefer small, fast ships and however many it takes to crew that ship, that's how many pirates are present. Whatever the size, one bandit captain is present as the pirate captain.

Treasure: If these pirates have taken another ship before this one, its stolen treasure will be on board. Roll on the Treasure Hoard table appropriate to the total CR of the encounter. Consider that there is also a 20% chance that the pirates have with them a high-value captive whom they intend to ransom. The identity of this captive is left to you as DM, as it should depend on local circumstances and fit into your campaign world.

Sahuagin. Sahuagin lurking beneath the waves spot the ship carrying your party and decide that it is, at the very least, an item of interest to them. If there are enough of them (see Scaling the Encounter), they split into two groups and attack from both port and starboard. A small group may just be a scouting party, but a larger group has plunder in mind. They give the ship's passengers a chance to surrender, but they'll take anything worth having one way or another.

Scaling the Encounter: The encounter group consists of two sahuagin for each multiple of 3 in your party's average level. You may substitute one sahuagin priestess for four sahuagin. If you party's average level is 10 or higher, add one sahuagin baron to the group as its leader.

Shipwreck. Someone on board spies the remains of a ship lost at sea — bits of wreckage, a ship's boat — with 1d12 survivors in it or clinging to it. Roll on Table 8.4.1 to determine the kind of ship that went down and guidance regarding the nature of the survivors, how grateful they might be for rescue, and what they might offer your party as thanks:

Shipwreck survivors come in all shapes and sizes.

TABLE 8.4.1
Shipwreck Survivors - Ocean

d8	ENCOUNTER
1	Explorer
2	Fisherman
3-5	Merchant
6	Military
7	Pirates
8	Smugglers

Smugglers. Though they also work the troublesome side of the law, smugglers are not the same as pirates. They already have valuable goods in hand, and they're trying to sneak them into a place where they can exchange them for money. A small, fast vessel comes into view of your party's ship, but its crew does not want their company. If your party's ship runs them down, they may try to play it off and pretend that they're doing nothing illegal; they may try to bribe your party into leaving them alone; or they may try to eliminate your party as witnesses to their crime.

Treat smugglers as bandits equipped only with shortswords.

Scaling the Encounter: The size of the encounter group should depend on the size of the smugglers' vessel. However many it takes to crew that ship, that's how many smugglers are present. Whatever the size, one bandit captain is present as the leader of the smuggling ring.

TABLE 8.5
Watch Out! - Ocean

d12	CATEGORY
1	Blazing Sun
2	Dead Calm
3	Fog
4-5	Man Overboard!
6-7	Storm
8	Whirlpool

Blazing Sun. The hot sun in a cloudless sky glaring down on the open ocean takes its toll. Each party member must make a Constitution saving throw. All who fail suffer one exhaustion level for the next six hours or until sunset, whichever comes first, to a maximum of

Exhaustion 5; in other words, this extraordinary exposure to the sun can debilitate, but it won't kill.

If your roll this encounter at night, re-roll for a different encounter.

Dead Calm. The winds cease entirely, for whatever reason. If your party's ship uses sails, it cannot move under sail for the next six hours or until you roll again for a random encounter, whichever comes first.

Fog. A sudden fog sets in, greatly reducing visibility. The area around the ship becomes heavily obscured for the next six hours or until you roll again for a random encounter, whichever comes first.

Man Overboard! One of the crew has fallen into the ocean. What does your party do about it? Rescuing the unfortunate sailor would earn his or her gratitude, as well as gratitude from the rest of the crew. What form that takes is up to you as GM.

Storm. Your party's ship sails into stormy weather. For the next four hours, the ship operates under storm conditions.

Whirlpool. Your ship approaches a point where shifting currents produce a whirlpool that could put the crew and passengers at some hazard. It's not a maelstrom powerful enough to doom the ship by itself — that's a major feature that should be saved for a fixed encounter. However, it could capsize a ship's boat that gets too close to it.

A ship's lookout (or, at your discretion, one of your party members) may make a DC 15 Wisdom (Perception) or Wisdom (Survival) check to see the whirlpool from a distance in time to steer away from it without problem. Otherwise, the ship gets too close to extricate it easily; steering clear at this point requires a successful DC 15 Dexterity or Strength check on the part of the ship's helmsman.

Failure means that the ship is caught in the vortex and lists heavily enough so that each party member should make a DC 10 Strength (Athletics) or Dexterity (Acrobatics) check to grab hold of something firm and avoid falling overboard. Anyone who falls overboard is affected as if caught in the whirlpool effect of the spell *control water*, spell save DC 15. A lifeline thrown from the ship eliminates the need to swim away from the whirlpool to avoid its effects.

"Desolate and Empty Is the Sea"

Admittedly, the ocean does not offer a lot of options for encounters compared to other environments. Again: This is a reflection of the current SRD. If you have your own ideas for ocean-going encounters, feel free to modify the tables in this chapter to accommodate them.

Whirlpools are a hazard best avoided entirely.

TUNDRA

CHAPTER NINE

Tundra

What is Tundra?

Far enough from the lethal cold at the poles, but not so far that the ground ever fully thaws out in summer, the tundra presents adventuring heroes with an environment that is harsh, but not impossible, and it is certainly distinctive. Whether or not it describes a noticeable part of your campaign world is up to you. But if it does, this chapter gives you some guidance about what your party could encounter there.

However, it's worth noting that you're not going to find a wide assortment of creatures in the tundra. The soil is rich in nutrients, but between the permafrost, the cold and the lack of precipitation, it doesn't support trees and plant life is restricted to grasses, shrubs, moss and lichen. There's enough flora to support large herbivores like elk and caribou, and enough of them to support predators like winter wolves, wyverns and remorhazes. But it literally takes a special breed to live here and like it, so there just isn't the same degree of biodiversity as you would find in, say, a tropical forest.

But you find frost giants and their associates, as well as certain humanoids who have come here with a specific purpose in mind. Human habitation is likely sparse, consisting of nomadic and semi-nomadic groups that hunt and herd for sustenance.

What Do You Find in Tundra?

When you determine that a random encounter is in order, roll on Table 9.1 to determine the category:

TABLE 9.1

Encounters - Tundra

d20	ENCOUNTER
1-8	Aggressive Creatures (Table 9.2)
9-13	Neutral Creatures (Table 9.3)
14-15	Humanoids (Table 9.4)
16-17	Humans (Table 9.5)
18-20	Watch Out! (Table 9.6)

Then, roll on the appropriate table to determine the creature, person or thing encountered.

Tundra is relatively flat and open, so it's likely that encounters will start at a distance, unless local cover like boulders create cover. Unless conditions that limit visibility — such as some of those described in Table 9.6 — are in force, your party should be able to see what they're up against while it's still a ways away. However, there may be low hills that affect line of sight and create high ground, especially on islands.

TABLE 9.2

Encounters - Tundra

d100	ENCOUNTER
1-3	Air Elemental
4-9	Birds of Prey
10-12	Bulette
13-15	Chimera
16-20	Cougar
21-23	Ettin
24-27	Grick
28-32	Griffon
33-42	Insects
43-45	Manticore
46-49	Mephits
50-52	Ogre
53-56	Phase Spider
57	Purple Worm
58-62	Remorhaz
63	Roc
64-68	Saber Toothed Tiger
69-71	Troll
72-80	Undead
81-85	Will-o'-Wisp
86-91	Wolf
92-93	Worgs
94-95	Wyvern
96-100	Yeti

Air Elemental. That bitter, sub-arctic blast of wind headed for your party is, in fact, an air elemental. It is disoriented from being cut off from its native plane. It's cold. And it is none too happy about either circumstance. It takes out its anger by attacking your party.

Scaling the Encounter: If your party's average level is lower than 5, an elemental may be more than you want to throw at them. Feel free to re-roll for a different encounter. Conversely, if your party's average level is 10 or higher, feel free to add one water elemental to the encounter.

Birds of Prey. Snow owls survive in this frigid land year-round, but the same cannot be said for other birds, most of whom can thrive here only after the spring thaw. If you strive for ornithological accuracy, feel free to re-roll a bird of prey encounter if it takes place in the late fall or winter.

Otherwise, roll on Table 9.2.1, because a bird of prey — or a flock of them — has spotted something in your party as food — a familiar or small summoned creature is an obvious choice, but it could also be travelers rations, like strips of cured meat left in the open. Your party sees them wheeling in sky overhead, but then they dive and strike.

TABLE 9.2.1
Birds of Prey - Tundra

d10	ENCOUNTER
1-2	Eagle
3	Giant Eagle
4-5	Blood Hawks
6-7	Hawks
8-9	Owl
10	Giant Owl

Eagle. One eagle swoops down on your party, aiming itself at something it has identified as food.

Giant Eagle. A giant eagle has spotted your party. Giant eagles are intelligent and may respond if your party tries to flag them down. Though it cannot speak when spoken to, a successful DC 15 Charisma (Persuasion) check by someone who speaks Common or Auran persuades it to do your party a service, if it is within its power to accomplish it. This may involve delivering a written message or token, or guiding your party to a place that it knows, or even traveling with them for a while as an airborne lookout.

Blood Hawks. A flock of 2d4 blood hawks swoops down on your party. They concentrate on a single target — most likely a pack animal, but they may settle for a small humanoid as the next best thing.

Hawk. A flock of 2d6 hawks targets your party.
➤

They're probably going after the party's rations, but they may also have spotted rodents or small reptiles who are literally scurrying along the ground at your party's feet. To the extent that your party is in their way, the hawks attack them.

Owl. Owls hunt at night, so you should re-roll this encounter if it takes place during the day. Otherwise, one owl has spotted food as your party rests outdoors overnight. Most likely, it has spotted a small animal companion or familiar, or rations left out in the open.

Giant Owl. Likewise, a giant owl encounter is most suitable for night, so you should re-roll this encounter if it takes place during the day. One giant owl spots food in your party's camp.

Bulette. A land shark in the tundra is more likely to be active in the summer than in the winter, as it's easier to tunnel after the ground has thawed a bit. But it has to eat regardless of the season — and it has just spotted your party as its next meal. To create a little drama, you may require a successful DC 15 Wisdom (Perception) check to sense the ground rumbling beneath them; you may then allow a DC 15 Intelligence (Nature) check to identify it as a bulette before it breaches the surface.

Scaling the Encounter: A bulette may be a bit much for a lower-level party to handle, so if your party's average level is less than 5, feel free to re-roll for a different encounter. Conversely, if your average party level is higher than 10, you may add another bulette to make it more challenging.

Treasure: Bulettes hunt on the move, so treasure that belonged to its previous victims is scattered far and wide. However, you may allow your party a DC 10 Wisdom (Survival) check to follow the trail back to its last kill. If successful, roll on the Individual Treasure: Challenge 0-4 table to determine what they find.

Chimera. Your party spots a winged monstrosity with three different animal heads circling above them. This can only mean one thing: A chimera has spotted them as potential prey. You may allow your party a DC 15 Wisdom (Perception) check. If successful, they notice the chimera at a range of about 200 feet, allowing them a little time to react before they are within range of its attacks. If not, they first become aware of the chimera at a range of only 100 feet.

Scaling the Encounter: If your party's average level is lower than 6, a chimera may be more than you want to throw at them. Feel free to re-roll for a different encounter.

Alternately, you may consider that your party comes upon a chimera that has been injured in a fight with a manticore or a wyvern — and that your party witnesses the dazzling air-to-air combat from a safe distance. In this case, the chimera is reduced to half of its hit points by the time it drives off its enemy and turns on your party, deep gashes or embedded manticore spikes are still visible. It's wounded, but it's still hungry — in fact, perhaps it needs to feed in order to heal and your party looks like an easier target than one of its monstrous rivals.

Cougar. Your party crosses paths with 1d4 mountain lions that are hungry and on the prowl. Mountain lions like to ambush their prey, leaping down from a rock ledge or some other perch where they can have the high ground and conceal themselves. If they can find a spot like this in the flat tundra, you may allow your party a DC 15 Wisdom (Perception) or Wisdom (Survival) check to intuit that something is watching your party from above.

Otherwise, your party spots them at a distance, across open ground. This is not an ideal circumstance for mountain lions on the hunt. But they're at the far edge of their habitat, where food is hard to come by. They attack anyway.

Ettin. Your party hears two voices booming out across the tundra. Have your party make a DC 15 Intelligence (Nature) check to recognize that it's an ettin arguing with itself. If they choose not to avoid the ettin, it calls out to your party and demands that they help settle a dispute. It should be something that the party would find awkward or at least pointless to answer — for instance, if gnome steaks are marbled enough to make good eating. No matter what answer the party gives, one or both heads accuses them of unfairly favoring the other and the ettin attacks.

Alternately, the ettin stops short when it spots the party and realizes that it's hungry after arguing with itself for such a long time.

Scaling the Encounter: As amusing as ettins can be if you run the encounter with the right sense of humor, one is a bit much for a party with an average level of less than 4.

Treasure: The ettin carries some coins in a pouch looped around its loincloth. Roll twice on the Individual Treasure: Challenge 0-4 table.

Grick. Your party passes by two large rocks situated so close together that they might originally have been one boulder split apart by the continual cycle of freezing and thawing. One grick tries to hide, coiled into this crevice and waiting for a target such as your party to come along. If it fails, they notice that one oversized worm-like thing with a maw surrounded by four tentacles instead of a face is trying to squeeze itself down into that tight space. When someone from your party gets within striking distance, it strikes.

Scaling the Encounter: If you wish to make the encounter more challenging, the encounter group consists of one grick for each multiple of 4 in your party's average level, rounded up. If your party's average level is 15 or higher, consider adding one grick alpha to the encounter as the group's leader. Alternately, you may use an encounter group that consists of one grick alpha for each multiple of 10 in your party's average level.

Treasure: Since gricks are opportunity predators rather than hunters, your party may find treasure that has piled up from the belongings of former victims. Roll once on the Treasure Hoard: Challenge 0-4 table for each grick in the encounter group, and once on the Treasure Hoard: Challenge 5-10 table for each grick alpha.

The Cold, Hard Ground

Permafrost is one of the defining characteristics of tundra — it's so cold the year-round that below a certain depth, the soil just never thaws out. However, this chapter assumes that the larger and more fearsome burrowing predators will find away around that, either by staying above the permafrost or churning right through it, ice be damned. It stands to reason that if a purple worm can chew through solid rock, it can deal with frozen soil as well.

Griffon. One griffon has strayed from its normal hunting grounds in more fertile lands. Pickings are slim, however, and when it sees your party its deepening hunger drives it to go for one of their mounts or pack animals — or at least, it thinks it has spotted a mount or a pack animal.

Scaling the Encounter: If you wish to make the encounter more challenging, your party encounters a flock (or pack?) of griffons hunting together. There is one for each multiple of 3 in your party's average level, rounded up.

Insects. You may not think of insects as predatory, but they have a way of attacking without giving it much thought and they cause trouble in their own way. Your party should not be surprised if one swarm of insects — call them gnats, midges, mosquitos, whatever you will — descends upon them and makes life unpleasant. In spite of the cold, enough of them hang on through the frigid winter to reemerge with the spring thaw, seemingly more annoying than they were the previous year. In particular, mosquitos are bound to be a problem wherever there is stagnant fresh water, such as patches of marsh.

Scaling the Encounter: If you wish to make the encounter more challenging (or more of a nuisance, depending on how you look at it), the encounter group consists of 1d4 swarms of insects plus one additional swarm for each level in your party's average level.

Manticore. Your party spots a large winged beast in the sky. You may insist that they make a successful DC 15 Intelligence (Nature) check to recognize it as a manticore on the hunt before it gets close enough to attack.

Once it gets close enough to launch its spikes, it may choose to toy with its prey just to watch them squirm. In this case, it demands some kind of bribe in exchange for sparing them — a bargain it will keep, if your party makes the right offer. A suitable offer might take the form of treasure or humiliating servitude that amuses the manticore.

Alternately, perhaps it is the case that the manticore has information that might interest your party, and if your party gets the upper hand in combat, it offers that information in exchange for its life.

Scaling the Encounter: If you wish to make the encounter more challenging, consider that there are multiple manticores working as a team. In such a case, the encounter group consists of one manticore for each multiple of 5 in your party's average level.

Mephits. Which of these annoying elemental beings crosses paths with your party depends on the time of year. In the fall and winter, when the ground freezes, one ice mephit perches on a boulder or uses ice and snow for camouflage as it pelts your party with small rocks or snowballs (with rocks inside them) as it cackles contemptuously at someone who would intrude on its realm. This isn't enough to cause damage, but it refuses to stop.

In the spring and summer, when the ground thaws out, the encounter group consists of two mud mephits lounging in a marshy patch. They have slowly been driving each other mad with incessant and pointless complaints about everything and nothing, and they see your party as a diversion. They're too lazy to move, so they yell out to your party and start complaining to them about the weather — it's too hot, or too cold, too dry or too wet — or how they're too poor, or bored, or exhausted. They start to beg your party for handouts. All of this is in Aquan or Terran, of course. If your party ignores them, the mephits chase after them and eventually become exasperated enough to attack. If your party confronts them, they become agitated and attack.

Scaling the Encounter: If you wish to make the encounter more challenging, the encounter group consists of 1d4 ice mephits for each multiple of 2 in your party's average level, or 1d4 mud mephits plus one additional mud mephits for every level in your party's average level.

Ogres. Ogres are unlikely to find a lot of targets for raiding in the sparsely populated tundra. Your party crosses paths with a group that has most likely been driven out of warmer and more populous lands. Another possibility is that they have just escaped servitude to an unappreciative tribe of frost giants, and they are now casting about for what to do and where to go next. In either case, they're not particularly fussy about who they attack and what they can get from them. Something, anything, will do.

Scaling the Encounter: The encounter group consists of one ogre for each multiple of 3 in your party's average level. If your party is only 1st Level, consider that one half-ogre confronts them.

Treasure. These ogres are away from their lair. Add the CR of all ogres killed and roll on the appropriate Individual Treasure table.

Phase Spiders can jump to a warmer plane to avoid the cold.

Phase Spider. Spiders don't much like the cold, but a phase spider can console itself by jumping between the Material Plane and the Ethereal Plane, where it may be warmer — maybe they have space heaters in the Ethereal Plane. Your party walks by a jumble of rocks or a small cave that one phase spider claims as its own. You may allow your party a DC 20 Wisdom (Survival) check to sense that something is about to pop into the Material Plane at a point very close by them. However the phase spider cannot be surprised, as it has sensed their presence from the Ethereal Plane; that's why it returned.

Scaling the Encounter: A phase spider may be a bit too much for a beginning-level party. Feel free to re-roll for another encounter. Conversely, if you wish to make the encounter more challenging, the encounter group consists of one phase spider for each multiple of 5 in your party's average level.

Purple Worm. When the ground beneath your feet suddenly starts rumbling and quivering, it is seldom — if ever — a good sign. This is especially true if a purple worm burrowing through the permafrost is the cause. The worm has detected your party as prey and breaches the surface to attack them. The worm's approach should give them enough time to sense that something is amiss and do something about it; you may allow them a DC 15 Intelligence (Nature) check to realize that it's a purple worm causing the disturbance. Combat begins when it breaches the surface within striking distance of your party.

Scaling the Encounter: If your party's average level is lower than 15, a purple worm may be more than you want to throw at them. Feel free to re-roll for a different encounter.

Treasure: Cutting open and gutting a purple worm is quite a chore, but it should reveal valuables that belonged to its previous prey — and purple worms eat a lot. Roll on the Treasure Hoard: Challenge 11-16 table to determine total hoard.

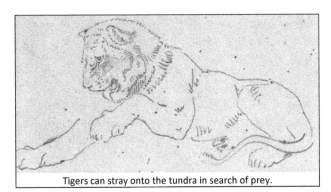
Tigers can stray onto the tundra in search of prey.

Remorhaz. Your party notices steam rising from the ground nearby. In summer, it may just look like mist rising as sunlight plays on a chilly marsh. In winter, it definitely looks like some source of heat is at work under the frozen soil. When they get as close to the spot as they dare, one remorhaz bursts up from beneath the ground. It may have mistaken your party for a polar bear or a small group of elk, but it views them as prey all the same.

Scaling the Encounter: If your party's average level is 5-10, a young remorhaz is most suitable for the encounter. If it is higher than 10, use a fully grown remorhaz. If your party's average level is lower than 5, however, a remorhaz of any age may be more than you want to throw at them. Feel free to re-roll for a different encounter.

Treasure: Since remorhazes swallow their prey whole, cutting open and gutting one should reveal valuables that it consumed. Roll on the Treasure Hoard table appropriate to the CR of the encounter to determine total hoard. You may also allow your party a DC 15 Wisdom (Survival) check to find a trail back to the remorhaz' nest and find 1d4 eggs.

Roc. Hunting in the tundra takes a roc far from its mountain eyrie, but the open sight lines and the presence of large prey animals often make the trip worthwhile. Human and humanoid prey are less common — but that makes your party all the more attractive as a rare delicacy.

Scaling the Encounter: Rocs are fearsome opponents. If your party's average level is lower than 11, a roc may be more than you want to throw at them. Feel free to re-roll for a different encounter.

Saber-Toothed Tiger. These predators occasionally stray onto the tundra from boreal forests in search of prey. They are fearless as well as skilled hunters, and if they're hungry enough to leave an area where there is more biodiversity (that is, more sources of food), they are hungry enough to attack your party. You may allow your party a DC 15 Wisdom (Perception) to notice that a saber-toothed tiger has been stalking them.

Scaling the Encounter: Saber-toothed tigers usually hunt by themselves. But if you wish to make the encounter more challenging, use an encounter group consisting of one saber-toothed tiger for each multiple of 3 in your party's average level.

Troll. Even though travelers to extort are rare in this part of the world, trolls still find enough victims to get by, strong-arming herders and hunters for food and personal possessions when they have to. Your party approaches a mound or a cave that a troll claims as its own.

Scaling the Encounter: If your party's average level is lower than 5, a troll may be more than you want to throw at them. Feel free to re-roll for a different encounter. Conversely, if your party's average level is 10 or higher, feel free to add one troll to the encounter — a tag-team of trolls.

Treasure: The troll's racket has worked well enough in the past: Its victims pay one way or another, and it has accumulated a decent hoard. Searching the area turns up its stash, thrown into a pile, on a successful DC 10 Wisdom (Perception) check. Roll on the Treasure Hoard: Challenge 5-10 table to determine the contents.

Undead. Few who perish in this hostile wilderness die peacefully and without suffering. Furthermore, the dry, frigid climate preserves their physical form astonishingly well, and this creates ample raw material for necromancy that animates them with its cruel imitation of life. Roll on Table 9.2.2 to determine the undead abomination that greets your party:

TABLE 9.2.2
Undead - Tundra

d10	ENCOUNTER
1	Ghost
2	Ghouls/Ghasts
3	Mummy
4-6	Skeletons
7	Wight
8	Wraith
9-10	Zombies

Ghost. That is not mist rising from the frozen ground; the ethereal form flitting across the wastes really is a ghost. It is most likely the remnant of a nomadic herder or hunter who died a cold and miserable death in the wilderness. Whatever the case, you may make this into a hostile encounter by having the ghost try to possess a member of your party so that it may resolve unfinished business from its former life.

Ghouls/Ghasts. An encounter with ghouls is most likely to take place at night. Two ghouls (or one ghast) approach your party, driven by mindless hunger for their flesh.

Mummy. Extreme cold has an uncanny ability to preserve the dead, and so the nomadic tribes that inhabit the tundra can create mummies — essentially, ritually prepared undead tasked with protecting their own burial places — with relatively little work. The nomadic tribes who treat their dead in this way inter them in cairns or naturally occurring caves. However, mummies encountered at random have wandered from their tombs, as if they have forgotten their original purpose, but the magic that created them as undead remains. Instinct drives them to attack, even though they no longer, strictly speaking, protect the place they were created to protect. ➤

Skeletons. Your party comes across the undead remnants of an ancient conflict: 1d6 skeletons carrying bows or broken spears and draped with fragments of hide or leather armor. It's unlikely that armies would have fought over this miserable patch of permafrost.

More likely, they were nomadic hunters killed by their prey, or who turned on each other, or fought with a rival tribe. Or perhaps they were from the losing side in a war in a far-off land, pursued by their enemies to the ends of the world and finally run to ground and wiped out here in this desolate place. Driven by necromantic echoes of the end of their lives, they're looking for a fight.

Wight. Your party makes camp for the night not far from a cluster of improvised cairns. Unfortunately for your party, at least one of the occupants has become a wight, and it rises from its tomb to attack them while they are most vulnerable.

Wraith. Even a hastily improvised cairn can house a wraith. As your party passes by, they can see that the ground around the site appears barren and blasted, even by the standards of the area. A clammy, charcoal-gray mist emerges and resolves itself into a wraith, which then attacks your party, acting out the resentment that it bore at the end of its natural life.

Zombies. Your party come across 1d4 zombies who have been programmed to kill every living thing they encounter. The source of the necromancy that created these zombies we leave to you. Perhaps they slipped the leash of their creator and they now wander the land mindlessly looking for victims.

Scaling the Encounter: Ghosts and wraiths always work alone. Also, if your party's average level is lower than 5, a wraith may be more than you want to throw at them. Feel free to re-roll for a different encounter.

Ghouls/Ghasts: If you wish to make the encounter more challenging, the encounter group consists of two ghouls (or one ghast) for each multiple of 4 in your party's average level. Feel free to mix and match ghouls and ghasts as long as you maintain the right proportion of total CR to average party level.

Mummy: A mummy may be a bit too much for a beginning-level party. Feel free to re-roll for another encounter. Conversely, if your party's average level is higher than 5, consider adding another mummy to the encounter. No more than that, though — a horde of ➤

stray mummies wandering from their tombs is a bit much to imagine as a purely random encounter. If your party's average level is 20 or higher, the wandering mummy is one mummy lord.

Skeletons: If you wish to make the encounter more challenging, the encounter group consists of 1d4 skeletons plus one additional skeleton for each level in your party's average level. You may substitute one warhorse skeleton for two skeletons.

Wights: A wight may be a bit too much for a beginning-level party. Feel free to re-roll for another encounter. Conversely, if you want to run a more challenging encounter for a higher-level party, use an encounter group consisting of one wight for each multiple of 5 in your party's average level.

Zombies: If you wish to make the encounter more challenging, the encounter group consists of 1d4 zombies plus one additional zombie for each level in your party's average level. If the average party level is 3 or higher, you may use an encounter group consisting of one ogre zombie for each multiple of 3 in the party's average level.

Treasure: Most likely, ghosts and mummies are encountered in or near what passes for a lair with them and you may consider that there they keep possessions that they had in life. Roll on the Treasure Hoard: Challenge 0-4 table for the contents of their stash. You may require a successful DC 15 Wisdom (Perception) check to find its exact location.

Likewise, wights and wraiths do not stray far from their places of burial, which are usually constructed as monuments to the dead. Therefore, their location should be self-apparent. Roll on the Treasure Hoard table appropriate to the total CR of the encounter

With ghouls, ghasts, skeletons and zombies, they may have with them some remains of what they had on their person at the time of their death. Roll on the Individual Treasure table appropriate to the total CR of the encounter (rounded up to the nearest whole number).

Will-o'-Wisp. Will-o'-Wisps are most active in the summer, when the topsoil thaws out and creates patches of bone-chilling marsh, some of which are quite treacherous. In one of these places, a luminous globe — all that is left of an unquiet soul who froze to death, or stumbled into the mire and drowned on a deceptively warm summer day long ago — dances and bobs above the boggy ground.

If you want to add some spice to the encounter, consider that this evil spirit tries to lure victims into a patch of quicksand-like bog to render them helpless. In this case, the will-o'-wisp restricts itself to a 50-foot diameter area. At the center of this area, the swamp turns into a 20-foot diameter pit of quicksand. If the will-o'-wisp is not already directly above the quicksand when it is engaged in melee combat, it retreats until it is above the quicksand, thus forcing its attacker to step into it in order to continue the melee.

Scaling the Encounter: If you wish to make the encounter more challenging, the encounter group consists of one will-o'-wisp for each multiple of 3 in your party's average level.

Treasure: Belongings from the will-o'-wisp's previous victims have been piling up here, with various valuables scattered in the muck. To determine the treasure, roll once on the Treasure Hoard: Challenge 0-4 table for each will-o'-wisp present.

Wolves. Winter wolves are most at home in the tundra, but all types of wolves find just enough food here to make a predatory go of it. The cold and occasional deprivation makes them tougher and meaner on the whole than their cousins who live in more hospitable lands. Wolves are confident predators in the best of times, but they are even more dangerous when hungry and desperate. Even though the flat, open terrain should allow your party to see them coming, they attack.

Roll on Table 9.2.3. to determine the wolves encountered:

TABLE 9.2.3
Wolves - Tundra

d6	ENCOUNTER
1-2	Dire Wolves
3-5	Winter Wolves
6	Wolves

Scaling the Encounter: The encounter group consists of one dire wolf for each multiple of 2 in your party's average level; or one winter wolf for each multiple of 3 in the party's average level, rounded up; or 1d4 wolves for each level in your party's average level.

Treasure: Furriers in your world may be willing to pay for wolf pelts. How much is ultimately up to you, but 2 gp is a reasonable baseline price for a normal wolf pelt; 3 gp for a dire wolf pelt; and 5 gp for a winter wolf pelt.

Worgs. Your party comes across one worg prowling the desolate landscape. Most likely, it has abandoned its goblin masters, or set to wandering after its rider met an untimely end. It is hungry and your party looks like food.

Scaling the Encounter: If you wish to make the encounter more challenging, the encounter group consists of a pack of worgs, 1d4 for each multiple of 2 in your party's average level. A pack of worgs might have defected *en masse*, or been left to their own devices after an entire tribe of goblins was slaughtered.

Wyvern. A wyvern on the hunt, ranging far afield from its mountain lair, spots your party from above. It swoops down to attack despite the odds.

Scaling the Encounter: If your party's average level is lower than 6, a wyvern with its blood up may be more than you want to throw at them. Feel free to re-roll for a different encounter.

Yeti. Your party may well hear a yeti's roar well before seeing the creature itself, especially since its white fur provides excellent camouflage. Yeti are ferocious when hungry and on the prowl, so they attack as soon as they identify a suitable target. Your party crosses paths with one yeti in just such a humor.

Scaling the Encounter: A yeti may be a bit too much for a beginning-level party. Feel free to re-roll for another encounter. Conversely, if you want to run a more challenging encounter, consider using an abominable yeti if your party's average level is 10 or higher.

TABLE 9.3
Neutral Creatures - Tundra

d20	ENCOUNTER
1	Awakened Shrub
2-3	Bear
4-6	Caribou
7	Dragon
8-9	Elk
10	Giant
11	Goats
12	Hippogriff
13	Mammoth
14	Pegasus
15-16	Pony
17-18	Tundra Mice
19-20	Weasels

Awakened Shrub. Trees cannot take root in soil that is always frozen, but grasses and shrubs can make do with what sustenance the tundra provides. Resilient and filled with a strong life force, or deliberately enchanted somehow, some of these develop sentience. Your party comes into contact with one or more such awakened shrubs. Perhaps a party member takes advantage of it to answer the call of nature. Perhaps it produces berries that look appetizing. Perhaps your party is looking for kindling for the campfire. These or similar actions cause the shrub to express alarm.

Awakened shrubs are feistier than awakened trees, but less intimidating — not unlike the bark of a small dog compared to that of a large dog. An encounter with them is not necessarily hostile, even if your party has done mischief to it. If your party asks it for help, a successful DC 10 Charisma (Persuasion) check wins it over, but the DC is 15 if your party has harmed it in some way. Help from an awakened shrub includes providing knowledge of the surrounding area and its history.

Scaling the Encounter: If you wish to make the encounter more challenging, the encounter group consists of one awakened shrub for each multiple of 3 in your party's average level, rounded up.

Bear. It's the tundra. There's a bear. Should that come as any surprise? Roll on Table 9.3.1 to determine the species of bear that your party encounters:

TABLE 9.3.1
Bear - Tundra

d8	ENCOUNTER
1	Black Bear
2-3	Brown Bear
4-8	Polar Bear

Black/Brown Bear. Black bears and brown bears hibernate, so during the winter an encounter with one would have to take place in a cave. It remains asleep as long as your party makes a successful DC 15 Dexterity (Stealth) check to avoid disturbing it. If it wakes up, it awakens in a foul mood and attacks.

On the other hand, during the rest of the year, it's warm enough for the bear to be out and about and looking for food. The smell of your party's travelers' rations draw its attention. To scare it off, have your party make a DC 15 Intelligence (Nature) or Wisdom (Survival) check. Success means that the bear takes the hint and lumbers away. Failure means that the bear charges them. ➤

Polar Bear. Polar bears do not hibernate, so the season does not affect their behavior. They're always active, and they're always hungry. Your party spots a polar bear prowling around for food. If they are resting, the bear comes sniffing around, drawn by whatever rations they are carrying. To scare it off, have your party make a DC 15 Intelligence (Nature) or Wisdom (Survival) check. Success means that the bear takes the hint and lumbers away. Failure means that the bear charges them.

Caribou. Caribou are smaller than elk (see below) and both males and females have antlers. They abound in a place where most creatures would struggle to sustain themselves, and they are both hunted and herded. Your party comes across 1d6 bulls and 2d6 cows; whether they are wild or somehow separated from a local herd is up to you as DM. If the latter, those herders are sure to be grateful for help in locating them — or angry if your party tried to poach them.

If your party attacks, only the male fights, covering the females while they flee. Even if your party does not behave in a threatening manner, you may have your party make a DC 10 Intelligence (Nature) or Wisdom (Survival) check. Failure means that the male reads your party as hostile, and it attacks.

Treat caribou as deer.

Treasure: Nomadic tribes that draw sustenance from this harsh land hunt elk and caribou to meet their needs, and generally have no need to buy meat from strangers. However, antlers and other body parts may be of ritual or medicinal use to them, in which case they may be willing to pay or barter to the equivalent of 1d6 gp, depending on the item and their actual need for it.

Dragon. Your party notices a shadow in the sky. It's a dragon on the prowl. To determine what kind of dragon roll on Table 9.3.2:

These encounters are surprising but not necessarily fatal.

TABLE 9.3.2
Dragon - Tundra

d12	ENCOUNTER
1-2	Black
3	Blue
4	Green
5	Red
6-7	White
8	Brass
9	Bronze
10	Copper
11	Gold
12	Silver

To determine its age, see Scaling the Encounter, below.

To be clear, this need not be a hostile encounter. The dragon is not defending its lair, so — being a highly intelligent creature — it may just be curious about your party. It may have more important things to do and decline to take notice of them at all. Or it may be hungry and on the hunt, or it's angry because your party has intruded on territory it claims as its own.

Alternately, you may present your party with a scenario that you can weave into the larger story of the campaign. It may even serve as the main thrust of the campaign. Your party finds a dragon wyrmling sprawled on the frozen ground, steam rising from spatters of dragon blood. It's obviously in a bad way — gashed open, bleeding profusely (or it has almost bled out), barely conscious. Assume that it has stabilized after being reduced to 0 hp, and that it now has 1 hp.

How it got that way is up to you, and it may depend on how dragons fit into your campaign world. Perhaps it fled from a fight in which it was badly wounded. Who would its enemies be, and why were they fighting? Were any of this dragon's relatives or companions killed?

How your party decides to deal with this child in distress could open up possibilities for later in your campaign. If they rescue it, will its kin reward them later? Conversely, what are the consequences if they put it out of its misery, like scavengers roaming a medieval battlefield? Will its kin seek retribution, or will its enemies treat your party as allies?
➤

Scaling the Encounter: Because dragons get tougher with age, the age of the dragon encountered should depend on your party's average level — especially if you decide that this is going to be a hostile encounter. If your party's average level is 10 or lower, they encounter a wyrmling. If their average level is 11-18, they encounter a young dragon. If their average level is 19-25, they encounter an adult dragon. If their average level is higher than 25, they encounter an ancient dragon.

Elk. Your party spots a herd of 1d4 bulls and 2d6 cows searching for forage. If your party attacks them, only the males fight, covering the females while they flee.

Even if your party does not behave in a threatening manner, you may consider that there is a chance that the males mistake their actions for a threat and attacks anyway. Have your party make a DC 15 Intelligence (Nature) or Wisdom (Survival) check. Failure provokes the males to charge.

Scaling the Encounter: If you wish to make the encounter more challenging, your party sees a lone (and rare) giant elk at a distance. As they approach it they realize that it's larger than it seemed. Confident in its power as an alpha of its kind, it attacks your party if it senses any hostile intent (remember that giant elk have the ability to understand certain languages).

Perhaps it is bad luck in your campaign world to hunt a giant elk. If your party kills it, each party member is cursed as if affected by the spell *bane*, except that the effect lasts indefinitely — until it is magically dispelled, or until those who did the deed atone for it. Also, the nomads who live here may regard giant elk as sacred and turn hostile to someone who has killed one.

Treasure: Nomadic tribes that draw sustenance from this harsh land hunt elk and caribou to meet their needs, and generally have no need to buy meat from strangers. However, antlers and other body parts may be of ritual or medicinal use to them, in which case they may be willing to pay or barter to the equivalent of 1d6 gp, depending on the item and their actual need for it.

Giant. The frozen wastes are most hospitable to frost giants, but they are not the only giants you may find roaming the tundra. It may seem odd to classify giants as "neutral" rather than "aggressive," but the fact is that giants cover a wide range of attitudes and behaviors, and some are quite intelligent. To determine the giant(s) encountered, roll on Table 9.3.3:

TABLE 9.3.3
Giants - Tundra

d8	ENCOUNTER
1-5	Frost Giant
6	Hill Giant
7	Stone Giant
8	Storm Giant

Frost Giant. You probably won't find a frost giant fortress plopped down in the middle of a flat stretch of tundra, but your party may encounter one frost giant from a stronghold sited on nearby high ground. It's acting as a scout for its clan, or as a messenger on its way to another frost giant clan. Unless your party can persuade it that they mean no harm, it takes them as a potential enemy that must be eliminated, even it's just to be on the safe side. You may allow your party a successful DC 20 Charisma (Persuasion) check to talk their way out of a fight.

Hill Giant. Hill giants encountered in the tundra either came here as mercenaries serving more powerful giants, or as their thralls. Either way, your party crosses paths with one disgruntled hill giant who has escaped from its frost giant masters. It's in a bad mood, and it is putting some distance between itself and the stronghold from which it escaped. Depending on how you want to play it, the giant is either suspicious that your party are bounty hunters hired to return it to its former masters, or it asks for their help in getting clean away. In the latter case, it's also willing to provide local knowledge and, if your party in interested in a sidequest, the hill giant tells them all about the frost giant fortress, including the best ways to sneak in.

Stone Giant. Like their hill giant cousins, stone giants come to the tundra at someone else's behest, not for their own reasons. Hacking deposits of metal, marble or other rare minerals out of the permafrost is hard work, and whoever wants it done may pay specialists like stone giants to do it. They may be hirelings or servants of frost giants.

Your party crosses paths with one stone giant who is on its way to meet its new employer, or setting out for a quarry or mining site. If it serves a frost giant tribe currently at war, the stone giant treats your party as a possible enemy. Under other circumstances, it is not interested in fighting your party, but persuading it to help them means overcoming its lack of interest➤

one way or another. Either way, you should require a DC 20 Charisma (Persuasion) check from your party if they want to get on the stone giant's good side.

Storm Giant. Your party comes upon one storm giant taking a long, contemplative walk from its palace, which is likely to be located on a faraway mountain or below the icy waters of the ocean. Despite the fact that it has come to this remote and desolate place to get away from it all, it greets your party with good cheer — perhaps it's starting to tire of solitary contemplation. Storm giants have a unique gift for taking in the big picture and looking into the future.

Think of it as a chance to share important information with your party and influence their course of action.

Scaling the Encounter: Even the lowliest giant is formidable foe for a low-level party. Feel free to re-roll for a different encounter.

Otherwise, you may add to the encounter group if you have a high-level party and want to increase the challenge. As a rough guideline, the total CR of the encounter group should be no higher than equal to your party's average level. You can tinker with the CR by adding more of the same giant, or by adding companions. All giants may have ogre underlings with them. Stone giants may have a pet black bear on a leash.

Treasure: Giants always have some personal possessions of note on them. If encountered away from their lair, roll on the appropriate Individual Treasure table for each giant present.

Goats. Your party comes across a small herd of 1d4 billies and 2d4 nannies looking for what grazing is available. Perhaps they are wild goats — or perhaps they have gotten separated from a larger herd, and somewhere nearby there is a goatherd who would give a reward for their safe return. In any event, billies can be ornery beasts and if your party approaches them, you may require your party to make a DC 15 Intelligence (Nature) check to avoid setting off an attack in which the males charge to cover the fleeing females.

Scaling the Encounter: If you wish to make the encounter more challenging, use a herd of wild (and potentially irritated) giant goats instead. The encounter group should consist of 1d4 giant goats for each multiple of 2 in your party's average level with the same 1:2 ratio of males to females. Giant goats are quite wild; there is no chance that they are being kept by someone else.

Hippogriff. Your party sees a hippogriff circling overhead, looking for its next meal, or on the ground dealing with its prey. Hippogriffs are not as aggressive as birds of prey or top predators like saber toothed tigers, and it is no sure bet that they would attack your party on the hope that it could make off with a pack animal or their stash of rations. Whether or not this is a hostile encounter is a matter of your discretion.

However, hippogriffs may be a kind of prey as easily as they could be predators. If hippogriffs are used as mounts in your world, it must follow that captive adults have value as breeding stock, and chicks captured from the wild also have value because they are still young enough to be tamed. To that end, you may allow your party a DC 15 Wisdom (Survival) check to trace a path to the hippogriff's lair, which is likely to be located in the nearest high ground. To subdue an adult hippogriff to the point where it can be bound and held captive, it must be successfully grappled and kept in grappled condition for 10 consecutive rounds.

Scaling the Encounter: If you want to stage a hostile encounter with hippogriffs and you need to make it more of a challenge for a higher-level party, consider that the encounter group consists of one hippogriff for each multiple of 3 in your party's average level.

Mammoth. Mammoths roam the tundra. While they are hunted for food, they also pose a significant threat when they feel they have to defend themselves. Your party comes across one mammoth looking for forage. Unless they make an effort to steer clear of it, they come face-to-face with a huge beast with large, sharp tusks. You may allow your party a DC 15 Intelligence (Nature) or Wisdom (Survival) check. Failure means that a party member has made a false move that provokes the mammoth. It charges.

Scaling the Encounter: A mammoth may be a bit too much for a beginning-level party. Feel free to re-roll for another encounter. Conversely, if you want to run a more challenging encounter for a higher-level party, consider that your party has encountered a mated pair of mammoths if your party's average level is 8 or higher.

Treasure: Nomadic tribes that roam the tundra hunt mammoths and may feel no need to pay for its meat. On the other hand, they may buy from or barter with someone who has already done the work — its beats getting gored or trampled while hunting for yourself. They may be willing to pay 5 gp or its equivalent in goods or services for a carcass, and 10 gp for its tusks.

However, the tusks will fetch more money in distant lands, where mammoth are not found — use the going rate for ivory in your campaign world. Also, mammoth steaks are a delicacy in lands where there are no mammoth to hunt. A preserved carcass may fetch as much as 20 gp from a butcher.

Pegasus. Pegasi are no more fond of the cold than any other creature, but the tundra may offer them a remote place where they can keep a lair in high ground without anyone bothering them.

Your party sees one pegasus wheeling in the sky. It does not attack, even if it sees evil creatures. However, it may be flagged down by signaling or calling to it and making a successful DC 15 Charisma (Persuasion) check. If your party can get the pegasus' attention, it may be persuaded to render some kind of aid to your party — such as taking a party member to a nearby location — with a successful DC 20 Charisma (Persuasion) check. For good-aligned creatures who can speak Celestial, Elvish or Sylvan the DC is 15.

Scaling the Encounter: If you wish to make the encounter more challenging, the encounter group consists of one pegasus for each multiple of 3 in the party's average level.

Who in Their Right Minds Would Live Here?
A fair question, when applied to humanoids whom you might find while stomping through the tundra. Let's face it: In fantasy roleplaying games, humanoid races are generally associated with a type of landscape or particular activities that characterizes them. That's what defines them by comparison to humans, who are the proverbial jacks of all trades, and masters of none. As the designer of your campaign world, you can always develop your own particular reasons why humanoids would be present here to an extent that makes them viable as random encounters. But by their various definitions, humanoids just don't fit here as well as humans, who are more adaptable.

Pony. Horses have a hard time of it in the tundra, but certain breeds of pony — compact in build, with short, stout legs and heavy coats — have adapted to survive here in spite of the cold and scarce forage. Your party comes across a small herd of 2d8 ponies grazing, or moving across the landscape at a walk. It's up to you to decide whether they're wild, or if they belong to someone — and if the latter, is their owner nearby (see Table 9.5) or have they escaped from someone who would pay a reward for their return?

If they are wild, they can be wrangled. To wrangle a pony, it must be successfully grappled and kept in

grappled condition for 3 consecutive rounds. At that point, it becomes docile and whomever grappled it may ride it or use it as a pack animal. Only one medium-size creature may try to grapple a pony at any given time.

Tundra Mice. Small rodents that make themselves a nuisance live everywhere, even in a place this cold and desolate. They prefer to be called tundra mice instead of rats, thank you very much, and they get very aggressive when food is scarce. They get hangry. While your party stops to rest, they emerge as if out of nowhere and go for their packs, or wherever they keep their rations. If they are not stopped, they eventually consume all of your party's food.

Treat tundra mice as a swarm of rats.

Scaling the Encounter: If you wish to make the encounter more challenging, the encounter group consists of one swarm of rats for each level in your party's average level.

Weasels. Someone at the front of your party's march order accidentally steps into a burrow housing enough weasels to cause trouble when they get angry and defend their home. You may allow your party a DC 10 Wisdom (Perception) or Wisdom (Survival) check to spot the burrow in time to avoid it or give warning to whomever is about to disturb it. However, if this happens while there is snow on the ground, you may consider that it's impossible to see the burrow, and that a DC 15 Wisdom (Survival) check to intuit its presence is more appropriate. The burrow houses a pack of 3d6 weasels.

Scaling the Encounter: If you wish to make the encounter more challenging, substitute giant weasels for normal-sized weasels.

Treasure: There is a 10% chance that they are actually mink, and their pelts would be of some value to furriers — 1 gp for normal-sized mink, and 5 gp for a giant mink. You may require a successful DC 15 Intelligence (Nature) check for your party to tell the difference between mink and weasels.

TABLE 9.5

Humanoids - Tundra

d8	ENCOUNTER
1	Bugbear
2-3	Dwarves
4	Gnomes
5	Hobgoblins
6-7	Lycanthropes
8	Orcs

Bugbear. Bugbears don't like the cold any more than anyone else. Chances are, the group that your party encounters here auxiliary soldiers attached to a unit of hobgoblin mercenaries operating in the area. At the moment, they are detached from their hobgoblin officers, patrolling or scouting. Whatever the case, they're in a surly mood and they might pick a fight with your party just to vent their aggravation.

Scaling the Encounter: A beginning-level party should only have to cope with one bugbear. If you wish to make the encounter more challenging, the encounter group consists of two bugbears for each multiple of 3 in your party's average level. If your party's average level is 10 or higher, add one bugbear chief as the group's leader.

Dwarves. It's uncommon, but not unknown, to find dwarves in this part of the world. They're rugged enough to deal with the cold, and the prospect of finding metal deposits are sufficient to draw some adventurous souls out of their homes under mountains and hills. Perhaps they have come here to look for lumps of iron with magical properties that are said to have fallen from the sky and buried themselves in the permafrost.

Your party crosses paths with a small party of dwarves, 1d8+2 of them. Treat them as commoners armed with battleaxes and war picks, and the weapon proficiency to use them. If they are taking loads of ore from a nearby mine for smelting, treat them as commoners leading an equal number of ponies. Or they might be a war party on the alert, having clashed with nomads or enemy humanoids — in which case, treat them as guards armed with battleaxes.

In any event, they could offer your party a sidequest, offering weapons or even ingots of precious metal in exchange for their help in dealing with monsters or other enemies.

Gnomes. Your party crosses paths with a small party of gnomes, consisting of 1d4+1 commoners and one priest. They're probably mechanics who have been hired to help a mining operation. Or they may be traders, driven by speculation (or desperation) to acquire art objects from local nomads for resale as curiosities. In either case, they have brought along a priest of one of their patron deities as their sole protection.

The gnomes are not aggressive. It won't take much prompting to get them to trade with your party and share local knowledge. Their priest may be willing to help your party with spells if they are willing to pay the going rate for such services.

Treasure: If these gnomes are traveling merchants, they should carry trade goods and/or coins in addition to their personal treasure. Roll on the Treasure Hoard: Challenge 0-4 table.

Hobgoblins. Hobgoblins would no more set up permanent bases here than most other humanoids, so the hobgoblins that your party encounters here are most likely mercenaries pursuing a defeated foe on behalf of their employers. As such, they're a business-like, no-nonsense bunch with strong leadership. They may be suspicious of your party — are they friend or foe? But they won't attack for unprofessional reasons, such as wanton cruelty or boredom.

However, the hobgoblins do interrogate your party closely, looking for information that will help them wind up the current operation. They'll let your party go if they're convinced your party is not a foe, but you may require that your party make a DC 15 Charisma (Persuasion) check to make it so.

Scaling the Encounter: The baseline encounter group should consist of 1d4 hobgoblins for each multiple of 2 in your party's average level. If your party's average level is 10-19, add a hobgoblin captain as the group's leader, accompanied by two goblin servants or one bugbear aide. If your party's average level is 20 or higher, add instead one hobgoblin warlord with two bugbear aides.

Lycanthrope. To determine what manner of werebeast your party encounters, roll on Table 9.4.1:

TABLE 9.4.1
Lycanthrope - Tundra

d6	ENCOUNTER
1-2	Werebear
3	Wererat
4-6	Werewolf

All lycanthropes assume their animal form if the encounter comes down to combat, although they may choose their hybrid form instead if they have access to a weapon.

Werebear. In this part of the world, werebears usually appear as polar bears in their animal form. Your party comes across a werebear has staked out the top of a low hill or a cave as its domain and the place for which it is the custodian. As soon as it sees your party, it assumes its human form. It is not automatically hostile to your party, especially if there are no evil characters present, and it may be willing to provide them with useful information about the surrounding area. ➤

On the other hand, an encounter could create difficulties for your party if the werebear decides that someone in your party would make a good apprentice (and successor to its self-appointed duties as the local guardian). Once it realizes that there is a druid or a ranger in your party, a light goes on in its head — and it won't take "No" for an answer.

Wererat. In this part of the world, wererats appear as tundra mice in their animal form. One wererat appears to your party in its humanoid form, pretending to be a hunter in distress or a herder who got separated from his flock. It asks to travel with your party for protection until that supposed time when it can rejoin its tribe. It tries to slip toward the back of the march order and waits for a moment when everyone's back is turned to it.

Werewolf. In this part of the world, werewolves usually appear as winter wolves in their animal form. One spots your party and cannot turn down the opportunity to claim more victims. However, it is clever enough to approach them in its human form, pretending to be a hunter or herder in distress. Once your party gets close and drops its guard, it attacks.

Scaling the Encounter: A single lycanthrope can offer a stiff challenge to a low-level party. If your party's average level is 3 or less, feel free to re-roll the encounter. Alternately, if you want to make a werewolf encounter more challenging for a higher-level party, use a pack of them consisting of one werewolf for each multiple of 5 in your party's average level, rounded up.

Orcs. You're not going to find orcs setting up a permanent dwelling in the tundra. Orcs encountered here are most likely raiding at the outer margins of their geographical comfort zone, or they have been defeated and driven into exile. To them, your party looks like a good source of plunder right now, so they fan out and attack without bothering to parlay.

Scaling the Encounter: The baseline encounter group should consist of 1d4 orcs for each multiple of 2 in your party's average level. If your party's average level is 5-9, add an orog as the group's leader. If your party's average level is 10 or higher, use an orc war chief as its leader. If you don't want to run a mass encounter but you still want to provide a higher-level party with a meaningful challenge, feel free to substitute one orog for four orcs as much as you like.

TABLE 9.5

Humans - Tundra

d10	ENCOUNTER
1	Adventurers
2	Explorers
3-4	Fishermen
5-6	Herders
7-8	Hunters
9	Shaman
10	Trappers

Adventurers. Unless your party contains all of the adventurers in your campaign world, it's at least theoretically possible that they'll run into another adventuring party even on the barren, frozen tundra. Perhaps they're pursuing the same objective as your party. Perhaps they have a different mission; perhaps they're headed for a site that your party knows nothing about (like ancient ruins said to hold lost treasures). Perhaps they're half-frozen and starving, or wounded, or cursed.

How they react to your party depends on a variety of factors. Are they rivals pursuing the same goal? If not, perhaps this party is willing to share useful information. In fact, if your party is stuck and having a hard time advancing the storyline of your campaign, a friendly encounter like this can help steer them in the right direction. Differences in alignment may also shape how the two parties react to each other.

Composition of this rival party is up to you and can vary according to circumstance. Any party in the wilderness would be well-advised to have someone accomplished in Survival, such as a ranger, with them. Conversely, a party that is struggling may be in a bad way precisely no one is well-versed in Survival or Nature.

Scaling the Encounter: Unless there is some possibility that this encounter turns hostile, the relative level of the party is mainly a matter of affect. A higher-level party might project self-confidence and calm (or arrogance), while beginning-level party might stumble about, unsure of themselves. If you're leaning towards a hostile encounter, however, consider that the total CR of the party should be roughly two-thirds of your party's average level.

Explorers. Your party crosses paths with a small human party who appear to be well-bundled up against the cold. They are explorers, driven by restlessness and curiosity to seek the very ends of the world — and so here they are. The party consists of 1d4 scouts and 1d4 tribal warriors — local nomads whom they have hired as guides.

Such an encounter is not likely to be hostile. Instead, you may treat this as an opportunity for your party to receive some help from a knowledgeable stranger — the explorer is likely to have excellent maps of nearby areas (and knowledge of those areas) and is willing to share them. Conversely, an expedition that has been in the field for a while may be running short on cartography supplies or other necessaries and may be willing to pay well if your party can help supply what they lack. Also, if your party is in the mood for a sidequest, an explorer may offer one: If the expedition is headed into particularly dangerous territory, it may need additional guards to keep it safe.

Fishermen. Your party comes across 1d6 anglers engaged in their occupation by a pond or stream. If it's winter they're ice-fishing, dropping their bait into a hole carved into the frozen surface of a pond. If it has been a good day and they have fish in hand, they're willing to sell from their catch for half of what a tavern meal would cost — the hitch being, of course, that you have to clean and smoke or cook it yourself before it goes bad. With just bit of coaxing, they're also happy to provide your party with local knowledge, including tales of monsters nearby and of course, stories of the one that got away.

Treat fishermen as commoners.

Herders. A herd of caribou is not an uncommon sight here in this part of the world. Nor is it rare to see amongst and around them 2d4 herders, who belong to a nomadic or semi-nomadic tribe and keep these animals for the benefit of their kith and kin. Your party startles them, but they are not necessarily hostile; it's just that, as natives familiar with this area, they thought they would avoid any sort of trouble bringing their animals here. If you wish, you may require your party to make a DC 10 Charisma (Persuasion) check to calm them.

That being said, the herders can provide your party with helpful local knowledge. They know all the nearby sources of food and fresh water, the places where monsters are reputed to reside, places to shelter from the cold, gossip from their tribe and perhaps other tribes in the area. They may even have specific knowledge that can help your party get where they want to go.

Treat herders as tribal warriors. They wear heavy fur jackets that function (more or less) as hide armor.

Hunters. Some of the local tribes hunt for game rather than herd animals to keep themselves fed. Your party comes across a group of 2d4 hunters on their way to a familiar hunting ground. Depending on your party's appearance, they may act with caution, even suspicion at first. Despite the fact that they are armed with bows, they know that they are operating in wilderness and there are always strange folk about. However, if your party is not hostile to them they are willing to help by trading goods and supplying food and local knowledge. If your wish, have your party make a DC 10 (Charisma) Persuasion check to get on their good side.

Treat hunters as scouts.

Shaman. Your party comes upon an elder from a local tribe who has gone into the wilderness to commune with its deities. This shaman performs a religious rite dressed in ceremonial garb that may incorporate elements from creatures native to the area, such as antlers, feathers, or animal skins, and it involves entering a trancelike state in which he or she may receive prophetic visions. At your discretion, 1d6 tribal warriors accompany the shaman, serving as assistants and bodyguards. They consider it their sacred duty to prevent your party from interfering with the ritual.

How the shamanic group reacts depends on your party's actions. Maintaining a respectful distance while the ritual plays itself out could gain their trust and lead to helpful contacts with the rest of the tribe — trade, local knowledge, gifts of food and/or survival gear. On the other hand, they may resent your party seeing something that was not meant for their eyes. That is up to you as DM.

If your party interrupts the rite before it plays out, the shaman — still in an altered state of consciousness — turns on your party and attacks.

Treat the shaman as a druid.

Trappers. Your party comes across 1d4 trappers who are out here for pelts that they can sell to furriers in the nearest settlement. However, they may encounter their traps before they meet the trappers themselves. If you wish, have your party make a DC 15 Wisdom (Perception) or Wisdom (Survival) check to note the presence of a leg trap before someone in the front of the march order sets it off.

The trap is a vise on a chain staked to the ground; stepping into it causes 1d4 piercing damage and whoever set it off cannot move more than 5' from the anchor chain. A successful DC 18 Strength (Athletics) check by someone else pries it open; otherwise, the victim has to wait for the trappers, who have a key that opens it by resetting the spring.

The trappers themselves are surprised to meet your party, but not necessarily hostile. If your wish, have your party make a DC 10 (Charisma) Persuasion check to get on their good side. If successful, they are willing to share local knowledge and supplies with your party. They may also offer them a business proposition if trapping has treated them well; rather than carry all of these pelts back to civilization, they'll sell your party what they have on hand — 1d6 wolf pelts or 2d6 mink pelts — at half of the price described in the entries for wolves and weasels, respectively. In other words, your party will have the chance to double their money by reselling the pelts to the nearest furrier; this allows the trappers to stay out in the wild and keep working.

Treat the trappers as scouts.

TABLE 9.6
Watch Out! - Tundra

d10	ENCOUNTER
1	Blizzard
2-3	Bog
4	Call of the Wild
5-6	Fog
7	Loose Ground
8	Mirage
9	Tracks
10	Tripping Hazard

Blizzard. The tundra doesn't get much precipitation in a typical year. But that doesn't mean that it never snows, or that it never snows hard. A sudden blizzard brews up and makes life miserable for your party. For the next d6 x10 minutes, heavily-obscured conditions prevail in the area around them, all movement allowances are halved and no aerial movement is allowed except with a successful DC 20 Strength (Athletics) check.

Bog. In the spring and summer, the ground thaws out in spots so that it becomes squishy and treacherous underfoot. In some some places, it's treacherous enough so that you'll sink into it completely without hitting the permafrost underneath. Your party stumbles into such a patch. Have them make a DC 15 Intelligence (Nature) or Wisdom (Survival) check to spot the hazard before one party member at the front of the march order steps right into it. Treat it like quicksand at that point.

Call of the Wild. Sound can distort in the frigid air, so that its source appears to be much closer than it really is. Your party hears a noise made by a creature or natural phenomenon. It sounds very near — no more than 50

feet away. Have them make a DC 15 Wisdom (Survival) check to realize that this is an illusion, and the sound is coming from a source so far away that they cannot presently see it.

If you wish, roll on Table 9.6.1 for guidance on what your party thinks it hears:

TABLE 9.6.1
Call of the Wild - Tundra

d10	They Think They Hear...
1	Bear growling
2	Ghostly wail
3	Hoofbeats of herd animals
4	Permafrost/frozen ground crackling
5	Voices speaking in Common
6	Voices speaking in Giant
7	Whistle of bows being fired
8	Wolves snarling
9	Wyvern shrieking overhead
10	Yeti howling

Fog. A dense mist sets in suddenly, and your party is right in the middle of it. For the next 1d4 hours, heavily-obscured conditions prevail regardless of where your party goes and how far they travel during this time.

Loose Ground. The terrain undulates where your party is currently located, and they near the crest of a rise from which they can get a good view of the surrounding area. However, a party member — choose one, or a character who wants to get a good look around may literally step forward as the best candidate — steps onto a patch of loose soil. It gives way and the character takes a tumble, suffering 1d6 falling damage. A successful DC 15 Strength (Athletics) or Dexterity (Acrobatics) halves the damage. Whee!

Mirage. Draw on the geography of your campaign world and pick a feature of the landscape — such as a mountain, a boreal forest, the shoreline of a lake — that lies below the visual horizon in relation to your party's current location. In short, it's so far away that there is no way that your party should be able to see it. However, strange atmospheric conditions bend light so that they *can* see it; therefore it seems much closer than it really is. You may allow your party a DC 15 Wisdom (Survival) check to realize that this is a superior looming mirage, and the terrain feature is much farther away than it looks.

Tracks. Your party spots tracks in the frozen ground made by a creature of your choice. At your discretion, they may be fresh enough to lead to an encounter if followed; or you may allow your party to make a DC 15 Wisdom (Survival) check to realize that they are very old, and they will not lead to anything useful. If they fail, this may lead to an amusing (for you as DM, anyway) wild goose chase.

Tripping Hazard. Pick a party member at the front of the march order. That character trips over an unseen obstacle — perhaps a rock, animal bones or a pair of antlers anchored in the frozen ground. He or she must make a successful DC 10 Strength (Athletics) or Dexterity (Acrobatics) check to avoid a face plant onto the permafrost that causes 1d8 damage — and perhaps no small embarrassment in the eyes of the other party members.

Chill or Too Chilly?

Like the desert, tundra is an extreme environment that may or may not play much of a role in your campaign world. If your party has no reason to brave the cold near the poles, you may not need this chapter at all. If your campaign takes place during an ice age of your world, you may wear out these pages. Either way — or at some point in between — it's useful to know what creatures can haunt this frozen land as a point of comparison with more hospitable places.

WETLANDS

CHAPTER TEN

Wetlands

What are Wetlands?

You can call them swamps, marshes, fens or bogs. Or you can be polite and call them wetlands. Either way, they are places that are flooded for much of the year, if not year round, so that traveling through them either requires a shallow-draft vessel like a raft or a boat, or a muddy slog on foot. They occur next to rivers and large lakes that inundate them, although there are also saltwater wetlands next to oceans, so you may think of them as places that transition between water and dry land, with generous helpings of the former. This makes wetlands soggier than littoral, where the dividing line between water and land tends to be more sharply drawn.

It Sank into the Swamp. So...

It is to be admitted that visualizing a party of adventurers traveling through a swamp offers some mechanical challenges. Are they on dry land? In thick mud? Wading in shallow water, or waist-deep in it? Is the water deep enough so that it makes sense to travel by boat or raft? Wetlands encompasses all of these things. But exactly how an encounter plays out may depend on circumstance — which of the above applies to your party, and which to the creature? That's really up to you as DM — that is, how you envision this part of your campaign world — as well as how your players handle traveling through it.

In spite of the morbid gloom that often characterizes them, they support a wide range of fauna and flora — including monsters. In places, the water is deep enough to accommodate creatures as large is hydras, and to allow infiltration by aquatic humanoids like sahuagin. Some wetlands, like tropical mangrove swamps, support tree growth dense enough so that they feel like forests with waterlogged floors, while marshes and bogs content themselves with grasses and shrubs.

Wetlands can occur at almost any latitude, with the main difference between them being the degree of clamminess against your skin as you wade through the mire and water soaks your leggings. Is it merely uncomfortable, or can you feel the cold all the way down to your bones? However, wetlands in different climatic bands also differ in terms of the creatures that you encounter in them, so some of the tables in this chapter require die roll modifiers depending on your party's current location in your campaign world. For instance, you may find wolves in subarctic wetlands, but not in tropical swamps and marshes. Conversely, boa constrictors live among the vines and warm muck of tropical swamps, but they find cold bogs discouraging.

Wetlands support a surprising range of life.

What Do You Find in Wetlands?

When you determine that a random encounter is in order, roll on Table 10.1 to determine the category:

TABLE 10.1

Humans - Wetlands

d20	CATEGORY
1-7	Aggressive Creatures (Table 10.2)
8-12	Neutral Creatures (Table 10.3)
13-15	Humanoids (Table 10.4)
16-17	Humans (Table 10.5)
18-20	Watch Out! (10.6)

Then, roll on the appropriate table to determine the creature, person or thing encountered.

TABLE 10.2
Aggressive Creatures - Wetlands

d100	CATEGORY
1-3	Wolves
4-8	Bird of Prey
9	Chuul
10-11	Drider
12-13	Elemental
14-16	Ettercap
17-19	Ettin
20	Gibbering Mouther
21-23	Green Hag
24-26	Griffon
27-31	Harpy
32	Hydra
33-39	Insects
40	Kraken
41-43	Merrow
44-46	Mud Mephits
47-48	Ogres
49	Oni
50-52	Otyugh
53-55	Owlbear
56-58	Panther
59	Roc
60-62	Quippers
63-65	Scorpion
66-68	Shambling Mound
69-74	Snakes
75-78	Spiders
79-81	Toad
82-83	Troll
84-88	Undead
89-93	Will-o'-Wisp
94	Worgs
95-96	Wyvern
97-100	Crocodile
101-103	Tiger

+3 to the die roll in tropical wetlands.

Wolves. You will not find wolves in tropical swamps, but you will find them in temperate wetlands, and also in sub-arctic bogs (which are not unlike mushier versions of boreal forests). Roll on Table 10.2.1. to determine the wolves encountered:

TABLE 10.2.1
Wolves - Wetlands

d10	ENCOUNTER
1	Winter Wolves
2-3	Dire Wolves
4-7	Wolves

+1 to die roll in temperate and tropical wetland.

Scaling the Encounter: The encounter group consists of one dire wolf for each multiple of 2 in your party's average level, or one winter wolf for each multiple of 3 in the party's average level; or 1d4 wolves for each level in your party's average level.

Treasure: Furriers in your world may be willing to pay for wolf pelts. How much is ultimately up to you, but 2 gp is a reasonable baseline price for a normal wolf pelt; 3 gp for a dire wolf pelt; and 5 gp for a winter wolf pelt.

Bird of Prey. A bird of prey — or a flock of them — wheels overhead, then strikes at your party. Keen-eyed, but bird-brained all the same, it has spotted something in your party as food — a familiar or small summoned creature is an obvious choice, but it could just be travelers rations, like strips of cured meat left in the open. To determine which species, roll on Table 10.2.2:

TABLE 10.2.2
Birds of Prey - Wetlands

d10	ENCOUNTER
1-2	Eagle
3	Giant Eagle
4-5	Blood Hawks
6-7	Hawks
8-9	Owl
10	Giant Owl

Eagle. One eagle swoops down on your party, aiming itself at something it has identified as food.

Giant Eagle. A giant eagle has spotted your party. Giant eagles are intelligent and may respond if your

➤

party tries to flag them down. Though it cannot speak when spoken to, a successful DC 15 Charisma (Persuasion) check by someone who speaks Common or Auran persuades it to do your party a service, if it is within its power to accomplish it. This may involve delivering a written message or token, or guiding your party to a place that it knows, or even traveling with them for a while as an airborne lookout.

Blood Hawks. A flock of 2d6 blood hawks swoops down on your party. They concentrate on a single target — most likely a pack animal, but they may settle for a small humanoid as the next best thing.

Hawks. A flock of 2d10 hawks targets your party. They're probably going after the party's rations, but they may also have spotted rodents or small reptiles who are literally scurrying along the ground at your party's feet. To the extent that your party is in their way, the hawks attack them.

Owl. Owls hunt at night, so you should re-roll this encounter if it takes place during the day. Otherwise, one owl has spotted food as your party rests outdoors overnight. Most likely, it has spotted a small animal companion or familiar, or rations left out in the open, or a frog or other amphibian that has gotten in among your party.

Giant Owl. Likewise, a giant owl encounter is most suitable for night, so you should re-roll this encounter if it takes place during the day. One giant owl spots food in your party's camp.

Chuul. Your party crosses paths with one of these ancient horrors picking its way through the marshes. Whether or not it is associated with a nearby aboleth ruin is up to you as DM; it may be wandering without purpose, severed from its connection to its former masters for all practical purposes. Whatever the case, old instincts die hard and it attacks your party for their treasure.

Scaling the Encounter: A chuul may be more than you want to throw at a beginning-level party. Feel free to re-roll for another encounter. Conversely, if you want to run a more challenging encounter for a higher-level party, consider that the encounter group consists of one chuul for each multiple of 5 in your party's average level, rounded up.

Drider. In a densely forested corner of the wetlands, your party comes across a drider that has wandered far, far away from the nearest drow settlement. It has gone mad from its fate, and that it attacks anyone who disturbs its lonely exile. Perhaps it somehow thinks that killing an elf

or another enemy of the drow and presenting its head to a representative of the Spider Queen will somehow restore it to favor. Or perhaps hunger and insanity have given it a taste for human or humanoid flesh. Whatever motivation you give it, that should drive how it reacts to your party.

Scaling the Encounter: A drider may be a bit much for a lower-level party to handle, so if your party's average level is less than 6, feel free to re-roll for a different encounter.

Treasure: It is most likely that your party has stumbled upon a lone drider sulking in its lair. To determine its treasure, roll on the Treasure Hoard: Challenge 5-10 table.

Wetlands can spell disaster for the unprepared or overconfident..

Elemental. If your party is more than ankle-deep in water, a water elemental rears up before them from out of the swamp. If they're standing on mostly dry land, the ground beside them resolves itself into an earth elemental. In either case, the elemental being is disturbed by its proximity to an alien element. It's an unhappy camper, and it lashes out at your party.

Scaling the Encounter: If your party's average level is lower than 5, an elemental may be more than you want to throw at them. Feel free to re-roll for a different encounter. Conversely, if your party's average level is 10 or higher, feel free to add one elemental to the encounter.

Ettercap. Ettercaps lurk in parts of the wetlands that have heavy vegetation that can hide them — preferably trees, but dense shrubbery will also do, and they don't even mind partially submerging themselves in shallow water. A lone ettercap tries to ambush your party, attacking from behind once they have passed its hiding spot. You may allow a DC 15 Wisdom (Survival) or Intelligence (Nature) check to notice that something is trying to hide from your party as they approach. If no one spots the ettercap, it uses its *Web* ability to pin as many party members as possible, then closes to finish off each one with its *Web Garrote* attack.

Treasure: You may consider that the ettercap jumps your party from its habitual spot, and that meager treasure from a few previous victims lies scattered in the vicinity. Roll on the Individual Treasure: Challenge 0-4 table to determine what your party finds.

Ettin. Your party hears two loud voices coming from somewhere amongst the thick vegetation. Have your party make a DC 15 Intelligence (Nature) check to recognize that it's an ettin arguing with itself. If they choose not to avoid the ettin, it calls out to your party and demands that they help settle a dispute. It should be something that the party would find awkward or at least pointless to answer — for instance, whether forest fey or swamp fey taste more savory. No matter what answer the party gives, one or both heads accuses them of unfairly favoring the other and the ettin attacks. Alternately, the ettin stops short when it spots the party and realizes that it's hungry after arguing with itself for such a long time.

Scaling the Encounter: As amusing as ettins can be if you run the encounter with the right sense of humor, one is a bit much for a party with an average level of less than 4.

Treasure: The ettin carries some coins in a pouch looped around its loincloth. Roll twice on the Individual Treasure: Challenge 0-4 table.

Gibbering Mouther. Gibbering mouthers navigate swamps and marshes with ease. How a gibbering mouther got into this ecosystem in the first place is a matter unto itself, but there is no question that these abominations make themselves at home in the muck and find plenty of prey to satisfy their indiscriminate appetite.

Your party enters a gloomy part of the swamp, where they are likely to hear a gibbering mouther before they can see it. You may allow them a DC 15 Intelligence (Nature) check to realize what is making that maddening cacophony. Needless to say, it attacks your party without hesitation — it is simply in its nature to do so.

Scaling the Encounter: If you wish to make the encounter more challenging, the encounter group consists of one gibbering mouther for each multiple of 4 in your party's average level.

Treasure: Belongings from the gibbering mouther's previous victims might well remain trapped in its body, remaining intact while the flesh that once claimed them as its own has long since dissolved. Roll once on the

Treasure Hoard: Challenge 0-4 table for each gibbering mouther present.

Green Hag. Your party hears what sounds like the voice of a young woman crying for help. Upon inspection, they see her half-sunk into the mire, evidently struggling to get out. Unfortunately, it's really a green hag trying to lure them into a patch of the swamp so treacherous that it is, effectively, quicksand. She looks forward to the pleasure of watching them struggle, then perish. If necessary, she'll help the process along.

Scaling the Encounter: Even a lone green hag may be a bit too much for a beginning-level party, especially combined with the quicksand hazard. Feel free to re-roll for another encounter.

Treasure: This bog is the hag's lair, and she keeps trophies from her previous victims here. To determine her treasure, roll on the Treasure Hoard: Challenge 0-4 table.

Griffon. The biodiversity of wetlands offer predators like griffons plenty of potential reward for traveling far from their eyries in mountains and hills. One such griffon spots your party and goes for one of their mounts or pack animals — or at least, it thinks it has spotted a mount or a pack animal.

Scaling the Encounter: If you wish to make the encounter more challenging, your party encounters a flock (or pack?) of griffons hunting together. There is one for each multiple of 3 in your party's average level.

That Sank into the Swamp
Given that swamps, marshes, bogs — whatever you want to call them — are basically liminal spaces between land water, it seemed appropriate to leave it entirely up to local circumstance whether your party hooks up with a water elemental or earth elemental here.

Harpy. A harpy's siren song sounds loud, clear and irresistible in the eerie stillness of the swamp. In wetlands, harpies make their lairs in large trees or on patches of solid ground that jut up from the swamp. Without fail, they choose locations very near treacherous ground that functions like quicksand, all the better to trap hapless passersby entranced by their song. Your party hears one siren. Can they resist it?

Scaling the Encounter: If you wish to make the encounter more challenging, the encounter group consists of two harpies for each multiple of 3 in your party's average level.

Treasure: By definition, a harpy's perch is its lair, so it's unlikely that this encounter takes place far from home. Roll on the Treasure Hoard table appropriate to the CR of the encounter to determine what your party finds with a routine search of the area.

Hydra. As your party navigates the swamp, they see monstrous reptilian heads rear up out of the murky water. They have come across one hydra that has come rather far inland to hunt — perhaps it has hunted out the fish and other aquatic creatures in its territory. Your party looks as edible to it as any land-based creature.

Scaling the Encounter: A hydra is probably too much for a low-level party. Feel free to re-roll for another encounter. Conversely, if you want to run a more challenging encounter for a high-level party, consider that your party has encountered a pair of hydras hunting together.

Insects. Insects are a constant nuisance in wetlands, especially during warm weather months. You may not think of them as predatory, but they feed without giving it much thought and they cause trouble in their own way. Some are viciously aggressive when they feel threatened. Roll on Table 10.2.3 to determine the insects encountered:

TABLE 10.2.3
Insects - Wetlands

d6	ENCOUNTER
1-4	Swarm of Insects
5-6	Giant Wasps

Swarm of Insects. One swarm of insects — call them gnats, midges, mosquitos, whatever you will — descends upon your party and makes their lives decidedly unpleasant.

Giant Wasps. Your party comes upon two giant wasps guarding a nest hanging from a tree branch. They attack anything that comes close to the nest.

Scaling the Encounter: If you wish to make the encounter more challenging (or more of a nuisance, depending on how you look at it), the encounter group consists of 1d4 giant wasps for each multiple of 2 in your party's average level, or 1d4 swarms of insects plus one additional swarm for each level in your party's average level.

Kraken. Swamps can be gloomy places as a matter of course, but when your party sees the sky above and the swamp water below suddenly darken because they're close to a kraken, it's a deeper order of gloom entirely. You may allow your party a DC 15 Intelligence (Nature) check to read the portents and figure out what is going on before an enormous tentacle, followed by the rest of the kraken, rears up out of the muck. For whatever reason, it has come inland from its home in the deep water to hunt. It is in a predatory mood; even if isn't looking to feed on your party, it feels like destroying them just for the sake of doing so.

Scaling the Encounter: A close encounter with a kraken may be too much for a lower-level party. If your party's average level is less than 20, feel free to re-roll for another encounter.

Merrow. One of these monstrous descendants of warped merfolk has infiltrated the swamp from its lair in the adjacent major river or other nearby body of water, intent on finding prey. Your party crosses paths with it, and it decides that taking them will be less trouble than trying to snatch someone from a settlement, where it might have to face down an entire village if caught in the act.

Scaling the Encounter: : If you wish to make the encounter more challenging, the encounter group consists of one merrow for each multiple of 3 in your party's level.

Mud Mephits. Unfortunately for all concerned, two mud mephits spot your party. They have slowly been driving each other mad with incessant and pointless complaints about everything and nothing, and they see your party as a diversion. They're lounging like couch potatoes in the muck of the swamp and they're too lazy to move, so they yell out to your party and start complaining to them about the weather — it's too hot, or too cold, too dry or too wet — or how they're too poor, or bored, or exhausted. They start to beg your party for handouts. All of this is in Aquan or Terran, of course. If your party ignores them, the mephits chase after them and eventually become exasperated enough to attack. If your party confronts them, they become agitated and attack.

Scaling the Encounter: If you wish to make the encounter more challenging, the encounter group consists of 1d4 mud mephits plus one additional mud mephits for each level in your party's average level. It's a veritable pity party of mephits!

Ogres. Ogres prefer dry land to the treacherous footing in wetlands, but they find enough targets to raid that you will encounter them here all the same. Your party crosses paths with a party of ogres looking for settlements of fisherfolk to plunder. Whether you want to stage any meaningful interaction with these undersized giants is up to you, but it should surprise no one if they decide that your party is as good a target as any they are likely to find in the near future, whether they are looking for treasure or food (or both).

Scaling the Encounter: The encounter group consists of one ogre for each multiple of 3 in the party's average level, rounded up. If your party is only 1st Level, consider that one half-ogre confronts them.

Treasure. These ogres are away from their lair. Add the CR of all ogres killed and roll on the appropriate Individual Treasure table.

Oni. An ogre mage roaming the wetlands likely does so for either of two reasons: It makes its living by infiltrating settlements in the marshes and is moving from one to another, or it has so worn out its welcome in another region that it has come here to hole up. Either way, your party crosses paths with one oni. Once it spots your party, it uses its *Change Shape* ability to disguise itself as someone trustworthy and inoffensive; use a form that is unlikely to arouse your party's suspicions. Maybe it claims to have a raft or a boat that will help your party get where they want to go. Maybe it pretends to be a traveler in distress. If they allow the oni to travel with them, it bides its time until they make camp for the night. It volunteers to take the first watch, then it strikes once everyone else is asleep.

That friendly stranger might be a hidden danger.

If you wish, you may allow your party a DC 20 Intelligence (Arcana) check to suspect that this apparently friendly stranger might be using magic to alter its appearance.

Scaling the Encounter: An oni may be a bit too much for a low-level party. Feel free to re-roll for another encounter. Conversely, if your party's average level is 10 or higher, consider that your party has encountered two oni working together.

Otyugh. An otyugh could be anywhere in a swamp. There's decaying plant and animal matter just about everywhere, and the muck gives it plenty of places to hide. Given how easily an otyugh could conceal itself, it should come as no surprise (ironically, given that they attack from concealment) if one of these monstrosities lashes out from beneath the mire as your party passes.

Scaling the Encounter: If your party's average level is lower than 5, an otyugh may be more than you want to throw at them. Feel free to re-roll for a different encounter.

Treasure: The belongings of the otyugh's previous victims lie scattered about its lair. Roll on the Treasure Hoard: Challenge 5-10 table to determine its contents. The coins are mostly collected in heaps, as their containers are rotting or have rotted away.

Owlbear. This encounter is most likely to take place at night, when owlbears hunt. Your party hears its terrible shriek echo through the swamp; you may require a DC 15 Intelligence (Nature) check to recognize it. If it is daytime, you can either re-roll for a different encounter or consider that your party has stumbled upon its lair in a place where the vegetation is so heavy that it blots out the sun, and it is currently resting. If hunting, it attacks; if disturbed in its lair it fights.

Scaling the Encounter: An owlbear may be a bit too much for a beginning-level party. Feel free to re-roll for another encounter. Conversely, if you want to run a more challenging encounter for a higher-level party, consider that your party has encountered a mated pair of owlbears.

Treasure: If the encounter takes place in the owlbear lair, roll on the Treasure Hoard: Challenge 0-4 table to determine what it has taken from its previous victims. If it involves a pair of owlbears, roll twice.

Panther. Your party draws the attention of a panther on the prowl, most likely for either of two reasons. Perhaps they have startled prey it was stalking — in which case, they see the prey animal dart across its path, and they hear an angry snarl off to one side. Or the panther has targeted one of the party's pack animals as its prey.

Quippers. Not all of the small fish that inhabit the 'wet' in wetlands are harmless and submit quietly to being caught for food. Some of them take a quite opposite attitude: If you step into the water, you are their food. If some or all of your party wades into the swamp where it's deep enough to support fish, one swarm of quippers sees their next meal and attacks. You may allow your party a DC 15 Wisdom (Perception) or Wisdom (Survival) check to notice a school of fish with sharp teeth close to shore in the turbid waters.

Scaling the Encounter: If you wish to make the encounter more challenging, the encounter group consists of two swarms of quippers for each multiple of 3 in your party's average level, rounded up.

Roc. A roc has roamed far afield from its mountain or hilltop eyrie in search of food, and the diversity of offerings in wetlands make up for traveling so far from home. If anything, the roc has learned that someone on a boat or a raft has nowhere to run from a powerful aerial predator, so travelers and local fishermen are easy pickings. When it spots your party, they look pretty tasty, so it attacks.

Scaling the Encounter: Rocs are fearsome opponents. If your party's average level is lower than 11, a roc may be more than you want to throw at them. Feel free to re-roll for a different encounter.

Scorpions. Not that they would ever do this intentionally, but your party disturbs a nest of scorpions hidden in the vegetation. 1d8 scorpions attack your party. They have stingers, and they don't hesitate to use them.

Scaling the Encounter: If your party's average level is 5 or higher, consider that your party has disturbed one or more giant scorpions concealed in the undergrowth. In this case, the encounter group consists of one giant scorpion for each multiple of 5 in your party's average level.

Shambling Mound. As your party makes its way through a part of the swamp with dense vegetation, they may or may not realize that a shambling mound has spotted them as a possible food source. You may require your party to make a DC 15 Wisdom (Perception) or Wisdom (Survival) check to realize that that jumble of plant growth off to the side just moved. Success means that your party may then make a DC 15 Intelligence (Nature) check to realize that it's a shambling mound.

Scaling the Encounter: If your party's average level is lower than 5, a shambling mound may be more than you want to throw at them. Feel free to re-roll for a different encounter.

Treasure: Shambling mounds feed on the move, but it's quite possible that its previous prey's less perishable possessions remain inside it. Roll on the Individual Treasure: Challenge 5-10 table.

Snakes. Venomous snakes occur in tropical and sub-tropical climates, and they feel very much at home in wetlands. They possess an unfortunate combination of traits: On the one hand, their coloration makes them hard to spot amid vegetation and in dim light, but on the other hand they tend to lash out if you get too close to them. This is what happens to your party. You may allow your party a DC 15 Wisdom (Perception) or Wisdom (Survival) check to realize that the front of the march order is about to step on a snake. This should give them enough time to take evasive action, although you may consider that this simply means they aren't surprised when the snake lashes out.

Constrictor snakes are found only in tropical regions where it's hot and humid enough for a large cold-blooded creature to survive. But where they do occur, they are awe-inspiring predators.

Roll on Table 10.2.4 to determine the size of the snake(s) encountered:

TABLE 10.2.4
Snakes - Wetlands

d10	ENCOUNTER
1-5	Swarm of Poisonous Snakes
6-8	Poisonous Snake
9-10	Giant Poisonous Snake
11-12	Constrictor Snake
13	Giant Constrictor Snake

+3 to die roll in tropical wetlands

Swarm of Poisonous Snakes. Your party comes across a shallow depression which is, literally, a snake pit with one swarm of poisonous snakes present. You may decrease the DC to notice the snakes to 5, to reflect the facts that there are more snakes present and the terrain feature is relatively easy to notice.

Poisonous Snake. Your party comes close to stepping on one poisonous snake.

Giant Poisonous Snake. Your party comes across one giant poisonous snake. You may decrease the DC to notice the snakes to 10 to reflect its size.

Constrictor Snake. One constrictor tries to sneak up on your party and make a meal of one of its members.

Giant Constrictor Snake. One *really big* constrictor tries to sneak up on your party and make a meal of one of its members.

Spiders. If your party runs afoul of spiders in a swamp, it is probably because the spiders have built large webs among dense stands of vegetation. It may be an empty web, as in Table 10.6: Hampering Web, or it may be crawling with spiders — or it may be that just one very big and dangerous spider calls it home and hunting ground. Roll on Table 10.2.5 to determine the spiders encountered:

TABLE 10.2.5
Spiders - Wetlands

d10	ENCOUNTER
1-5	Spider
6-8	Giant Spider
9-10	Phase Spider

Spider. These spiders are small, but their venom packs a punch. Your party finds 1d4 spiders in this web. They won't leave their web, but if someone in your party gets close enough, they'll attack.

Giant Spider. Giant spiders live alone, so your party encounters one in its web.

Phase Spider. Phase spiders are quite fearless, and they use their ability to jump back and forth between planes to conduct hit-and-run attacks, wearing the party down until they are all incapacitated or dead.

Scaling the Encounter: Larger spiders live alone or together in small numbers, as too much weight would drag down their web. Also, a phase spider may be a bit too much for a beginning-level party. Feel free to re-roll for another encounter in that case.

However, you may want to create a populous web of spiders to provide higher-level parties with more of a challenge. In this case, the web swarms with 1d4 spiders for each multiple of 2 in your party's average level, rounded up.

Treasure. With larger spiders, they may have trapped humanoid-sized victims in the past and left some of their valuables caught in their web. You may roll on the Individual Treasure: Challenge 0-4 table if you wish.

Toad. These amphibians are not naturally aggressive, but they need to eat — and when they get this big a lot of different creatures look like food. In a freshwater marsh (toads are not much fond of salt water), your party comes across one giant toad that is hungry enough to eat anything it can swallow. Assuming that at least someone in your party can be swallowed by a giant toad, the toad attacks.

Scaling the Encounter: If you wish to make the encounter more challenging, the encounter group consists of two giant toads for each multiple of 3 in your party's average level.

Troll. A troll has staked out this corner of the swamp as its own. It emerges from the shadows of the trees and demands a fee in order to let your party pass through. Perhaps it demands one of the party's pack animals as its toll, or a suitable amount of coins. It fights rather than let anyone pass for free.

Scaling the Encounter: If your party's average level is lower than 5, a troll may be more than you want to throw at them. Feel free to re-roll for a different encounter. Conversely, if your party's average level is 10 or higher, feel free to add one troll to the encounter — a tag-team of trolls.

Treasure: The troll's racket has worked well enough in the past: Its victims pay one way or another, and it has accumulated a decent hoard. Searching the area turns up its stash, thrown into a pile, on a successful DC 10 Wisdom (Perception) check. Roll on the Treasure Hoard: Challenge 5-10 table to determine the contents.

Undead. Of course there are undead here, lurking all around. It would be a surprise if they were not. The deep gloom and air of decay that permeates swamps, especially where the vegetation is thick and crowds out the sun, make them natural homes for the undead. Wetlands are as remote and dangerous as any wilderness environment, so they offer plenty of opportunities to die an unfortunate death, and for unquiet souls to be kept restless by dark magic of mysterious origin. Besides, swamps just feel creepy. Roll on Table 10.2.6 to determine the undead abomination that greets your party:

Undead are found wherever there is an untimely death to be had.

TABLE 10.2.6
Undead - Wetlands

d12	ENCOUNTER
1	Banshee
2	Ghost
3-7	Ghouls/Ghasts
8	Shadows
9	Specter
10	Wraith
11-12	Zombies

Banshee. Assuming that elves are a part of your campaign world, it's possible that they live, or at least once lived in this swamp. This banshee is a relic of evil deeds and tragic events from their history. Perhaps your party hears its forlorn wail from a distance, and they only confront it if they investigate. Or perhaps they stumble upon its domain, and in its madness and despair it demands that they hand over their valuables, particularly their jewelry.

Ghost. A ghost encountered in the swamp — whether glimpsed flitting between the trees, or whether it rears up suddenly out of the gloom — is most likely the remnant of someone who died a miserable death in this forsaken place. Perhaps that unfortunate person got lost; or died while fleeing from pursuers; or ended his or her own life in loneliness and despair. Whatever the case, you may make this into a hostile encounter by having the ghost try to possess a member of your party so that it may resolve unfinished business from its former life.

Ghouls/Ghasts. An encounter with ghouls is most likely to take place at night, although a gloomy part of the swamp, thick and dark with mangrove trees, may work well enough for that purpose. Two ghouls (or one ghast) approach your party, driven by mindless hunger for their flesh.

Shadows. One sees plenty of shadows in the gloom of wetlands with heavy vegetation. However, sometimes a shadow is more than just a shadow — it's an undead creature! Without thinking or feeling, it attacks the nearest party member, eager to drain the life from another victim and create one more of its own kind.

Specter. Specters can find enough gloom to suit them where heavy plant growth blocks out the sun in a patch of swamp. It isn't darkness, but it's close enough. Your party comes upon one specter that was once someone who perished in the wilderness, but all

➤

connections to who and what it was in life no longer exist. Only blind hatred of the living drives it to attack your party on sight.

Wraith. As your party passes by, they can see a bit of swamp ringed by barren and blasted ground with only withered plants and perhaps a dead tree to show that it once supported life. A cold, charcoal-gray mist emerges and resolves itself into a wraith, which then attacks your party, acting out the resentment that it bore at the end of its natural life.

Zombies. Your party come across 1d4 zombies who have been programmed to kill every living thing they encounter. The source of the necromancy that created these zombies we leave to you. Perhaps they slipped the leash of their creator and they now wander the wetlands mindlessly looking for victims.

Scaling the Encounter: Banshees, ghosts and wraiths always work alone. The base encounter group for specters also consists of only one of its kind.

A banshee or a wraith may be too much for a beginning-level party, so feel free to re-roll the encounter in that case. With specters, you may create a more challenging encounter by using two for each multiple of 3 in your party's average level, with all of them being part of a group that perished *en masse*.

Ghouls/Ghasts: If you wish to make the encounter more challenging, the encounter group consists of two ghouls (or one ghast) for each multiple of 4 in your party's average level. Feel free to mix and match ghouls and ghasts as long as you maintain the right proportion of total CR to average party level.

Shadows: The encounter group consists of two shadows for each multiple of 3 in your party's average level.

Zombies: If you wish to make the encounter more challenging, the encounter group consists of two zombies for each of your party's average levels. If the average party level is 3 or higher, you may use an encounter group consisting of one ogre zombie for each multiple of 3 in the party's average level.

Treasure: Most likely, banshees, ghosts and wraiths are encountered in or near what passes for a lair with them and you may consider that there they keep possessions that they had in life. Roll on the Treasure Hoard: Challenge 0-4 table for the contents of their stash. You may require a successful DC 15 Wisdom (Perception) check to find its exact location.

➤

With ghouls, ghasts and zombies, they may have with them some remains of what they had on their person at the time of their death. Roll on the Individual Treasure table appropriate to the total CR of the encounter (rounded up to the nearest whole number).

Will-o-'Wisp. Will-o'-wisps can be found virtually anywhere in wetlands, so it should not seem out of place if your party spots a luminous globe dancing and bobbing above the mire. It's the remnant of an unquiet soul that perished here. Perhaps it was a pirate who tried to get away through the swamp after stealing from his comrades became a monster's terrorized prey.

If you want to add some spice to the encounter, consider that this evil spirit tries to lure victims into a patch of quicksand to render them helpless. In this case, the will-o'-wisp restricts itself to a 50-foot diameter area at the center of the clearing. At the center of this area, the swamp turns into a 20-foot diameter pit of quicksand. If the will-o'-wisp is not already directly above the quicksand when it is engaged in melee combat, it retreats until it is above the quicksand, thus forcing its attacker to step into it in order to continue the melee.

Scaling the Encounter: If you wish to make the encounter more challenging, the encounter group consists of one will-o'-wisp for each multiple of 3 in your party's average level.

Treasure: Belongings from the will-o'-wisp's previous victims have been piling up here, with various valuables scattered in the muck. To determine the treasure, roll once on the Treasure Hoard: Challenge 0-4 table for each will-o'-wisp present.

Wyvern. They don't live in wetlands, but the abundance of prey in this environment makes it worthwhile for wyverns to travel from their hilltop lairs to hunt here. One such wyvern spots your party from above. It is either very hungry or very aggressive, so it swoops down to attack despite the odds.

Scaling the Encounter: If your party's average level is lower than 6, a wyvern with its blood up may be more than you want to throw at them. Feel free to re-roll for a different encounter.

Crocodile. Crocodiles are very much at home in temperate and tropical wetlands, where they can conceal themselves in shallow water right until it's close enough to strike. One crocodile, bold (or hungry) enough to strike even when outnumbered leaps out of the swamp at your party, teeth bared.

Scaling the Encounter: If you wish to make the encounter more challenging, consider that your party comes across a bask of crocodiles, all of whom are hungry enough to eat your party. The encounter group consists of one crocodile for each level in your party's average level. Or, you may substitute one giant crocodile for six crocodiles.

Tiger. Your party draws the attention of a tiger prowling the marsh, most likely for either of two reasons. Perhaps they have startled prey it was stalking — in which case, they see the prey animal dart across its path, and they hear an angry snarl off to one side. Either that, or the tiger has targeted the party's pack animals as its prey.

TABLE 10.3

Neutral Creatures - Wetlands

d100	ENCOUNTER
1-4	Elk
5-10	Black Bear
11-14	Awakened Plant
15-19	Axe Beaks
20-24	Bats
25-28	Boar
29-34	Centipede
35-38	Cockatrice
39-44	Crabs
45-49	Deer
50	Dragon
51-52	Elephant
53-57	Fey
58-62	Fire Beetles
63-68	Frog
69-73	Hyenas
74-77	Jackals
78-81	Lizards
82-87	Rats
88	Unicorn
89-92	Water Weird
93-98	Weasels
99-105	Vultures
106-110	Rhinoceros

+8 to die roll for temperate wetlands.
+10 to die roll for tropical wetlands.

Elk. Elk inhabit sub-arctic and temperate wetlands, where the climate agrees with them and they find enough vegetation to support them. Your party spots a herd of 1d4 bulls and 2d6 cows grazing. If your party attacks them, only the males fight, covering the fleeing females.

Even if your party does not behave in a threatening manner, you may consider that there is a chance that the bulls mistake their actions and attack anyway. Have your party make a DC 15 Intelligence (Nature) or Wisdom (Survival) check. Failure means that someone has made a false move that sets off the males and they charge.

Scaling the Encounter: If you wish to make the encounter more challenging, your party sees a lone (and rare) giant elk at a distance. As they approach it they realize that it's larger than it seemed. Confident in its power as an alpha of its kind, it attacks your party if it senses any hostile intent (remember that giant elk have the ability to understand certain languages).

Perhaps it is bad luck in your campaign world to hunt a giant elk. If your party kills it, each party member is cursed as if affected by the spell *bane*, except that the effect lasts until it is magically dispelled, or until those who did the deed atone for it.

Treasure: Elk are hunted for food wherever they share territory with humans. Perhaps a butcher will pay 2 gp or thereabouts for a fresh carcass.

Black Bear. Black bears roam sub-arctic and temperate wetlands, and your party spots one prowling the swamp for food. If your party just wants to scare it off, require a DC 15 Intelligence (Nature) or Wisdom (Survival) check. Success means that the bear takes the hint and lumbers away. Failure means that someone has made a false move, provoking the bear to attack.

Awakened Plant. Roll on Table 10.3.1 to determine whether your party comes across an awakened shrub or an awakened tree drawing sustenance from the rich muck of the swamp:

TABLE 10.3.1
Awakened Plant - Wetlands

d6	ENCOUNTER
1-4	Awakened Shrub
5-6	Awakened Tree

Awakened Shrub. Your party comes into contact with one awakened shrub. Perhaps a party member gets
➤

tangled up in it while picking his or her way through the swamp. Perhaps it produces berries that look appetizing. Perhaps your party is looking for kindling for the campfire. These or similar actions cause the shrub to express alarm. An encounter with them is not necessarily hostile, even your party has done mischief to it. If your party asks it for help, a successful DC 10 Charisma (Persuasion) check wins it over, but the DC is 15 if your party has harmed it in some way. Help from an awakened shrub includes providing knowledge of the surrounding area.

Awakened Tree. Your party has some sort of physical contact with a particularly large tree looming over the surrounding bog. Perhaps someone stumbles over a root and falls heavily against it. Perhaps someone just leans against it to rest. Perhaps someone breaks off a branch, or carves a sigil into the trunk, or does some other casual mischief. Whatever it is, the tree expresses its alarm.

An awakened tree is not necessarily hostile. If your party asks it for help, a successful DC 10 Charisma (Persuasion) check wins it over. If your party includes someone visibly carrying an axe of some sort, the DC is 15. If the party has harmed the tree in any way, the DC is 20. Help from an awakened tree includes providing knowledge about the immediate area, or even accompanying your party as an ally as long as this doesn't mean going very far.

However, an awakened tree instinctively reacts to open flame with hostility. Lighting a torch or starting a campfire causes it to attack.

Scaling the Encounter: If you wish to make the encounter more challenging, the encounter group consists of one awakened shrub for each multiple of 3 in your party's average level or one awakened tree for each multiple of 4 in your party's average level.

Axe Beaks. Your party comes across a hunting pack of 1d4+2 of these odd-looking, bad-tempered flightless birds. They don't like having their hunt interrupted, but it's not a sure thing that they'll attack. You may have your party make a DC 15 Intelligence (Nature) or Wisdom (Survival) check. Failure means that a party member has made a false move that angers the axe beaks, which then attack the party.

Bats. Your party passes a dead tree, its trunk apparently hollowed out, in a gloomy corner of the swamp. They hear odd noises, like squeaking or chattering, coming from inside. If they so much as take look into the open cavity, they see a colony of swamp bats — one swarm of bats — in the hollow. Have your party make a DC 15 Intelligence (Nature) or Wisdom (Survival) check. Failure means that someone has made a false move, and the bats attack.

Scaling the Encounter: If you wish to make the encounter more challenging, consider that the bats are so aggressive and persistent that it's worth treating them as multiple swarms, one swarm for each level in your party's average level. Either that, or there are *a lot* of bats.

Boar. Your party spots 1d4 wild boar rooting around in the undergrowth for food. Boar are popular targets for hunters. They'll fight back if attacked — indeed, the challenge they present is part of the appeal of hunting them. But they have also developed a fight-or-flight instinct, and if your party wishes to avoid a fight, have them make a DC 15 Wisdom (Survival) or Intelligence (Nature) group check to scare the boar off.

Scaling the Encounter: If you wish to make the encounter more challenging, use an encounter group consisting of one giant boar for each multiple of 3 in your party's average level. Giant boar are even more aggressive than their smaller cousins and they charge anyone who disturbs them.

Treasure: Boar meat is good eating for many folk. Perhaps a nearby butcher will pay 2 gp or thereabouts for a fresh carcass. The price might go up to 5 gp for a giant boar.

Centipede. Have your party make a DC 15 Intelligence (Nature) or Wisdom (Survival) check. Failure means that no one notices one giant centipede wending its way across their path — in the dim light, its dark color makes it hard to distinguish — and someone in the front of the march order comes dangerously close to stepping on it. It responds by attacking that character. Success means that they notice the giant centipede in time to avoid provoking it, thus making a hostile encounter purely optional.

Cockatrice. Your party comes across one cockatrice poking around the undergrowth for food, or padding about the swamp as it chases down a prospective snack. If your party wishes to avoid a fight, require a DC 15 Intelligence (Nature) or Wisdom (Survival) check. Failure means that someone in your party has made a false move that sets off the beast, and it attacks.

Scaling the Encounter: If you wish to make the encounter more challenging, use an encounter group that consists of 1d4 cockatrices plus one additional cockatrice for each level in your party's average level.

Crabs. While wading through shallow water — not a particularly unusual thing to have to do in a swamp — your party runs afoul of 2d4 giant crabs. They attack only if they feel threatened, so have your party make a DC 15 Intelligence (Nature) or Wisdom (Survival) check. Failure means that a party member has made a false move that sets the crabs' pincers snapping.

Treasure: If crab meat is a delicacy in your campaign world, live giant crabs could fetch 2-5 gp each at a seafood market, but they would have to be sold live and they cannot survive out of water for very long. The easiest way to trap a crab is to lure it into a container. Grappling is much more difficult; it requires someone to maintain a grapple on the crab while someone else binds its claws, which requires an action and a successful DC 15 Strength check.

Deer. Your party spots 1d8 bucks and 2d6 does grazing. If your party attacks, only the male fights, covering the females while they flee.

Even if your party does not behave in a threatening manner, there is a chance that the males mistake their actions and attack anyway. Have your party make a DC 10 Intelligence (Nature) or Wisdom (Survival) check. Failure means that someone has made a false move that sets off the males and they charge.

Treasure: Anyone for venison? Perhaps a nearby butcher will pay 2 gp or thereabouts for a fresh carcass.

Dragon. Your party notices a shadow in the sky. It's a dragon on the prowl. To determine what kind of dragon roll on Table 10.3.2:

TABLE 10.3.2
Dragons - Wetlands

d12	ENCOUNTER
1-2	Black
3	Blue
4	Green
5	Red
6	White
7	Brass
8	Bronze
9	Copper
10-11	Gold
12	Silver

To determine its age, see Scaling the Encounter.
➤

To be clear, this need not be a hostile encounter. The dragon is not defending its lair, so — being a highly intelligent creature — it may just be curious about your party. It may have more important things to do and decline to take notice of them at all. Or it may be hungry and on the hunt, or it's angry because your party has intruded on territory it claims as its own.

Alternately, you may present your party with a scenario that you can weave into the larger story of the campaign. It may even serve as the main thrust of the campaign. Your party finds a dragon wyrmling sprawled on the ground. It's obviously in a bad way gashed open, bleeding profusely (or it has almost bled out), barely conscious. Assume that it has stabilized after being reduced to 0 hp, and that it now has 1 hp.

How it got that way is up to you, and it may depend on how dragons fit into your campaign world. Perhaps it fled from a fight in which it was badly wounded. Who would its enemies be, and why were they fighting? Were any of this dragon's relatives or companions killed?

How your party decides to deal with this child in distress could open up possibilities for later in your campaign. If they rescue it, will its kin reward them later, or will its enemies confront them on the principle that, "The friends of my enemy must also be my enemy?" Conversely, what are the consequences if they put it out of its misery, like scavengers roaming a medieval battlefield? Will its kin seek retribution, or will its enemies treat your party as allies?

Scaling the Encounter: Because dragons get tougher with age, the age of the dragon encountered should depend on your party's average level — especially if you decide that this is going to be a hostile encounter. If your party's average level is 10 or lower, they encounter a wyrmling. If their average level is 11-18, they encounter a young dragon. If their average level is 19-25, they encounter an adult dragon. If their average level is higher than 25, they encounter an ancient dragon.

Elephant. Your party comes across one elephant grazing on swamp grass, or perhaps relaxing in the mud on a hot day. However, it is always the case with elephants in the wild that avoiding a stampede requires some care. If they want to avoid a confrontation with the elephant, require a DC 15 Wisdom (Survival) or Intelligence (Nature) check. Failure means that someone has made a false move, triggering an attack.

Scaling the Encounter: If your party's average level is lower than 4, a hostile elephant encounter may be more than you want to throw at them. Feel free to re-roll for a different encounter. Conversely, if you want to run a more challenging encounter, the encounter group is a small herd of elephants, consisting of one for each multiple of 5 in your party's average level.

Fey. Fey are creatures of the deep forest, but they can be found in mangrove swamps and any other wetland environment where there are plenty of trees about. They mean no harm. But they have agendas of their own that can work at cross-purposes with that of adventurers pursuing fortune and glory. To determine which fey creature your party comes across, roll on Table 10.3.3:

TABLE 10.3.3
Fey - Wetlands

d8	ENCOUNTER
1-2	Dryad
3-4	Pixies
5	Satyr
6-8	Sprite

Dryad. One dryad spots your party and develops an instant crush on the party member with the highest Charisma. It uses its *Tree Stride* ability to move among the trees without being detected and waits for a moment when the object of its affection separates from the rest of the party. If necessary, it uses its *Speak With Beasts and Plants* ability to create a distraction and its *entangle* innate spell to trap that character. Then it uses *Fey Charm* to turn him or her into its prisoner of love.

Pixies. Your party crosses paths with 1d4 pixies, but most likely only the pixies know this at first. Shy around strangers but curious all the same, they remain invisible while taking your party's measure by playing (mostly) harmless pranks on them and judging their reaction. Exactly what pranks they pull is up to you as DM, but it makes the most sense that they should use their *Innate Spellcasting* abilities somehow.

It's also up to you whether your party wins over the pixies because of (or in spite of) their reactions. They may decide that these strangers are too dangerous to deal with, in which case they use their abilities to disable your party and cover their own retreat. If they decide they like your party, on the other hand, they reveal themselves and offer to share their local knowledge and provide material assistance — though what material assistance tiny-sized creatures can offer is an open question. ➤

Satyr. Your party comes upon one bored satyr looking to party. Everyone hears a melody created by its *Panpipes* ability coming from the trees. Anyone affected by the *Charming Melody* forgets his or her purpose and joins the satyr, who now emerges into view, in dancing and drinking to the exclusion of any other activity.

If anyone in your party turns hostile, the satyr switches from *Charming Melody* to *Gentle Lullaby*. If that does not pacify them sufficiently, it switches to *Frightening Strain* and retreats.

Sprites. Your party stumbles into territory claimed by a colony of sprites. Out of nowhere, a guard post of 1d4 sprites challenges them. One appears and demands that your party state their business, while the others (if present) remain invisible until combat starts or they decide your party is friendly.

Scaling the Encounter: Dryads and satyrs work alone.

If you wish to make a hostile encounter with sprites more challenging, they raise an alarm to summon reinforcements. The reinforcement pool consists of 1d4 sprites for each level in your party's average level. 1d6 arrive on scene each turn after combat begins until the reinforcement pool has been exhausted.

Treasure: Dryads take those who have succumbed to their charms back to their lair, where they keep souvenirs of their previous paramours. Treasure may also be a factor in sprite encounters, since their colony is bound to have a central repository of its belongings. In both cases, roll on the Treasure Hoard: Challenge 0-4 table.

Fire Beetles. Your party comes across 1d8 giant fire beetles scuttling along a patch of dry land. Perhaps your party notices them glowing in the gloom of an overgrown patch of the swamp. Fire beetles are not aggressive, but they defend themselves if threatened — if they're hunted for their luminous glands, for instance.

Frogs. Frogs are not aggressive predators, but even so an amphibian's got to eat. Making their way through the swamp, they draw the attention of 1d4 giant frogs, half-submerged and watchful. If any party member is small or smaller, or there is a familiar or other animal companion present, the frogs lash out instinctively and the first frog to stick out its tongue tries to swallow it. They leave alone anyone of medium or larger size.

Scaling the Encounter: If you wish to make the encounter more challenging, add one giant frog for each level in your party's average level. That is a lot of humanoid-sized frogs to be gathered in one place, and it is bound to make things awfully crowded on the lily pads.

Hyenas. Hyenas are clever predators, and they know well enough to pick their targets carefully. A hunting pack of 2d8 hyenas comes across your party, but they do not attack unless they are at least twice as numerous as your party, or unless they can isolate a party member and use their pack tactics ability — perhaps one character has gone ahead to scout the lay of the land, or lagged behind after having difficulty with the swampy terrain. Otherwise, they hover about on the flank of the party, looking for an opportunity to strike. If they find none, they eventually tire of the hunt and move off.

Scaling the Encounter: If you wish to make the encounter more challenging, the encounter group consists of two giant hyenas for each multiple of 3 in your party's average level.

Jackals. Your party comes across a small pack of 2d4 jackals scavenging a carcass. It's a feast compared to nosing through the muck for small animals, so they're keen to protect their find. If your party wishes to avoid a fight, have them make a DC 15 Wisdom (Survival) check. Failure means that someone has made a move that the jackals take as a threat, and they attack.

Lizards. Your party crosses paths with 1d4 giant lizards foraging for large insects and smaller lizards among the vegetation. They may be wild, or they may be pack animals left at the water's edge by smugglers who transferred their goods to a vessel and found they didn't have room for the beasts.

In the former case, the giant lizards can be wrangled and trained to serve as pack animals or mounts. To wrangle a giant lizard, it must be successfully grappled and kept in grappled condition for 10 consecutive rounds. At that point, it becomes docile and submits to whomever grappled it. Because of its size, two medium-size creatures may grapple with the same giant lizard simultaneously, and as long as one of them maintains its grappled condition, this counts toward the requirement for wrangling it.

Rats. Keen and nimble, even large rats have no trouble making their way around a swamp. Roll on Table 10.3.4 to determine the nature of the rat encounter:

Lizards are not above eating their own, if opportunity knocks.

TABLE 10.3.4

Rats - Wetlands

d6	ENCOUNTER
1	Lone Rat
2-4	Swarm of Rats
5-6	Giant Rats

Lone Rat. A single rat, perhaps foraging by itself or perhaps lost from its nest, approaches your party while they take a rest. It's not much of a threat, but if someone in your party is looking for a familiar or even just a pet, this is an opportunity. Interacting with the rat — especially earning its trust with food — and making a successful DC 10 Intelligence (Nature) check earns its loyalty as a pet.

Swarm of Rats. Your party has stopped to rest near a nest of rats hidden in the undergrowth. Drawn by the party's rations, one swarm of rats makes for the nearest source of food. They don't attack party members who don't interfere with their basic mission of acquiring food. But unless they are stopped, they eventually account for all of your party's rations, making off with what they don't eat on the spot.

Giant Rats. In this case, the rats drawn by the food your party carries are giant rats. There are 2d4 of them.

Scaling the Encounter: Rat encounters are more of a nuisance than anything else. But if you want to make them more of a challenge, use an encounter group consisting of one swarm of rats or 1d8 giant rats plus one giant rat for each level in your party's average level.

Unicorn. One of these celestials has staked out a forested corner of the wetlands and defends the place's sanctity against all comers. It uses its innate spell casting to *detect evil and good,* and it marks down anyone who registers as good as a probable friend and anyone who registers as evil as a probable enemy. However, even good characters who appear to be harming the forest in some way — chopping down a tree, for instance — rouse its suspicion. A successful DC 15 Intelligence (Nature) check by a good character who tries to interact with it, or a successful DC 15 Charisma (Persuasion) check by someone who speaks one of its known languages, helps turn the unicorn to your party's side. It may even join a predominantly lawful good party as an ally for a short time, but it refuses to leave the swamp.

If your party can't defuse the unicorn's hostility, it may come down to a fight. If killing a unicorn is a horrific act in your campaign world, then your party will just have to deal with the consequences.

Scaling the Encounter: If your party's average level is 10 or higher and you suspect that a meeting with a unicorn will turn hostile, consider adding one unicorn to the encounter to make it more challenging.

Water Weird. Your party comes upon a place that is guarded by a water weird — an elemental tasked with safeguarding a specific location. In a swamp, there are bound to be pools, creeks and the like that would make logical places for a water weird's care. As an elemental, it acts instinctively and treats your party as intruders. However, its actions vary according to the alignment it has absorbed from its surroundings, so consider that there is a 50% chance that it is neutral good and guarding a sacred site and 50% that it is neutral evil and bound to a befouled site.

Scaling the Encounter: If you wish to make the encounter more challenging, consider that more than one water weird has been bound to this place. The encounter group consists of one water weird for each multiple of 5 in your party's average level, rounded up. At your discretion, you may require your players to say, "one weird water weird" three time fast.

Treasure: Since the water weird is bound to the spot, it stands to reason that belongings from others who have run afoul of it would be located here. Roll on the Individual Treasure table appropriate for the total CR of the encounter.

Weasels. On dry ground, someone at the front of your party's march order accidentally steps into a burrow housing enough weasels to cause trouble when they get angry and defend their home. You may allow your party a DC 10 Wisdom (Perception) or Wisdom (Survival) check to spot the burrow in time to avoid it or give warning to whomever is about to disturb it. The burrow houses a pack of 3d6 weasels.

Scaling the Encounter: If you wish to make the encounter more challenging, substitute giant weasels for normal-sized weasels.

Treasure: There is a 10% chance that they are actually mink, and their pelts would be of some value to furriers — 1 gp for normal-sized mink, and 5 gp for a giant mink. You may require a successful DC 15 Intelligence (Nature) check for your party to tell the difference between mink and weasels.

Vultures. Your party comes across 1d6+2 vultures picking at a carcass. It could be an animal — or it could be a humanoid or a human. How they respond depends on how they interpret your party's actions. You may have your party make a DC 10 Intelligence (Nature) or Wisdom (Survival) check. Failure means that someone has made a false move that persuades the vultures to attack, thinking that they need to defend the buffet table.

Scaling the Encounter: If you wish to make the encounter more challenging, consider substituting giant vultures for the vultures. The encounter group then consists of two giant vultures for each multiple of 3 in your party's average level. Giant vultures may be hunting instead of feeding. Perhaps they — mistakenly or not — spotted your party as hapless travelers on their last legs, in which case they swoop down to try to hasten their demise.

Rhinoceros. Rhinoceros are not a common sight in wetlands, but they find enough grasses and other plants here to survive. Your party interrupts one rhinoceros as it grazes. It is not aggressive — as an herbivore, it does not hunt for food. But if it feels threatened, it becomes a dangerous foe. Have your party make a DC 15 Intelligence (Nature) or Wisdom (Survival) check. Failure means that someone has made a false move that the rhinoceros interprets as a threat. It charges.

Scaling the Encounter: If you wish to make the encounter more challenging, your party faces a herd of potentially angry rhinoceros, one for each multiple of 3 in your party's average level.

TABLE 10.4

Humanoids - Wetlands

d20	ENCOUNTER
1	Bugbear
2-4	Elves
5-6	Gnolls➤

7-8	Gnomes
9-10	Goblins
11	Hobgoblins
12-15	Lizardfolk
16	Lycanthrope
17-18	Orcs
19-20	Sahuagin

Bugbear. Your party crosses paths with one or more bugbears (see Scaling the Encounter). They could be mercenaries on their way to join a larger goblinoid army operating in these wetlands, or they could be detached from that larger army, acting as scouts or chasing a defeated foe. If there is no such war in which they could take part, they're out for some casual plunder, or perhaps on their way to shake down a hobgoblin tribe that once employed them.

Their interest in fighting your party should vary according to the reason why they're here. For instance, marching to war means they have a larger purpose in mind than victimizing your party. If they're looking to strongarm some hobgoblins, they may even offer your party a cut of the take in exchange for adding to their strength in numbers.

Scaling the Encounter: A beginning-level party should only have to cope with one bugbear. If you wish to make the encounter more challenging, the encounter group consists of two bugbears for each multiple of 3 in your party's average level. If your party's average level is 10 or higher, add one bugbear chief as the group's leader.

Elves. Wetlands with lots of trees may house a native elf population. Your party encounters a group of elves from a nearby community. Their purpose in being here could fit any of a vast number of plausible possibilities. Perhaps they are just hunting or gathering, or they're on a routine patrol to look out for possible threats to their community. Perhaps they're a war party, acting on information that a hostile group of orcs or goblins is about. Perhaps they are pursuing a criminal, or looking for one of their own who has gone missing. Much should depend on what else is going on in this corner of your campaign world. Make it fit as closely as you like.

How the elves react to your party depends a lot on their mission and your party's composition. Obviously, a party with elves in it is more likely than not to receive friendly treatment. Conversely, they regard a party with traditional enemies of the elves in it with suspicion or even hostility. However, if your party establishes a rapport with this group, they may be willing to provide local lore, or they may even offer your party a sidequest by asking for their help with their mission.

Scaling the Encounter: The encounter group consists of one elf scout and one elf spy for each multiple of 2 in your party's average level. You may substitute one spy for two scouts to keep the size of the encounter group manageable, if you wish. If your party's average level is higher than 5, substitute one elf priest or one elf veteran for one spy as the group's leader.

Gnolls. Your party comes across a small band of gnolls scouting out the swamp, looking for targets that their tribe can raid. They try to intimidate your party into giving up what they know about the area, especially the location of fishing villages and if they have spotted any merchants lately. Either that, or they just decide to separate your party from their possessions by force.

If the gnoll group is relatively large (see Scaling the Encounter) this may be the actual raiding party, headed for the nearest settlement. Or they may be on their way back from a successful raid, spattered with blood and taking with them captives to sacrifice to their deity. In either case, they ignore your party if your party declines to interfere with them, guided as they are by their primary purpose.

Scaling the Encounter: The baseline encounter group should consist of two gnolls for each multiple of 3 in your party's average level. If your party's average level is 7-9, add a gnoll pack lord to the mix as the group's leader. If your party's average level is 10 or higher, feel free to substitute one gnoll pack lord for four gnolls as much as you like if you don't want to run a mass encounter.

Treasure: If the gnolls are coming back from a successful raid, you may roll on the Treasure Hoard: Challenge 0-4 table to determine the fruits of their labor. This is in addition to the individual treasure they carry.

Gnomes. Your party comes across a small group of 1d6 gnomes paddling a small boat or poling a raft as they navigate the swamp. They're most likely a team of freelance mechanics who travel between settlements, selling their services. But they could also be traders, with goods to sell instead of services.

In either case, they don't give your party any trouble unless provoked. They're willing to share local knowledge and trade useful items. They may also offer your party a sidequest if they feel like they could use an armed escort until they reach the next village.

Treat the gnomes as commoners. If you wish, you may add a gnome acolyte or priest to the encounter as a cleric

tagging along to give protection and aid, and who can offer help to your party in the form of divine spells.

Goblins. Goblins tend to make their lairs elsewhere, but they come to the marshes as a good place to find isolated victims that they can slaughter and loot, or take captive and torture for their amusement. Your party crosses paths with a such a goblin foraging party.

With a large encounter group (see Scaling the Encounter), the uneven terrain breaks up their formation, so that at some of them are likely to fall behind. In such cases, the leading goblins try to buy time for the laggards to come up and eventually work their way around the flanks by parlaying with your party (or at least making a show to intimidate them).

Scaling the Encounter: Use an encounter group of 1d4 goblins for each level in your party's average level. If you don't want to run a mass encounter but you still want to provide a higher-level party with a meaningful challenge, feel free to substitute one goblin boss for four goblins as much as you like.

Hobgoblins. Wetlands are not particularly friendly to military operations, so the hobgoblins that your party encounters here are most likely mercenaries scouting or pursuing a scattered foe on behalf of their employers. As such, they're a business-like, no-nonsense bunch with strong leadership. They may be suspicious of your party — are they friend or foe? But they won't attack for unprofessional reasons, such as wanton cruelty or boredom.

However, the hobgoblins do interrogate your party closely, looking for information that will help them wind up the current operation. They'll let your party go if they're convinced your party is not a foe, but you may require that your party make a DC 15 Charisma (Persuasion) check to make it so.

Scaling the Encounter: The baseline encounter group should consist of 1d4 hobgoblins for each multiple of 2 in your party's average level. If your party's average level is 10-19, add a hobgoblin captain as the group's leader, accompanied by two goblin servants or one bugbear aide. If your party's average level is 20 or higher, add instead one hobgoblin warlord with two bugbear aides.

Lizardfolk. Your party has entered a patch of swamp claimed by a lizardfolk tribe. A patrol or war party from that tribe spots them. In their overdeveloped reptilian brains, they identify your party first as intruders, then as possible captives to be sacrificed or eaten later. So they attack.

Scaling the Encounter: The encounter group consists of one lizardfolk for each level in your party's average level. You may substitute one lizardfolk shaman for four lizardfolk. If you party's average level is 10 or higher, add one lizardfolk king/queen to the group as its leader.

Lycanthrope. To determine what manner of werebeast your party encounters, roll on Table 10.4.1

TABLE 10.4.1
Lycanthrope - Wetlands

d8	ENCOUNTER
1	Werebear
2	Wereboar
3-4	Wererat
5	Weretiger
6-8	Werewolf

All lycanthropes assume their animal form if the encounter comes down to combat, although they may choose their hybrid form instead if they have access to a weapon.

Werebear. Your party comes across a werebear that has claimed this corner of the wetlands as its domain. Perhaps it was once a druid, or a wandering ranger who volunteered for this fate to protect the creatures and plants therein from harm. It is not automatically hostile to your party, especially if there are no evil characters present, and it may be willing to provide them with useful information about the surrounding area.

On the other hand, an encounter could create difficulties for your party if the werebear decides that one of the player characters would make a good apprentice (and successor to its self-appointed duties as the local guardian). Once it realizes that there is a druid or a ranger in your party, a light goes on in its head — and it won't take "No" for an answer.

Wereboar. A wereboar met by chance in the swamp was most likely an unfortunate resident of a nearby settlement who went hunting or fishing alone and ran afoul of a wereboar. It goes about looking for victims to share its fate, hoping that a lone boar will lure an unwary hunter, as was once done to it. A party of adventurers could offer it an even more attractive target — confident in its ability to take at least one of them and drive the others off, it attacks.

Wererat. One wererat appears to your party in its humanoid form, pretending to be a hunter or

▶

fisherman from a nearby community in distress. Perhaps it claims to be lost and it asks to travel with your party for protection until it can regain its bearings. It tries to slip toward the back of the march order and waits for a time when everyone's back is turned to it.

Weretiger. Your party crosses paths with a weretiger on the hunt. If it's hungry, it may stalk and attack your party, though it is more likely to focus on driving off the party members and taking the pack animals than on hunting the party members themselves. Otherwise, it may assume human form and treat your party as fellow travelers, content to barter with them and exchange information about unknown places.

Werewolf. One werewolf spots your party and cannot turn down the opportunity to claim more victims. However, it is clever enough to approach them in its human form, pretending to be a hunter in distress. Once your party gets close and drops its guard, it morphs into its hybrid form and attacks.

Scaling the Encounter: A single lycanthrope can offer a stiff challenge to a low-level party. If your party's average level is 3 or less, feel free to re-roll the encounter. Alternately, if you want to make a werewolf encounter more challenging for a higher-level party, use a pack of them consisting of one werewolf for each multiple of 5 in your party's average level, rounded up.

Orcs. Orcs are not particularly comfortable living in a swamp, but they do visit looking for raiding targets. Wetlands elven communities are particularly attractive to them. A small group orcs could be a scout party out to get the lay of the land, while a larger group would be an actual raiding party on its way to — or on its way back from — its target.

Your party crosses paths with these orcs, but if they have such a fixed purpose in mind, it's no guarantee that they'll pay your party much attention. Their leader may look your party over and decide that they're not worth the bother. But they may also decide to interrogate your party for information about the surrounding area, and they'll resort to violence without hesitation if your party is too slow to cooperate. They are less likely to give your party a break if there are elves in it, and they'll make elf characters a special focus of hostility in any interactions with them.

Scaling the Encounter: The baseline encounter group should consist of 1d4 orcs for each multiple of 2 in your party's average level. If your party's average level is 5-9, add an orog as the group's leader. If your party's average level is 10 or higher, use an orc war chief as its leader. If you don't want to run a mass encounter but you still want to provide a higher-level party with a meaningful challenge, feel free to substitute one orog for four orcs as much as you like.

Treasure: If the orcs are coming back from a successful raid, you may roll on the Treasure Hoard: Challenge 0-4 table to determine the fruits of their labor. This is in addition to the individual treasure they carry.

Sahuagin. When sahuagin come to wetlands in search of raiding targets, they tend to stay out of shallow water for as long as they can. They are creatures of deep water, and that's where they feel most comfortable. As a result, this gives them the element of surprise, creating the impression that they have arrived out of nowhere when they do come up on land. Chance has your party crossing paths with sahuagin raiders who have arrived on land, or are close to coming ashore (in which case, they're only partially visible above the water's surface). A small group may just be a scouting party, but a larger group has a target and plunder in mind. It's possible — if not likely — that they view your party as a target of opportunity.

Scaling the Encounter: The encounter group consists of two sahuagin for each multiple of 3 in your party's average level. You may substitute one sahuagin priestess for four sahuagin. If you party's average level is 10 or higher, add one sahuagin baron to the group as its leader.

TABLE 10.5

Humans - Wetlands

d20	ENCOUNTER
1	Adventurers
2-5	Bandits/Pirates
6	Druid
7	Exiles
8	Explorer
9-13	Fishermen
14	Fugitives
15-17	Hunters
18-19	Merchants
20	Military

Adventurers. Unless your party contains all of the adventurers in your campaign world, it's at least theoretically possible that they'll run into another

adventuring party navigating the swamp. Perhaps they're pursuing the same objective as your party. Perhaps they have a different mission; perhaps they're headed for a site that your party knows nothing about (like ancient ruins said to hold lost treasures). Perhaps they're lost and starving, or wounded, or cursed.

How they react to your party depends on a variety of factors. Are they rivals pursuing the same goal? If not, perhaps this party is willing to share useful information. In fact, if your party is stuck and having a hard time advancing the storyline of your campaign, a friendly encounter like this can help steer them in the right direction. Differences in alignment may also shape how the two parties react to each other.

Composition of this rival party is up to you and can vary according to circumstance. Any party in the wilderness would be well-advised to have someone accomplished in Survival, such as a ranger, with them. Conversely, a party that is struggling may be in a bad way precisely no one is well-versed in Survival or Nature.

Scaling the Encounter: Unless there is some possibility that this encounter turns hostile, the relative level of the party is mainly a matter of affect. A higher-level party might project self-confidence and calm (or arrogance), while beginning-level party might stumble about, unsure of themselves. If you're leaning towards a hostile encounter, however, consider that the total CR of the party should be roughly two-thirds of your party's average level.

Bandits/Pirates. Whether you call them bandits or swamp pirates, armed robbers find no shortage of places to hole up and hide in wetlands. There are plenty of narrow inlets and creeks where only small boats fit, and which require intimate knowledge of the waterways to avoid getting snagged or running aground. Mangrove swamps and other wetlands with heavy vegetation offer concealment from unwelcome company, too.

Even though a party of adventurers like yours is better-armed than their typical target, it's not out of the question that they'll attack. They're used to traveling to busy waterways to find victims, so when someone like your party arrives in their front yard, they may figure that they might as well save themselves the travel. Also, they're bound to be suspicious of strangers. They may think that your party is a posse sent out after them — or that they're out to rob them of what they robbed from others.

Scaling the Encounter: As a rough guideline, the encounter group should contain 1d8 of these villains for each level in your party's average level. If your party's average level is 4 or higher, add a bandit captain as their leader. If you don't want to run a mass encounter but you still want swamp pirates to provide a higher-level party with a meaningful challenge, feel free to substitute one thug for four bandits as much as you like.

Treasure: If your party finds the bandits' hideout, roll on the Treasure Hoard table appropriate to the total CR of the encounter. Do so also if you decide that the bandits encountered are laden with booty from a successful raid. Consider that there is also a 20% chance that the bandits have with them a high-value captive whom they intend to ransom. The identity of this captive is left to you as DM, as it should depend on local circumstances and fit into your campaign world.

Druid. Your party crosses paths with one druid in his or her native element. Druids in the wild may wander, with no fixed abode, but it's at least as likely that they protect a patch of wetlands with fierce devotion. How druids react to your party depends almost entirely on whether or not they think your party represents a menace to the natural environment. A druid who is persuaded that your party's intentions are benign may be willing to help by providing local lore, casting spells for their benefit, or even joining them as a friendly NPC as long as it does not involve leaving the wetlands.

Scaling the Encounter: If you wish to make this a hostile encounter (or at least suspect that it will turn hostile), consider increasing the CR to make it more of a fight for a higher-level party. In this case, the encounter group is a veritable coven of druids devoted to protecting the same territory, and it consists of one druid for each multiple of 3 in your party's average level.

Exiles. Your party encounters a group of 1d6 people in a ragged state who could serve as a source of adventure hooks. They have fled their home for any of a variety of reasons: perhaps they are royalty or nobility who have been usurped; perhaps the opposite is the case and they are failed usurpers themselves and they now fear for their lives. Or perhaps they have gotten caught up in some kind of blood feud in their homeland and that's why they fear for their lives. Whatever the circumstance, they have come to the swamp because they need some place to hide.

No matter their reason for being here, they should offer your party an adventure hook of some sort. It may involve protecting the exiles from their real (or imagined) pursuers. It may involve returning to their former home and securing an important item that was left behind (a family heirloom, a badge of office), perhaps even helping them return home and force their way back into their former position of prominence. At the very least, exiles can provide your party with information about their

former home territory, which in turn could be a key location in your campaign.

Explorers. Your party bumps into a small human party, driven by the curiosity that characterizes their kind, to map and describe this wetlands system that has been mostly untouched by human hands. The group consists of one commoner — the scholar who leads the expedition — and one scout or druid acting as guide and bodyguard. Perhaps they are here thanks to the sponsorship of an academy or a ruler eager to know more about the world, or perhaps the explorer is a wealthy eccentric who undertook this expedition on his or her own.

Such an encounter is not likely to be hostile. Explorers are open and curious, despite the fact that the swamp has more than enough hazards to keep them on their guard. Instead, you may treat this as an opportunity for your party to receive some help from a knowledgeable stranger — the explorer is likely to have excellent maps of nearby areas (and knowledge of those areas) and is willing to share them. Conversely, an expedition that has been in the field for a while may be running short on cartography supplies and other necessaries and may be willing to pay well if your party can help supply what they lack. Also, if your party is in the mood for a sidequest, an explorer may offer one: If the expedition is headed into particularly dangerous territory, it may need additional guards to keep it safe.

But the Fourth One Stayed Up

Conducting military operations in a swamp is hard. The ground is too unsteady for an army to stand and fight, but at the same time the water is too shallow to support deep-draft warships. As the King of Swamp castle in *Monty Python and the Holy Grail* unwittingly reveals, it's quite difficult building a fortress in wetlands.

Yes, Alfred the Great of England famously waged war on the Viking invaders from the marshes of Somerset. So you may consider that bands of irregular fighters may operate from hiding places in wetlands, if there's something like that going on in your world. But more often, armies deploy on solid ground and if there's a swamp present, they'll use it to anchor their flank as effectively as a major river. Hence, soldiers encountered in wetlands are likely to be engaged in more peripheral activities, like scouting or pursuing fugitives.

Fishermen. Your party comes across 1d6 fishermen from a nearby settlement using spears or bows. It looks more like hunting than fishing with bait, but they're after prey that swims. They fish from dry land or from rafts or boats. They're used to being left alone in this treacherous environment, and because they have to get fairly close to their targets, they're always on the alert for predators like crocodiles and quippers. So they may react to your party with suspicion, even hostility. You may require your party to make a DC 10 Charisma (Persuasion) check to win them over.

On the other hand, if they're friendly and they have fish in hand, they're willing to sell fish from their catch for half of what a tavern meal would cost — the hitch being, of course, that you have to clean and smoke or cook it yourself before it goes bad. With just bit of coaxing, they're also happy to provide your party with local knowledge, including tales of monsters in the water nearby and of course, stories of the one that got away.

Treat fishermen as commoners armed with either javelins or shortbows. In both cases, the projectiles are tethered to the fisherman, allowing them to pull in their prey. However, this also limits their range to 50 feet.

Fugitives. Your party crosses paths with 1d6 ragged people stumbling through the swamp. They look to be in less-than-optimal shape, but they're moving as fast as the difficult terrain permits. Most, if not all of them have a manacle around one wrist, with the other manacle dangling on its chain. They're escaped prisoners who have fled into the swamp. From whom they are fleeing and why they were imprisoned in the first place is up to you, and ought to depend on where in your campaign world this encounter takes place.

How the encounter plays out depends entirely on how your party reacts, but one thing on which you may rely is that these fugitives did not go to the trouble of a jailbreak just to allow a bunch of strangers to take their freedom back from them. Each of them has learned whip their freed manacle by the chain and wield it as a club.

Treat the fugitives as bandits, but without weapons or armor.

Treasure: Fugitives have no treasure.

Hunters. Your party comes across a group of 2d4 hunters searching the swamp for birds and game. They're always on the alert for predators like crocodiles and quippers, and they're not used to encountering strangers in this thinly-populated wetlands. So they may react to your party with suspicion, even hostility. You may require your party to make a DC 10 Charisma (Persuasion) check to win them over, after which point they are willing to help by trading goods and supplying food and local knowledge.

Treat hunters as scouts.

Merchants. Your party spots some merchants moving their goods through the swamp by raft or boat. The group consists of 1d6 merchants and 1d6 guards. Traveling merchants could help your party by selling them necessary items, exchanging hard money for treasure items or providing knowledge of just about anywhere in your campaign world (where are these traders going, and where did they originate?). They may also be interested in hiring your party as additional guards if they fear pirates.

Treat the merchants as commoners. Treat the guards as guards, although you may substitute veterans for as many guards as you wish.

Treasure: Roll once on the Individual Treasure: Challenge 0-4 table for each merchant or guard. In addition, roll once on the Treasure Hoard: Challenge 0-4 table for each merchant present to determine the value of goods and/or hard money in the caravan. You may substitute valuable goods — spices, fine cloth, expensive hardwood, rare animals, etc. — for art objects or coin as you wish.

Military. Wetlands are not friendly to large-scale military operations. The terrain makes it too difficult to move whole armies, not to mention the supplies that they need. However, if war touches this corner of your campaign world, your party may cross paths with outriders from one side or another who are looking for useful information. In fact, they may be pursuing a foe that their side has defeated, assuming that fleeing soldiers have entered the swamp. They won't attack your party without provocation. However, they do stop your party to grill them for information, and possibly enlist their help with their mission.

Scaling the Encounter: The encounter group should consist of one scout for each level in your party's average level. If you want to create a more challenging encounter, add one spy for each multiple of 4 in your party's average level.

TABLE 10.6
Watch Out! - Wetlands

d20	ENCOUNTER
1	Did You Hear That?
2-4	Falling Branch
5	Falling Tree
6	Hampering Web
7-11	Quicksand
12-13	Submerged Log ➤

14	Swamp Gas
15-16	Thick Mist
17	Tracks
18-20	Tripping Hazard

Did You Hear That? Swamps — especially those with heavy vegetation that block lines of sight — have a way of playing tricks on the mind. The mangrove trees close in on you, and the prevalent air of decay and death brings out your anxieties and fears. It shouldn't come as a surprise if your party falls prey to acoustic illusions, thinking that they hear something that isn't there.

Choose a party member to make a DC 15 Wisdom (Survival) or Intelligence (Nature) check. Failure means that that character believes that he or she has heard a noise made by creature or natural phenomenon to which it presently has no line of sight. It can be as consequential as a dragon's roar in the distance, or as eerily intimate as muttering in Orcish coming from behind those rocks. A successful check means that that party member realizes that this is an illusion; either it's not as close as it seems or it isn't real at all.

If you wish, roll on Table 10.6.1 for guidance on what your party thinks it hears:

TABLE 10.6.1
Did You Hear That?

d10	They Think They Hear...
1	Banshee wailing
2	Giant insects buzzing
3	Human or humanoid calling for help, water splashing
4	Large amphibian croaking
5	Large (or larger) creature splashing through the swamp
6	Panther or other predatory cat snarling
7	Voices speaking in Common
8	Voices speaking in Draconic, with a lizardfolk accent
9	Voices speaking in elvish
10	Voices speaking in Sylvan

Falling Branch. Look out below! A high branch falls from a tree as your party passes by. Perhaps the tree is dead, or perhaps the branch is diseased. Perhaps the tree has been injured in some way. Whatever the cause, the branch is heavy enough, or it falls from high enough, to smart if it hits you.

Determine the party member closest to the tree in question, or pick one at random. Treat the falling branch as a melee attack with a +0 bonus that causes 1d6 bludgeoning damage.

Falling Tree. Timber! The decayed remains of a dead tree topples over just as your party nears it. Choose the tree's position relative to the party and the angle at which it falls onto them. Or roll a d12 to determine the tree's bearing: 12 o'clock means that it is dead ahead; 1 o'clock means that its bearing is 30 degrees to the right; 6 o'clock means that it falls onto the party from directly behind, etc. The tree falls onto the party from that bearing. The trunk — the part heavy enough to cause damage — is 20 feet long. Anyone in the path of the trunk must make a successful DC 15 Strength (Athletics) or Dexterity (Acrobatics) check to get out of the way. Anyone who fails takes 2d8 bludgeoning damage. Anyone who succeeds must move out of the spaces into which the tree falls; if this means moving into a space occupied by someone else, that character must make a successful DC 15 Strength (Athletics) or Dexterity (Acrobatics) check to avoid a collision, or else take 1 damage and fall prone.

Hampering Web. There is a finely-woven spider's web between two trees, or among particularly dense and tall ground cover. Either way, it's right in your party's path. But there is no spider present. Your may allow your party a DC 15 Wisdom (Perception) or Wisdom (Survival) check to spot the web before someone at the front of the march order walks right into it. Anyone who fails to avoid the web is stuck and becomes restrained.

The restrained character may attempt to escape by making a DC 20 Strength (Athletics) or DC 20 Dexterity (Acrobatics) check. Other party members may try to free their restrained colleague by making a total of three successful attack rolls with a slashing weapon against the web, which has AC 15. But for each attempt, there is a 10% chance, cumulative with each new attempt, that one giant spider appears enters the web from an overhanging tree branch to see what it caught this time. Each attack roll counts as an attempt.

Quicksand. Your party stumbles into a patch of swamp so treacherous underfoot that it functions like quicksand. Have your party make a DC 15 Intelligence (Nature) or Wisdom (Survival) check to spot the quicksand before someone in the front of the march order steps right into it.

Submerged Log. Your party sees something partially submerged — but what is it? It could be the head of a crocodile, or part of an even more dangerous predator, like a hydra! Have your party make a DC 15 Wisdom (Survival) check to realize that it is actually a hollow log stuck in the mud and angled so that the top part can be seen above the water. It's quite harmless — unless you as the DM decide that there is a crocodile or some other predator lurking inside it.

Swamp Gas. As they make their way through the swamp, your party notices the terrible smell of decay and rot, and it just keeps getting worse and worse. Swamp gas is especially strong and noxious here. Have each party member make a DC 15 Constitution check to avoid being sickened by the stench. Everyone who fails is poisoned for the next 1d4 hours — that is, until your party gets clear of the swamp gas and everyone has had the chance to get fresh air back into their lungs.

Consider that there is a 10% chance that the swamp gas spontaneously combusts while your party is in its midst. Pick a random unoccupied space adjacent to at least one party member and treat it as the target of the spell *flaming sphere*, except that the area of effect expands by one space each turn (the direction of spread is random) for the next 10 turns, at which point the fire burns itself out.

Thick Mist. A dense mist suddenly sets in over the swamp, and your party is right in the middle of it. For the next 1d4 hours, heavily-obscured conditions prevail regardless of where your party goes and how far they travel during this time.

Tracks. Your party spots tracks in the frozen ground made by a creature of your choice. At your discretion, they may be fresh enough to lead to an encounter if followed; or you may allow your party to make a DC 15 Wisdom (Survival) check to realize that they are very old, and they will not lead to anything useful. If they fail, this may lead to an amusing (for you as DM, anyway) wild goose chase.

Tripping Hazard. Pick a party member at the front of the march order. That character trips over an unseen obstacle — perhaps a rock or animal bones stuck in the ground, or a tangle of vines that was hard to spot. He or she must make a successful DC 10 Strength (Athletics) or Dexterity (Acrobatics) check to avoid a hard fall that causes 1d4 damage — if not caused by the soft ground, the victim falls against a hard object like a tree trunk — and perhaps no small embarrassment in the eyes of the other party members.

If you prefer an incident more challenging to your players, consider that the character who trips and falls

lands in a mire so treacherous that it is, effectively, quicksand.

And That's What You're Gettin', Lad....

If the sidebars in this chapter throw you, consider *Monty Python and the Holy Grail* your assigned viewing. The fact that swamps are neither wholly land or wholly water makes them a challenging environment in which to run your party because you should always be aware of which element predominates in a given place, or if one predominates at all. The fun part of wetlands is that they offer a range of creatures (and folk) to encounter as exotic and fantastical as you'll find in the deep forest and the underground.

INDEX

CPSIA information can be obtained
at www.ICGtesting.com
Printed in the USA
JSHW050730270621
16225JS00004B/17